The 25th Anniversary Edition

ANN PETRY

A BIO-BIBLIOGRAPHY

(with a new introduction and more than 500 new annotations)

ANN PETRY

A Bio-Bibliography

(with a new introduction and more than 500 new annotations)

Hazel Arnett Ervin

J. H. Publishing Company
Research Triangle Park, NC

The 25th Anniversary Edition, Ann Petry: A Bio-Bibliography
Hazel Arnett Ervin

Copyright (c) 2021 by Hazel Arnett Ervin and J. H. Publishing Company

ALL RIGHTS RESERVED. No part of this book may be reproduced or transmitted in any form or by any means, electronic or mechanical, including photocopying, recording or by any information storage and retrieval system without permission in writing from the author and publisher.

J. H. Publishing Company
600 Park Offices Drive, Suite 300, Research Triangle Park, NC 27709-1109
www.jhpublishing.org.   info@jhpublishing.org

Library of Congress Cataloging - in - Publication Data

ISBN: 979-8-9863593-3-5

The 25th Anniversary Edition, Ann Petry: A Bio-Bibliography
by Hazel Arnett Ervin

1. Petry, Ann, 1908-1997; biography and bibliographical references (with an Index).
2. Women and literature - 20th Century.
3. Major African Americans in literature.
4. New Englanders in literature.

The paper used in this publication meets the minimum requirements.

Published in the United States of America

for Mom and Dad

and

HU professors, Dr Lettie Austin and Dr. Theodore R. Hudson

Contents

Acknowledgments
Epigraphs
Chronology — i
Introduction — xi

Primary Works — 1
Secondary Works — 15
Interviews — 159
Index — 191
About the Editor

Acknowledgments

The compiler gratefully acknowledges permission to reprint interviews from the following periodicals and books:

American Institute of the History of Pharmacy Collection, Kremers Reference Files, University of Wisconsin School of Pharmacy for "A Visit with Ann Petry."

Artspectrum, a newsletter published by the Windham Regional Arts Council of Willimantic, Connecticut, for " An Interview with Ann Petry."

The Crisis, for James Ivey's "Ann Petry Talks about First Novel," which appeared in vol 53, no 2 (February 1946).

MELUS, the Journal of the Society for the Study of the Multi-Ethnic Literature of the United States, for the "MELUS Interview: The New England Connection" by Mark K. Wilson (vol 15, no 2).

Reprint from *Interviews with Black Writers*, edited by John O'Brien, by permission of John O'Brien and Liveright Publishing Corporation. Copyright(c) 1973 by Liveright Publishing Corporation.

With a knowledge of the name comes a distincter recognition and knowledge of the thing.   Thoreau

The least we owe the writer . . . is an acknowledgment of her labor.

Barbara Christian

Black Feminist Criticism

Without great audiences, we cannot have great literature.

Sterling A. Brown

"Our Literary Audiences"

Chronology

1908

Ann Lane (Petry) is born Anna Houston Lane on October 12 in Old Saybrook, Connecticut, to Peter Clark Lane and Bertha Ernestine James Lane, and is the younger of two children

1912

Enters Old Saybrook Elementary School

1922

Begins to write short stories

1925

Graduates from Old Saybrook High School

1931

Receives Ph.G. degree from Connecticut College of Pharmacy in New Haven (now School of Pharmacy at the University of Connecticut, Storrs)

Works as clerk and manager, respectively, in family drugstores in Old Saybrook and Old Lyme, Connecticut, until 1938

1938

Marries (on February 22) George D. Petry, who is a native of New Iberia, Louisiana. Resides at 2 East 129th Street, New York, until 1946; then for a year at 2816 Bronx Park East, New York, 67, New York

Works as salesperson in advertising and as a journalist for New York's *Amsterdam News* until 1941

1939

Publishes first short story, "Marie of the Cabin Club," which is a suspense-romance, in *Afro American* (Baltimore), under the pen name Arnold Petri and receives a check for $5

1940

Joins the American Negro Theatre in New York. For over a year, performs as Tillie Petunia in *On Striver's Row* at the Schomburg Center for Research in Black Culture. For two years, experiences "firsthand the way in which the dialogue in a play further[s] the action"

1941

Works for New York's *People's Voice* as editor of the woman's page and also works as a reporter until 1944

From 1941 to 1943, writes the weekly column, "The Lighter Side," which evolves into a mixture of commentary and announcements of various cultural, social, and political events. From the column, the fictitious characters Miss Jones and Miss Smith emerge

Studies painting and drawing at New York's Harlem Art Center, while concentrating on "people, landscapes . . . everything"

1942

Attends for two years, Mabel Louise Robinson's workshop and course in creative writing at Columbia University; learns to critique her own and other people's works

Helps to organize the Negro Women, Inc., a Harlem consumers' watch group that provides working-class women with "how-to" information for purchasing food, clothing, and furniture; holds various offices until 1947

Helps to prepare skits and programs for children of laundry workers for number of years; works out of the educational office of the Laundry Workers Joint Board

1943

Publishes in *The Crisis*, under her own name, "On Saturday the Siren Sounds at Noon." An editor at Houghton Mifflin reads the short story and inquiries whether Petry is working on a novel. She suggests Petry apply for the Houghton Mifflin Literary Fellowship Award. Petry responds that she is not working on a novel but perhaps by the time the next award is offered, she might be able to submit one. The following year, the same editor at Houghton Mifflin sends Petry all the information about the Literary Fellowship and an application

Prepares newspaper releases as well as recruits volunteers for Harlem-Riverside Defense Council while serving as an assistant to the secretary of the council

Prepares the newspaper releases for National Association of Colored Graduate Nurses while serving as its publicity director

Joins Harlem's Play Schools Association Project at Public School No.10 at St. Nicholas Avenue and 116th Street as recreation specialist and helps to "develop a community program for parents and children in problem areas"

1944

Competes for the Houghton Mifflin's Literary Fellowship in fiction; as instructed includes in her application an outline and several chapters of *The Street*

Publishes short story, "Doby's Gone" in *Phylon*

1945

Wins Houghton Mifflin's Literary Fellowship Award in fiction; stipend is $2400

Publishes "Olaf and His Girl Friend" and "Like a Winding Sheet" in *The Crisis*

1946

Publishes *The Street* and dedicates the novel to her mother, Bertha James Lane

Interviews with James Ivey for *The Crisis*

The Best American Short Stories, 1946, which is edited by Martha Foley, is dedicated to Ann Petry. Included in the collection is Petry's "Like a Winding Sheet"

Is placed by critics in the "School of Wright" or the "Chicago Renaissance," primarily because of certain naturalistic elements found in *The Street*

Is honored by New York's Women's City Club for her "exceptional contribution to the life of New York City"

Responds to query of Alain Locke, the America's spokesperson for African-American writers; Shares her plans for a second novel (See Alain Locke's papers in the Manuscript Division of the Moorland-Spingarn Research Center at Howard University)

Responds to Rosey Poole's request for biographical and bibliographical information for publications abroad (See Rosey Poole's papers in the Manuscript Division of the Moorland-Spingarn Research Center at Howard University)

1947

Publishes *Country Place* and dedicates the novel to both her father, Peter C. Lane, and to her husband, George D. Petry

Relocates with her husband to Old Saybrook, Connecticut

Publishes the following short stories: "The Bones of Louella Brown" in *Opportunity*; "Solo on the Drums" in *The Magazine of the Year*; and "In Darkness and Confusion" in *Cross Section*, edited by Edwin Seaver

Donates autographed copies of *The Street* and *Country Place* to the Countee Cullen Memorial Collection, Trevor Arnett Library, Atlanta University (now Atlanta University Center, Woodruff Library)

Agrees to turn over manuscript for *The Street* to Carl Van Vechten for inclusion in the James Weldon Johnson Memorial Collection of Negro Arts and Letters, Beinecke Rare Book and Manuscript Library, Yale University

Is announced by *New York Amsterdam News* as follows: Petry's *The Street* is being considered for motion picture production

1948

Donates letters, autographed publications (in English and in numerous translations), reviews, photographs, and the manuscript for *Country Place* to the James Weldon Johnson Memorial Collection of Negro Arts and Letters at the Beinecke Letters at the Rare Book and Manuscript Library, Yale University

1949

Birth of daughter, Elisabeth Ann Petry

Death of father, Peter Clark Lane

Launches career as a writer for children and young adults with *The Drugstore Cat.* The work is dedicated to her grandmother, Anna Houston Bush, and to her aunt, Anna Louise James

1953

Publishes *The Narrows* and dedicates the novel to Mabel Louise Robinson

1955

Publishes *Harriet Tubman, Conductor on the Underground Railroad* and dedicates the biography to her daughter, Elisabeth Ann

1956

Death of mother, Bertha James Lane

Joins other writers and signs The American Civil Liberties Union's "Statement on Censorship Activity by Private Organizations and the National Organization for Decent Literature" which, among others, protests the censorship of *The Narrows*

1957

Is principal speaker, "The Problems of Writing Fiction and Biography" as she joins nine other Columbia University writers who pay tribute to former mentor, Dr. Mabel Louise Robinson

1958

Works as a writer for Columbia Pictures in Hollywood; Is assigned to adapt Charles Williams' novel *Hill Girl* to a screenplay for Kim Novak's film *That Hill Girl*

Publishes short story, "Has Anybody Seen Miss Dora Dean?" in *The New Yorker*

1960

Under the auspices of the Library of Congress, *Harriet Tubman, Conductor on the Underground Railroad* is transposed into braille

Harriet Tubman, Conductor on the Underground Railroad is reprinted as *That Girl Called Moses* by Methuen in London

1963

Publishes short story, "Miss Muriel" in *Soon, One Morning: New Writings by American Negroes, 1940-1962*, edited by Herbert Hill

1964

Publishes *Tituba of Salem Village* with Thomas Y. Crowell and dedicates the biography to her uncle Frank P. Chisholm

Under the auspices of the Library of Congress, *Tituba of Salem Village* is recorded for the Division for the Blind

Delivers lecture, "The Common Ground, " in the Central Children's Room at the New York Public Library at the Fifty-Fourth Annual Exhibition of Children's Books

1965

Is reelected to the Board of Directors of the Author's League Fund (the Author"s League of America)

Publishes short story, "The New Mirror" in *The New Yorker*

1967

Publishes short story, "The Migraine Worker" in *Redbook*

1968

Donates the following to the "Ann Petry Collection" located in Special Collections at Mugar Library, Boston University: autographed publications (in English and in numerous translations); letters; "numerous" newspaper clippings of articles and reviews; manuscripts, galleys, and research notes; photographs; and miscellaneous memorabilia

1970

Publishes *Legends of the Saints* and dedicates the work to her sister, Helen L. Bush

Publishes biographical article on Harriet Tubman for *Encyclopedia Britannica*

1971

Publishes short story, "The Witness" in *Redbook*

Publishes *Miss Muriel and Other Stories*, the first collection of short stories by an American black woman writer, and dedicates the collection to her brother-in-law, Walter J. Petry

1972

Lectures at Miami University in Ohio

1973

Interviews with John O'Brien for *Interviews with Black Writers*

Delivers lecture on her life and works at Suffolk University: "This Unforgettable Passage"

1974

Serves as Visiting Professor of English at the University of Hawaii

Is interviewed by *The Honolulu Advertiser* and appears on local television

Biography is entered in *Who's Who of American Women*

1976

Publishes first poems, "Noo York City 1," "Noo York City 2," and "Noo York City 3" in *Weid: The Sensibility Revue* (Bicentennial Issue H, American Women Poets)

1977

Biography is entered in *Who's Who Among Black Americans*

1978

Is awarded creative writing grant by the National Endowment for the Arts

1981

Adaptation of "Solo on the Drums" is aired on PBS television as an episode in a series with Ossie and Ruby. Giants Ossie Davis and Ruby Dee read from the text while accompanied by Billy Taylor on piano and Max Roach on drums

Publishes the poems, "A Purely Black Stone" and "A Real Boss Black Cat" in *A View from the Top of a Mountain*

1982

Delivers lecture at the Fourth Annual Richard Wright Lecture at Yale University

1983

Receives Doctor of Letters from Suffolk University

1984

Receives award for literature from Connecticut Historical Society, "Black Women of Connecticut: Achievements Against the Odds"

1985

Delivers lecture "Writers Speak III: New England as Region and Idea" at Symposium held at the University of Massachusetts

Receives a citation for her literary achievements from the City of Philadelphia (9 April)

The Street is reprinted by Beacon Press (Black Women Writers' Series)

1986

Biography is entered in the *Great Women in Connecticut History* (Hartford, CT: The Permanent Commission on the Status of Women)

Publishes the contemporary short story, "The Moses Project" in *Harbor Review* (English Department, University of Massachusetts)

1988

Interviews with Mark Wilson for *MELUS*

Death of sister, Helen L. Bush

Receives a citation from the United Nations Association of the United States of of America (28 January)

Receives honorary Doctor of Letters from University of Connecticut

The Narrows and *The Drugstore Cat* are reprinted by Beacon Press (Black Women Writers' Series)

Lectures at the University of New Hampshire in Durham

1989

Interviews with Hazel Arnett Ervin for *Ann Petry: A Bio-Bibliography*

Receives the Lifetime Achievement Award at the Fifth Annual Celebration of Black Writers' Conference during a reception held at the Friends of the Free Library in Philadelphia (4 February)

Receives honorary Doctor of Humane Letters from Mount Holyoke College

Biography is entered in *Who's Who in Writers, Editors and Poets*

Miss Muriel and Other Stories is reprinted by Beacon Press (Black Women Writers' Series, 1990)

Joins playwright Alice Childress and poets Gwendolyn Brooks and Sonia Sanchez at the Hartford College for Women Conference, "Prophets for a New Day," and reads from works

1991

Tituba of Salem Village is reprinted by Harper Collins

1992

The Street is reissued by Houghton Mifflin

Reads from her writings during the thirty-minute evening broadcast of "Connecticut Voices" on Connecticut Public Radio in Hartford. Is the first of thirteen (13) widely known Connecticut writers invited to participate in the thirteen-week project, sponsored jointly by The Connecticut Center for the Book and the *Northeast Magazine* in Hartford (14 November)

Delivers Keynote Speech at the Twenty-Fifth Anniversary of Old Saybook Library

Receives the Connecticut Arts Award from the Connecticut Commission of the Arts

Is honored at "Tribute to Ann Petry" Conference, held at Trinity College in Hartford, Connecticut. Guest speaker is Gloria Naylor. Is attended by scholars from numerous colleges and universities who make presentations, followed by discussions

Contributes story "My First Real Hat" to *When I Was a Child*, a publication by the Children's Literature Association

Reveals in *American Visions* (June/July), an extensive list of personal reading preferences

1993

Receives honorary degree from Trinity College

Donates autographed copies of all works to the Ann Petry Collection located in the African-American Research Center at Shaw University. Includes in the collection several hundreds of difficult-to-find reviews and articles

Receives a copy of Hazel Arnett Ervin's dissertation, which is the first post-structuralist study that reveals a hidden feminist text in both her 1940's novels, *The Street* and *Country Place*; this dissertation helps measurably to move Petry's criticism from the Wright School of Naturalism

1997

Death of the acclaimed writer, Ann Petry, on 28 April. Is buried in Cypress Cemetery, Old Saybrook, Connecticut

Life of Ann Petry is celebrated at a Memorial Service held at the First Congregational Church, which is located in Old Saybrook, across the street from the once family-owned drugstore; the same drugstore is often referenced in Petry's short stories and the novel, *Country Place*

Is honored posthumously during the dedication of the "Ann Petry Reading Room" at the Acton Public Library in Old Saybrook, Connecticut (Note: this location is Ann Petry's hometown library). The guest speaker is Hazel Arnett Ervin, a Petry bibliographer. Other guests include Elisabeth Ann Petry, Petry's daughter and current biographer; city dignitaries; and family, friends, and other members of the community

Is remembered posthumously on the Congress floor of the United States Senate by Connecticut's Senator Dodd via "In Memory of Ann Petry" which also is posted in the *U. S. Congressional Record Daily Edition*

1999

Is inducted posthumously into The Literary Hall of Fame for Writers of African Descent

Introduction

In 1939, Ann Petry receives $5.00 for her short story "Marie of the Cabin Club" from the *Afro-American*, a newspaper in Baltimore, Maryland. Published under the pseudonym Arnold Petri, the suspense-romance, with its multitude of coincidences which include espionage, kidnapping, attempted murder, and finally the rescue of a female in distress, is, according to Petry, the "first" in her long literary career (1). Four years later, after completing a creative writing workshop and a class at Columbia University, using her real name, Petry publishes the short story, "On Saturday the Siren Sounds" in the periodical, *The Crisis* (2). An editor from Boston's Houghton Mifflin reads the somewhat probing story which tells of a grieving father who loses his favorite child in a house fire, murders his wife because of her neglect of the child, and then takes his own life. The editor approaches Mrs. Petry about applying for Houghton's Literary Fellowship Award in fiction. The following year, Petry makes application and she wins, receiving a stipend of $2,400. In February of 1946, Houghton Mifflin publishes *The Street*. The novel soars to best-seller status, and Ann Petry becomes the first African American woman to achieve such a distinction of literary success.

Since the 1940s, seldom has Petry needed an introduction as celebrated novelist, short story writer, essayist, and author of juvenile and children's books, but as literary critic Barbara Christian instructs, "The least we [always] owe the writer ... is an acknowledgment of her labor" (3). Or, as Sterling A. Brown, the noted sage of African American literary criticism, advises, "Without great audiences [critics, editors and researchers], we cannot have great literature" (4). In 1993, *Ann Petry: A Bio-Bibliography* becomes the first formal acknowledgment of Petry's life and works. It's aims are strategic:

> to promote accuracy in Petry's biography, bibliography, and criticism
> - supported by the book's chronology; annotations of primary and
> secondary works; interviews; cross-references located in the
> annotations of secondary works; and an index.
>
> to increase documentation and cross-references of scholarly interests
> in Petry and critical approaches to Petry's primary and secondary
> works

In numerous ways, the 1993 edition also initiates a guide: Who are Petry's critics, editors, and researchers? How do they acknowledge Petry's life and labor? When are such acknowledgments published - in the 1940s, 1950s, 1960s, 1970s, 1980s, or 1990s? How are such acknowledgments delivered - in articles in peer-reviewed journals, book reviews, articles within collections, interviews, etc? Also as a guide, the 1993 edition directs critical and close readings and re/readings of Ann Petry, uncovering as well as restructuring approaches to Petry's scholarship and criticism.

The 25th Anniversary Edition, Ann Petry: A Bio-Bibliography speaks volumes to the aims and to the excellences of the seminal 1993 edition. Also, found in the anniversary edition is that Petry's critics, editors, and researchers stand on the shoulders of earlier critics, editors and researchers - uncovering, challenging, correcting, expanding, enhancing, documenting, and, acknowledging Petry's biography, bibliography, and criticism *with* aesthetic and theoretical imaginations. The latest edition also reveals a growing Petry audience which, to paraphrase Sterling A. Brown, has not failed to equate great scholarship and criticism with the writer:

- considerable increases in the number of re-issuances of Petry's novels, short stories, and juvenile works in print, braille, and audiobook;

- substantial increases in the number of theses on the writer and on her literary works at undergraduate and graduate levels;

- recognizable increases in the number of summer research fellowships awarded to under-graduates in humanities and interdisciplinary studies for summer research-based studies of Petry's oeuvre;

- translations of Petry's short and long fiction by scholars from almost all of the continents;

- archival information on Petry's life, craft, and literary works deposited not only in public research centers, but also with national public radio; national public television; and historical societies;

- recognizable increases in online monographs on both the writer's primary and secondary works;

- substantial increases in theoretical and comparative studies of the writer and her novels, short stories, and juvenile works - found largely, at this printing, in undergraduate and graduate theses, peer-reviewed articles, and in comparative studies in book collections. Note: book collections devoted solely to Ann Petry are less than ten;

- scholarship and criticism which include interdisciplinary, comparative, post-structuralist, global readings and re-readings of the author and her works (again, found largely, at this printing, in undergraduate and graduate theses, peer-reviewed articles, and comparative studies in book collections). Note: book collections devoted solely to Petry are less than ten;

- excerpts from Petry's major works continue to be anthologized by publishers in the United States and abroad

- supplemental readings of Petry's plots, characters, themes, settings, and stylistics are found in study guides, encyclopedias, dictionaries, and handbooks via print, digital, and video;

- podcasts and audiobooks;

- assigned readings of Petry's novels and several short stories by book clubs;

- attempted adaptations in film and stage of *The Street*; successful adaptations of the short story, "Solo on the Drums";

- blogs which focus on black women writers, including Petry; and

- honoree in the Hall of Fame for African American writers.

With the exception of an Ann Petry literary society, which does not exist at this printing, Ann Petry's critics, editors, and researchers - who now are more diverse and global than ever - strive collectively in the pages that follow, using aesthetic and theoretical imaginations, to provide a "distincter recognition" of the life and labor of one of America's most acclaimed African American women writers.

Biography

The 25th Anniversary Edition, Ann Petry: A Bio-Bibliography includes a Chronology, which was first edited by Mrs. Petry for the 1993 publication (5). The aim of the Chronology remains "to correct errors" that have been perpetuated by critics, editors, and researchers, such as Petry's birthdate, her marital status, her actual publications, when she graduated from high school, college, and professional school, and where she has lectured and received honorary degrees (6). As achieved in the 1993 edition, the Chronology also aims to frame Petry's literary development - using dates, people, and places. For instance, Petry uses landscapes as titles for her published novels, and she uses landscapes for settings in many of her short stories. To assist readers in drawing correlations between landscapes and Petry's artistic style, the Chronology establishes, for instance, that in 1938, shortly after the would-be artist arrives in New York City, she studies visual painting. As Petry confirms, as a literary artist, her choices are to concentrate on "people, landscapes... everything" (7).

Petry's scholarly audience is generally the first to applaud her "swift and moving style." The Chronology includes the fact that during Petry's two years with the American Negro Theatre, she experiences "firsthand the way in which the dialogue . . . further[s] the action" (8). And, of course, there are those years that Petry studies under Mabel Louise Robinson at Columbia University. As the Chronology underscores, it is under the tutelage of Robinson that Petry learns to critique her own techniques as well as other people's works (9). The Chronology concludes with Petry's death and a number of posthumous events that seem significantly biographical and fitting for someone of her literary stature - e.g., a memorial service at the famous First Congregational Church in Old Saybrook, Connecticut, which brings together family, friends, literary critics, editors, journalists, civic figures, and others from the community for remembrance and celebration of the life of the writer; a dedication ceremony held at The Acton Public Library in Old Saybrook, Connecticut, where Petry is honored with the naming of the "Ann Petry Reading Room"; on the Senate floor of the U. S. Congress, a moment of remembrance is led by Connecticut's Senator Dodd who delivers "In Memory of Ann Petry"; and recorded in the *U. S. Congressional Records Edition* is the congressional event honoring Petry (10).

In this anniversary edition, the primary and secondary works are also sources of biography. For instance, under Primary Works, there is Petry's autobiographical essay - encouraged and supported by the Contemporary Author Series with Gale Research. Under "Non-Fiction," several articles also provide glimpses of Petry's personal nuances: "The Common Ground"; "The Great Secret"; and "The Novel as Social Criticism." In the introductions to most of the interviews for this edition, critics such as James Ivey and John O'Brien offer character sketches as well as family sketches. Especially, in his *MELUS* interview, "Ann Petry - The New England Connection," critic Mark K. Wilson includes questions to Petry about her childhood and her parents. In three additional interviews, all of which are re-printed from the 1993 compilation, especially in "An Interview with Ann Petry" and "A Visit with Ann Petry," Petry is questioned extensively about her life. Under Secondary Works to the anniversary edition, added are three new interviews. Though brief in content, these are the most recent additions to interviews which provide in Petry's own words her preferences for creative writing: Jill Krementz's "Ann Petry"; Peggy Dye's "The New York Newsday Interview with Conrad Lynn and Ann Petry"; and Maria Gallagher's "City Fetes Ann Petry: Her Novel 'Street' Sold 1 Million Copies and - At 80 - She's Still Writing" (11).

    Petry's biography is further enhanced in this edition by perhaps her most familial critic and researcher - Elisabeth Ann Petry, who is Ann Petry's daughter. At this writing, in her two books, Elisabeth shares intimate conversations and experiences between mother and daughter; strives to clarify the effects of privacy on Petry's personality and craft; and shares remembrances and reflections of the writer by family and friends. Reviewers of Liz's works expound on the daughter's biographical observations and on the facts and reflections of historical events in the life of Ann Petry. According to some critics, such observations and reflections are significant when researching the effects of Petry's personality on her craft, especially her desire for privacy. Under Secondary Works, see the daughter's entries, *At Home Inside: Daughter's Tribute to Ann Petry* (2008) and *Can Anything Beat White? A Black Family's Letters* (2005); see also the reviews of both works (12). At this printing, efforts are somewhat underway by the family to turn the family letters into a documentary.

    Under the Secondary Works, bountiful also are more diverse renderings of biographical information on Petry - e.g., transcripts from recorded segments of PBS - public television stations and public radio programmings; feature articles on Petry cited by the Connecticut Historical Society and other Connecticut women's organizations; reflective articles by editors over the years at New York's *Amsterdam News* on Petry's work as a journalist in the 1930s and following her death in 1997 (Note: This is Petry's employer when she first arrives in New York in the late 1930s); and insightful articles by the *Hartford Courant*, a major Connecticut periodical which remains quite supportive of its native daughter even after her death. Last, captured under Secondary Works are rising numbers of international Petry critics who speak volumes about the writer through their biographical selections when introducing Petry to international audiences - e.g., see the articles and book reviews that appear in, among others, *London's Daily Mail*, *Guardian* and *The Daily Telegraph*; in the *West Indian Caribbean Studies*; and in periodicals from Canada, France, Germany, Japan, South Korea, and India. Also see online introductions to Petry's biography and criticism by critics from Nigeria and the Middle East (13).

Bibliography

Ann Petry's life and labor as novelist, short story writer, essayist, poet, and author of juvenile and children's literature are also acknowledged through her bibliography. In the 1993 edition, there are 389 entries which include Petry's Primary and Secondary works. In the anniversary edition, there are a total of 910 entries which establish Petry's Primary and Secondary Works. Because the 910 entries, more or less, address plot, characterization, style and stylistic technique, theme, setting, and language, readers are encouraged to review all of Petry's critics, editors and researchers, so to ensure deeper understanding and appreciation of Petry's labor, which, according to Petry, inevitably does begin for her with character, plot, setting, style, and theme. Too, readers are directed to the Index entry "Petry, Ann" which documents and acknowledges more personal accounts of the artist's bibliography, such as: pharmacist, recreation specialist, literary forerunner, realist, naturalist, journalist, columnist, storyteller, and Hollywood screenwriter. In addition, the Index entries document and acknowledge more comprehensively the bibliography of the artist:

- rhetorical and critical readings of Petry's novels, *The Street*, *Country Place*, and *The Narrows*; the short stories in *Miss Muriel and Other Stories*; the juvenile works, *Harriet Tubman, Conductor on the Underground Railroad*, *Legends of the Saints*, and *Tituba of Salem Village*; and the children's literature;

- case studies, study guides, encyclopedias, dictionaries, handbooks, and book collections;

- theses for the doctorate, Master's, Master's of Science (one), and A.B. Honor's;

- comparative studies;

- concentrations of tropes;

- concentrations of themes;

- concentrations of theoretical approaches;

- interviews;

- audiobooks, podcasts, and videos on Petry and writings. [Note: at this printing, the focus of one audiobook is on *The Street* (see, Sapphire elsewhere in this edition) and another focus is on Petry's unpublished short story, "Checkup" which is read by Shayna Small. Most podcasts include Petry's daughter, discussing some of her mother's works];

- translations; and

- international book reviews and introductory articles, published by Petry's critics not only from Canada, France, Italy, Germany, United Kingdom, Japan, South Korea, India, Brazil, and the Caribbean, but also online by her critics from the Middle East and Nigeria.

Criticism

Ann Petry's critics, editors, and researchers of the twenty-first century stand on the shoulders of those who came before them. To recognize just how interconnected are Petry's critics, editors, and researchers - that is, how well they "talk back" to one another - required is a chronological review of Petry's criticism, from the 1940s and 1950s to the present:

In the 1950s, two full-length critical studies of major black novelists - Carl Milton Hughes's *The Negro Novelist, 1940-1950*, a *Discussion of the Writings of American Negro Novelists 1940-1950* and Robert Bone's *The Negro Novel in America* - set the patterns of critical approaches to Petry, and those are sociological and formalist. Because of Hughes's and Bone's book-length critiques, which are often quoted and excerpted well into the 1970s, critics focus on Petry's *The Street* as an indictment of a racist society, or they insist she is a naturalist or a disciple (often a less-than-adequate disciple) of Richard Wright (14). Furthermore, when analyzing *Country Place* as Petry's "raceless" novel, critics insists she is an assimilationist (15). Lesser - known critiques of Ann Petry's writings appear between 1946 and the late 1950s in newspapers and in popular magazines. During this time, critics work to move Petry's criticism beyond the realms of naturalism and the Wright School. For example, in the 1940s in the *Pittsburgh Courier*, one critic calls the writer "Harlem's adopted daughter" (16). For another critic, in the *New York Herald Tribune*, because of her style, Petry is referred to as an "unblushing realist" (17).

Introduction

For a third critic, with the *Chicago Defender*, Petry is an artist who approaches her characters with the "penetration of a psychiatrist . . . [and the] delicate care of a mother" (18). In *The New York Times Book Review*, reviewer Alfred Butterfield looks at the actions of Lutie Johnson in *The Street*, and he encourages further examinations of the narrative as Lutie's "personal epic" (19). In the *Birmingham News*, writer Mary Ellen Crane introduces thoughts of Lutie's "free will" (20), while in the *Boston Chronicle*, writer William Harrison suggests comparing the actions of Lutie and others in *The Street* with the actions of Greek tragedies by Sophocles and Euripides (21). Jose Yglesias in *New Masses*, questions whether *Country Place* is a "morality tale" (22).

In the 1950s, lesser-known critics continue to approach Petry outside of any naturalistic or protest tradition. For instance, in *The Nation*, Diana Trilling explores "class" in *The Street* and encourages additional criticism - perhaps Marxist criticism - on how, in the novel, "class feelings . . . [are] ingrained in the black community" (23). In *The New York Times Book Review*, Wright Morris encourages a comparison of Petry's Mamie Powther in *The Narrows* with James Joyce's Molly Bloom in *Ulysses* (24), while in the *Hartford Courant*, Sidney Clark sees similarities between Faulkner's Lena Groves in *Light in August* and Petry's Abbie Crunch in *The Narrows*. Clark also suggests the Pulitzer Prize for Petry's love story in the same novel. In the late 1950s and early 1960s, Petry's most academic critics appear oblivious to the critiques which appear in newspapers and popular magazines of the 1940s and 1950s; nonetheless, they do call for re-evaluations of Petry's novels. For example, in "Perhaps Not So Soon One Morning," Addison Gayle, Jr., refutes Herbert Hill's conclusion in *Soon One Morning* that James Baldwin and Ralph Ellison are the only capable forerunners of black writers entering the mainstream of American literature. In further disapproval, Gayle concludes that Baldwin's Ida Scott has been drawn more artistically by Petry in *The Street* (25). Although critic Vernon E. Lattin in "Ann Petry and the American Dream" and editor David Littlejohn in *Black on White: A Critical Survey of Writing by American Negroes* are reluctant to dismiss all naturalistic or protest tendencies in Petry's novels, Lattin does insist that readers "look at [Petry's] novels freshly and . . . reevaluate." Then he shows how Petry undermines cultural notions in America that with a little effort anyone can make it (26). David Littlejohn also offers for review Petry's sympathetic identifications with her character sketches (27), and women critics such as Mary Helen Washington in "Black Women Image Makers" (28) and Barbara Smith in "Toward a Black Feminist Criticism" (29) go a step further to claim Petry as a forerunner of the black women writers' literary tradition.

By the 1980s and early 1990s, critics and editors are speaking in persistent and concordant voices, insisting that Petry's criticism be moved beyond naturalistic visions and the Wright School. In an article on Petry for the *Nethula Journal*, Joyce Ann Joyce clarifies the manner with which critics are to move Petry's criticism beyond sociological approaches. She urges Petry critics to trust Petry's *donnee* - her given subject or idea (30). Other critics do concur by "trusting" Petry's given subject or idea, which is observable in their titles: Margaret B. McDowell in " 'The Narrows': A Fuller View of Ann Petry" (31); Bernard Bell in "Ann Petry's "Demythologizing American Culture and Afro-American Character" and "The Triumph of Naturalism" (32); Thulani Davis in "Family Plots: Black Women Writers Reclaim their Past" (33); Trudier Harris in "On Southern and Northern Maids: Geography, Mammies, and Militants" (34); Thelma Shinn in "The Women in Ann Petry's Novels" (35); and Joyce Hope Scott in "Commercial Deportation as Rite of Passage in Black Women's Novels" (36). Included here also should be the numerous Petry critics in the special 1994 issue of *Callaloo* (guest editor is Lindon Barrett). There are also critics and editors who choose to focus on Petry's responses to particular themes. For instance, Sybille Kamme-Erkel looks at "marriage" in *The Street* (37); Nellie McKay in the Introduction to the reprint of *The Narrows* by the Black Women Writers' Series at Beacon Press directs readers to Petry's interest in patriarchal ideology and black feminine consciousness during the 1940s and 1950s (38). In her essay, " 'Patterns against the Sky': Deism and Motherhood in Ann Petry's *The Street*," Marjorie Pryse adds another theme for Petry's criticism - "motherhood" (39). Academic scholars and editors of *But Some of Us Are Brave* include syllabi by leading professional black women writers/critics, so to offer thematic approaches to Petry's fiction (40).

Introduction

Not all of Ann Petry's literary criticism has been favorable. For example, in the 1940s, in "Mrs. Petry's Harlem," James Ivey criticizes the writer's failure in *The Street* to depict "normal and responsible people in the [African American] community." Ivey insists that Lutie fails because of her naivete and because of her poor choices of male friends - not because of Petry's "street" (41). In articles appearing in *The Christian Science Monitor* (42) and *Catholic World* (43), unidentified writers question why Petry as an African American gives such a "deplorable" impression of Harlem life. The unidentified reviewer in *Catholic World* also predicts that the sex and violence in the novel will be objectionable by some African Americans (44). As for Petry's *Country Place*, early critics unfavorably suggest that the novel's style is contrived and melodramatic, or that the work is simply not another *The Street*. In the 1950s, unfavorable criticism of *The Narrows* is concerned with the novel's interracial lovers - Link, a black man, and Camilo, a white woman. Critic Charles Nichols finds Petry's overall effect or style in the novel "disappointing" (45). Over the years, with reprints of *The Street* and *The Narrows*, which began in the mid-1980s, critical objections continue. For instance, in the 1987 essay, " 'Infidelity Becomes Her': The Ambivalent Woman in the Fiction of Ann Petry," critic and editor Mary Helen Washington takes a feminist perspective and faults Petry's insistence on environmental determinism as an explanation for the "dead-end lives" of her characters. Furthermore, Washington objects to Petry's ignoring certain realities for women such as women's "relationships with their families" or women's own "suppressed creativity" (46). In her review of the reprint of *The Street*, writer Sherley Anne Williams never really states any objections; yet, after significant efforts by previous Petry critics to move the writer beyond the shadows of Richard Wright, Chester Himes, Theodore Dreiser, or James Farrell, Williams appears to return Petry's criticism to such prescribed notions at mid-century when she writes that the novel earns Petry "an abiding place among American naturalist novelists" (47).

Throughout the mid-1990s and early 2000s, there are consistent efforts by a number of new researchers and critics and future editors to use their dissertations, peer-reviewed articles, interviews, and books to "talk back" objectively to earlier critics and editors - via reexaminations of reviews of the 1940s and 1950s; reevaluations of positions taken by editors of collections out of the 1960s, 1970s, and 1980s on black writers such as Petry; and reassessments of research series from the 1980s and early 1990s on black women writers at work. Throughout the mid-1990s and early 2000s, Petry's researchers, critics and editors never lose site of Petry's *donnee*, or even keywords that are often associated with Petry and her literary works - e.g., class, race, gender, realism, forerunner, the American Dream, Harlem, morality, psychology of characters, community, ideology, or suggestions for comparative studies of Petry and other major male and female writers. These researchers, critics and editors make use of "close readings" - how Petry uses language - and they apply more modernist, post-modernist, structuralist, and post-structuralist theories to their "close readings." As a result, they usher in new directions in Petry's scholarship and criticism - e.g., see Lindon Barrett's book *Blackness and Value: Seeing Double: Cambridge Studies in American Literature and Culture* (1999), which pulls from his dissertation on Petry as a revisionist of black values and identity; Keith Clark's article "A Distaff Dream Deferred? Ann Petry and the Art of Subversion," which pulls from his dissertation on detailed and observable techniques of subversion in Petry's novels and short stories; Hilary Holladay's *Ann Petry* (1996) which pulls from a dissertation that details thematic aesthetics of Petry's novels and short stories, and which calls for more comparative studies of "communities," "neighborhoods" and "relationships" between Petry and other major male and female writers; Hazel Arnett Ervin's dissertation, "The Subversion of Cultural Ideology in Ann Petry's *The Street* and *Country Place*" (1993), which uncovers a hidden feminist text in Petry's 1940's novels and, via Petry's echoes, contradictions and gaps in her works, deconstructs 1940's ideology to raise a new level of feminine consciousness. Such outcomes authorize Ervin's editions of "firsts" such as *Ann Petry: A Bio-Bibliography* (1993), *Ann Petry's Short Fiction: Critical Essays*, (with Hilary Holladay in 2004), and *The Critical Response to Ann Petry* (2005). Also, in the 2000s, critic Kimberly Drake pulls from her dissertation and generates through her articles new and diverse directions in Petry studies which are literary, cultural, and theoretical - e.g.," 'Women on the Go': Blues, Conjure, and Other Alternatives to Domesticity in Ann Petry's *The Street* and *The Narrows*" (48). Also, Kari J. Winters' contribution promotes new directions in Petry's scholarship and criticism, as is suggested in the title of her article: "Narrative Desire in Ann Petry's *The Street*" (49). Like the earlier Petry critics (Barrett, Clark, Holladay, Ervin, Drake, and Winters), later Petry critics work collectively, in the early to mid-2000s, to ensure new directions in Petry studies - cultural, literary, and theoretical - and they make applications of new terminology - e.g., Muriel W. Brailey, who devotes a dissertation to the writer and then an article to Petry's short stories in the late 1990s; Rita Dandridge (who might be seen as earlier and later theoretical critic/editor); Martin Japtok and later Gene Jarrett who illustrate how one might reexamine and theorize about "whiteness" in Petry's short and long New England fiction; and Carol E. Henderson, Heather Hicks, John C. Charles, Rose Marie-Garland Thomson, and Joy Myree-Mainor who literally focus and publish on "the text" in Petry's fiction (50). Include, among others, Gladys J. Washington, who devotes several articles, from the 1980s to the early 2000s, to "the multiplicity of tendencies, attitudes, desires, and determinations" of Petry's characters in Petry's short fiction when closely viewed through Petry's "interweaving" of folk traditions into the "fabric of the fiction." In essence, to echo Sterling Brown, well into the twenty-first century, great audiences can equate great literary criticism to the acclaimed writer Ann Petry.

As stated earlier in this introduction, Petry's critics, editors, and researchers of the twentieth century do not go unrecognized by Petry's critics, editors, and researchers of the twenty-first century, who, again, are more diverse and global than ever. As a result, *The 25th Anniversary Edition, Ann Petry: A Bio-Bibliography* is diverse and inclusive of critics, editors, researchers, and others who, therefore, "look back and then go forth"- documenting, challenging, correcting, expanding, enhancing, acknowledging and promoting Petry's scholarship and criticism with aesthetic and theoretical imaginations. Expect, therefore, to find, among others, the following in the anniversary edition:

- *critical, theoretical approaches* of Petry's life and works that move her scholarship and criticism from rhetorical and formalist to more theory-driven critiques: archetypes, architectural aesthetics, aural aesthetics, authenticity, authority, black futilitarianist, body as text, the theory of dwelling, eco-criticism, geo-criticism, Gothicism, green reading, intersectionality, intertextuality (of class, race, and gender), liberal humanism, literacy, Marxism, masquerade narratives, matriarchal narratives, narrative authority, narrative desires, objective correlatives, the politics of listening, queer desires, representation, spatiality, scars as text, signification, spectatorship, subversion, surveillance, the 'teller' and the telling, trauma theory, useable past, whiteness, and white panopticism, to name a few;

- *comparative studies* between Petry and other major, male writers such as Achebe, Baldwin, Clark (Austin), Crane, Dickens, Dreiser, Ellison, Faulkner, Hardy, Hawthorne, Hayden, Himes, James, Joyce, Kafka, Lawrence, Malamud, Melville, Norris, Steinbeck, and Wright; or between Petry and other major, female writers such as Brooks, Butler, Cather, Chopin, Childress, Cisneros, Cofer, Cruz, Faust, Hansberry, Hurston, Jackson, Jewett, Kingston, Larsen, Marshall, Meriwether, Morrison, Naylor, Olsen, Porter, Stein, Walker, West, Wharton, Wright, and Woolf, to name a few;

- *stylistic* use of cultural and linguistic codes, so to enhance storytelling or plot structure, characterization, setting, and theme in novels and short stories - e.g., music such as jazz, the blues, and hip hop; singing; film; dance such as Lindy Hop and Cakewalk; theatre; and conjure;

- *tropes* that represent a commonality and a diversity of words or expressions in Petry, such as: black mourning, city, community, domesticity, double consciousness, the forties, Harlem, home, immigration, Jane Crow writing, marriage and domesticity, maternal myth, matriarchal myth, memory, merit myth, migration, place, prejudice, poverty and space, railroad blues, riot as ritual, scars, space, street literature, urban spaces, urban street literature, voice, and womanist, to name a few; and

- *themes* that represent common recurrences of ideas or topics in Petry, including: the American Dream, anti-lynching literature, black intimacy, city, community, criminal justice in literature, the forties, geography, identities, irony, labor, law and literature; literature and medicine, literature of exile, loneliness in cities, marginalization, masculinity, migration, motherhood, mothers of incarcerated sons, oppression, prodigal daughter, race and sexuality, seven deadly sins, smellscapes, social realism, social work and literature, state of innocence, stereotypes, totalitarianism literature, urban realism, values, violence, war and citizenship, and women war literature, to name a few.

Ann Petry was asked once to identify the works for which she wanted to be remembered, and she responded, "I want to be remembered for everything I've written" (51). She followed up with this remark: "I try to write so that what I've written will be remembered, whether it's a character or a situation or believable dialogue that will leave a lasting impression" (52). As a reminder, prior to her death, Petry's published works consist of three novels, sixteen short stories, five poems, one children's book, three juvenile works, and collectively, more than twenty-five book reviews and articles. The most reviewed work by Ann Petry is *The Street*. The least reviewed include the children's work, *The Drugstore Cat*; the juvenile work, *The Legend of the Saints*; and Petry's five poems.

In *The 25th Anniversary Edition, Ann Petry: A Bio-Bibliography*, Petry's critics, editors, and researchers of the twentieth and twenty-first centuries measurably strive to acknowledge collectively - in English and in translations - "everything" that the gifted writer has written. Petry's critics, editors, and researchers also *witness* for others who seek to understand the responsibilities of critics, researchers, and editors who are immensely interested in remembering and in acknowledging the life and labor of writer Ann Petry - yesterday, today, and tomorrow.

Hazel Arnett Ervin, Ph.D.

(c) 2021

Notes

A Note of Gratitude

As stated in the first edition of this compilation, I remain forever appreciative to a number of particular people, now either in memory or in the present for their support. First, I want to express immense gratitude to the late Mrs. Petry who is remembered by so many as a literary forerunner, heroine, friend, and teacher. I appreciate Petry who provided interviews and articles which I had no knowledge. Nor had I ever seen certain Petry pieces in other bibliographies. Thus, I am grateful to James Lee Hill in *Bibliography of the Works of Chester Himes, Ann Petry, and Frank Yerby* for his early compilation of numerous secondary sources on Petry; to Carol Fairbank and Eugene Engeldinger for their compilation of secondary works on Petry in *Black American Fiction: A Bibliography*; and to those persons who included bibliographies on Petry in their dissertations. The latter served to disclose many other sources of Petry's bibliography prior to 1993. Next, I want to thank the thoughtful librarians at the following universities: Atlanta University Center, Boston, Duke, Fisk, Howard, North Carolina Central, the University of Minnesota, and Yale. From the group, I am especially grateful to Janet Sims-Woods (prior to her retirement) and to others at the Moorland-Spingarn Research Center at Howard University; to curators, Patricia Willis and others at the Beinecke Rare Book and Manuscript Library at Yale; Bettye McCullough in Archives/Special Collections at the Woodruff (Atlanta University Center) Library; and to the staff both at the Schomburg Center for Research in Black Culture in New York City and the Martin Luther King, Jr. Public Library in Washington, D.C. A heartfelt thank you to Charles Niles and all others in Special Collections at the Mugar Library at Boston University. Thank you to Dr. Alphonso Frost at Howard University for his English translation of the German writer Sabine Brock and her study of *The Street*, and to Michel Fabre in Paris, France, for his prompt response to my query on Chester Himes. The great Professor Lettie Austin at Howard taught us to confirm *and* to reconfirm our sources. After reconfirming Fabre's scholarship on Himes, I can now exclude Chester Himes's review of *The Street* which had been recorded by most of Petry's critics as "missing." In a letter dated 7 November 1991 from Michel Fabre, who, at the time, was compiling Chester Himes's bibliography, I learned that Himes's review of *The Street* was actually unpublished. Thank you, E. Ethelbert Miller, Christopher Arnett, Kevin Ervin, Antionette Kerr, Ann Shockley, Blyden Jackson, Stephen Henderson, and Jon Woodson. To the many people whom I spoke to at conferences, over the telephone, or via email, requesting information, articles, books, and/or photographs of Petry for the first edition, again in memory or in the present, I thank you for your selfless contributions. Finally, a sincere thank you to David Faldet and Jacqueline S. Wilkie who recently provided me a copy of their article which includes Petry. Ann Petry was someone who really disliked photographs. She believed pictures took away from one's spirit and reality. In 1993, I chose to honor her request, and the many pictures collected for the edition were removed; I have chosen again in this edition to exclude pictures.

Notes to the Introduction

1. Letter dated 12 May 1988 from Ann Petry to Hazel A. Ervin which also includes copies of newspaper clippings, articles, letters, etc., which are significant to the Chronology, Primary Works, and Secondary works.
2. Ann Petry, "On Saturday the Siren Sounds at Noon." *Crisis* 50.12 (December 1943): 368-369. See #16 in this edition.
3. Barbara Christian, *Black Feminist Criticism: Perspectives on Black Women Writers* (New York: Pergamon, 1985), xi.
4. Sterling A. Brown, "Our Literary Audiences." In *African American Literary Criticism, 1773 to 2000.* Edited by Hazel Arnett Ervin. (New York: Twayne Publishers, 1999), 51.
5. Letter dated 12 May 1988 from Ann Petry to Hazel A. Ervin which also includes copies of newspaper clippings, articles, letters, etc., which are significant to the 1993 edition.
6. Ibid
7. *Ann Petry, Contemporary Authors: Autobiography Series*, vol 6 (Detroit: Gale Research, 1988).
8. Ibid.
9. Ibid.
10. "In Memory of Ann Petry" is the announcement of her death shared on the floor of the United States Senate. See #431 in this volume.
11. See new interviews with Petry since the 1993 edition: see Jill Kremantz.
12. Elisabeth Ann Petry in the daughter of Ann Petry. See # 637 and #638 elsewhere in this edition.
13. International critics have appeared in, among others, the following periodicals: *London Daily Mail*, #637; *Guardian*, #468; *Times Literary Supplement*, #549; and *The Daily Telegraph*, #606; *New Korean Journal of English Language and Literature*, #287; *KIU Interdisciplinary Journal of Humanities and Social Sciences* (Nigeria), #7; *Caribbean Studies*, #168; *Research Scholar*, #276; *Cahiers Charles*, #183; *Canadian Review of American Studies*, #143; *La Poesie Americaine: Construction Lyriques*, #180; and 영미문학페미니즘 *Feminist Studies in English Literature*, # 214 to name a few.
14. Carl Milton Hughes, #425 and Robert Bone, #150 are editors of works which include Petry.
15. Ibid.
16. James E. Fuller, "Harlem Portrait," *Pittsburgh Courier*, 9 February 1946 [Special Collections, Boston University].
17. Arna Bontemps, "Tough, Carnal Harlem," *New York Herald Tribune Weekly Book Review*, 10 February 1946, 4.
18. Ben Burns, "Off the Book Shelf," *Chicago Defender*, 9 February 1946 [Special Collections Boston University].
19. Alfred Butterfield, "The Dark Heartbeat of Harlem," *New York Times Book Review*, 10 February 1946, 6.
20. Mary Ellen Crane, "Life in Harlem," *Birmingham News*, 9 March 1946 [Special Collections, Boston University].

21. William Harrison, review of The Street, *Boston Chronicle*, 23 February 1946 [Special Collections, Boston University].
22. Jose Yglesias, "Classy-Type People," *New Masses*, 9 December 1947 [Special Collections, Boston University].
23. Diana Trilling, "Class and Color," *The Nation* 162 (9 March 1946): 290-291.
24. Wright Morris, "The Complexity of Evil," *New York Times Book Review*, 16 August 1953, 4.
25. Addison Gayle, Jr., "Perhaps Not So Soon One Morning," *Phylon* 26 no. 4 (Winter 1968): 397.
26. Vernon E. Lattin, "Ann Petry and the American Dream," *Black American Literature Forum*, 12, no. 2 (Summer 1978): 69-72.
27. David Littlejohn, *Black on White: A Critical Survey of Writing by American Negroes* (New York: Viking, 1966).
28. Mary Helen Washington, "Black Women Image Makers," *Black World* 23, no. 10 (August 1974): 11.
29. Barbara Smith, "Toward a Black Feminist Criticism," *Conditions: Two* 1, no. 2 (October 1977): 25-42.
30. Joyce Ann Joyce, Ann Petry, *Nethula Journal* 2 (1982): 16-20. Joyce's use of the word "donnee" is defined further by that of Henry James in "The Art of Fiction."
31. Margaret B. McDowell, " 'The Narrows': A Fuller View of Ann Petry," *Black American Literature Forum* 14, no 4 (Winter 1980): 135-141.
32. Bernard W. Bell, "Ann Petry's Demythologizing of American Culture and Afro-American Character," *Conjuring: Black Women, Fiction, and Literary Tradition*, ed. Marjorie Pryse and Hortense J. Spillers (Bloomington: Indiana University Press, 1985); "The Triumph of Naturalism," *The Afro-American Novel and Its Tradition* (Amherst: University of Massachusetts Press, 1987. Reprint. 1989).
33. Thulani Davis, "Family Plots: Black Women Writers Reclaim Their Past," *The Village Voice* 32, no 10 (10 March 1987): 14-17.
34. Trudier Harris, "On Southern and Northern Maids: Geography, Mammies and Militants," *From Mammies to Militants: Domestics in Black American Literature* (Philadelphia: Temple University Press,1982).
35. Thelma J. Shinn, "Women in the Novels of Ann Petry," *Critique, Studies in Modern Fiction* 16, no.1 (1974): 110-120.
36. Joyce Hope Scott, "Commercial Deportation as Rite of Passage in Black Women's Novels," *Matatu* 3, no. 6 (1989): 127-154.
37. Sybille Kamme-Erkel, *Happily Ever After?: Marriage and Its Rejection in Afro-American Novels* (New York: Peter Lang, 1989).
38. Nellie McKay, Introduction, *The Narrows* (Boston: Beacon, 1988). See Also Nellie Y. McKay, "Ann Petry's The Street and The Narrows: A Study of the Influence of Class, Race, and Gender on Afro-American Women's Lives" in *Women and War: The Changing Status of American Women from the 1930's to the 1950's,* ed. Maria Diedrich and Dorothea Fischer-Hornang (New York: Berg, 1999); 39.
39. Marjorie Pryse, " 'Patterns against the Sky:' Deism and Motherhood in Ann Petry's The Street" in *Conjuring: Black Women, Fiction, and Literary Tradition*,

ed. Marjorie Pryse and Hortense J. Spillers (Bloomington: Indiana University Press, 1985).
40. Gloria T. Hall, Patricia Bell Scott, and Barbara Smith, eds. *All the Women Are White, All the Blacks Are Men, But Some of Us Are Brave* (Old Westbury, NY: The Feminist Press, 1982).
41. James Ivey, "Mrs. Petry's Harlem," *Crisis* 53, no. 5 (May 1946): 154-155.
42. M. W., "The Latest Negro Novel," *Christian Science Monitor*, 8 February 1946, 14.
43. Review of *The Street*, *Catholic World* 163 (May 1946): 187. For additional critiques that might be considered unfavorable, see Petry in the Index to this book.
44. Ibid.
45. Charles H. Nichols, "New England Narrative," *Phylon* 14, no. 4 (Fourth Quarter 1953): 437.
46. Mary Helen Washington, " 'Infidelity Becomes Her': The Ambivalent Woman in the Fiction of Ann Petry" in *Invented Lives: Narratives of Black Women, 1860-1960* (Garden City, NY: Anchor/. Doubleday, 1987), 298. One might add, however, that Washington's criticism simultaneously encourages further feminist readings of Petry. After all, she follows her critical comments with an excerpt from *The Narrows* - an excerpt that highlights the assertive and individualistic Mamie Powther - and she titles the excerpt simply, "Mamie."
47. Sherley Anne Williams, Review of *The Street*, *MS* (23 September 1986), 23.
48. See Kimberly Drake, #285, #286.
49. See Kari J. Winters, #889.
50. See Gladys J. Washington, #860, #861; Muriel W. Brady, #160, #161; Rita Dandridge, #250, #253; Martin Japtok, #449, #450; Gene Jarrett, #451, #452, Carol E. Henderson, #389, #392; Heather Hicks, #397, #398; John C. Charles, #209, #210, #211; Rose Marie Garland Thomson, #824, #825, #826; and Joy Myree-Mainor, #585, #586, #587.
51. See Hazel Arnett Ervin, "Just a Few Questions More, Mrs. Petry" in this edition.
52. Ibid

ANN PETRY

A Bio-Bibliography

Primary Works

Fiction

1

"The Bones of Louella Brown," *Opportunity: Negro Journal of Life* 25.4 (October - December 1947): 189-192, 226-230. Also appears in *Miss Muriel and Other Stories* by Ann Petry. Boston: Houghton Mifflin, 1971. Reprint. Boston: Beacon, 1989. *Great Short Stories by African American Writers*. Edited by Christine Rudisel and Robert Blaisdell. Mineola, NY: Dover Publication, 2015. Foreign Reprint: Los huesos de Louella Brown y otros relatos. Translated by Teresa Lancer Demaso Lonez Garcia. Hoorn, The Netherlands: Palabrero Press, 2016.

  A Harvard graduate student attempts to study the bone structure of white and black women and inadvertently mixes up the "astonishingly" identical remains of two women: the Countess of Castro, a white woman, and Louella Brown, a black women and laundress to the Countess. Which of these women will be buried in Boston's all-white Bedford Abbey Cemetery? Several Bostonian conservatives are faced with such a perplexing question - that is, until the ghost of Louella Brown returns.

2

Country Place. Boston: Houghton Mifflin, 1947. Reprint. London: Michael Joseph, Ltd., 1948. Chatham, NJ: Chatham Bookseller, 1971. Reissued. Evanston, Il: Northwestern University Press, 2019. Foreign Reprint. Tempeste. Translated by V. E. Bravetta. Roma: Jandi Sapi, 1949.

  Like the powerful thunderstorms that disrupt the pastoral town of Lennox, uncontrollably disruptive are also the lives of several characters when their lives become intertwined with the lives of others in this New England setting.

3

" Doby's Gone." *Phylon* 5. 4 (Fourth Quarter 1944): 361-66. Also appears in *Miss Muriel and Other Stories* by Ann Petry. Boston: Houghton Mifflin, 1971. Reprint. Boston: Beacon, 1989. *The Third Woman*. Edited by Dexter Fisher. Boston: Houghton Mifflin, 1980. *The Unforgetting Heart: An Anthology of Short Stories by African American Women, 1859-1993*. Edited by Asha Kanwar. San Francisco: Aunt Lutebooks, 1993.

  A close relationship between six-year-old Sue Johnson and her imaginary friend, Doby, comes to an end when Sue enters the first grade.

4

"Has Anybody Seen Miss Dora Dean?" *New Yorker* (October-November 1958): 41-48. Also appears in *Miss Muriel and Other Stories* by Ann Petry. Boston: Houghton Mifflin, 1971. Reprint. Boston: Beacon, 1989.

    A young and nameless female narrator is summoned to the home of Sarah Forbes - an old friend of the narrator's parents - to honor Sarah's death wish. The story is told as the narrator, who in route to the Forbes's home, recollects the circumstances surrounding Sarah's death - her marriage to Peter Forbes and, three weeks later, their living in separate quarters because Forbes had to return to his live-in employment with Mrs. Wingate. Then, there are Forbes's promiscuous activities with beautiful girls in Shacktown, followed by his suicide. The title of the short story is a tune made famous by Bert Williams and George Walker during the twenties, suggesting "cakewalks, beautiful brown girls, and ragtimes." The tune becomes a leitmotif for Peter Forbes throughout the story.

5

"In Darkness and Confusion." In *Cross Section*. Edited by Edwin Seaver. New York: L. B. Fisher, 1947, 98-128. Also appears in *Black Voices*. Edited by Abraham Chapman. New York: New American Library, 1968. Reprint. 1978. *Right On: An Anthology of Black Literature*. Edited by Bradford Chambers and Rebecca Moon. New York: New American Library, 1970. *Harlem*. Edited by John Henrik Clarke. New York: New American Library, 1970. Reprinted. Brooklyn, NY: A & B Books Publishers, 1993. *Miss Muriel and Other Stories* by Ann Petry. Boston: Houghton Mifflin, 1971. Reprint. Boston: Beacon, 1989. Foreign Reprint. *Harlem Story*. Edited by Giichi Ouchi and Mikio Suzuki. Tokyo: Kaibunsha Ltd., n.d.

    The story involves psychological probes, particularly into the minds of three oppressed characters who purge themselves of built-up frustrations and anger when they participate in a riot that becomes ritualistic.

6

"Like a Winding Sheet." *Crisis* 52.11 (November 1945): 317-318, 331-332. Also appears in *A World of Fiction: Twenty Timeless Short Stories*. Edited by Sybil Marcus. White Plains, NY: Pearson/Longman, 2006. *American Working-Class Literature: An Anthology*. New York: Oxford University Press, 2007. *Best American Short Stories*. Edited by Martha Foley. Boston: Houghton Mifflin. 1946. *Black Literature in America*. Edited by Houston A. Baker. New York: McGraw-Hill, 1971. *From the Roots: Short Stories by Black Americans*. Edited by Charles L. James. New York: Dodd, Mead,1970. *Miss Muriel and Other Stories* by Ann Petry. Boston: Houghton Mifflin, 1971. Reprint. Boston, Beacon, 1989. *Black Writers of America: A Comprehensive Anthology*. Edited by Richard Barksdale and Keneth Kinnamon. New York: Macmillan, 1972. *New Cavalcade: African American Writing from 1760 to Present*. Edited by Arthur P. Davis, J. Saunders Redding, and Joyce Ann Joyce. Vol.1. Washington, DC: Howard University Press 1991. *Revolutionary Tales: African American Women's Short Stories From the First Story to the Present*. Edited by Bill Mullen. New York: Dell Publisher, 1995.

    With continuous references to his hands, Petry introduces main character Mr. Johnson, and foreshadows his violent outcome. After a racially motivated incident, the stressed and discontented Mr. Johnson loses his self-control, and, with his hands, murders the one person who has been his long-time companion throughout the story - his wife.

7

"Marie of the Cabin Club." *Afro-American* (Baltimore), August 19, 1939, 14.

    This suspense-romance, written under the pseudonym Arnold Petri, is Petry's first publication in short fiction. Marie, a cigarette girl at the Cabin Club, is kidnapped by a villainous English spy and used to entrap her friend Georgie Barr, a musician at the jazz club and a spy for France. When Barr refuses to turn over secret intelligence to the Englishman, he and Marie are told they will die. The New York police, however, intervenes. Once out of danger, Georgie confesses his love for Marie and he asks her to marry him.

8

"The Migraine Workers." *Redbook* (May 1967): 66-67, 125-127. Also appears in *Miss Muriel and Other Stories* by Ann Petry. Boston: Houghton Mifflin, 1971. Reprint. Boston: Beacon, 1989. *Feminine Fiction from Across America*. Edited by Tettuo Yamaguchi and Midori Sasaki. Tokyo: Bunri Co., Ltd., n.d.

    The owner of a service station feeds a poor and undernourished migrant worker who escapes his migratory job in order to survive. Before the story ends, the simple act of turning the migrant worker over to his employer becomes a painful decision for the service station owner.

9

"Miss Muriel." In *Soon One Morning: New Writings by American Negroes, 1940- 1962*. Edited by Herbert Hill. New York: Knopf, 1963, 166-209. Reprint. 1965. Also appears in *Stories in Black and White*. Edited by Eva Kissin. Philadelphia: Lippincott, 1970. *Miss Muriel and Other Stories by Ann Petry*. Boston: Houghton Mifflin, 1971. Reprint. Boston: Beacon, 1989. *Nine Short Novels by American Women*. Edited by Elizabeth McMahan, Susan Day, and Robert Funk. New York: St Martin's Press, 1993.

    A nameless child who lives a protected and carefree life in a small, New England town loses this state of innocence when she chooses to take a stand against her uncle and his friend for deliberately running out of town her friend Mr. Bemish - a white man - because Mr. Bemish wants to marry her Aunt Sophronia - a black woman.

10

"The Moses Project." *Harbor Review* (English Department, University of Massachusetts), 5/6 (1986): 52-61.

    Contemporary trickster Joe Cooper is sentenced to weekend house arrest for neglecting to pay $300 in fines for traffic tickets. A transmitter attached to Cooper's leg monitors his movements and beeps whenever he goes outside his confined space. Cooper, however, who is a skilled mechanic and an expert locksmith, outwits the authorities. He freely spends his weekends away from his home.

11

"Mother Africa." *Miss Muriel and Other Stories* by Ann Petry. Boston: Houghton Mifflin, 1971. Reprint. Boston: Beacon,1989. *African American Short Story, 1970 to 1990*. Edited by Wolfgang Karrer and Barbara Puschmann. Wissenschaftlicher Verlag Trier, 1993.

    The main character, Mannie, an "everyman," idolizes a female statue that he calls the sable Mother Africa. The statue, however, is really an "alive-looking [white female] statue," used by the omniscient narrator to satirize the colonization of the African American mind.

12

The Narrows. Boston: Houghton Mifflin, 1953. Reprint. London: 16. Gollancz, 1954. Reprint. New York: Signet, 1955. Reprint. London: Ace Books Limited, 1961. Reprint. New York: Pyramid, 1971. Reprint. Boston: Beacon, 1988. Reprint. Evanston, Il: Northwestern University Press, 2017 (Keith Clark, Contributor). Reprint. New York: The Library of America, 2019 (Farah Jasmine Griffin, Editor). Also appears as excerpt, "Mamie," in *Invented Lives: Narratives of Black Women 1860-1960.* Edited by Mary Helen Washington. Garden City, NY: Anchor/Doubleday, 1987. Foreign Reprint. *Link and Camilo.* Berlin: Propylaen-Verlag, 1955.

A black man and a white woman are in love. Yet, for reasons extending as far back as slavery, such an affair is taboo, even in New England America.

13

"The Necessary Knocking at the Door." *The Magazine of the Year 1947* (August 1947): 39-44. Also appears in *Miss Muriel and Other Stories* by Ann Petry. Boston: Houghton Mifflin, 1971. Reprint. Boston: Beacon, 1989. *Strange Barriers.* Edited by J. Vernon Shea. New York: Lion Library Editions, 1955.

Early in the day at a religious convention, the southern conservative Mrs. Gib Taylor hurls the two-syllable hate "N" word at main character Alice. Late in the night, Alice overhears Mrs. Taylor moaning as if she were seriously ill, and she is seriously ill. But after Mrs. Taylor's racial epithet earlier in the day, Alice cannot force herself to knock, to enter, and to inquire. By morning, Mrs. Taylor is dead. The story ends, raising questionings about the actions of both women.

14

"The New Mirror." *New Yorker* (29 May 1965): 28-36, 38, 40,43-44, 46, 49-50, 52, 55. Also appears in *Miss Muriel and Other Stories* by Ann Petry. Boston: Houghton Mifflin, 1971. Reprint. Boston: Beacon, 1989. *By Women: An Anthology of Literature.* Edited by Linda Kirschner and Marcia McClintock Folson. Boston: Houghton Mifflin, 1996. *Out of Our Lives: A Selection of Contemporary Black Fiction.* Edited by Quandra Stadler. Washington, DC: Howard University Press, 1975.

The "private" lives of the Layen family - " those rare laboratory specimen [of] black people who [run] the [only] drugstore in the white town of Wheeling, New York" - are interrupted when father Layen disappears for almost a day. His wife and sister-in-law do not know that he has secretly gone to get a set of false teeth; they must decide whether to inform the police and the public that someone from their private world is missing.

15

"Olaf and His Girl Friend." *Crisis* 52. 5 (May 1945): 135-137,147. Also appears in *Miss Muriel and Other Stories* by Ann Petry. Boston: Houghton Mifflin, 1971. Reprint. Boston: Beacon, 1989.

Told from the perspective of an observant painter is one man's courageous and successful attempts to be reunited with the woman he loves. The grandmother of Belle Rose prevents Belle from marrying the Barbadian Olaf by resettling the girl in Harlem. Yet, after crossing the ocean, Olaf finds Belle Rose and reclaims her as his only love.

16

"On Saturday the Siren Sounds at Noon." *Crisis* 50.12 (December 1943): 368-369. *Spooks, Spies and Private Eyes: Black Mystery Crime and Suspense Fiction.* New York: Doubleday, 1996.

Minutes before the nameless protagonist commits suicide by jumping in front of a moving train, the sound of a siren and the sight of metallic train tracks evoke memories of his return home from work to find the charred and still body of his favorite child, and the terribly burned bodies of his other two children. The children had been locked inside their tiny Harlem apartment by their mother who went out. The protagonist murders the negligent mother, and as the story comes full circle, he commits suicide. This short story is the first to appear under Petry's real name.

17

"Solo on the Drums." *The Magazine of the Year 1947* (October 1947): 105-110. Also appears in *Miss Muriel and Other Stories* by Ann Petry. Boston: Houghton Mifflin, 1971. Reprint. Boston: Beacon, 1989. *American Negro Short Stories.* Edited by John Clarke. New York: Hill and Wang, 1966. *Best American Short Stories: A Century of the Best.* Edited by John Henrik Clarke. New York: Hill and Wang, 1998. *Harlem's Glory: Black Women Writing, 1900-1950.* Cambridge, MA: Harvard University Press, 1997. *Hot and Cool: Jazz Short Stories.* New York: Plume, 1990. *Intercultural Journeys through Reading and Writing.* Edited by Marilyn Smith Layton. NY: Harper Collins, 1991.

This story, with its familiar theme of boy loses girl, includes the influences of jazz stylistics on characterization. Shortly before his performance, drummer Kid Jones discovers that his wife plans to leave him for the piano player in the musical group. Enraged and humiliated, Jones manages to go on stage and to perform. His "pulse beat . . . becomes one with the drums" and by the end of the performance (and the story), he has purged himself of his anger, pain, and humiliation.

18

The Street. Boston: Houghton Mifflin, 1946. Reprint. New York: Pyramid, 1946. 1961. Reprint. London: Michael Joseph, Ltd.,1947. Reprint. New York: Signet, 1947. Reprint. Boston: Beacon, 1985. Reissue. Boston: Houghton Mifflin, 1992. Reissue. Boston:Houghton Mifflin, 2014. Reissue. London, UK: Penguin Books, 2019. Reissue. New York: The Library of America, 2019 (Farah Jasmine Griffin, Editor). Reissue. Boston, MA: Mariner Books. Houghton Mifflin Harcourt, 2020.Reissue. London: Virago Press LTD, 2020 (Tayari Jones, Contributor). In condensations. *Afro-American Literature: Fiction.* Compiled by William Adams, Peter Conn, and Barry Slepian. Boston: Houghton Mifflin, 1970. *African American Literature: Voices of a Tradition.* Chicago: Holt, Rinehart and Winston, 1992. *Cavalcade: Negro American Writing from 1760 to the Present.* Edited by Arthur P. Davis and J. Saunders Redding. Boston: Houghton Mifflin, 1971. *City Women.* Edited by Liz Hera. Boston: Beacon Press, 1993. *Great American Novels You've (Probably) Never Read.* Edited by Karl Bridges. Westport, CT: Libraries Unlimited, 2007. *The Ghetto Reader.* Edited by David P. Demarest and Lois S. Lamdin. New York: Random House, 1970. *Negro Digest* 4, no 7 (May 1946): 84-98. *The Harlem Reader: A Celebration of New York's Most Famous Neighborhood, from the Renaissance Years to the Twenty-First Century.* Edited by Herb Boyd. New York: Three Rivers Press, 2003. *Intimate Relationships:Marriage, Family and Lifestyles through Literature.* Edited by Rose M.Somerville. Englewood Cliffs, NJ: Prentice-Hall, 1975. *The Norton Anthology of African American Literature.* Edited by Henry Louis Gates, Jr. and Valerie Smith. New York: W. W. Norton & Company, 2016. *The Prentice Hall*

Anthology of African American Literature. Edited by Rochelle Smith, Sharon L. Jones, Kevin Everod Quashie, and Stewart L. Twite. Upper Saddle River, NJ: Prentice Hall, 2000. *Racism and Anti-Racism in American Popular Culture: Portrayals of African Americans in Fiction and Film*. Edited by Catherine Selk and John Selk. Manchester, UK: Manchester University Press, 1990. Foreign Reprints. *A Rua.* Translated by Ligia Junqueira Smith. Sao Paulo, Brazil: Companhia Editoru Nacional, 1947. *De Straat.* Translated by Vertaald Door and H. W. J. Schaap. Amsterdam: N.Y. De Arbeiderspers, 1948. *De Stratte.* Berlin: Druck and Veratbeitung. *Die Strabe Roman.* Uda Stratling: Veriag Nagel & Kimche A G. Zurich. Zurich Nagel & Kimche, 2020. *Die Strasse*. Translated by von Marinette Chenaud. Bern, Switzerland: Verlag Hallwag Bern, n.d. *En Kvinne I Harlem.* Translated by Oversatt Av Erik Farland. Oslo: Tiden, 1947. *Gaden*. Copenhagen: Aschenog Dansk Forlag Kobenhaun, 1946. *Gatan*. Translated by Olof Hogstadius. Stockholm: Ljus, 1947. *La Calle*. Translated by Julio Vacarezza Argentina: Ediciones Penser, n.d. *La Rehob*. Translated by Aaron Amir. Tel-Aviv: N. Tversky Publishing House, Ltd., 1947. *La Rue*. Translated by Martine Monod, Nicole Soupault, and Philippe Soupault. Paris: Charlot, 1948. Reprinted. *La Rue*. Translated by Martine Monod, Nicole Soupault, and Philippe Soupault. Paris: Charlot, 2018. Reprinted. *La Rue*. Translated by Martine Monod, Nicole Soupault, and Philippe Soupault. Paris: Charlot, 2019. *The Street*. Translated by Ryo Namikawa. Tokyo: Kaizo Sha, 1950. Foreign Excerpts. *L'Arche* 4, no 23 (Janvier1947): 47-86 (translated by Nicole and Philippe Soupault). *L'Arche* 6, no 24 (Fevrier 1947): 42-79. *L'Arche* 7, no. 25 (Marche 1947): 61-96. *L'Arche* 8, no 26 (Avril 1947):71-106. *Omnibook* (March 1946): 1-40; *Omnilibro* 8 (August 1946): 113-144. Audible Audiobook.Thalia Book Club (Sapphire, Narrator; and Sharifa Rhodes-Pitts, et al, 2013).

In this best-seller, protagonist Lutie Johnson is defeated in her attempts as an honest, hard-working, single parent to improve conditions for herself and her eight-year-old son. When faced with her last option to survive - to become a prostitute - Lutie adamantly refuses to do so, even if it means committing a murder.

19

"That Hill Girl." Hollywood, CA: Columbia Pictures, 1958.

Is a script that is, according to Mrs. Petry, probably still filed away at Columbia Pictures in Hollywood.

20

"The Witness." Redbook (February 1971): 80-81, 126-134. Also appears (slightly revised) in *Miss Muriel and Other Stories* by Ann Petry. Boston: Houghton Mifflin, 1971. Reprint. Boston: Beacon, 1989. *Children of the Night: The Best Short Stories of Black Writers 1967 to the Present*. Boston: Back Bay Books, 1997. *Studies in the Short Story*. Edited by Virgin Scott and David Madden. Chicago: Holt, Rinehart and Winston, 1976. *The World of Fiction*. Edited by David Madden. Chicago: Holt, Rinehart and Winston, 1990.

A group of white, middle-class youth and a black, middle-class educator, Mr. Woodruff, commit a crime. The egregious actions of the white youth include kidnapping and physically and sexually assaulting a young, white female. Mr. Woodruff, who comes upon the youth, is kidnapped and implicated in the crime a a witness. While he is a witness, he sees himself merely as a black man who might be accused of raping a white woman. Therefore, once released by the youth, Mr. Woodruff leaves town; he abandons the female victim to her executioners.

Collection

21

Miss Muriel and Other Stories. Boston: Houghton Mifflin.1971. Reprint. Boston: Beacon, 1989. Evanston, IL: Northwestern University Press, 2017.

    Short stories written by Petry - as early as 1943 and as late as 1971 - are gathered in the first collection of short fiction by an African American woman writer. The characters are said to be recognizable by contemporary readers. A foreword is provided in the latest issuance by Jamilah Lemie.

Juvenile

22

Harriet Tubman, Conductor on the Underground Railroad. New York: Crowell, 1955. Reprint. New York: Washington Square,1971. Reprint. New York: Amistad Press, 2018. New York: Harper Collins Publishers, 2018. Also London: Methuen, 1960 (published as T*he Girl Called Moses: A Story Biography of Harriet Tubman* with illustrations by Judith Valentine). Also appears in Braille Book for Juvenile Readers. Washington, DC: Library of Congress, 1960. Excerpt: *Projection in Literature*. America Reads Series. Chicago: Scott, Foresman, 1967. Foreign Reprint. *Het Leven van Harriet Tubman*. Translated by Geschiedenis Voor Jenge Mensen. Amsterdam: C. P. J. Van der Peet.

    A poignant historical biography that traces the development of the woman who would lead 300 American slaves to freedom and would become known as the "Moses"of her race. Each chapter concludes with information that is factual and relevant to either Harriet Tubman's personal development or to the abolitionist cause.

23

Legends of the Saints (illustrations by Anne Rockwell). New York: Crowell, 1970.

    This text shows that saints come in all nationalities, even African-American.

24

Tituba of Salem Village. New York: Crowell. 1964. Reprint. New York: Harper, 1988. Reprint. Princeton, NJ: Recorded. Division for the Blind. Washington, DC: Library of Congress, 1964. Recording for the Blind & Dyslexia, 2005. Reprint. Newbury: Open Road Media Teen and Tween, 2015.

    According to this biography, the Salem trials for witchcraft were not restricted to only white Americans.

Children

25

The Drugstore Cat (illustrated by Susanne Suba). New York:Crowell, 1949. Reprint. Boston: Beacon, 1988.
      Buzzie, a short-tempered cat, redeems himself when he saves his owner's drugstore from a "potential disaster."

Poetry

26

"Noo York City 1." *Weid: The Sensibility Revue* (Bicentennial Issue II, American Women Poets) 12, nos. 45, 46, 47 (December 1976): 125
      Cockroaches "keep comin' forth" on the buses in New York City. The speaker tells why.

27

"Noo York City 2." *Weid: The Sensibility Revue* (Bicentennial Issue II, American Women Poets) 12, nos. 45, 46, 47 (December 1976):126
      A laundryman's concerns, that simply are about survival, are captured in repetitive lines.

28

"Noo York City 3." *Weid: The Sensibility Revue* (Bicentennial Issue II, American Women Poets) 12, nos. 45, 46, 47 (December 1976):127
      Auntie Jennifer Jones's health is critical to the speaker because "she so old/ she so black."

29

"A Purely Black Stone." In *A View from the Top of the Mountain*. Edited by Tom Koontz and Thom Tammaro. Daleville, IN: Barnwood Press Cooperative, 1981, 75.
      The deceased Mr. Ed is mourned by employees at the "laun-de-ree store." On the grave of the deceased, there is to be placed "a purely black stone." In artistic form, this poem is reminiscent of New Black poetry.

30

"A Real Boss Black Cat." In *A View from the Top of the Mountain*. Edited by Tom Koontz and Thom Tammaro. Daleville, IN: Barnwood Press Cooperative, 1981, 76.

    The speaker is overheard wishing to be like the real boss black cat that "can fly." In artistic form, this poem is reminiscent of New Black poetry.

Autobiography

31

"Ann Petry." In *Contemporary Authors: Autobiography Series*, vol 6. Detroit: Gale Research, 1988.

    In detailed and lengthy recollections, Petry talks about living among colorful, proud, and ingenious family members; about how she develops as a writer, and about how she manages her success. She frequently calls herself a survivor and a gambler. Family photographs are also provided.

32

"My Most Humiliating Jim Crow Experience." *Negro Digest* 4.8 (June 1946): 63-64.

    Petry recalls that at age seven while on a Sunday school picnic at a beach she and members of her class are forced to leave the premises because she is black.

Nonfiction

33

"Actress Says Coast Takes War in Stride." *People's Voice,* February 14, 1942, F18.

    Reporter Ann Petry takes the reader to the New York apartment of Hollywood actress Fredi Washington, better known as Peola in "Imitation of Life." Offscreen, Petry's character sketches of Washington are drawn from a descriptive narrative interview. Presented also are Washington's brief comments on how "Negro" troops and other members of her race on the West Coast are managing after Japan's attack on Pearl Harbor.

34

"Ann Petry on Roy De Carava's and Langston Hughes's 'The Sweet Flypaper of Life.' "In *Rediscoveries II*. Edited by David Madden and Peggy Bach. New York: Carrol and Graf, 1972.

    A review of Langston Hughes's 1955 publication, *The Sweet Flypaper of Life*, which includes photographs by Roy De Carava. Petry calls attention to the disclaimer found in most bibliographies and in the front of *The Sweet Flypaper of Life* - the work is a novel. Petry concludes, to the contrary; says that Hughes has created "a believable home," and she expresses her hope that the book remains forever in print.

35

"Annice Hairston Succeeded with Energy and Imagination." *People's Voice*, April 18, 1942, 18.

    Reveals how Annice Hairston turns a hobby (knitting) into a thriving business in downtown New York - Hairston's Knitting Nook. Annice's regular clientele is around 500; some are as far away as Florida.

36

"A Letter from Ann Petry." *Crisis* 54.5 (May 1947): 156.

    Petry informs the editors at *Crisis* that she has sold to the Danish the serial rights to "Like a Winding Sheet." The short story first appears in *Crisis*.

37

"A Novel about a Writer Who Tried Being a Jew." *PM* (2 March 1947): 15-16.

    A book review of Laura Z. Hobson's *Gentlemen's Agreement*. Petry predicts that for some time to come, readers will squirm and argue over the evidence that has been gathered by Hobson's gentile character who finds, upon pretending to be a Jew, anti-Semitism in the professional business world.

38

"An Open Letter to Mayor La Guardia." *People's Voice*, May 22, 1943, 4.

    Seeks the mayor's assistance in reopening the Savoy Ballroom. Reminds the mayor that in the past the facility has been a place of entertainment for the black community as well as a place for civic organizations like the National Association for the Advancement of Colored People (NAACP) and the National Urban League which both hold events that benefit the community.

39

"Canalboat to Freedom." *New York Times Book Review*, August 14, 1966, 24.

    A brief review of Thomas Fall's *Canalboat to Freedom*, an historical novel that is said to show "clearly" the working of the historical underground railroad.

40

"Clues to Creativity in Written Expression." Report of Instructional Research Institute on Written English. Westbrook, CT: State Department of Education (sponsored jointly by the Boards of Education in Haddam, Lyme, Middlefield, Salem, and Westbrook), 1966.

    Petry shares what she calls "two unforgettable experiences" with two former English teachers when responding to the questions: "How to recognize creative writers? How to encourage writers? How to foster talent in the classroom? In response, Petry suggests to the educators that they begin by getting "youngsters to think with their own minds."

41

"The Common Ground." *The Horn Book Magazine* 41 (April 1965): 141-151. Also appears in *Horn Book Reflections*. Edited by Elinor W. Field. Boston: Horn Book, 1969.

Petry reveals why she wrote both *Harriet Tubman, Conductor on the Underground Railroad* and *Tituba of Salem Village*.

42

"David in Silence." *New York Times Book Review,* May 8, 1966, 32.

Petry reviews briefly Veronica Robinson's *David in Silence*, a short novel about a deaf youth from England who gains for himself "hard-won" respect.

43

"Doomed Boys May Live Due to Layman's Plea." *People's Voice*, June 26, 1943, 13.

Reports that clemency may be granted to three Puerto Rican youth found guilty of murdering a soldier who had sought a prostitute in the youths' neighborhood.

44

"The Great Secret." *The Writer* 6 (July 1948): 215-217.

Analogies are used by Petry to explain how she wrote her first two novels. She equates herself to a shoemaker and a mechanic, both needing specific tools in order to accomplish their jobs. Petry's tools are the following: "words; a better-than-average knowledge of people; and a first-class storytelling technique."

45

"Harlem." *Holiday* (April 1949): 110-116, 163-166, 168.

Is Petry's essay of descriptive accounts of Harlem's "thousand varied faces"- from its aspiring Sugar Hill to desolate Hollows. Photographs depict how the wealthy and the poor live.

46

"Harlem Urged to Attend First Meeting of Women, Inc." *People's Voice*, May 2, 1942, 17.

Announces the first meeting of Women, Inc., a consumer information and action group in Harlem. Includes an agenda which addresses the concerns of women interested in themselves and in Harlem as a place to live "during the war and after the war is over."

47

"Harlem Woman Wax Indignant Over Latest 'Crime' Campaign." *People's Voice*, August 15, 1942, 3.

Polls the opinions of "Negro" women from Harlem about an article carried in the white-owned *Daily News*. The article tells of how white soldiers are being barred from Harlem because of prostitution among Harlem's black women.

48
"I, Juan De Pareja." *New York Times Book Review*, August 22, 1965, 18.

Is a review of Elizabeth Borton de Trevino's *I, Juan de Pareja* - an historical novel about Pareja, a slave who wins his freedom from Spanish master and artist Velazquez; and later, who gains recognition himself as a talented artist.

49
"The Lighter Side" (weekly column) *People's Voice,* March 7, 1942- May 8, 1943.

Weekly column by Petry which focuses on art, literature, music, and "who's who" in middle-class black America. Like Addison and Steele in their eighteenth-century *The Spectator* or like Samuel Johnson in *The Rambler*, in "The Lighter Side" Petry's Miss Smith and Miss Jones comment on art, literature, music and a variety of issues.

50
"Miss Halsey Feelingly Records an Interracial Experiment." *PM* (22 September 1946):15.

Is a review of Margaret Halsey's *Color Blind*. Calls an "enormous service for both Negroes and whites," particularly the study of interracial relations at the Stage Door Canteen - a nondiscriminatory social club for servicemen located off Broadway in 1940s.

51
"The New American Outlaws." *Saturday Review of Literature* (23 December 1950): 21.

A book review of Philip B. Kaye's *Taffy* - a novel about a male protagonist named Taffy who grows up in Harlem and becomes a hoodlum and a murderer by age eighteen. Petry contrasts the strong characterizations of Taffy and his gang to the weak characterizations of Taffy's law-abiding family.

52
"New England's John Henry." *Negro Digest* 3.5 (March 1945): 71-73.

Legends, anecdotes, and quotations compile a portrait of New England's own John Henry - Venture Smith. Once a slave who labored with his own nine-pound axe, Smith buys his freedom, a shipping business, and rich fertile New England land.

53
"No Mobs, No Fiery Crosses." *New York Herald Tribune Weekly Book Review*, April 10, 1949, 4.

A book review of Bucklin Moon's *Without Magnolias*. Petry disapproves of Moon's "downplay" or "real drama" in everyday life. She concludes, however, that the novel paints an "accurate, realistic picture" of the "delicate balance of race relations in the South," and that it presents recognizable characters.

54
"The Novel as Social Criticism." In *The Writer's Book*. Edited by Helen Hull. New York: Harper and

Brothers, 1950.

    Petry argues against the idea that the novel becomes less art and more propaganda when it is used to serve moral or political ends. She says the novel will "always" reflect the economic, social, and political times in which it is created. For Petry, the socially conscious novelist is merely "a man or a woman with a conscience." She praises the novel of social criticism and concludes that it too has aroused interest in social reforms, even the passage of civil rights legislation.

55

"Race Betrayal." *Saturday Review of Literature* (25 February 1950):18.

    Is a book review of J. Saunders Redding's *Stranger and Alone*. Petry proclaims that the novel "evokes pity and terror." She calls central character Sheldon Howden "more frightening than a lynch victim." As superintendent of New York's black schools, Howden responds to unwritten codes that govern relations between blacks and whites and he reinforces the theory that members of his race are inferior to whites.

56

Review of *Youngblood. New York Herald Tribune Book Review*, July 11, 1954, 8.

    Reviews briefly John Oliver Killens's *Youngblood*. Approves of his "good development" of the major and minor characters. However, disapproves of scenes of racially-inspired violence, calling them too repetitive.

57

"System of Control Is not Intricate." *People's Voice*, January 9, 1943, 6.

    Explains how to use the special ration book issued in the 1940s by the Office of Price Administration (OPA) of the United States' government.

58

"This Writing Business." *Author's Guild Bulletin* [Special Collections, Boston University], 1965.

    Includes miscellaneous comments on Petry.

59

"Tribute to Mr. Gentry." *Connecticut Pharmacist.* 3 (November 1946): 5-42.

    An imaginary druggist named Mr. Gentry symbolizes small-town druggists. In his actions, he suggests that the contributions of small-town druggists range from medical to social and political.

60

"Tubman, Harriet." *Encyclopedia Britannica*, vol 22, 1970, 302.

    Provides a biographical sketch of black female abolitionist and activist Harriet Tubman. As the "Moses" of her people, Tubman successfully guides over 300 slaves from bondage in the United States to freedom in Canada.

61
"U. S. Will Fail as World Leader If Ruled by Jimcro - Mrs. F.D.R." *People's Voice*, May 8,1943, 7.

    Covers a lecture-concert sponsored by the New York City Committee to honor Mrs. Mary McLeod Bethune and to benefit Bethune-Cookman College. Guest lecturer is Mrs. Franklin D. Roosevelt who says Mrs. Bethune "symbolizes a spirit of courage, love, endurance and hope that is very necessary in the present world." As for race relations in the 1940s in the United States, Mrs. Roosevelt says "prejudice is due to ignorance and lack of education." The First Lady concludes that the country has an opportunity to lead at the present time but will fail as a leader if it is controlled by ignorance.

62
"What's Wrong with Negro Men?" *Negro Digest* 5. 5 (March 1947): 4-7.

    Provides a satirical point of view. Petry concludes that male attitudes discussed in her article come straight out of the Dark Ages.

Secondary Works

63

"A Harlem Suite for Three Women." New York: *New York Times* (online), 25 September 2013.

    Provides a review of Farah Jasmine Griffin's book, *Harlem Nocturne: Women Artists and Progressive Politics During World War II*; provides also an interview with Griffin. In the interview, Griffin gives historical, political, cultural, literary, and artistic reasons for her narrative/study of three accomplished women who lived and flourished in New York City and abroad during the 1940s: novelist, Ann Petry; dancer and choreographer, Pearl Primus; and pianist and composer, Mary Lou Williams. Evoking the Chaucerian format, Griffin delivers a work which begins with a Prologue that is stylistic and methodical; it introduces and foreshadows the life experiences of the three accomplished women. The Prologue is followed by chapters, one chapter for each woman and her experiences; each chapter from within contextualizes the artistic, cultural, and political settings for each woman. Then in the book's conclusion, Griffin salutes the women collectively, reiterating how they "gave to [New York] city" - e.g., [they] "danced for it; wrote it; and set it to music."

64

A Study Guide for Ann Petry's The Street. Cengage Learning Gale. Farmington Hills: Gale, Cengage Learning, 2016.

    Surveys Petry's first novel, focusing on literary history, audiences, themes, and stock characters.

65

"A Visit with Ann Petry." College of Pharmacy, University of Illinois of Chicago. Deposited in Kremers Reference Files. Madison: University of Wisconsin School of Pharmacy, 1984.

    Provides an intriguing conversation/interview between Petry and pharmacy students at the University of Illinois at Chicago. [see interview elsewhere in this edition].

66

Abston, Carmen Patrice. "Representation and Signification: *The Street* and *Dutchman* as Revisions of Richard Wright's Portrayal of Black Identity and Experience in *Native Son*." Ph.D. Diss., University of Southern Mississippi, 2005.

    Emphasizes textual comparisons between Richard Wright's *Native Son* and Ann Petry's *The Street*, and between Wright's *Native Son* and Amira Baraka's *Dutchman*. Outlines different views by the writers on representations of black identity and black experiences. Illustrates why at times Petry and Amira Baraka feel the need to revise and to reverse elements of *Native Son*. Also seeks to promote *Native Son*, *The Street*, and *Dutchman* as links in a signifying chain of tropes and themes that reach all the way back to slave narratives as early as 1770.

67

Adams, George. "Riot as Ritual: Ann Petry's 'In Darkness and Confusion.' " *Black American Literature Forum* 6.2 (Summer 1972):54-58. Reprint. In *Ann Petry's Short Fiction: Critical Essays*. Edited by Hazel Arnett Ervin and Hilary Holladay. Westport, CT: Praeger, 2004.

    Provides thematic and archetypical readings of "In Darkness and Confusion." Outlines breakout of the riot, and how the protagonist is "born again [through sacrifices]" and through the "ritualized shedding of the past."

68

Adams, William, Peter Conn and Barry Stepian, eds. *Afro-American Literature: Fiction*. Boston: Houghton Mifflin, 1970.

    Provides an excerpt from *The Street* under the subtitle "The Family." The excerpt is followed by study questions.

69

Ader, Melissa Susan. " 'Walled in': Race, Motherhood and Labor in Ann Petry's *The Street*." A.B. Honors in History and Literature, Harvard University, 2009.

    Provides a Lacanian reading of Petry's *The Street* to meet requirements for undergraduate A. B. Honors.

70

Ajimuda, O.S. and O. Aminu. "Art for Art's Sake: Death of the Author in the 21st Century." *KIU Interdisciplinary Journal of Humanities and Social Sciences* 1.2 (2020): 68-78.

    Provides an intellectually in-depth discussion of the functionality of art and the roles of author and critic via schools, principles, thoughts and theories. Interjects Petry and her essay, "The Novel as Social Criticism" in the discussion and asks for considerations of a new literary creed such as "art for life's sake" or at least "for the sake of community." After providing in-depth discussions of "aesthetics poetics" and "critical poetics," the writers seem to return critics to the "critical poetics" when critiquing African American literature, meaning unfortunately, dependence on "history" and a set of "sociological rules" in the guise of African American literary criticism. See also entries #316 and #469 where other critics recommend that readers "trusts the text" and not the author.

71

Alexander, Sandra Carlton. Ann Petry. In *Dictionary of Literary Biography. Afro-American Writers, 1940-1955*. Vol 6. Edited by Trudier Harris. Detroit: Gale Research, 1988.

    Insists that Petry is a "study in contrast." Says Petry demonstrates the versatility of African Americans in her writings which are set in urban and rural New England cities. With the exception of erroneously citing "The Common Ground" as a book, provides accurate chronological listings of Petry's fiction and juvenile works. Includes plot summaries and, in some instances, critical analysis of characters.

72

Alvarez-Wilson, Sonia. "Beyond the Borders of Exile: Exile, Immigration, and Migration in U.S. Women's Writing." Ph.D. Diss., University of North Carolina at Greensboro, 2015.

    Argues for a study of literature of exile. Insists on an analytical focus on tropes in Petry such as trauma, healing, and memory rather than the familiar focus on ethnicity or national origins. Seeks to reveal discursive strategies that transcend cultural borders. For example, the writer examines common threads of folk medicines in Ann Petry's *The Street* and Judith Ortiz Cofer's *The Line of the Sun*. Argues that traditional faith practices, primarily brought to America through the slave trade, are utilized by women authors such as Petry and Cofer and are sources of empowerment for their characters. Emphasizes literary considerations across cultural lines to suggest a powerful counter-hegemonic strategy that is prominent in the landscape of exile survival. Applauds the community of exile portrayals by U.S. women authors like Petry and Cofer for their transnational and transcultural connections.

73

American Masters. "*The Street* by Ann Petry: Black Single Mother Seeks the American Dream." Novel Reflections on the American Dream. WNET Television Station: New York: New York. (Also notice: Video is for the Grades 9-12 Collection). See https:www.pbs.learningmedia.org

Presents a video that introduces Petry's novel *The Street* and heroine Lutie Johnson to high school students in Grades 9-12. Note: In its introduction of Petry to high school students, the video comes with a warning: "This resource contains material that may be sensitive for some students."

74

"An Interview with Ann Petry." *Artspectrum* (Windham-Regional Arts Council, Willimantic, CT), September 1988, 3-4.

Poses familiar interview questions. However, there are two exceptions: Petry's role as a feminist and her position which take on the Civil Rights Movement. [See full interview in this edition].

75

An, Jee Hyun. " ' There was a Whole Lot of Grayness Here': Modernity, Geography and "Home" in Black Women's Literature, 1919-1959." Ph.D. Diss., The University of Chicago, 2003.

Examines representations of "place," "home," and "domesticity" in urban, modern America. Says such a focus in literature fills a void in literary criticism by moving beyond familiar examinations of modernization and urbanization of male narratives (e.g., Richard Wright, Chester Himes, Ralph Ellison) and in examining the differences and similarities of black women writers of Chicago and New York City from 1919 to 1959 within the contexts of modernization and urbanization (e.g., Jessie Fauset, Nella Larsen, Ann Petry, Gwendolyn Brooks, Lorraine Hansberry, Paule Marshall, and Marita Bonner). Offers critiques of Fauset and Larsen; Brooks and Bonner; and Marshall and Hansberry. Critiques singularly Petry, focusing on the female writer's uneven geography of America in *The Street*. Also includes more specific studies of differences and similarities between Petry's black, female Lutie Johnson of New York City in *The Street* and the white, female Mrs. Chandler of Connecticut in Petry's *Country Place*.

76

Andrew, Joseph Hines. "Understanding Criticism: An Institutional Ecology of U. S. American Literary Criticism." Ph.D. Diss., Vanderbilt University, 2015.

Argues that too often the dominant narrative of black intellectuals has concealed the critical, literary practices employed by intellectual writers like Melvin B. Tolson, Langston Hughes, Parker Tyler, and Ann Petry. Proposes that Tolson, Hughes, Tyler and Petry do not rely on institutionally endorsed methods of literary reading. Puts these black intellectuals into conversations with white critics who have been long understood as pivotal in formulating literary criticism (e.g., Allen Tate, John Crowe Ransom, Cleanth Brooks, and Robert Penn Warren). Urges broadening the network of critics and critical practices, so to deliver access to an expanded archive of interpretations of and approaches to African American literature - e.g., to the interdisciplinary perspectives of ecology.

77

Andrews, Larry R. "At Home Inside: A Daughter's Tribute to Ann Petry." *African American Review* 43.4 (2009): 757-758.

    Reviews favorably Elisabeth Petry's contributions to the scholarship of writer, Ann Petry, in her book which blends effectively biography, memoir, journals, and letters. Says the daughter of Ann Petry fulfills the many aims of her book, which include the following: to communicate Petry's early years and her obsession with privacy; to illustrate Petry's experiences between life and creative work; to reveal the close bond between mother and daughter; and to acknowledge Petry's illness which leads to her death. Calls the work, *At Home Inside*, a companion to the daughter's first book about her mother: *Can Anything Beat White: Black Family's Letters* (2005). Applauds the invaluable service of *At Home Inside* which amplifies the writer's sparse biography.

78

_____. "Revising the Blueprint: Ann Petry and the Literary Left. " *African American Review* 42. 3/4 (Fall/Winter 2008):772-773.

    Reviews Alex Lubin's collection *Revising the Blueprint: Ann Petry and the Literary Left* (2007), calling it a contribution to Petry's scholarship. While critics in *Revising the Blueprint* explore Petry's relations to the "literary Left," critics also reveal Petry's ambivalence toward Marxist thought and her resistance to political and literary categorizations. Suggests there is, however, a new and interesting thread in several of the essays from *Revising the Blueprint*, which outline Petry's effective use of popular culture to demystify white power and racism.

79

_____. "The Sensory Assault of the City in Ann Petry's *The Street*." In *The City in African American Literature*. Edited by Yoshinobu Hakutani. Madison,NJ: Fairleigh Dickinson University Press, 1995. Reprint. In *The Critical Response to Ann Petry*. Edited by Hazel Arnett Ervin. Westport, CT: Praeger, 2005.

    Provides in-depth interpretations of the role of the city in urban American literature within the contexts of naturalism, class oppression, racism, and sexism.

80

Angelou, Maya. *Black Women Writers at Work*. Edited by Claudia Tate. New York: Continuum, 1983.

    Pays tribute to Petry. Says that she (Angelou) would walk "fifty blocks in high heels" for something written by Petry (p. 60).

81

Ann Petry. In *African American Literature, Voices in a Tradition*. Orlando, FL: Holt Rinehart and Winston, 1992.

    Is a textbook that is first introduced to secondary schools in urban cities such as Detroit and Memphis. In this textbook, provided are the following: African American literary maps; history and literary terms; a chronological listing of African American literature from the beginning to present; thematic approaches to writers; photographs of well-known African American writers and other African artifacts; and paintings by African American artists. Unit Six ("From Renaissance to Mid-Forties") includes opening paragraphs from Petry's *The Street*. Discussion questions follow. Also provides a 1946 photograph of Petry.

82

Ann Petry. In *Black Writers*. Senior editor, Linda Metzger. Detroit: Gale Research, 1989.

> Offers a chronological listing of Petry's first three novels and excerpts from book reviews, dating from the 1940s to the 1970s.

83

Ann Petry. In *Call and Response: The Riverside Anthology of the African American Tradition*. Edited by Patricia Liggins Hill et al. Boston: Houghton Mifflin Harcourt, 1998.

> Includes Petry's short stories, "Like a Winding Sheet" and "Miss Muriel."

84

Ann Petry. In *Contemporary Authors*. Edited by Barbara Harte and Carolyn Riley. Vols 5-8. Detroit: Gale Research, 1963. Reprint 1969.

> Provides vitals on Petry, her hobbies, and an abbreviated writing list.

85

Ann Petry. In *Contemporary Authors: Autobiography Series*. Vol 6. Detroit: Gale Research, 1988.

> Notes that Petry calls herself a survivor in the literary sense and an advocate of children's literature. Introduces family photographs. Offers comments on Petry's novels.

86

Ann Petry. In *Contemporary Literary Criticism*. Edited by Carolyn Riley. Detroit: Gale Research, 1973.

> Provides literary analysis of *Country Place* and of short stories from *Miss Muriel and Other Stories*. Quotes Carl Milton Hughes, Robert Bone, Alfred Kazin, and Houston Baker, Jr.

87

Ann Petry. In *Contemporary Literary Criticism*. Edited by Phyllis Carmel Mendelson and Dedria Bryfonski. Detroit: Gale Research, 1977.

> Presents excerpts of critical writings on Petry's style and structure in her short and long fiction. Quotes David Littlejohn, Thelma J. Shinn, and William Peden.

88

Ann Petry. In *Contemporary Literary Criticism*. Edited by Sharon R. Gunton. Vol 18. Detroit: Gale Research, 1981.

> Reprints excerpts from reviews of *Country Place*, *The Narrows*, and the short story "In Darkness and Confusion," which are written respectively by Author P. Davis, Arna Bontemps, and George R. Adams.

89

Ann Petry. In *Current Biography*. Edited by Anna Rothe. New York: H. W. Wilson, 1946.

> Provides a biographical sketch of the writer and includes the phonetic spelling of the writer's surname, which has a long "e" (pee-tree). A photograph is included.

90

Ann Petry. In *Dictionary of American Children's Fiction, 1960-1984*. Edited by Alethea K. Helbig and Agnes Regan Perkins. New York: Greenwood, 1986.

> Acknowledges Petry's biographies for youth (*Harriet Tubman, Conductor on the Underground*

Railroad and *Tituba of Salem Village*); provides, however, only an extensive plot summary for Tituba. Complains about the narrative structure of Tituba, calling it brief summaries of events, particularly those following the trial of Tituba.

91
Ann Petry. In *Harlem Renaissance and Beyond*. Edited by Lorraine Elena Roses and Ruth Elizabeth Randolph. Boston: G. K. Hall, 1990.
    Calls Petry a "bridge figure between the Harlem Renaissance and the black writers after mid-century." Considers Petry to be a precursor to Toni Morrison and Gloria Naylor. Says that contrary to the "forced" comparisons between the 1940's best-selling works of Richard Wright and Chester Himes, Petry's *The Street* has "a poetic breadth all its own." Offers answers to "why critics are made so uncomfortable by Petry's works."

92
Ann Petry. In *Historical Negro Biographies* by Wilhelmina S. Robinson. New York: Publishers Co. Inc. [under the auspices of The Association for the Study of Negro Life and History], 1967.
    Provides a brief biography of Petry - which is with errors.

93
Ann Petry. In *Interviews with Black Writers*. Edited by John O'Brien. New York: Liveright, 1973.
    Discusses the author's craft with her. [See full interview in this bibliography].

94
Ann Petry. In *Portraits in Color*. Edited by Gwendolyn Cherry, Ruby Thomas, and Pauline Willis. New York: Pageant, 1962.
    Draws comparisons between Petry and earlier writers of the "problem novels" to show how Petry differs, particularly saying that in *The Street* and in *Country Place*, Petry presents "strong storyline, brilliant characterization, and fast-moving plot."

95
Ann Petry. In *Reader's Encyclopedia of American Literature*. Edited by Max Herzberg. New York: Thomas Y. Crowell, 1962.
    Is an abbreviated biography with listings of Petry's novels. Calls *The Street* the "best ever written about Harlem."

96
Ann Petry. In *The Chelsea House Library of Literary Criticism: Twentieth Century American Literature*. General Editor Harold Bloom. Vol 5 (M-P). New York: Chelsea House, 1987.
    Provides critiques of Petry's craft via excerpts from the following: David Littlejohn's *Black on White*; Robert Bone's *The Negro Novel in America*; and Arthur P. Davis's *From the Dark Tower*.

97
Ann Petry. In *The Norton Anthology of African American Literature*. Edited by Henry Louis Gates and Nellie McKay. New York: W.W. Norton, 1997.
    Includes Petty under the section: "Realism, Naturalism and Modernism."

98

Ann Petry. In *Twentieth Century Authors: A Biographical Dictionary of Modern Literature*. Edited by Stanley J. Kunitz. New York: H. W. Wilson, 1955.

    Offers quotes by the author on her biography and bibliography. Reveals that the author's surname is pronounced with a long "e" (pee-tree).

99

Ann Lane Petry. 190[8] -[19]97 *MS.* 3.2 (May 1997): 148.

    Provides one Black/White photograph. There is, however, an error in the year of Petry's birth.

100

"Ann Petry Acclaimed author dies at 88." *Jet* 92.1, 1997.

    Announces the death of the author and reminds readers that Petry wrote the "first literary portrait of Harlem."

101

"Ann Petry Gets Warm Reception at Book Fair." *Hampton Bulletin* (January 1956): 3.

    Announces Petry as a speaker at the first all-community Book Bazaar at Hampton Institute (now University). Records that Petry advises prospective writers "to practice self-discipline and to read." Petry suggests "liberal reading, but with emphasis upon the Greek tragedies, the Bible, and the great works of the 18th Century Western Europe."

102

"Ann Petry Services Set June 14 [1997]." *Hartford Courant* [Hartford, Conn], 5 June 1997, B.11.

    Announces memorial services for Ann Petry which is held at the First Congregational Church of Christ in Old Saybrook, Connecticut - the same church that is fictionalized in several of Petry's literary works. Memorial donations are directed to the Authors League Fund, 330 W. 42nd Street, New York, NY, 10036.

103

"Ann Petry Tells Parley of Need for Play Schools." *New York Herald Tribune Book Review*, 14 April 1946, 5.

    Identifies Petry's role as a recreation specialist in Harlem's Play School Association, an association that provides community programs for minority parents and their children.

104

"Ann Petry's Lasting Legacy." *Hartford Courant* [Hartford, Conn], 1 May 1997, A 18.

    Eulogizes Petry in the Hartford Courant which often features articles on Petry when she is alive. The writer who dies on April 27 of 1997 is remembered as a "rarity in pre-civil rights America," largely because she becomes a best-selling black female novelist in the 1940s. Petry is also called a "prophetic storyteller," largely because of her first novel *The Street* - "a heartbreaking and important literary work for its compelling insight into urban poverty and broken family life."

105

"Ann Petry's New Book Tells Story of a Heroic Negro Woman Who Led Slaves to Freedom." *New Era* (29 September 1955): 1.

Reviews *Harriet Tubman, Conductor on the Underground Railroad*. Calls the work an "absorbing" reader and more than a "factual biography." Applauds Petry for her "delicate" and "evocative" words which help recreate "the fear of being sold into deeper misery" and "the hopeless insecurity of the slaves' lives." Tubman is said to become "a living figure" in this work.

106

"Ann Petry's ' *The Street*.' " Transcript. NPR: All Things Considered, June 16, 2008.

Provides a documented transcript of a conversation between NPR host, Robert Siegel, and Gretchen Holbrook Gerzina, a professor at Dartmouth College. According to Gerzina, Petry's *The Street* is a classic that raises passion in readers, including herself. Says the work is still relevant today: "It makes us think about what it [is] like to be a single mother raising a black son to believe he [is] worthy of all the best this country can offer."

107

"Ann Petry's *The Street* Is May's Book Club Pick: Now Read This." *New York Times* (online), 9 January 2018.

"Now Read This" is a book club, sponsored jointly by PBS News Hour and *The New York Times*. Each month, at the beginning of the month, members pick a work of fiction or non-fiction that is thought to help them to make sense of the present world. Petry's *The Street* is such a selection. Prior to monthly meetings, posted are questions and other materials related to the book, including reviews. Readers join via Facebook and Google. "Now Read This" encourages local book clubs to join its monthly book discussions. [See also entry 616].

108

"Ann Petry's '*The Street*' Is Sugar-Coated Problem Novel." *Afro-American* (Baltimore), 2 February 1946, 14.

Announces the February release of *The Street* and quotes Petry's reasons for writing the novel.

109

Annas, Pamela and Suzy Groden. *The Street*. *Radical Teacher* [Brooklyn] 113 (Winter 2019): 6-7, 122.

Says *The Street* provides powerful, complex ways that sex, race, and class intersect. Announces four teachers at the University of Massachusetts-Boston using Petry's novel in "Foundations in Law and Justice," an 8-credit hour interdisciplinary writing course for freshmen. Says novel presents complex social issues that "clearly, subtly, and metaphorically" shape class discussions around social justice.

110

Anonymous. Review of *Ann Petry's Short Fiction: Critical Essays* (2004). Edited by Hazel Arnett Ervin and Hilary Holladay. *Reference and Research Book News* [Portland] 19.3 (August 2004), n/a.

Highlights favorably topics of interest to critics: folk traditions, rewriting innocence into experience, multiple masculinities, riot as ritual, migration, feminist ally, and traumatic reenactments.

111

Asher, Jacqueline Colleen. "Kept Boys: Scenes of Masculine Dependency in American Literature and Culture." Ph.D. Diss., University of California, Riverdale, 2008.

Investigates the "kept boy" as organizing anxieties across lines of class, gender, race, and nationality in American culture. Focuses on figure of the "kept boy" - i.e., a structuring anxiety that haunts representations of masculine individualism - from texts by Herman Melville, Henry James, Richard Bruce Nugent, Ann Petry, and James Baldwin, and on counterpart - the "self-made" man (pulled from Benjamin Franklin). Raises questions about what masculine "keptness" offers as enduring counter-cultural narrative? How representations of slavery, racial blackness, and the prospects of boundless "keeping," which are born of legacy, show-up in the texts by same writers?

112

Autry, Thea. "Writing the Gaze: Race and Visual Poetics in Postwar U. S. Fiction." Ph.D. Diss., Vanderbilt University, 2020.

Broadens criticism and examinations of post-war American fiction within historical and cultural contexts, especially as powerful, visual exchanges to construct meaning; narrative representation of the racialized gaze; and as an intertextual trope (the construction of racial identity). Works of interest include: Chester Himes' *If He Hollers Let Him Go*; Ann Petry's *The Street*; William Faulkner's *Intruder in the Dust*; and James Baldwin's *Another Country*. Includes other contextual studies: the black aesthetics, black enfranchisement, existential philosophy, changing racial relationships, and urban spaces.

113

Babb, Valeria. *A History of the African American Novel*. Cambridge: Cambridge University Press, 2017.

Traces the history of the African American novel; keeps the genre in conversations with other documents, including with Petry's novels.

114

Babenko, Olga Alexandrovna. "How Can We Use Post-Colonial and African American Literary Criticism in Contemporary Text Analysis." International Visible Conference on Educational Studies and Applied Linguistics. Tishk International University, Erbil Kurdiston Region, Iraq, April 26-27, 2019.

Presents the observations of participants teaching foreign language and literature in multicultural classrooms in Ukraine, the Kingdom of Saudi Arabia, and the Kurdistan Region of Iraq at different educational levels. Offers several possible ways for development of: comparative studies, intercultural competence: time management; appropriate selection of literary tools for analysis; and ways of synthesizing information. Petry's "Like a Winding Sheet" surfaces and is required.

115

Baker, Henry. "Witchcraft: The Idea Is Both Old and Modern." *Middletown Press*, 6 January 1970 [Special Collections, Boston University].

Summarizes a speech by Petry which is delivered at a meeting of the Old Saybrook Historical Society. Presents research data from Petry on witchcraft which informs Petry's juvenile work, T*ituba of Salem Village*.

116

Baker, Houston A., Jr., ed. Overview. In *Black Literature in America*. New York: McGraw-Hill, 1971.

    Discusses Petry in his Overview. Calls her characters "complex human beings." Concludes that Petry writes unflinchingly in a "realistic tradition." Includes a reprint of her short story, "Like a Winding Sheet."

117

Balliett, Whitney. "Imagining Music." *New Yorker* (18 June 1990): 93-94.

    Mentions favorably Petry's short story, "Solo on the Drums" and how as a jazz writer Petry has imagined the music. Concludes that Petry's "jilted drummer makes his big boss' drum growl."

118

Balshem, Maria. *Looking for Harlem: Urban Aesthetics in African American Literature*. Sterling, VA: Pluto Press, 2000.

    Calls attention to an "urban aesthetics." Uses numerous essays, elegies, and fiction as well as identifiable city streets, subways, hotels, and cabarets to contextualize Harlem as follows: "space," "race," "identity," "passing," "gender," "domesticity," and "urbanites." Frequently references the fiction of Petry.

119

Bande, Usha. "Murder as Social Revenge in *The Street* and *The Women of Brewster Place*." *Notes on Contemporary Literature* 23.2 (January 1993): 4-5.

    Continues thematic interests in representations of "violence" in literature by African American women writers, including Ann Petry.

120

Barrett, Lindon. *Blackness and Value: Seeing Double. Cambridge Studies In American Literature and Culture*. Cambridge (England): Cambridge University Press, 1999.

    Encourages criticism that goes beyond historical and sociological approaches to African American literature. Suggests studying interrelations between race and value - e.g., the literate/illiterate; the sighing/singing voice; time/space; civic/criminal; and academy/street. Also encourages other theoretical ways of telling- which means, other ways of looking at race, gender, and queer studies. Offers relevant and fresh readings of Petry's *The Street* and *The Narrows*.

121

_____. "(Further) Figures of Violence: '*The Street*' in the American Landscape." *Cultural Critique* Issue 25 (1993): 205-232.

    Contends the story in Ann Petry's *The Street* addresses urban revisionary attempts in the twentieth-century to "redefine black Identity." Concludes that *The Street* ends, so to speak, where Richard Wright's *Native Son* begins.

122

_____. "In the Dark: Issues of Value, Evolution, and the Authority in Twentieth - Century Critical Discourse." Ph.D. Diss., University of Pennsylvania, 1990.

    Encourages viewing value as a theoretical model and as a way to investigate African American expressive traditions. Suggests defining value as a process within Petry's novels. Concludes that, among others, Petry troubles the notion of a clear and discrete separation between American suburbs and African American ghettos.

123
Barry, Michael. " 'Same Train Back Tomorrow': Ann Petry's *The Narrows* and the Repetition of History." *MELUS* 24.1 (Spring 1999). Reprint. In *The Critical Response to Ann Petry*. Edited by Hazel Arnett Ervin. Westport, CT: Praeger, 2005.

Raises the question whether black writers can make any distinctions between politics and art when writing about the African American experience? Then, using Petry's narrative, *The Narrows*, presents a favorable response and confirmation. Draws attention to Petry's artistic techniques such as irony, repetition, cyclical (versus linear) narration, and resistant imagery of the blues.

124
Bartter, George C. Review of *The Street*. *Book Find* News 2 (April 1946): 16.

Writes that *The Street* is "a rich, smooth-flowing novel filled with people you know and understand." Rejects criticism that Petry's characters are criminals.

125
Battat, Erin Royston. *Ain't Got No Home: America's Great Migration and the Making of an Interracial Left*. Chapel Hill, NC: The University of North Carolina Press, 2014.

Studies mass migrations by African Americans and southern whites during the Depression-era, giving close attention to inter-connected responses to capitalist collapse and political upheavals during the early twentieth century. Encourages re-readings of classic black and white writers and other creative artists and their migration stories, songs, histories and ethnographies that specifically bolster a black-white Left alliance - e.g., Ann Petry, William Attaway, John Steinbeck, Sanora Babb, Dorothea Lange, and Elizabeth Catlett. Also seeks to recover the literary and visual culture of the 1930s and 1940s; expand understanding of the migration narrative by uniting the political and aesthetic goals of the black and white literary Left; and illuminate striking interrelationships between American populism and civil rights.

126
Beach, Terry. "Embedding the Canon in the Inner-City Classroom: Finding Relevancy in the Classics through a Study of the Contemporary." *Notes on American Literature*, vol 20 (2011): 12.

Offers a pedagogical approach to characterization, using Petry's Lutie Johnson.

127
Belilgne, Maleda. "Bodily Trespass: An Ecology of the Fantastic in Twentieth-Century African American Literature." Ph.D. Diss., Duke University, 2011.

Situates the fantastic as a discourse of spatial production, erupting the fantastic in realist and surrealist narratives and ameliorating the spatial constructions that inform African American subjectivity in most African American texts. Says that as a literary mode in the Todorovian sense, fantastic identifies the real as a production of the "unreal" and calls attention to ideological and institutional apparatuses which sustain the dominant order. Concludes that imaginative space extends to the task of recording and refuting the racial discourse which articulates urbanity. Supports outcomes "to depict the racially encoded urban geographies as corporeally informed psychosocial interfaces" with Himes' *The Real Cool Killers*; Petry's *The Street*; and Brooks' *Maud Martha*.

128
Bell, Bernard W. "Ann Petry's Demythologizing of American Culture and Afro-American Character." In *Conjuring: Black Women, Fiction, and Literary Tradition*. Edited by Marjorie Pyrse and Hortense J. Spillers. Bloomington: Indiana University Press, 1985. Reprint. In *The Critical Response to Ann Petry*. Edited by Hazel Arnett Ervin. Westport, CT: Praeger, 2005.
  Says Petry moves "beyond the naturalistic vision of Wright and Himes" when she explores "the black community's place in time and space [and] its relationship to the American past and future." Concludes Petry's "realistic delineation of cultural myths," also "debunks the myths of urban success and progress, of rural innocence and virtue, and of pathological black women and men."

129
_____. "The Triumph of Naturalism." In *The Afro-American Novel and Its Tradition*. Amherst: University of Massachusetts Press, 1987. Reprint. 1989.
  Insists Petry's "most invaluable achievement in the tradition of the Afro-American novel" is her successful move "beyond the naturalistic vision of Himes and Wright to the demythologizing of American culture and Afro-American character."

130
Benoit, Larry. "Introducing Two Small-Town Druggists," 1946 [Special Collection, Boston University].
  Focuses on Petry's father, Peter C. Lane and aunt, Anna L. James, as druggist.

131
Benton, Loron Melinda. "Interior Spaces, Spiritual Traces: Theorizing the Erotic in the Cultural Works and Creative Lives of Black Women Writers and Artists, 1930-1970." Ph.D. Diss., University of California, Los Angeles, 2020.
  Offers spiritual eroticism, once engaged by Audre Lorde, in creative epistemologies and narratives by African American women writers and artists who illustrate analytical points of inquiries on the interior, social, and hopeful modalities of African American female experiences in life. Discusses poet and novelist Sarah Wright; journalist and author Ann Petry; and songwriter, pianist, and vocalist Aretha Franklin.

132
Bergman, Jill. "Charlotte Perkins Gilman and a Woman's Place in America."*Studies in American Literary Realism and Naturalism*.Tuscaloosa: University of Alabama Press, 2013.
  Compiles a collection of perspectives on Charlotte Perkins Gilman in the following topic chapters: 1) Geography and Biography: Places in and of Gilman's Life; 2) Know Your Place; 3) Limits on Women's Freedom and Power; and 4) Reclaiming and Redefining a 'Woman's Place.' Makes frequent references to Ann Petry's *The Street*.

133
_____. *The Motherless Child in the Novels of Pauline Hopkins*. Baton Rouge: Louisiana State University Press, 2012.
  Illuminates the trope of "motherlessness" in African American literature, using Pauline Hopkin's

novels as exemplary models, but also promotes "motherless child literature" as a literary tradition, using comparative readings by Olaudah Equiano, Frederick Douglass, Countee Cullen, Nella Larsen, Alice Walker, and Ann Petry (*The Street*). Unearths patterns of "motherlessness" but also the desire for interdisciplinarity.

134

Bernard, Emily. "Nothing New Under the Sun: Ann Petry's *The Street* and *The Narrows*." *The Yale Review* 107.2 (April 2019):53-63.

Insists that while Petry writes about racism as a systemic injustice with devastating impacts on both black and white minds, Petry also writes about four characters as human beings whose experiences are the choices they make in life, or what they refuse to acknowledge, or to see in front of them. Says there is "no novel more satisfying to teach in the age of #Me Too Movement than Petry's *The Street*."

135

_____. " 'Raceless' Writing and Difference: Ann Petry's *Country Place* and the African-American Literary Canon." *Studies in American Fiction* 33.1 (Spring 2005): 87-117.

Draws attention to the book cover of *Country Place* - its pictures, probing questions, and statements. Theorizes about publisher's attempt in the 1940s to authorize Petry's geographical shift and her authorship and authority in writing about white characters. To authenticate Petry's authority and authorship in writing her second novel, Bernard provides a comprehensive reading of *Country Place* with substantial analyses of plot, characterizations, and settings. She insists that, in lieu of the publisher's marketing via the book's cover, readers should move beyond the whiteness of *Country Place* and see just what is innovative and subversive about the narrative text.

136

Binggeli, Elizabeth Cara. "Hollywood Dark Matter: Reading Race and Absence in Studio Era Narrative." Ph.D. Diss., University of Southern California, 2005.

Elucidates the narrative culture of Hollywood studios and the greater American culture. Provides comparative and critical analysis of Hollywood's rejection of supposedly "unacceptable" texts by authors Zora Neale Hurston, Richard Wright, and Ann Petry and the adaptation of supposedly "acceptable" texts by William Faulkner, Marjorie Kennan Rawlings and Ellen Glasgow.

137

_____. "Burbanking Bigger and Bette the Bitch." *African American Review* 40.3 (Fall 2006): 475-492.

Examines the political as well as the sexual threat that "black skin" brings to the Hollywood screen in the 1940s. Uses Richard Wright and Ann Petry in Hollywood to point out the hypocrisy of film studios.

138

Bixler, Paul. "Freedom Takes Time." *Antioch Review* 7.2 (1946): 269-74.

Provides a comparative analysis of Petry's "limited intrusion" and "objectivity" in *The Street* and Richard Wright's "intrusive voice" and "indicting tone" in *Native Son*. Concludes that Petry knew considerable security in her life and had not been subjected to Lutie's "way of living all her life"; therefore, the novelist is horrified at what she sees in Harlem and is "able to translate" her horror "straight . . . into terms . . . instantly recognized and widely understood." Also briefly compares Petry and Zola.

139

_____. "She Tried to Flee Harlem: Tragic Tale in the Great Tradition of Naturalism." *Chicago Sun Book Week*, 10 February 1946 [Special Collections. Woodruff Library, Atlanta University Center].

Writes that after Petry's *The Street* neither Zola, Dreiser, nor James Farrell had material "better fitted to the naturalistic hand." Refutes critics who label Petry's characters as "simply evil." Says the "environment and the urge to survive" help Petry's characters to share their behaviors. Criticizes the middle of Petry's novel, however, calling the work's intent "unsure" and its pace "uneven." Concludes with favorable comments. For instance, says the novel is "one of the most powerful . . . of the past decade."

140

Black, Leslie. "The New Negro Novelist and His Development." M.S. Degree, Kansas State College, 1949.

Examines African American writers and their novels, from slavery to the end of the Harlem Renaissance, in chronological order of reviews: history, literary audiences, themes, and stock characters. Female novelists include Petry, Zora Neale Hurston and Dorothy West. Male novelists include Wright, Yerby, and Himes, to name a few.

141

Bloom, Harold. *American Women Fiction Writers, 1900 – 1960*. Philadelphia: Chelsea House Publishers, 1997.

Provides a brief profile of Petry and existing criticism of major works.

142

Bloomquist, Katherine Mary. "American Women Writers, Visual Vocabularies, and the Lives of Literary Regionalism." Ph.D. Diss., Washington University in St Louis (Mo), 2012.

Calls for re/readings of Sarah Orne Jewett, Willa Cather, and Ann Petry and a focus on how texts by these women (essays and fiction) illuminate the lives of the "other" through visual vocabularies and local color. Says re/readings also illuminate how Jewett, Cather, and Petry ground literary regionalism in the politics of their writings and in the art of life realities and practices which circulate in the literary marketplace of the late nineteenth century - e.g., slave narratives, suffragist autobiographies, and travel narratives.

143

Bold, Christine. "American Studies Dissertations in Canada: In Progress and Completed Since 1993." *Canadian Review of American Studies* 25.1 (1995): 147-172.

Documents global interests in race, gender, and identity in the academy at the doctorate level; documentations suggest there is an interest in the works of Ann Petry.

144

Bonadies, Genevieve Terese. "Viewing Post-War Black Politics through a New Lens: Tracing Changes in Ann Petry's Conception of the Mother-Child Relationship, 1943-1965." A.B. Honors in History and Literature and Women, Gender, and Sexuality, Harvard University, 2008.

Provides a thematic re/reading of Petry's critical approaches to mother-child relationships in literature. Also meets the undergraduate requirement for A. B. Honors.

145

Bond, E.G. "Imagining War and Peace: American Women's Short World War II Fiction." Ph.D. Diss., Lehigh University, 1996.

Strives to increase attention to "women's war literature" and its literary qualities, especially in short fiction written between 1935 and 1953. Calls for further studies of such literature, so to explore 1) insights into literary development; 2) post-war American thoughts; and 3) romanticized and demythologized truths about the war. Includes in the study, short fiction written between 1935 and 1953 by writers Ann Petry, Katherine Ann Porter, Bessie Brauer, Shirley Jackson, and Dorothy Porter.

146

Bond, Gregory. "Recovering and Expanding Mozella Esther Lewis's Pioneering History of African-American Pharmacy Students, 1870-1925." *Pharmacy in History* 58.1-2 (2016): 3-23.

Focuses on Petry's Aunt Anne Louise James, providing biography, struggles, and triumphs in the life of this female who dares to become a pharmacist in a male-dominated profession during the nineteenth century. Petry who is first trained in pharmacy and earns a degree in pharmacy provides accurate accounts of this recovered text of her aunt.

147

Bond, Gwenda. Review of *The Street. Publishers Weekly* 255, 14 June 2019.

Announces release of the 75th anniversary edition of *The Street* in January of 2021. Includes a book review by Tayara Jones who highlights the remarkable pre-sales of the novel following its press release - e.g., an increase in "six translation sales." As a result, a new announcement follows, changing the re-issuance of the novel to January of 2020.

148

Bond-Hutto, Patricia Claudette. "Determined Players in a Fixed Game: A Study of the Black Heroine in Selected Urban Novels by African American Women Writers." Ph.D. Diss., Emory University, 1993.

Calls for new ways to examine critically the African American heroine in literary urban environments found in novels from 1900 to the 1950s. Directs attention to the dominant motif - "the city" - and to the metaphoric phrase "determined player in a fixed game." Offers re- interpretations of the heroine as a "determined player" in novels with city settings by Jessie Fauset, Nella Larsen, Dorothy West, Ann Petry, and Paule Marshall.

149

Bone, Robert. "Black Writing in the 1970s." *Nation* 227 (16 December 1978): 677-679.

Identifies important trends in major African American writings of the 1970s. Under short story, includes Petry's *Miss Muriel and Other Stories*, calling her short fiction and collection, "outstanding."

150

_____. *The Negro Novel in America.* New Haven: Yale University Press, 1958. Revised. 1965.

Calls Petry a disciple of Richard Wright and her work *The Street* an "environmentalist" novel. Says Petry's novel lacks the "historical sweep" and the synthesizing of racial and social protest found in Wright's *Native Son*. Favors Petry's second novel, *Country Place*, for its "forceful characterization"; its "tight and economical style"; and its "well-executed design." Classifies *Country Place* as the "best" of the assimilationist novels in the African American literary canon.

151
Bonner, Emily Anne. "Subversive Speculations: Reading Ann Petry's *The Street* and Octavia Butler's *Kindred* Across the Sensory Line." M.A., The University of Tennessee-Knoxville, 2018.
    Encourages theoretical readings of the parallel utilization of speculative by Petry in *The Street* and Octavia Butler in *Kindred*. Suggests these writers create a bridge for readers to actively interact with their texts on multiple levels - as voyeur, sympathizer, and speculator. Includes useful language for active readings and interactions: intersectional oppression, matrix of domination, color line, sonic color line, marginalization of individuals based on race and gender, and constrained identity.

152
Bontemps, Arna. "Awakening." In *Story of the Negro*. New York: Knopf, 1969.
    Provides explanations for how ideology has shaped twentieth-century African American arts and literature. Cites Petry as a successful mainstream.

153
_____. Introduction. *Five Black Lives: The Autobiographies of Venture Smith, James Mars, William Grimes, The Rev. G. W. Offley, and James L. Smith*. Edited by Arna Bontemps. Middletown: Wesleyan University Press, 1958.
    Is a collection of ex-slave narratives which span 150 years in time, from 1729 to 1870. Bontemps' first subject is Venture Smith, a native of Africa who in the end becomes the owner of a shipping business in East Haddan, Connecticut; the subject also appears in Petry's 1945 article, "New England's John Henry" (see #52).

154
_____. "The Line." *Saturday Review of Literature* (22 August 1952):11.
    Says Petry elects to be a "neighborhood novelist" in her controlled yet "electrifying" novel, *The Narrows*. Suggests Petry's style is New England.

155
_____. "Tough, Carnal Harlem." *New York Herald Tribune Weekly Book Review*, 10 February 1946, 4.
    Calls Petry an "unblushing realist" who "leaves out none of the essential character" of the street.

156
Bourgeois, Ashley. "In-Between Black Self and White Desire: Mobility and Liminality in Ann Petry's *The Street*." *South Carolina Review* 46.2 (Spring 2014): 103-114.
    Examines the feminist theories of spatiality and the ways in which space operates in relations to the intersectionality of race, gender, sexuality, and class. In this examination, centers protagonist Lutie Johnson and focuses on the challenges of identity for Lutie who rejects black family space and inevitably denies her sense of belonging which cloud her objectivity and decision-making. Says Petry leaves Lutie suspended between white and black worlds. Lutie is erroneously referenced as Lutie Brown.

157
Boyd, Herb. "Famed Novelist and A Former News Reporter." *New York Amsterdam News*, 17 April 2014.
   Chronicles the literary development of Ann Petry as a bestselling novelist via her work as a journalist and as a community activist in Harlem during the 1930s and 1940s. Analyzes Petry's best-selling novel *The Street* within its contexts of Harlem life in the 1930s, the 1940s, and modern times.

158
_____. "Famed Author of *The Street*, Ann Petry, is Dead at 88." *New York Amsterdam News* (10 May 1997): 34 1.
   Announces that Petry, a former journalist at *Amsterdam News* in the 1930s and 1940s, has died. Reminds readers that Petry's novel *The Street*, which the reviewer calls a "vivid portrait of street life in Harlem in the 1940s," is the work that leads to Petry's fame as a bestselling African American novelist. Boyd inadvertently errors on the date Petry dies which is April 27, 1997.

159
Boynton, Anthony, Morgan L. McComb, Venie Omni, and Kyndall Delph. "Reclaiming the Black Body: Women Writing Women." University of Kansas: *Kansas Scholarly Works*, 2018.
   Exhibits posters and the works of eleven (11) authors in an aim to open up a new conversation about physical violence against the female black body. Says the authors selected for the exhibit tell a different story about agency and self-ownership; about women making and remaking themselves; and about women actively reclaiming their own bodies. The eleven authors featured in the exhibit are Janet Mock; Suzan-Lori Parks; June Jordan; Ann Petry; Yaa Gyasi; Octavia Butler; Alice Dunbar-Nelson; Angela Davis; Assata Shakur; Marita Bonner; and Nnedi Okorafor. Petry's readings for the exhibit are from Petry's *Miss Muriel and Other Stories* and from *The Street*.

160
Brailey, Muriel W. "Necessary Knocking: The Short Fiction of Ann Petry." Ph.D. Diss., Miami University, 1997.
   Calls for improved critical attention to Ann Petry's short fiction. Argues that to overlook the writer's short fiction is to overlook much of what defines her as a writer. Examines themes and literary techniques in Petry's short fiction, especially the African American oral tradition which helps to shape the writer's voice. Also underscores the following: How Petry's writing style is as crucial as what Petry writes. Reminds readers that Petry's artistic purpose is not only "to entertain" but also "to teach" - using lessons about African American survival and empowerment.

161
_____. "The Witness." *Identities & Issues in Literature*, September, 1997, 1.
   Provides a summary and critical analysis of Petry's short story, "The Witness."

162
Bramwel, Jacqueline Patricia. "Marginality and Subservience in Selected Works." M.A., University of the West Indies (Jamaica), 1994.
   Examines marginality and subservience in Erna Brodber's *Jane and Louisa Will Soon Come Home*; Toni Morrison's *Sula*; and Ann Petry's *The Street*.

163
Brauer, Sabine Franziska. "Strategies for Survival in African American Women's Literature." M.A., Southwest Texas State University, 1993.

    Focuses on "survival in literature" by women writers Nella Larsen, Louise Meriwether, Gwendolyn Brooks, and Ann Petry.

164
Brock, Sabine, ed. " 'The Street' ---Kein Ort. Nirgends." *Der entkolonisierte Korper. Die Protagonistin in der afroamerikanischen weiblichen Erzahl-tradition der 30er bis 80er Jahre (The Decolonized Body, The Female Protagonist in the Afro-American Woman's Narrative Tradition from the 1930s to the 1980s)*. New York: Campus Verlag, 1988.

    Requires German translation. Brock adds to Petry's title "Kein Ort. Nirgends," which means "No Place. No Where." Says *The Street* suggests that the mainstream dream from the woman's perspective is impossible because society does not offer a place for black women. Calls Petry "sharpest contrast" to Hurston and Paule Marshall.

165
Brooks, Michael W. *Subway City: Riding the Trains Reading*. New York: Rutgers University Press, 1997.

    Historicizes "the subway" and the writers and artists who make queries about the New York City subway in their writings from the 1920s, 1930s, 1940s, and 1950s. Says numerous writers and artists turn to "the subway," not to dramatize civic and emotional failures but to provide an optimistic testing ground for citizens who survive their exposures to "the subway." Petry utilizes "the subway" in her short and long fiction.

166
Brown, Carolina. "Hot Venus, Cool Modern: Voice, Body, and the Hungry Gaze as Sites of Black Feminist Re-Inscription in Ann Petry's *The Narrows*." *Feminist Modernist Studies* 1.1 (2019): 21-43.

    Encourages a review of Petry's cultural and aesthetic experimentations in *The Narrows*: Petry's investments in the blues and the African American musical tradition; the incorporation of cinematic conventions of film noir; attention to rich aesthetic details; the art of subversion; and social realism. Calls the novel exemplary of "hybrid modernisms."

167
Brown, Jacqueline Elaine. "The Mother as Teacher in Selected Novels by African American Women Writers." M.A., University of Louisville, 1991.

    Analyzes the "mother as teacher" in literature by Zora Neale Hurston, Gwendolyn Brooks, Sarah Wright, Kristin Hunter, and Ann Petry.

168
Brown, Lloyd W. "Tituba of Barbados and the American Conscience: Historical Perspectives in Arthur Miller and Ann Petry." *Caribbean Studies* 13.4 (January 1974):118-126.

    Compares and contrasts Arthur Miller's *Crucible* and Petry's *Tituba of Salem Village*, paying attention to their "major" treatments of Tituba Indian, a slave woman in the seventeenth century, accused of being a witch. Concludes that Petry's treatment of Tituba's is "ethical and social"; her drawing of Tituba's character is "convincingly human."

169

Brown, Stephanie Lynne. "Constructing and Contesting Authenticity in the Postwar African-American Novel." Ph.D. Diss., Columbia University, 2002.

    As the title suggests, the question of "authenticity" in writings about the African American experience is being reexamined, especially during the literary period of 1945-1962. Questions are being raised about whose voice is sufficiently "authentic" to translate the black experience, especially for a white readership and mainstream publishers? Also, Is there a co-option of the black experience by white writers who conflate class and ethnic identity with race? Do writers such as Ann Petry use identity and class to force reconsiderations of "authentic" black writing? In essence, Petry critics are encouraged to determine what are the reliable textual markers that exist for "authentically black" narratives, including Petry's writings.

170

Brown, Sterling A. "A Century of Negro Portraiture in American Literature." *Massachusetts Review* 7.1 (Winter 1966): 73-96. Reprint. In *Black and White in American Culture: An Anthology from the Massachusetts Review*. Edited by Jules Chametzky and Sidney Kaplan. Amherst: University of Massachusetts. 1969. Reprint. In *Black Voices*. Edited by Abraham Chapman. New York: New American Library, 1968.

    Includes Petry in this chronicle of African American literary history. Calls *The Street* an "authentic" slice of Harlem life and a "refutation" of the exotic.

171

Brown, Thomasine Corbett. "Elements of Naturalism in Ann Petry's *The Street*." M.A., University of North Carolina at Chapel Hill, 1966.

    Uses reviews and critical studies of *The Street* to support the thesis that naturalistic and artistic qualities co-exist in the novel. Discusses separately the naturalistic and artistic elements of the novel (plot, setting, point of view, characters, and theme) but insists that both naturalistic and artistic qualities apply in the narrative.

172

Brown, Tia La Shauna. "The Oppressive Use of Difference." M.A., Radford University, 1996.

    Conducts a psychoanalytical reading of Petry's *The Street*, giving attention to "difference," "oppression," and "discrimination."

173

Bryant, Jacqueline K. " 'Clothed in my Right Mind': The Foremother Figure in Early Black Women's Literature." Ph.D. Diss., Kent State University, 1998.

    Traces the stereotypical "mammy" figure found in early fiction by white women writers such as Harriet Beecher Stowe, Carolyn Henta, and Kate Chopin. Also traces portrayals of the foremother and mulatta figure found in the fiction by black women writers Harriet Jacob, Frances Harper, Pauline Hopkins, and Jessie Fauset. Finally focuses on Zora Neale Hurston, Ann Petry, and Gloria Naylor who confirm a consistency in repositioning the foremother and the mulatta in twentieth-century writings.

174
_____. "Postures of Resistance in Ann Petry's *The Street*." *CLA Journal* 45.4 (June 2002): 444-459.
　　Says jazz is used by African American writers as more than just a creative mode of African American cultural expression. Discusses Petry's use of jazz in *The Street* as a commercial medium - subject to economic, racial, and gender politics.

175
_____. *The Foremother Figure in Early Black Women's Literature: Clothed in my Right Mind.* New York: Routledge, 2018.
　　Provides studies to confirm the repositioning of literary foremother and mulatta figures in works by Zora Neale Hurston, Ann Petry, and Gloria Naylor.

176
Buchanan, Jemima D. "The Destruction of Black Masculinity in Ann Petry's Short Fiction." Ph.D. Diss., Morgan State University, 2012.
　　Raises questions about what causes black men in Petry's short fiction to retaliate against their women? Contends that black women are the motivating force behind the destruction of black masculinity, citing examples and evidence in selected short fiction by Ann Petry. Calls Petry's "On Saturday the Siren Sounds at Noon" a blueprint for such a study.

177
Buell, Ellen Lewis. "A Tempery Cat." *New York Times Book Review*, 6 November 1949, 24.
　　Provides a very brief summation of what is called "a beguiling story which catches the essence of kitten nature." Criticizes the illustrator whose pictures sometimes do not accompany the story line in *The Drugstore Cat*.

178
_____. "The Deliverer." *New York Times Book Review*, 16 October 1955, 34.
　　Reviews *Harriet Tubman, Conductor on the Underground Railroad*. Calls the work insightful and stylish. Praises also the brief historical summaries at the end of each chapter. Compares Petry's biography of Harriet Tubman to the biographical work of Dorothy Sterling in "Railroad to Freedom," concluding that Petry's work is "more introspective."

179
Buncombe, Marie H. "From Harlem to Brooklyn: The New York Scene in the Fiction of Meriwether, Petry, and Marshall." *MAWA Review* 1.1 (Spring 1982): 16-19.
　　Chooses to discuss *The Street, Daddy Was a Number Runner*, and *Brown Girl, Brownstones* as "a trilogy," and concludes that from this trilogy comes two major statements about setting: 1) records a history of black life in New York City, particularly of working-class black women in Harlem and in boroughs such as Brooklyn; and 2) serves as a "tarnished symbol" of a "land of opportunity" - especially for black women in America who have had to swallow their pride, face reality, and get jobs.

180
Burgess, Francoise. "The White Woman: The Black Woman's Nemesis." *Revue Francaise D'Etudes*

Americaines. No. 67, *La Poesie Americaine: Constructions Lyriques* (Janvier 1996): 99-107.

    Centers racism and sexism as matters of power and control, and supports the position, using critical writings by Zora Neale Hurston, Toni Morrison, Paula Giddings, and Mary Helen Washington. Also includes supportive critical interpretations from Ann Petry's novel *The Narrows*.

181

Burns, Ben. "Off the Book Shelf." *Chicago Defender*, 9 February 1946 [Special Collections, Boston University].

    Defines "the street" as an "octopus-like monster" and as "one of the most terrible villains ever described in a book." Petry is said to approach her characters "with the penetration of a psychiatrist and the delicate care of a mother." The mood and tempo in *The Street* are said to be comparable to mood and tempo in Edgar Allen Poe's "Pit and the Pendulum." Petry is also said to have avoided one shortcoming that marred Richard Wright's *Native Son* - melodrama.

182

Burns, Mary Patricia. "Testing the Seams of the American Dream: Minority Literature and Film in the Early Cold War." Ph.D. Diss., University of Texas at Austin, 2011.

    Explores the inability of novelists and filmmakers of color of the 1940s to envision racial equality and the American Dream. Includes Petry and her novel *The Street*.

183

Bus, Heiner. " 'All I am and All I Know is Rooted in your Streets' : Women in the Barrio Streets as Depicted in Recent Chicano Writing." *Cahiers Charles* v.20 (1996): 179-192.

    Insists that "literature and city exist in a dialogic relationship" - e.g., architectural design, geography, ecology, economy, environment, sociology, psychology, demographics, town planning, political governances, and ultimately gender, class, and race. Broadens scope of urban studies in Chicano poetry and prose. Invokes characterizations found in Richard Wright's *Native Son*, Ann Petry's *The Street*, and Ralph Ellison's *Invisible Man* whose characters fail to conquer the streets.

184

Busby, Margaret. *Daughters of Africa: An International Anthology of Words and Writings by Women of African Descent from the Ancient Egyptian to the Present*. New York: Ballantine Books, 1994.

    Includes samples of Petry's writing; welcomes international comparative studies.

185

Butcher, Margaret Just. "Regional Nationalism in American Culture." In *The Negro in American Culture* [based on materials left by Alain Locke]. New York: Knopf, 1968.

    Names Petry along with a list of male writers (Richard Wright, Willard Motley, Ralph Ellison, and James Baldwin) for achieving universal portrayals of characters "who simply happen to be colored."

186

_____. "The Negro in Modern American Fiction." In *The Negro in American Culture* [based on materials left by Alain Locke]. New York: Knopf, 1968.

    Mentions Petry favorably and cites her novels *The Street* and *Country Place*.

187

Butcher, Philip. "Our Raceless Writers." *Opportunity: Journal of Negro Life* 26.3 (July-September 1948): 113-115.

    Traces the tradition of raceless novels written by African American writers. Includes Petry's *Country Place* in the discussion. Offers a brief review of the work, calling it a "study of the deteriorating small town." Also points out Petry's carelessness - e.g., Johnnie gets inside the front of the Weasel's car, but he is viewed by the Weasel through the rearview mirror. Also criticizes Petry's varying points of view.

188

Butkovic, Matea. "Druga Svetovna Vojna in Crnci V Ameriski Knjizevnosti: doktorska disertacija (World War II and the Blacks in American Literature)." Ph.D., Diss., Univ V Ljubljani, 2017.

    Examines the communal and individual Black experience, captured by Richard Wright, Ann Petry, and Chester Himes within the historical contexts of the World War II period and (Richard) Wright's School of Protest. Translation is required.

189

Butterfield, Alfred. "The Dark Heartbeat of Harlem." *New York Times Review*, 10 February 1946, 6.

    Discusses *The Street*, drawing attention to protagonist Lutie Johnson's struggles against her own race and neighborhood while attempting to provide a safe and comfortable home for herself and her son. Calls Lutie's experiences a "personal epic."

190

Butts, Jonathan J. "Community and Social Justice in New Deal - Era Urban Literature." Ph.D. Diss., Syracuse University, 2006.

    Explores intersections of urban literature and liberal debates about community from 1920s to the 1950s. Studies literature and debates that promote urban renewal in tandem with a new sense of national community. Also examines novels and documentary writings about New York City written by male Jewish-American and African American writers as well as by male, modernist novelists and leftwing radicals. Petry is the only female writer included.

191

Byrd, Rudolph P., ed. *Generations in Black and White: Photographs from the James Weldon Johnson Memorial Collection*. Athens: University of Georgia Press, 2014.

    Includes photographs of Petry as chemist.

192

Cahill, Susan, ed. *Women and Fiction.* New York: New American Library, 1975.

    Is a collection of twenty-six short stories written by women. Includes Petry's "Like a Winding Sheet" for its "vision and craft." Encourages comparative studies of this Petry story with either Edith Wharton's "A Worn Path" or Katherine Anne Porter's "Rope."

193

Cakirtas, Onder. "Ann Petry Ve Amerikan Romanind A Etnisite Ve Irkcilik." *Bingol Universitesi Sosyal*

Bilimler Enstitusu Dergisi 2.3 (2012): 87-92.

    Clarifies the social and psychological impacts of racist discrimination in the lives of African Americans. Focuses on Petry's protagonist in *The Street* and her attempts to survive against social and racial injustices. Says protagonist helps to expose identity problems in American communities with women who become victims of racist behavior just because of their skin color. Requires translation.

194

Caldwell, Katrina Myers. " 'It Will be Social': Black Women Writers and the Post War Era 1945 – 1960." Ph.D. Diss., University of Illinois at Chicago, 2009.

    Uses a critical Black feminist framework to examine conditions that influence the production of black women's fiction during the postwar era. Includes readings of novels by Ann Petry, Dorothy West and Paule Marshall, referencing them as artifacts shaped by the cultural and political period in question. Concludes that because of contributions to the rich black feminist literary tradition by Petry, West, and Marshall, the postwar fiction writers are important foremothers to later generations of black women artists.

195

Callahan, Cynthia. "Adopted or Married: Families of Choice in Ann Petry's *The Narrows*." *MELUS* 43. 2 (Fall 2018): 103-123.

    Draws attention to Petry's unusually progressive approach to kinship; to the anticipations of psychic effects and rewards of an adoptive kinship, especially from the perspectives of African American males. Centers adoptive kinship in *The Narrows*.

196

Campbell, Donna. "American Literary Naturalism: Critical Perspectives." *Literature Compass* 8.8 (2011): 499-513.

    Provides an overview and reinterpretation of American literary naturalism as practiced by classic naturalists (Stephen Crane, Frank Norris, Theodore Dreiser, and Jack London); later naturalist (John Steinbeck); and other contributors to naturalist texts, especially writers of color (Paul Laurence Dunbar and Ann Petry). Draws attention to key features of naturalism in this study (urban poverty, violence, parody, theories of heredity and capitalism, social Darwinism and determinism, and racial atavism and primitivism). Insists on recovering naturalistic texts as diverse means of interpreting a tradition.

197

_____. *Bitter Tastes: Literary Naturalism and Early Cinema in American Women's Writing*. Athens: University of Georgia Press, 2015.

    Encourages re-readings of classic naturalists such as Frank Norris and Stephan Crane and of the modernist naturalist Ann Petry within the contexts of less familiar topics: naturalist depictions of sex work, reproductive issues, sexual danger for women, etc.

198

Carby, Hazel. *Reconstructing Womanhood: The Emergence of the Afro-American Woman Novelist*. New York: Oxford University Press, 1987.

    Calls for a "rethinking of black feminist criticism and theory." Traces ideologies of womanhood to reveal alternative discourse for black womanhood. Confronts the general history of Anglo-American feminist theory and black feminist criticism and theory to seek an existence of an American sisterhood between black and white women. Measures the achievement of black women writers on the basis of cooptation of the conventions of sentimental novels in regard to their own politically corrective projects - e.g., black womanhood in Ann Petry's *The Street*.

199
Carden, Mary Paniccia. "Sons and Daughters of Self-Made Men: Nation Building and Gender Construction in Modern and Contemporary American Novels." Ph.D. Diss., State University of New York at Binghamton, 1998.
Studies male-centered narratives in American history and identity in modern and contemporary American literature, giving attention to the interpenetration of sexed spaces and subjects; the collapse of space and subject which has gendered an imagined community; and the paradoxes of self-making nation-building constructions which insistently lead to cultural and individual amnesia. Writers studied are Petry, Cather, Faulkner, Wideman, Jane Smiley, and T. Coraghessan Boyle.

200
_____. *Sons and Daughters of Self-Made Men: Improvising Gender, Place, Nation in American Literature*. Lewisburg, PA: Bucknell University Press, 2010.
Discusses ideology, patriarchy, self-determination, group identity, and national characteristics in American literature.

201
Carey, Alice. "Harlem Revisited." *Boston Herald* (Boston, MA),19 July 1992, 013.
Contrasts the "storybook street" in Old Saybrook, Connecticut, that Petry lived on for nearly half a century with "the streets" of Harlem, New York, which made Petry famous. Reminds readers that Petry's first novel *The Street* is published by Houghton Mifflin via a literary award - an honor which Petry also shares with Robert Penn Warren, Philip Roth, and Edward Hoagland. Quotes Gloria Naylor, a fellow female novelist, who calls *The Street*, a "painfully honest and wrenching ... American classic." Also quotes Coretta Scott King, the internationally-known civil rights' activist, who insists: "To this day, few works of fiction have so clearly illuminated the devastating impact of racial injustice."

202
Carter, Michael. " ' There's No Humor in Fear and Poverty': Ann Petry." *Afro-American*, 16 May 1946.
Discusses with Ann Petry the background for her best-selling novel, *The Street*, including "the streets" of Harlem, the people of the city, and their lives.

203
Carter-Sanborn, Kristin. "A Question of Agency: American Women Writers, Feminism, and the Gender of Violence." Ph.D. Diss., University of California, Los Angeles, 1995.
Historicizes and theorizes about "violence" within contemporary [African American] and American feminist traditions. Applies both to Nella Larsen's *Passing*; Ann Petry's The *Street*; and Toni Morrison's *Beloved*.

204
Cataliotti, Robert H. "The Songs Became the Stories: The Music in African American Fiction 1970-2000."

Studies in African American History and Culture. New York, NY: Routledge, 2019.

Provides a comprehensive and historical analysis of representations of African American music in works by African American authors - from the nineteenth century to the 1960s and the Black Arts Movement. Traces the dramatic metamorphous of the representations of music in black fiction, written between the nineteenth century and the Black Arts Movement - e.g., from William Wells Brown to Leroi Jones/Amiri Baraka. Analysis includes Ann Petry and her writings of the 1940s. This work begins as a dissertation.

205

_____. "The Music in African American Fiction: Representing Music in African American Fiction." Ph.D. Diss., State University of New York Stony Brook, 1993.

Identifies black writers who capture the pivotal role of music in African American culture and then examines how these writers have exemplified the spirit and sensibilities of African American music and culture in their writings. Illustrates through the use of music paradigms of literary and cultural traditions in African American literature. Includes authors and fictional works from the nineteenth century to the 1960s and the Black Arts Movement. Includes Petry's short and long fiction published in the 1940s and 1950s,.

206

Chambers, Bradford and Rebecca Moon, eds. *Right On! An Anthology of Black Literature*. New York: New American Library, 1970.

Includes Petry's short story "In Darkness and Confusion" under a section entitled "Oppression." Says Petry's work exemplifies a "modern urban ghetto."

207

Chambers, Veronica. "Ann Lane Petry 190[8]-97: The Passing of a Sister Griot." *Essence* (New York) 28.4 (August 1997): 148.

Shares personal reflections and a conversation between Petry and a college professor on becoming a creative writer. Also provides analytical readings of Petry's longer fiction.

208

Chandler, Zala. "Interview with Toni Cade Bambara and Sonia Sanchez." In *Wild Women in the Whirlwind: Afra-American Culture and the Contemporary Literary Renaissance*. Edited by Joanne M. Braxton and Andree Nicole McLaughlin. New Brunswick, NJ: Rutgers University Press, 1990.

Quotes Sonia Sanchez who says Petry among other women writers in the African American literary tradition has been an inspiration. Says because of Petry and others, she can "feel" history.

209

Charles, John C. "The Home and the Street: Ann Petry's 'Rage for Privacy'." *Abandoning the Black Hero: Sympathy and Privacy in the Postwar African American White Life Novel*. New Brunswick: Rutgers University Press, 2012, 55-85.

Calls attention to the binaries that govern the reception of Petry's works. Offers comparative readings of Petry's *Country Place* and her short stories, "The Bones of Louella Brown" and "In Darkness and

Confusion" to demonstrate the following: striking continuities in Petry's works; an interracial sympathy (in failures and successes); and desires for privacy.

210

_____. "The Home of the Street: The Dialectics of Racial Privacy in Ann Petry's Early Career." *Revising the Blueprint: Ann Petry and the Literary Left.* Edited by Alex Lubin. Jackson: University Press of Mississippi, 2007, 97-119.
    Examines Petry's relationship with left-wing political critics after World War II.

211

_____. "Talking like White Folks: The Rise of the Post World War II African American White-Life Novel." Ph.D. Diss., University of Virginia, 2007.
    Argues that following social transformations of the Great Depression and World War II, there are major African American writers who begin to explore a wide range of subjects and themes beyond cultural expectations and political obligations. Illustrates how Petry is one of those writers who chooses to depict all-white characters in her 1947 novel, *Country Place.*

212

Chenier, Felicia Antoinette. "*Incidents in the Life of a Slave Girl, Passing*, and *The Street*: Women Diverging from the Norm." Ph.D. Diss., Morgan State University, 2011.
    Examines the representation of African American women across literary periods in three seminal texts: Harriet Jacobs' *Incidents in the Life of a Slave Girl;* Nella Larsen's *Passing*; and Ann Petry's *The Street*. Takes feminist and theoretical approaches to examine the struggles of the protagonists created by these women writers, especially their struggles with physical freedom, social identity, and economic advancement in a male-dominated society. Determines that each protagonist steps away from her moral compass in order to survive.

213

Childress, Paulette. "A Womanist Social Protest Tradition in Twentieth Century African-American Literature: Fiction by Marita Bonner, Ann Petry, Dorothy West, and Gwendolyn Brooks." Ph.D. Diss., Wayne State University, 1998.
    Promotes Ann Petry's *The Street*, Dorothy West's *The Living is Easy*, Gwendolyn Brooks' *Maud Martha*, and the short fiction of Marita Bonner as womanist texts. Cites the writers' theoretical representations of gender, race, and class with special attention given to the social, political and economic aspects of the black women writers' womanist tradition.

214

Choi, Yoon Young. "Failing Face of a Nation: The Anxiety of Miscegenation in Ann Petry's *The Narrows*." 영미문학페미니즘 *Feminist Studies in English Literature* 22.3 (2014):5-32.
    Urges a critical reading of Petry's *The Narrows* within the contexts of "miscegenation"; racial anxiety and paranoia in American society; and "racial repression." Says Petry inverts such approaches within the historical reality of the novel. Provides an examination of the relationship between racial stereotypes and what is called Petry's "over-determination of plot and character" in *The Narrows*. Concludes

by encouraging from readers a closer theoretical look at "fantasy" and "representation" in the writer's third novel.

215
Christian, Barbara T. " A Checkered Career - *The Street* by Ann Petry." *The Women's Review of Books*, July 1992.

    Chronicles the availability and lack of availability of marketing for Petry's novels, largely from the 1950s to the 1980s within the backdrop of the availability of Richard Wright's *Native Son*; literature of the Black Arts Movement; and literature courses which include largely black male writers. Provides thematic discussion topics for other Petry critics: proletarian novel which is from the point of view of a woman; space, ghetto, and oppression; lack of opportunity; violence; rape; and the intersectionality of class, gender, and race.

216
_____. "From the Inside Out: Afro-American Women's Literary Tradition and the State." CHS Occasional Paper, Number 19, Minneapolis: University of Minnesota, Center for Humanistic Studies, 1987.

    Taking her title from a line in June Jordan's "Declaration of an Independence I Would Just as Soon Not Have," Christian identifies several African American women writers who deny essential aspects of black womanhood in their writings in order to subvert definitions of black womanhood set by "others." In a later discussion of the political significances of African American women writers on womanhood, Christian briefly mentions Petry in *The Street*, especially for the writer's emphasis on the effects of "poverty and oppression on black women."

217
_____. " Images of Black Women in Afro-American Literature: From Stereotype to Character (1975)." In *Black Feminist Criticism: Perspectives on Black Women Writers*. New York: Pergamon,1985. Reprint. 1989.

    Calls *The Street* functional in its capacity to displace the typical tragic mulatto by introducing a complex, urban heroine. Thinks, however, that protagonist Lutie Johnson reinforces certain stereotypes of black women: the "domestic worker"; the "struggling single mother"; and the "tragic mulatto." Concludes that because of Petry's setting and tone, African American women writers are brought into the twentieth century.

218
_____. "Ordinary Women: The Tone of the Commonplace." In *Black Women Novelists: The Development of a Tradition, 1892-1976*. Westport, CT: Greenwood, 1980.

    Writes there is a tone of the commonplace in *The Street*: "a selection of details and seemingly trivial struggles that poor women can seldom avoid." Recognizes *The Street* as one of the first novels to present a "struggling, urban black mother attempting to create a better life for herself." Encourages comparisons of novels by Petry and other male and female African American writers.

219
Clark, Graham. "Beyond Realism: Recent Black Fiction and the Language of ' The Real Thing.' " In *Black Fiction: New Studies in the Afro-American Novel Since 1946*. Edited by A. Robert Lee. New York: Barnes

and Noble, 1980.

 Focuses on the "black modernist voice" in fiction after 1957. Takes time to refute Robert Bone's earlier denouncement of "tired and worn racial prescriptions" in African American writings after *Native Son*. Suggests that when Bone's call for a "new style" - most obviously a black modernist voice - such a style and voice are being developed "in precisely the tradition of Afro-American realist writing[s] which Bone saw as so worn and frenzied." Directs readers to Petry and early works of Chester Himes.

220

Clark, Keith. "A Mighty Queer Place": Textual and Sexual Dis-Ease in Ann Petry's *Country Place*." *African American Review* 49. 2 (Summer 2016): 93-110.

 Places Petry with a number of African American writers (from Dunbar and Hurston to Wright and Baldwin) who examine whites and their lives, "lay[ing] bare not simply the disease of whiteness but [that which is considered 'normative'] and [which] manifold anxieties therein."

221

_____. A Distaff Dream Deferred? Ann Petry and the Art of Subversion." *African American Review* 26. 3 (Fall 1992): 495-505.

 Provides a post-structuralist reading of *The Street*, which is influenced by Petry's depiction of black women in pursuit of the American Dream, but who must subvert the quest [the Dream], so to fulfill their own versions of it. Is an extension of his dissertation.

222

_____. " ' From a Thousand Different Points of View' : The Multiple Masculinities of Ann Petry's 'Miss Muriel'." In *Ann Petry's Short Fiction: Critical Essay*s. Edited by Hazel Arnett Ervin and Hilary Holladay. Westport, CT: Praeger, 2004.

 Contends that Petry asks readers to consider the meaning of black men accepting and reenacting the very oppressive behaviors that have enervated them throughout history. Insists, however, in Petry's short and long fiction that the writer adds and critiques "layered" portrayals of male characters and dimensions of black male subjectivity.

223

_____. *The Radical Fiction of Ann Petry.* Baton Rouge: Louisiana State University Press, 2013.

 Cites various, new theoretical directions for Petry's criticism. Introduces for discussion an analysis of Petry's radical aesthetic agenda in *The Narrows* and several of her short stories. Directs critical attention to the writer's emphasis on storytelling, especially on relationships between the teller and the tale. Also directs attention to Petry's techniques of multiple points of view via discontinuities and breaks in her narratives as well as by way of jazz sensibilities.

224

_____. (Contributor). *The Narrows: A Novel* (Paperback). Evanston, IL: Northwestern University Press, 2017.

 Provides an analytical introduction to Petry's third novel which is reissued.

225

Clarke, Deborah. *Driving Women: Fiction and Automobile Culture in Twentieth-Century America.*

Baltimore, MD: The Johns Hopkins University Press, 2007.

    Explores origins of "automobile culture" and the gendering of it into early twentieth century fiction from many perspectives: historical, psychological, economic ethnic, etc. Reads women writers against male writers and their creations and cultivations of "automobile culture" in fiction. Petry is included with a number of mainstream and period women writers: Dorothy Allison, Julia Alvarez, Kay Boyles, Joan Didion, Louise Erdrich, Jessie Fauset, Leslie Feinberg, Christina Garcia, Zora Neale Hurston, Cynthia Kadohata. Michelle Kennedy, Barbara Kingsolver, Rose Wilderhane, Erika Lopez, Bobbie Ann Mason, Toni Morrison, Joyce Carol Oates, Flannery O'Conner, Marge Piercry, Danzy Senna, Leslie Marmon Silko, Mona Simpson, Jane Smiley, Gertrude Stein, Helena Viramontes, and Edith Wharton.

226

Cloutier, Jean-Christophe. *Shadow Archives: The Lifecycles of African American Literature*. New York: Columbia University Press, 2019.

    Questions the state and availability of 20th century American literary archives. Promotes several critical objectives: 1)"Analyz[e] both [the] archival function that novels serve - the way they can stand as alternative, expanded or even counter-factual sites of historical preservation - and the role that novelists have played as archivists and record creators"; 2) "explore authors' own appraised strategies and record-creating processes and at times, their own research practices to uncover how their archival sensibilities inform their novelistic practices"; and 3) focus on "how novelist amass and create other ways … to negotiate civic, social, and national estrangement; how and what they choose to document and record [to] reflect the kind of nation they are working to redefine, both in the present moment and for posterity." Makes a personal observation of the "neglect" of critical appraisals and explorations of the archival function of Ann Petry's largest collection - which, at the time, is at Boston University. Suggests possible projects for Petry enthusiasts: "Petry's personal notebooks and manuscript drafts [which] would invariably uncover a fount of new knowledge not only about her novelistic practice and archival sensibility, but … the unique perspective of a black, female artist-activist."

227

Coffey, Michael. "Black Writers Debate 'Being Human in the 20th Century' (5th Annual Celebration of Black Writing)." *Publishers' Weekly* (17 February 1989): 17.

    Mentions briefly that Ann Petry is guest of honor at the Fifth Annual Black Writers' Conference and that she is also honored later in the evening at a reception at the Free Library of Philadelphia. Includes a photograph of Petry.

228

Coleman, James W. Review of *The Radical Fiction of Ann Petry* by Keith Clark. *African American Review* 48.3 (Fall 2015): 385-387.

    Reviews Keith Clark's *The Radical Fiction of Ann Petry*, calling it "ground-breaking study." In particular, details how Clark is able to illustrate that Petry's novels and short stories such as "Like a Winding Sheet" are "substantively deeper and richer than naturalism" ; that Petry is far ahead of her time in the exploration of black male ontology; and that Petry anticipates gothic conventions to display horrors of racism in African American life.

229
Collins, Patricia Hill. "Shifting the Center: Race, Class, and Feminist Theorizing about Motherhood." In *Mothering: Ideology, Experience and Agency*. Edited by Evelyn Nikon Glenn, Grace Chaney, and Linda Ronnee Foray. New York: Routledge, 2016, 45-65.

    Insists "For women of color, the subjective experience of mothering/motherhood is inextricably linked to the sociocultural concern of racial ethnic communities - one does not exist without the other." Calls for a richer feminist theorizing about motherhood, recognizing that experiences of African Americans, Native Americans, Hispanics, and Asian Americans might yield markedly different themes - e.g., survival, power, and identity.

230
"Color and Conflict." *The Times* (London), 27 August 1954 [Special Collections, Boston University].

    Reviews *The Narrows* for an international audience. Says Petry represents the new African American writer who is able to examine her race, its characteristics, and problems "without the underlying current of resentment." Says that *The Narrows* has familiar defects and qualities of the Wolfe-Faulkner school - "poetry, rhetoric, diffuseness and colour."

231
"Color in Connecticut." *Time* (17 August 1953): 94-96.

    Proposes that setting in *The Narrows* is most "remarkable," especially when compared with other elements of the novel. Says plot is seriously told, but prefers the "rich parallel story" of Malcolm Powther. Predicts that Malcolm and Mamie Powther's story will help to sustain *The Narrows* - more so than the "fictional survival" of Link Williams and Camilo Sheffield.

232
Colson, Don. Review of *The Radical Fiction of Ann Petry* by Keith Clark. *Studies in American Naturalism* 9.1 (Summer 2014):111-114.

    Reviews favorably Keith Clark's *The Radical Fiction of Ann Petry*, classifying the work as a recovery and a re-evaluation of Petry's fiction. In particular, the reviewer calls attention to what Clark requires of critics: re-readings of Petry's fiction for its complexity, including its unique adoptions of American gothic conventions; nuanced feminism and anti-racism; and most importantly, its essentiality, including approaches to masculinity. The reviewer intentionally calls attention to Clark's deployment of the word "radical" in his title; he explains that the word does not denote a tie to the Left. Rather, the word is meant to move the writer out of the marginalized shadows of Richard Wright, Ralph Ellison, Toni Morrison, and Alice Walker.

233
"Commentary." In *The World of Fiction*. Edited by David Madden. Chicago: Holt, Rinehart and Winston, 1990.

    Comments on Petry's literary strategies in her short story "The Witness,"particularly her point of view, characterization, and theme. "The Witness" is reprinted, followed by questions, assignments, and "writing suggestions."

234
Connor, J. D. "The Language of Men: Identity and Existentialism in the American Postwar." Ph.D. Diss.,

The Johns Hopkins University, 2000.

    Challenges postwar discourse on the repression and eruption of identity in a subversive Cold War hegemony. Argues that the postwar era is a time in American literary history when identities proliferate and become interchangeable. Provides evidence of language in postwar social-problem novels that offer the chance to change the hegemonic social order by perfecting the order of words. Petry is referenced along with an exhaustive list of major, prolific writers of American and world literature who also achieve the latter with language.

235

Conrad, Earl. "A Woman's Place in Harlem." *Chicago Defender,* 2 February 1946, 13.

    Concludes that Petry, who is an award-winning novelist and a wife, is the "most apt symbol" of the African American question concerning the woman's place. Underscores Petry's discussion of the status of the African American woman, both in literature and in the real world. Also discusses Petry's efforts in *The Street* to portray women more realistically.

236

Constantakis, Sara. *Novels for Students*, Volume 33: Presenting Analysis, Context, and Criticism on Community Studies Novels. Detroit: Gale, 2010.

    Presents critical overviews of literary periods. Includes discussions of authors' plot structures, characterizations, themes, and cultural and the historical significances of literary texts. Petry is included in these discussions.

237

Contributions of Black Women to America (The Arts, Media, Business, Law, Sports). Edited by Marianna W. Davis. Vol 1. Columbia, SC: Kenday, 1982.

    Pays tribute to Petry for her fiction. Includes a picture, courtesy of *Ebony*.

238

Cook, William W. "College Composition and Communication."*National Council of Teachers in English* 44.1 (February 1993): 9-25.

    Provides a substantial and critical reading of "voice" in Ann Petry's *The Street*, and then contextualizes what can happen when "voice" is passive rather than active.

239

Cooke, Michael. "Introduction: Building on 'Signifying' and the Blues." *Afro-American Literature in the Twentieth Century: The Achievement of Intimacy.* New Haven: Yale University Press, 1984.

    Moves African American literature outside of "signifying" and outside of the blues. Contends that there are "four major modes and stages" in African American literature: self, veiling, solitude, kinship, and intimacy, etc. Petry's protagonist Lutie appears in the "solitude" section.

240

Corbett, Jane. "Store Porch Gossip." *Times Educational Supplement*, 19 September 1986, 40.

    Acknowledges the literary contributions of Zora Neale Hurston and Ann Petry to African American literature.

241

Cosgrove, Mary Silva. "In Tune with Their Times." *Book Work* 2 (1 November 1964): 28.

    Calls *Tituba of Salem Village* "in tune" with American seventeenth-century Salem Witch. Says reminiscent of Elizabeth George Speare's *The Witch of Blackbird Pond*.

242

Crafty, Bryant J. "Fighting 'forced relationship' : Rape and Manslaughter in Ann Petry's *The Street*." In *Some Educational Implications of Movement*. Seattle, WA: Special Child Publications, 1970.

    Demonstrates aligning social work and literature to study relationships and rape.

243

Crane, Mary Ellen. "Life in Harlem." *Birmingham News* 9 March 1946 [Special Collections, Boston University].

    Notes the "wonderous personalities" that emerge in *The Street* due to the characters' relationships to "the street," particularly Min, who is thought to be "the most successful portrait of them all." Applauds Petry's "treatment of loneliness in cities" and Lutie's "struggle to prove the existence of free will."

244

Crescenza, Michele. "Poor Lutie's Almanac: Reading and Social Critique in Ann Petry's *The Street*." In *Reading Women: Literary Figures and Cultured Icons from the Victorian to the Present*. Edited by Janet Badia and Jennifer Phegley. Toronto: University of Toronto Press, 2005, 215-235.

    Argues that Petry's novel encourages studies of ways in which "literacy" simultaneously functions as liberation of and limitation for black women. Theorizes social critiques of Petry and her authorial concerns for black women's uncritical reading practice - e.g., Lutie's naïve and mis-reading of Benjamin Franklin's credo.

245

_____. "Reading Women Reading: Literacy and Consciousness in Four American Novels." Ph.D. Diss., Emory University, 2005.

    Provides a comparative study of Frances Newman's *The Hard-Boiled Virgin* and Petry's *The Street* to demonstrate, among others, how women's uncritical reading practices simultaneously function as liberation and limitation.

246

Crystel, Pinconnat. *Traduire la puissance du blanc. Du gothique dans "Native Son" de Richard Wright et "The Street" d'Ann Petry. DeGrand Inquisiteur a Big Brother Arts, science et politique*. Edited by Anna Saignes, Agathe Salha. Classiques Garnier, 2013.

    Is a collection of essays on Richard Wright and Ann Petry. Requires translations.

247

Currier, Isabel. " '*The Street* ' is Realistic Literature." *Boston Herald* 20 February 1946 [Special Collections, Boston University].

    Insists *The Street* is "as unpretty as the horror films from Germany's mass-murder concentration camps." Says it is the "painful duty" of all who earnestly seek peace to read this novel. Criticism is also directed towards Petry's lack of balance for truth: her story "has only one dimension"; her "prose spills out in colloquial violence"; her characters other than Lutie are "dwarfed by the monstrosities of their separate and collective natures."

248

Curry, Stephanie Juanita. " ' Much Smaller than His Shadow': A Gothic Analysis of Black Masculine Figures in Ann Petry's *The Street*, 'Like a Winding Sheet,' and 'The Witness.' " Ph.D. Diss., Texas Southern University, 2018.

    Insists many of Petry's short and long texts are latent with elements of Gothicism, revealing the psychological effects of racism and intra-racial discrimination on black men (i.e., the disruption of the black male psyche). Applies Carl Jung's psychoanalytical theory to deconstruct the lives of men in Petry's novel and short stories to show how their actions and choices are the direct result of the traumatized and disrupted black male psyche.

249

Daltry, Patience M. Review of *Tituba of Salem Village*. *Christian Science Monitor*, 25 February 1965, 7.

    Praises the work, but not without calling attention to the wordiness of its style and its melodramatic conclusion.

250

Dandridge, Rita B. *Black Women's Blues: A Literary Anthology, 1934-1988*. New York: G. K. Hall & Co, 1992.

    Is a socio-historical and psychological anthology of twentieth-century African American women writers, from the Depression era to the present. Provides a wide range of genres, including poetry, plays, letters, essays, novels, short stories, and autobiographies. Petry is included. Maintains that selections were chosen to play off each other and to complement each other in such a way that the writings "coalesce to form … black women's blues, representing, as do the blues, both the pain of the struggle and the need to tell of it." Again, Petry is mentioned.

251

_____. "Male Critics/Black Women's Novels." *CLA Journal* 23. 1 (September 1979):1-2.

    Discloses how male critics review novels by African American women writers with "apathy, chauvinism, and paternalism" and cites as an example David Littlejohn's discussion of Petry and Richard Wright, James Baldwin, and Ralph Ellison in Black on White. Dandridge applauds Petry's "creative sympathy."

252

_____. Review of *The Critical Response to Ann Petry*, edited By Hazel Arnett Ervin. *CLA Journal* 50.1 (September 2006):115-117.

    Provides a review of the collection. Applauds the editor for an "impressive … celebration of Ann Petry's [three] novels." Says the collection is "long overdue."

253

_____. " On Novels by Black American Women: A Bibliographical Essay (Authors)." *Women's Studies Newsletter* 6.3 (Summer 1978): 28-30.

    Comments on criticism of Black American women authors. Includes Petry.

254

Daniel, Thomas H. "Street in Harlem is Subject of New Book." *Columbia Record* (South Carolina), 7 February 1946 [Special Collections, Boston University].

    Calls *The Street* "a faithful portrayal of a segment of American life" that is not necessarily limited to African Americans. Calls Petry's style "Dickensian," particularly her emphasis on the temptations and struggles of Lutie in an environment filled with "poverty, degradation, and crime."

255

Dauterich, Edward, IV. "Violence and the Ideology/Utopia Dialectic in Wright, Petry, Ellison, and Hurston." Ph.D. Diss., Kent State University, 2006.

    Notes the following observations: Characters in novels by Wright, Ellison, Hurston, and Petry constantly waiver between ideological class, race, and gender-based restraints and the impulse to challenge those restraints. When the characters push too far toward utopia or are pulled too far into ideology, a violent event often occurs that shifts the balance of the dialectic back in the other direction.

    Takes an Hegelian dialectical approach to center violence and ideology in Wright, Ellison, Hurston and Petry, and encourages viewing violence as the mediator in the dialectic relationship, forcing readers and critics to move beyond simple judgments of the texts and to provide a critical vocabulary for discussing violence in new ways.

256

Davidson, Adenike Maria. "Ann Petry's *The Street*: A Fight for the Respect of Black Men and Women in 1940s America." M.A., University of California-Los Angeles, 1992.

    Studies "respect" - as a character merit of black men and women of 1940s.

257

Davis, Amanda J. "Shatterings: Violent Disruptions of Homeplace in *Jubilee* and *The Street*." *MELUS* 30.4 (Winter 2005): 25-51.

    Views Margaret Walker in *Jubilee* and Ann Petry in *The Street* as the two most important 20th century writers who have carefully examined and attempted to find and to maintain "the home" with some degree of comfort, belonging, and protection. Says such attempts are continuously met with violence and are thwarted via social and economic injustices that pervade the boundaries of home or that threaten to disrupt any resistance. Concludes Walker and Petry make clear that violence and discrimination have long informed struggles to construct viable and ultimately safe homes for African Africans.

258

Davis, Arthur P. "Current Literature." *Journal of Negro Education* 25.4 (Fall 1946): 649-650.

    Applauds *The Street* for its sound thesis and its universal appeal. Criticizes the novel for its melodramatic characterizations of Junto and Mrs. Hedges and its "forced ending."

259

_____. "Integrationists and Transitional Writers." In *From the Dark Tower: Afro-American Writers, 1900 to 1960*. Washington, DC: Howard University Press, 1974.

    Provides literary analysis of Petry's novels. Insists the literary strength of the "competent writer" lies in her children's works and short stories. Considers she "does several things well, but none superlatively." Believes short stories will "stand up best after the critical years have passed judgment."

260

_____. " Negro American Literature." In *Negro Year Book: A Review of Events Affecting Negro Life 1941-1946*. Edited by Jessie Parkhurst Guzman. Tuskegee, AL: Department of Records and Research, Tuskegee Institute, 1947.

Discusses the Harlem Renaissance and the effects of the movement on the "hard-boiled writers," including Petry, of the Chicago Renaissance. Considers Petry's *The Street* a "milder [and] less powerful New York version of *Native Son*."

261

Davis, Arthur P. and J. Sanders Redding, eds. *Cavalcade: Negro American Writing from 1760 to the Present*. Boston: Houghton Mifflin, 1971.

Renames an excerpt from *The Street* as "Dead End Street." Calls the Novel "one of the better . . . of the naturalistic school."

262

Davis, Arthur P., J. Saunders Redding and Joyce Ann Joyce, eds. *New Cavalcade: African-American Writing from 1760 to Present. Vol 1*. Washington, DC: Howard University Press, 1991.

Provides a brief biographical sketch of Petry. Reprints "Like a Winding Sheet."

263

Davis, Carole Boyce, ed. "Black Women's Writing: Crossing the Boundaries." *Matatu: Zeitschrift fur Afrikanische and Gesellschaft* 3.6 (1989): 1-4.

Includes Petry in her discussion of American black women writers.

264

Davis, Thulani. " Black Women Writers Reclaim Their Past." *The Village Voice* (online), 1 January 2020.

Includes Petry in a chronology and in discussions of writers.

265

_____. " Family Plots: Black Women Writers Reclaim Their Past." *The Village Voice* 32.10 (1987): 14-17.

Responds to critics who suggest contemporary African American women writers have "broken a silent pact among all African American writers to present positive images." Responds especially to critic Mel Watkins (*New York Times Book Review,* 15 June 1986), who traces "the portrayal of hostility between black men and women to the 1967 novel, *The Flagellants*, by Carlene Hatcher Polite." Davis returns to early African American novelists, or "motherlodes" like Jessie Fauset, Nella Larsen, Zora Neale Hurston, and Ann Petry to show that the impulses and concerns of these writers often parallel those of contemporary African American women writers. She concludes that together the "motherlodes" and the contemporary women writers help to create the "black women's tradition within the larger black literary tradition."

266

Debo, Annette. " Power, Destiny, and Individual Choice: Gloria Naylor's Naturalism." *CLA Journal* 44.4 (2001): 492-521.

Approaches Gloria Naylor, Richard Wright and Ann Petry as naturalistic writers. Insists, however, that Naylor promotes her own definition of naturalism which moves beyond Wright and Petry's scenarios that are seen as devoid of hope. Says in *The Women of Brewster Place, Linden Hills,* and *Mama Day,* Naylor's characters face the realization of other forces of destiny.

267
Delano, Page Dougherty. "Loose Lips Sink Ships": Women and Citizenship in Wartime Culture (World War II, Ann Petry, Chester Himes, Kay Boyle, William G. Smith, Gertrude Stein)." Ph.D. Diss.,The Graduate Center, City University of New York, 1996.

    Discusses a female citizenry - i.e., from women identifiable with the nation and women with critical identifications to women excluded from the national face. Evidence of such observations comes from memoirs of women writers of fiction, from Ann Petry and Kay Boyle to Gertrude Stein.

268
_____. " Making Up for War: Sexuality and Citizenship in Wartime Culture." *Feminist Studies* 26.11 (Spring 2000): 33-68.

    Discusses female makeup and the masculine imagination in American culture during World War II - e.g., women are intimately bound to sex, prostitution and rape; or overtly sexualized. Also discusses other ways to view wartime discourse on makeup: a sign of female agency which includes sexual power and citizenship. Includes interpretative readings of Petry's "In Darkness and Confusion" and "Like a Winding Sheet" where lipstick becomes the focal point of brutal wife beating.

269
Delcoco-Fridley, Lea Johanna. "Defining Motherhood: The Plight of the Non-traditional Mother in Multi-Ethnic American Women's Literature." Ph.D. Diss., Indiana University of Pennsylvania, 2004.

    Takes a cultural feminist/historical focus on the multi-ethnic American mother in the mid-to-late twentieth century and questions where does she fit in contemporary American society? Answers come in the form of additional questions: 1) How does multi-ethnic motherhood challenge the ideals set by American society, and do these ideals set the mother up for failure? 2) What influence has the multi-ethnic mother made on the American family, literature, and society in the late twentieth century? and 3) What does this impact say about motherhood in general? Literary works by the following writers are included in the study: Toni Morrison, Alice Walker, Maxine Hong Kingston, Ann Petry, and Sandra Cisneros.

270
Demarest, David P. and Lois S. Lamdin, eds. *The Ghetto Reader*. New York: Random House, 1970.

    Includes an excerpt from *The Street* entitled "Bub and Ben Franklin." In a very brief introduction, the editors call Lutie a "fictional rendering of the Negro Matriarchy." Encourages comparisons between Petry's matriarch and the sociological description of the matriarch recorded by sociological Kenneth Clark.

271
Demmler, Monika. "Biophilia and the Aesthetics of Blues, Jazz, and Hip-Hop Music in African-American Prose Fiction." Ph.D. Diss., der Universitat Augsburg, 2015.

    Pulls theories from African American literature and music (blues, jazz and hip-hop), reader response, and biophilia to study "emotional engagement in the reading process." After elaborate discussions of artistic productions as well as aesthetic receptions of African American prose fiction influenced by blues, jazz, or hip-hop music, sheds light on possible ecological healing effects through productions. Includes in the study Petry's short story, "Solo on the Drums."

272
Dempsey, David. "Uncle Tom's Ghost and the Literary Abolitionists." *Antioch Review* 6.3 (Fall 1946): 442-447.

    Gives Petry credit for displacing African American "types" in literature like "Uncle Tom," "poverty-stricken Willie," and "happy-go-lucky Josh." Applauds Petry for creating professionals and government workers with "much deserved intelligence, dignity, and courage." However, indicts Petry for the novel's murder, claiming that it lacks "poetic justice."

273
Dente, Shahara Tova V. " 'Creeping into the Conversation': Tracing Hip Hop Literature from Margin to Center." Ph.D. Diss., University of Alabama, 2015.

    Inspires intertextual studies and diverse conversations across a trajectory of African American literature - e.g., street literature and Hip Hop literature alongside canonical texts. Examines canonical texts such as Ann Petry's *The Street* and Toni Morrison's *The Bluest Eye* alongside "street literature" and Hip Hop literature, namely Sapphire's *PUSH* and Sister Souljah's *The Coldest Winter Ever,* allowing for reviews of cultural, racial, and political impacts on popular culture and on the academy.

274
Devers, Rebecca Allison. "The Iron Curtain in the Picture Window: The Cold War Home in American Fiction and Popular Culture." Ph.D. Diss., University of Connecticut, 2010.

    Examines domestic spaces represented in American Cold War literature, television, film, advertising, civil defense publications, and popular magazines between the years of 1945 and 1963; examines ways the post-war suburban boom and the dawning atomic age are working together to shift Americans' apocalyptic ideations away from traditional Christian moorings and towards a modern faith in science and technology. Petry is among the writers of Cold War literature included in this study.

275
Devlin, Paul. "Ann Petry, Ralph Ellison and Two Representations of Live Jazz Performances." *American Studies* 54.3 (2015): 115-126, 189.

    Suggests Ellison's inspiration for "Three Days Before the Shooting" is Petry's "Solo on the Drums," especially the jazz club scenes. Overall, provides a comparative study of narrative portrayals and the effects of jazz performances on literature and on how music is used to communicate political and cultural loss (Ellison and Petry) and personal betrayal of love (Petry). Asks readers to consider Petry as a sort of "alternative jazz critic."

276
Dhillon, Nargis. "*The Street* by Ann Petry: A Quagmire of Environmental and Economic Oppression." *Research Scholar (*An International Refereed e-Journal of Literary Explorations) 5.1 (February 2017): 1-81.

    Examines how and why protagonist Lutie Johnson is caught between the yearning to elevate her standards of living and the hindrances in her way -e.g., race, class, gender and relentless economic forces. Encourages applying eco-criticism to the reading of Petry.

277

Dingledine, Dan. " 'It Could Have Been Any Street ': Ann Petry, Stephen Crane, and the Fate of Naturalism." *Studies in American Fiction.* 34.1 (Spring 2006): 87-106. Reprint. *Reading America: New Perspectives on the American Novel*. Edited by Elizabeth Boyle and Anne-Marie Enew. Newcastle upon Tyne: Cambridge Scholars Publishers, 2008.

      Encourages comparative studies of Petry and white naturalists Theodore Dreiser, Frank Norris and Stephen Crane. Notes that such critiques are missing in Petry's scholarship. Illustrates how Petry engages Crane in her writing of *The Street* and how Crane's *Maggie* is an importantly early representation of urban poverty and a logical influence on Petry's best-seller. Calls for further examinations of the echoes and the key differences between the two texts.

278

Donahue, James J. and Jennifer Ann Ho and Shaun Morgan, eds. *Narrative, Race, and Ethnicity in the United States*. Columbus: Ohio State University Press, 2017.

      Collects essays that study the complexities of race and ethnicity (African American, Native American, Latino/a, Asian American, and queer) in American literature. Cautions that fields of study in American literature are not always in dialogue with one another, but while representations in the collection do point towards internal diversity, offered are new models of critical race narratology, suitable for scholars broadening disciplinary horizons. Petry is among a host of major African American writers included in the collective study.

279

Dorris, Michael. "Novel Still Holds Power After 50 Years." *Sun Sentinel* (Fort Lauderdale), 22 March 1992, 10F. Reprint. Dorris, Michael. "Where We've Been: *The Street* by Ann Petry." *Los Angeles Times*, 1 March 1992, 1.

      Provides critical commentary on Petry's *The Street*, especially on character Lutie Johnson, social realism, and Petry's artistry and techniques. Says Petry has a grand, impressive talent. Compares *The Street* favorably with the best of John Steinbeck, John Dos Passos and Upton Sinclair. Includes a photo of Petry and other book cover illustrations.

280

Dow, W. E. "Living on Paper: Disarticulating a Racialized Capitalism in Works by Richard Wright and Ann Petry." In *The Fictions of American Capitalism*. New York: Palgrave Macmillan, 2020.

      Traces the desires of Richard Wright and Ann Petry, both of whom were journalists and major novelists, so to move beyond the fictional charge of the African American novel and to capture the effects of racialized capitalism. Chronicles their narrative resistance to the destructive forces of capitalism and their contributions to realism and the need to change existing social orders.

281

_____ and Roberta S. Maquire, editors. *The Routledge Companion to American Literary Journalism*. New York: Routledge, 2019.

      Raises the following questions for consideration: Is journalism as art form or a profession? Is it an object of scholarship or a craft suitable for instructions? Does it belong among the faculties of the arts and sciences, or should it be taught in a free-standing school, like law, medicine, or business? Responses come in

35 essays which "interrogate the assumptions." Concerned contributors write to suggest ways that the past might inform those attempting to navigate the future. Petry who served as a journalist in New York before publishing *The Street* is included in the study.

282

Downing, Francis. *Commonweal* 47 (2 January 1948): 306-307.

    Takes issue with one critic who reviews *Country Place* as "real" [and] most compelling." Says Petry is "not clear" and not a "born storyteller." Approves naming Glory as the unfaithful wife. Through Glory's symbolic name Petry is saying that "what ruins our marriage is the adolescent and romantic process of falling in love."

283

Doyle, Sister Mary Ellen. "The Heroine in Black Novels." In *Perspectives on Afro-American Women*. Edited by Willa D. Johnson and Thomas L. Green. Washington, DC: ECCA (Division of Educational-Community Counselors Associates, Inc.), 1975.

    Includes Lutie Johnson from *The Street* in an analysis of black heroines in African American fiction. Says Petry joins a host of other black women writers who raise issues that are crucial to gender and race. Is not convinced, however, that Lutie's unsuccessful fight for security and respectability is "fully. . . tragedy."

284

Drake, Kimberly. "Women on the Go: Blues, Conjure, and Other Alternatives to Domesticity in Ann Petry's *The Street* and *The Narrows*." *Arizona Quarterly*, Spring, 1998. Reprint. In *The Critical Response to Ann Petry*. Edited by Hazel Arnett Ervin. Westport, CT: Praeger, 2005.

    Contends that Petry does not portray her minor characters as fallen or degenerate. Instead, through narrative support, Petry portrays characters with working-class morals and lifestyles, and she challenges white-identified bourgeois standards. Ends, calling Petry the first black woman writer to create literary space for the "legitimate" expression of black female sexuality.

285

_____. " ' Women on the Go': Double Consciousness, Domesticity, and the Street Culture in Ann Petry's Fiction." *Subjectivity in the American Protest Novel*. Basingstoke: Palgrave, 2011, 89-130.

    Traces depictions of marriage and domesticity, the "cult of true womanhood," and African American cultural experiences within comparative contexts by Nella Larsen in *Quicksand* and Petry in *The Street* and *The Narrows*.

286

Drake, Kimberly Sue. " ' Your Back Against a Wall': Home Invasion and Refigured Architecture in Depression-era Protest Novels." Ph.D. Diss., University of California, Berkeley, 1996.

    Analyzes the metaphor 'individual self and home' - a private space protected from the contaminating public realm. Traces versions of the metaphor in American literature, from Ben Franklin's self-sufficiency and Stowe's domestic ideology to twentieth-century writers of consumerism and self-making, including Ann Petry, Tillie Olsen, Richard Wright, and Sarah Wright.

287

"Dream Deferred or Dream Defeated?: Ann Petry's *The Street*." *The New Korean Journal of English Language & Literature* 56.1(2014): 127-147.

    Reinforces the following: Petry's critique of male-dominant ideology; protagonist, Lutie Johnson's reckless embrace of the American Dream; social injustice; and the double standards of American society.

288

Duane, Anna Mae. "Tituba of Salem Village." *Journal of the History of Childhood and Youth* (Baltimore), 5.1 (Winter 2012): 154-156.

    Says the book, which was first written in 1950s, offers a wealth of timely material designed for students in the twenty-first century.

289

Dubey, Madhu. "Narration and Migration: Jazz and Vernacular Theories of Black Women's Fiction." *American Literary History* 10.2 (Summer 1998): 291-316.

    Examines the historical and geographical directions of vernacular criticism in black women's fiction, with references to a specific moment in black cultural history - the Great Migration of the early twentieth century. The era is thought to have conditioned the subsequent development of black literature. As evidenced, focuses largely on Zora Neal Hurston, Alice Walker, and Toni Morrison, but because of the chronology of black women's literary tradition also mentions Petry.

290

Dubuk, Laura. "White Family Values in Ann Petry's *Country Place*." *MELUS* 29.2 (2004): 55-76.

    Creates space for Petry in studies of "whiteness," focusing on Petry's *Country Place* and the following: her interrogations of ideologies about gender, class, and national identity; her subversion of social constructions of postwar 'gendered white' subjects; and her reconsiderations of disenfranchised people of color (and disenfranchised white women). Adds Morrison's *Playing in the Dark* to help contextualize the studies of "whiteness."

291

Dubuk, Laura Jo. "White Family Fictions: Black Novelists and Cultural Narratives of Whiteness, 1942 - 1956." Ph.D. Diss., University of Iowa, Iowa City, 2001.

    Refers to Ann Petry, James Baldwin, Richard Wright, and Zora Neale Hurston as major African American authors who have written novels with primarily white characters; as important theorists on "whiteness" and the historical constructions of national identity. Examines Petry's *Country Place* and cautions that the underlying message is that women (and people of color) must not be consigned to a "place" but valued as important participants in the political and social life of the nation.

292

DuCille, Ann. *The Coupling Convention: Sex, Text, and Tradition in Black Women's Fiction*. New York: Oxford University Press,1993.

    Investigates the cultural climate from 1853 to 1948 and marriage conventions as a means of exploring questions of sexuality and relationships. Includes Petry in the investigation.

293
Dudley, John. "Naturalism and African American Culture." *Studies in American Naturalism* (University of Nebraska Press) 7.1 (Summer 2012): 1-6.
    Includes critical analysis of Petry and Wright, questioning: What is African American naturalism? What makes the naturalistic works of Wright and Petry simultaneously part of both African American and naturalist traditions?

294
Duneer, Anita. "Aesthetic Slippage in Realism and Naturalism." *The Oxford Handbook of American Literary Realism*. New York: Oxford University Press, 2019.
    Considers realist and naturalist aesthetics that transcend traditionally defined genres, terrains, and time periods; that examine inclusions and exclusions based on assumptions; that entail the divided self; and that contend with evolutionary discourse as well as environment. The latter includes discussions of Petry.

295
Dunne, Susan. "Connecticut's Famous African Americans: Black History Month Quiz." *Hartford Courant* (Hartford, CT), 13 February 2019, D1.
    Includes quiz questions and answers that appear under the photograph of Petry, such as:
Q. This Old Saybrook native wrote the 1946 novel "The Street," the first novel by an African American woman to sell more than a million copies.
A. Who was Ann Petry?

296
Dye, Peggy. "The New York Newsday Interview with Conrad Lynn and Ann Petry." *Newsday* (Long Island, NY), February 27, 1992, 93.
    Includes Petry's descriptive and succinct responses to interview questions.

297
Eby, Clare Virginia. "Beyond Protest: *The Street* as Humanitarian Narrative." *MELUS* 33.1 (Spring 2008): 33-53.
    Encourages re-readings of *The Street* as a humanitarian narrative, giving attention to "sympathetic passions" which "bridge the gulf between facts, compassion, and action."

298
Edgar, Anne E. "Come Together: Desire, Literature, and the Law of the Sexual Revolution." Ph.D. Diss., University of Kentucky, 2016.
    Focuses on litigations - e.g., *Brown v. DOE* in 1954 and *Loving v. Virginia* in 1967 - and the legal shortfalls of removing or changing racist stereotypes and categorizations of race. Analyzes interracial desire as depicted in Petry's *The Narrows*, Amira Baraka's *Dutchman*, and Eldridge Cleaver's *Soul On Ice*, showing how the legal and cultural history of racial desire can inform and often constrain African American literary characters. Encourages future studies of literary depictions of interracial desire and legal subjectivity in works by African American writers.

299
Egan, Jennifer. "By the Book." *New York Times* (online), 28 September 2017.

Gives the audience a tour of Egan's private book stacks from which she draws inspiration for her latest novel. Ann Petry, a fellow New England writer, is an inspiration.

300

Eisenger, Chester E. *Fiction of the Forties*. Chicago: University of Chicago Press, 1963.
Introduces *The Street* and calls the novel "tightly plotted."

301

Emanuel, James. "Ann Petry." In *Contemporary Novelists*. Edited by D. L. Kirkpatrick. London: St. James, 1972. Reprint. 1986.
Provides terse critiques of all three of Petry's novels. Calls *The Street* more than just another example of environmental determinism, overshadowed by its precursor, *Native Son*. Says *Country Place* is another one of Petry's attacks "against a cash-and-carry society hostile to moral beauty." Concludes that *The Narrows* is a novel "about love and its betrayal." Insists Petry's "craftsmanship, social truth, and humanity . . . deserve wider recognition."

302

_____. Ann Petry. In *Contemporary Novelists*. Edited by James Vinson. 2nd Edition. New York: St. Martin's, 1976.
Provides an analysis of Petry's first three novels, suggesting that the endings in *The Street* and *Country Place* are marred from the beginning due to their seemingly "conjured" theses. Calls for wider recognition, however, of Petry's craftsmanship and humanity.

303

Emanuel, James A. and Theodore L. Gross. Introduction. *Dark Symphony: Negro in Literature in America*. New York: Free Press,1968.
Mentions Petry's second and third novels, calling *Country Place*, with its metaphors and symbols, reminiscent of Hawthorne, and calling *The Narrows* a modification of the basically sociological approach taken with the family's environment in *The Street*.

304

"Emotional Impact in Novel on Slum-Shocked Negroes." Review of *The Street*. *Weekly People*, 13 April 1946 [Special Collections, Boston University].
Provides a Marxist critique of *The Street*. Says the "enlightened and class conscious worker . . . who can give his aroused emotions directions" benefits from Petry's "emotional-arousing novel."

305

Engel, Paul. "Heroine Keeps Her Integrity in Cruel Street." *Chicago Tribune*, 10 February 1946, 12.
Writes that *The Street,* with its realizations about the "actual forces of race and environment," is "stronger than any argument about the [Negro]." Concludes that the novel is proof that "Negroes" are equally human.

306

Epstein, Michael, Julie Sacks, and Patricia Clarkson. "American Masters: Novel Reflections on the

American Dream." WNET (Television Station: New York: New York), 2017.

Examines characters, plots, and themes in seven American novels that address poverty and wealth, and failure and success, in the context of the American Dream. Petry's *The Street* is one of the seven novels.

307

Erdheim, Cara Elana. "The Greening of American Naturalism." Ph.D. Diss., Fordham University, 2010.

Calls for a focus on nature as it pertains to culture in the socially-activist prose of Theodore Dreiser, Jack London, Frank Norris, Petry, Upton Sinclair, and Richard Wright. Argues politically charged and traditionally naturalistic writings of these writers should be studied as critical conversations about hunger and social stratification - i.e., ecological studies on access to food and air quality or about waste, water use. Incorporates phraseology "green reading of literature" and "environmental ethics informing literature."

308

Ervin, Hazel Arnett. "Adieu Harlem's Adopted Daughter: Ann Petry (12 October 1908 – 28 April 1997)." *Langston Hughes Review* 15.1 (Spring 1997): 71-73.

Takes the title from a 1940's review of Petry's best-selling novel, *The Street*, to write in memoriam about the pharmacist-turned-novelist who learned and perfected her craft while working in Harlem as a journalist and recreation specialist.

309

_____. "Ann Petry." *The Oxford Companion to African American Literature*. Edited by William Andrews, Frances Smith Foster, and Trudier Harris. New York: Oxford University Press, 1997. 570-572.

Combines biographical and bibliographical information approved by Ann Petry.

310

_____. "Chicago Renaissance." *The Handbook of African American Literature*. Gainesville, Fl: University Press of Florida, 2004.

Places Petry in the Chicago Renaissance, the literary movement (1935 to the early 1950s) influenced by the Great Migration, integration, modernism, the Chicago School of Sociology, theories of urbanization, and, although thought to be lost sometimes in ideology, indigenous folk forms. Often referred to as protest literature.

311

_____. Introduction. *Ann Petry's Short Fiction: Critical Essays*, edited by Hazel Arnett Ervin and Hilary Holiday. Westport, CT: Praeger, 2004.

Provides an overview of Petry's short stories, and examines their cultural, historical, and aesthetic dimensions. Encourages the following studies: diversity of backgrounds in philosophy, music, anthropology, and literary and women's studies.

312

_____, ed. Introduction. "The Novel as Social Criticism" by Ann Petry. In *African American Literary Criticism, 1773 to 2000*. New York: Twayne/Macmillan, 1999.

Quotes Petry and her call for writers to strive to achieve balance between art and propaganda; to guard against forsaking the story and manipulating characters to serve the interests of some political and social theme; and to refer to the writer as "a man or woman with a conscience."

313

_____. "Just a Few Questions More, Mrs. Petry." Philadelphia, PA: 1989 .

Poses questions to Petry left unanswered in other interviews and critiques, in an interview, following a Writer's Conference in Philadelphia; questions still left unanswered by Petry are addressed in written follow-up questions via mail [See full interview in this bibliography].

314

_____. "Legend." *The Handbook of African American Literature*. Gainesville, Fl: University Press of Florida, 2004.

Defines legend as a story that is handed down in oral traditions and that is usually based on myth or historical accounts of a figure or persona. Identifies historical accounts of folk hero John Henry in African American writings by John O. Killens, Ernest Gaines, James Alan McPherson, Margaret Walker, and Melvin B. Tolson. Adds Petry to this list of writers because of her adaptation of the folk hero John Henry to cast Venture Smith, a New England slave from Rhode Island and later Connecticut, who in real life labors with his axe to buy his freedom and eventually to start a very successful New England shipping business.

315

_____. "Protest Literature." *The Handbook of African American Literature*. Gainesville, Fl: University Press of Florida, 2004.

Chronicles literary discussions of protest literature - definitions, functions, techniques, etc., that are used to indict American society for its racial hatred, oppression, maltreatment of underprivileged groups, and hypocrisy of the American Dream. Cites major writers of the tradition - from early African American writers of 1773 to Ann Petry and James Baldwin. Quotes Petry from "The Novel as Social Criticism" who concludes that "the minute a writer begins to question the status quo, he is writing social criticism or protest."

316

_____. "Representation." *The Handbook of African American Literature*. Gainesville, Fl: University Press of Florida, 2004.

Chronicles literary discussions of representation - i.e., reality imitated in the literary text - from 1899 to the late twentieth century in African American literature. Includes Petry's position on character portrayals. Like major British and American writers before her, such as D. H. Lawrence and Henry James, Petry insists on allowing art to speak directly to the needs and aspirations of audiences. She, too, insists that novelists should not manipulate their characters to serve some theme or some other social or political end. Petry concludes that the writer must allow characters "[to]battle with themselves to save their [own] souls" because "[t]heir defeat or their victory [should] be … their own."

317

_____. Review of *The Radical Fiction of Ann Petry* by Keith Clark. *Tulsa Studies in Women's Literature* 34.2 (Fall 2015): 448-449.

Insists that Clark breathes new life into Petry's scholarship. Says that he succeeds in achieving the aim of his book: re-situating the female and New England writer in the annals of American and African American literary criticism through postmodernist approaches, including the much overlooked and radical aesthetic agenda visible in Petry's short stories and novels. Says Clark adds depth to his repositioning of Petry by providing substantive evidence pulled not only from Petry's short stories and novels but also from her non-fiction articles, interviews, autobiography and bio-bibliography. Like British giant D. H. Lawrence, Clark demonstrates what happens when readers learn to "trust the text" and not the teller.

318

_____ ed. *The Critical Response to Ann Petry.* Westport, CT: Praeger, 2005.

Compiles critical responses to Petry's novels, *The Street*, *Country Place*, and *The Narrows*, (via chronology, book reviews, reprinted articles, new articles, and a select bibliography) collected from 1946 to the present.

319

_____. " The Hidden Hand of Feminist Revolt in Ann Petry's *The Street*." In *The Critical Response to Ann Petry*. Edited by Hazel Arnett Ervin. Westport, CT: Praeger, 2005.

Takes the position that Petry writes in specific chapters in *The Street* recognizable portraits of domesticated women as wives, mothers, and homemakers, and then, by pointing out voids, contradictions and double standards of women's lives, or by the ironic circumstances of their social realities, especially as working-class black women, Petry subverts traditional attitudes and practices concerning the role and behavior of women in a patriarchal society. A new level of feminine consciousness is raised on behalf of women of the forties.

320

_____. "The Subversion of Cultural Ideology in Ann Petry's *The Street* and *Country Place*." Ph.D. Diss., Howard University,1993.

Takes the following positions in a post-structuralist study of Petry's 1940s novels: Coded in specific chapters in *The Street* and *Country Place* is Petry's discontent with patriarchal ideology concerning the "woman's place." From these chapters, and among Petry's women characters in these chapters, a new sense of feminine consciousness emerges, undermining patriarchal ideology. Such chapters mark measurable outcomes and a critical shift in Petry's scholarship and criticism.

321

_____. " Tituba of Salem Village." *The Oxford Companion to African American Literature*. Edited by William Andrews, Frances Smith Foster, and Trudier Harris. New York: Oxford University Press, 1997.

Directs historical, cultural, and aesthetic re-readings of *Tituba of Salem Village.*

322

Ewig, Elizabeth J. "Ann Lane Petry." Ph.D. Diss., Pennsylvania State University, Behrend College, 2001.

Writes four years after Petry's death about her life and works, bringing into focus the paternal family - the Lanes.

323

Farquharson, Katherine. "No Walls in Eden: Architecture in Twentieth-Century Fiction." Ph.D. Diss., University of Roehampton (London, UK), 2015.

Proposes investigating the figurative significance of "architecture" - i.e., exploring and evaluating the discursive interplay between text and architecture, or using architecture as a figure through which to interrogate the inside/outside dichotomy, both within twentieth-century short and longer fiction, and between fiction and seminal works of architectural theory. Analyzes, among others, Edith Wharton, Thomas Hardy, Virginia Woof, and Franz Kafka - with specific attention given to Ann Petry in *The Street* and Aya Rand in *The Fountainhead*, so to articulate the struggles of protagonists who seek to find the point of equilibrium between self and the world. Represents an international interest in Petry.

324

Fein, Esther B. "An Author's Look at 1940's Harlem Is Being Reissued." *New York Times*, 8 January 1992, C13.

Compares Petry's "the street" in 1946 with today's "the street," concluding conditions are not better. Reviews Petry's rise to "sudden fame" with the publication of *The Street* and her sudden departure from Harlem to New England's Old Saybrook. Photographs from 1946 and 1992 are also provided.

325

Feld, Rose. "Tragedy on Two Levels." *New York Herald Tribune Weekly Book Review*, 5 October 1947, 6.

Reviews *Country Place* briefly. Says Petry's motif of the returning soldier who discovers his wife has been unfaithful is one that is popular among novelists during the forties. Thinks *Country Place* is "exceedingly good," primarily because of the "feel of a small town, the integrity of dialogue, and the portrayals of Johnnie, Glory, [and] Mrs. Gramby." Concludes, however, that the novel has its flaw: Petry changes from first- to third-person narrator.

326

Fendt, Gene. "Apartheid among the Dead; Or, on Christian Laughter in Ann Petry's "The Bones of Louella Brown." In *Ann Petry's Short Fiction: Critical Essays*. Edited by Hazel Arnett Ervin and Hilary Holladay. Westport, CT: Praeger, 2004.

Reviews "The Bones of Louella Brown" as Petry's "comic masterpiece." Says the work provides readers with an unexpected approach to discussing " apartheid" and "racism."

327

Fikes, Robert Jr. "Escaping the Literary Ghetto: African American Authors of White Life Novels, 1946-1994." *Western Journal of Black Studies* 19.2 (1995): 105-112.

Reviews criticism levied against African American writers who choose to write a white - life novel. Concludes authors are true to their own thoughts and expressions.

328

"First Novel." *Ebony* (April 1946): 35-39.

Gives an account of the cocktail party sponsored in 1946 by the editors at Houghton Mifflin at the Biltmore Hotel in New York City in honor of Petry for her successful first novel, *The Street*. Includes photographs of Petry with notable critics, writers, and celebrities of stage and screen. Also includes biographical information.

329

Fisher, Dexter, ed. "Contexts and Narratives." In *The Third Woman.* Boston: Houghton Mifflin, 1980.

Contends that Petry's short story, "Doby's Gone" explains the "complexity of black female sensibility" by "magnifying the realities" of discrimination for even a child.

330

Fishkin, Shelley Fisher. *Writing America: Literary Landmarks From Walden Pond to Wounded Knee (A Reader's Companion)*. New Jersey: Rutgers University Press, 2015.

    Includes *The Street,* calling a literary landmark and "portrait of Harlem streets."

331

Fitzimmons, Lorna. "The Socially 'Forsaken Race': Dantean Turns in Ann Petry's *The Street*." *Notes on Contemporary Literature* (March 2000): 6-8. Reprint. In *The Critical Response to Ann Petry*. Edited by Hazel Arnett Ervin. Westport, CT: Praeger, 2005.

    Explores how Petry critiques racism in *The Street*, employing Dantean tropes to suggest that discrimination and prejudice in the U. S. society reduce African Americans to the "forsaken race" of the doomed in the Inferno.

332

Ford, Nick Aaron. "A Blueprint for Negro Authors." *Phylon* 11.4 (Fourth Quarter 1950): 374-377. Reprint. *Black Expression*. Edited by Addison Gayle, Jr. New York: Weybright and Talley, 1969.

    Suggests providing a blueprint for writers "who wish to accept the glorious opportunities and grave responsibilities of the next half century." Praises Petry for having demonstrated a mastery of craftsmanship and design in *The Street*, but then criticizes her for abandoning racial themes in *Country Place* in favor of universal themes. Says *Country Place* is greatly inferior to *The Street*.

333

"Fortitude Sustains Movement." *Hartford Courant,* 2 March 1986, A14.

    Outlines Petry's writing habits. Provides a very brief discussion of Petry's "first born" - *The Street*. Identifies the women in Petry's family who have contributed to her success.

334

Foster, Frances Smith. "African American Literary Study, Now and Then and Again." *PMLA* 115.7 (Dec 2000): 1965-1967.

    Addresses external perceptions of African American literature, responding to the question, Is there a constituency for this literature? Traces the African American literary tradition, giving attention to major African American writers and their works in the canon. Includes Petry.

335

Franklin, Marie C. "Kit Designed to Help Teachers Present Female Writers." *Boston Globe*, 27 December 1998.

    Responds to teachers who are seeking ways to include female writers in American literature classes. Directs teachers to "Scribbling Women," a multimedia education kit available through the Public Media Foundation. As a teaching tool, the kit includes ten (10) half-hour radio dramas of materials by the following 19th- and 20th- century women writers: Harriet Jacobs, Louisa May Alcott, Willa Cather, and Ann

Petry ("The Bones of Louella Brown"). In addition to focusing on classic women writers, the focus is also on promoting oral literature and listening skills.

336
"From Pestle to Pen." *Headlines and Pictures* (March 1946): 42-43.
      Features an essay/interview with Petry as well as a review of her first novel, *The Street*. Notes that in the novel, there are repeated testimonies of the hazards of single mothers raising children in "an environment of squalor and viciousness." In response to these repeated images in her work, Petry is quoted as saying that "women's problems have been [her] longtime interests." Petry shares that when she lived in Harlem, she observed the "problems of mothers leaving children [alone while they went] to work." The children "paid the price." The reviewer concludes that *The Street* is at its best when it is "pleading the cause of Negro women and children" and at its weakest when "its characters become enlarged in a melodramatic series of events."

337
"From Test Tube to Typewriter." *Afro-American* (Baltimore), 11 December 1948, 3.
      Traces Petry's career from pharmacist to novelist. Compares her with other "first" American women writers of literature - both black and white. Offers quotes by Petry.

338
Fuller, Edmund. " 'Unbelievable' Is Word for It." *Chicago Sunday Tribune*, 23 August 1953, 5.
      Gives a remorseful yet unfavorable review of *The Narrows*, calling it a "lurid. . . sensational . . . and sympathetic story." Finds the "tragic love" motif unbelievable. Calls Link and Camilo "demoralized persons, in their different ways."

339
Fuller, Hoyt W. "Contemporary Negro Fiction." In T*he Black American Writer. Vol I: Fiction.* Edited by C.W. E. Bigsby. Deland, Fl: Everett/Edwards, 1969.
      Writes that "the contemporary Negro novelist and playwright [are] heirs of Richard Wright." Calls Petry "the most promising novelist" and "a superb but uneven literary craftsman."

340
Fuller, James E. "Harlem Portrait." *Pittsburgh Courier,* February 9, 1946 [Special Collections, Boston University].
      Offers personal impressions of Petry: Calls her "serious but charming" and "Harlem's adopted daughter." Quotes Petry's reasons for writing *The Street.*

341
Gale, Erin Nicholson. "New York City Street Theater: Gender, Performance, and the Urban from Plessy to Brown." Ph.D. Diss., Graduate Center, City University of New York, 2015.
      Investigates the ordinary public performances of fictional female characters in novels set against the backdrop of legal segregation in Manhattan in the early to mid -1900s (e.g., Stephen Crane's *Maggie, A Girl of the Streets*; John Dos Passos' *Manhattan Transfer*; Nella Larsen's *Passing*; and Ann Petry's *The Street*). Cites ordinary performances central to interpreting race, gender, and class relations (from bragging

to racial passing). Ends by theorizing about the characters' "fantasies" about New York City as space of idealistic opportunities, safe harbor, financial security, etc.

342
Gallagher, Maria. "City Fetes Ann Petry: Her Novel 'Street,' Sold 1 Million Copies, and - At 80 - She's Still Writing." *Philadelphia Daily News*, 3 February 1989, 45.

    Discusses with Petry her schedule and strategies for writing; how she feels about being honored for success as a writer; her biggest disappointments as a writer; and other African American writers whom she enjoys reading.

343
Gannett, Lewis. Review of *The Street*. *New York Herald Tribune Book Review*, 7 February 1946, 21.

    Writes that while Petry's novel is swift and absorbing, its melodramatic ending is objectionable. Believes readers deserve solutions to the economic and racial problems that are so convincingly raised in *The Street*.

344
Garrett, Emma Isadore. "Undoing Home: Queer Space and Black Women's Writing 1865-1953." Ph.D. Diss., University of Michigan, 2013.

    Uses the trope "home" to analyze queer characters in the black community and black women's representation of queer space. As social and material constructions, "home" serves to symbolize both respect for and restrictions of black sexuality as well as for undoing racial and sexual boundaries. Petry is included in this study because of her violent portrayals of interracial heterosexuality.

345
Garrett, Lula Jones. *Afro-American* (Baltimore), 13 September 1958, 13.

    States that Petry is the "first woman scriptwriter invited to the West Coast" to be employed by Columbia Pictures as a journeyman for the screenplay *That Hill Girl*.

346
Garvey, Johanna X. "That Old Black Magic? Gender and Music in Ann Petry's Fiction." *Black Orpheus: Music in African American Fiction from the Harlem Renaissance to Toni Morrison*. Ed. Saadi A. Simawe. New York: Garland, 2000, 119-151. Reprint. In *The Critical Response to Ann Petry*. Edited by Hazel Arnett Ervin. Westport, CT: Praeger, 2005.

    Illustrates how music figures are central to plot, characterization, and themes throughout Petry's short and long fiction. Says music figures illuminate the African American experience, both urban and suburban. Adds that music figures in Petry are used to evoke a southern past with elements of black culture - gradually displaced, muted, or forgotten as the result of the Great Migration.

347
Gates, Henry Louis, and Nellie Y. McKay, eds. *The Norton Anthology of African American Literature*. New York: W.W. Norton, 2004.

    Includes Petry under the section, "Realism, Naturalism Modernism, 1940-1960."

348

Gayle, Addison, Jr. "Perhaps Not So Soon One Morning." *Phylon* 26.4 (Winter 1968): 397.

Refutes Hill in *Soon One Morning* who suggests that James Baldwin and Ralph Ellison are the most capable forerunners of African American writers entering the "mainstream" of American literature. Insists that Baldwin's Ida Scott has been drawn more artistically by Petry in *The Street*.

349

_____. *The Way of the New World: The Black Novel in America.* Garden City, NY: Anchor/Doubleday, 1975.

Defines Lutie in *The Street* as one of the "Black Rebel[s]" who follows Bigger Thomas in *Native Son*, but warns that *The Street* is not a carbon copy of *Native Son*. Rather, the novel is "a powerful and provocative work exploring areas that Wright, who took his readers for granted, did not venture to explore." Too, insists *The Street* moves beyond social Darwinists, relying upon the salvation of its people along classical lines: "change the society and there will be no Juntos, Boots Smiths, Mins, or Joneses." Furthermore, Gayle says the novel takes on "dimensions of a mock-heroic epic."

350

Gebhard, Ann O. "The Emerging Self: Young-Adult and Classic Novels of the Black Experience." *English Journal* 82.6 (September 1993): 50.

Reveals that themes of growing up black in the United States, of cultural identity, and establishing identities that are consonant with cultural ideals can be found in adolescent literature written by Alice Childress, Rosa Guy, and Walter Dean Myers. Points out that the works of Childress, Guy, and Myers also offer thematic connections to Petry, Larsen and Hurston.

351

Gelfant, Blanche Housman. *The American City Novel*. Norman: University of Oklahoma Press, 1954. Reprint. 1970.

Discusses the city novel as a literary genre and concludes that three forms of the city novel exist: the "portrait" study; the "synoptic" study; and the "ecological" study. Names works by Theodore Dreiser, John Dos Passos, and James T. Farrell to support this thesis. Briefly mentions Petry's *The Street* as an example of the "ecological" novel.

352

"General Courses." In *All the Women Are White, All the Blacks Are Men, But Some of Us Are Brave.* Edited by Gloria T. Hull, Patricia Bell Scott, and Barbara Smith. Old Westbury, NY: Feminist Press, 1982.

Provides a network of general topics, genres, and critical resources for teaching black women writers. Includes course outlines by Barbara Smith, Gloria T. Hull, Theresa R. Love, and Alice Walker as well as Fahamisha Shariat's "Blackwomen Writers of the U.S.A. - Who Are They, What Do They Write?" Recommends the short stories and novels by Petry.

353

Gholston, Tracey Marcel. "Tracing Zora's Janie: Reimagining Janie as an Archetypal Character in 20th - and 21st- Century Contemporary Literature." Ph.D. Diss., The University of Alabama, 2015.

Is inspired by Zora Neale Hurston's Janie Mae Crawford found in *Their Eyes Were Watching God* to review archetypes of African American women characters who are involved in quest fiction. Questions what becomes of Hurston's once-self-actualized Janie? Responds to the question by providing extensive literary and cultural analysis of Petry's *The Street* and Sister Souljah's *The Coldest Winter Ever* and *A Deeper Love Inside: The Porsche Santiaga Story*. Concludes that main female characters in Petry and Souljah are literary reiterations of archetypal Janie, and because the texts of Petry and Souljah span more than eight decades, and emphasize realistic social, cultural and political issues, the main characters are modernized versions of Janie in an archetypal quest story.

354

Giddings, Paula. Review of *The Street*. *Essence* (March 1989): 36.

    Calls Lutie's story in *The Street* one "with a message." Classifies Petry's novel as an "exciting mystery-murder thriller." Encourages a rereading.

355

_____. *When and Where I Enter: The Impact of Black Women on Race and Sex in America*. New York: William Morrow and Company, 1984.

    Insists on including Petry's novel *The Street* in studies on the impacts of race and sex on black women in America.

356

Gilbert, Sandra M. and Susan Gubar. "Fighting for Life." In *No Man's Land: Vol I, The War of the Words*. New Haven: Yale University Press, 1988.

    Questions whether "late nineteenth - and twentieth-century literary women transform[ed] their words into weapons in order to wrestle authority from [literary] men." Concludes that the "text . . . in the black tradition has enable[d] female artists to translate the comparatively subtle terms of sexual struggle into the more openly theatrical terms of . . . racial struggle." Further concludes that Petry's *The Street* is a "documentary text representing the battle of the sexes not only as a racial but also as a class struggle."

357

Giles, Sally Marie. "Who Cares? : Dependency and Domestic Labor in 20th- and 21st- Century U.S. Literature." Ph.D. Diss., University of California - San Diego, 2013.

    Studies the representation of African American, Chicana, and Latina women in "domestic and care work" in American literature from the 20th- and 21st- Centuries. Says support comes respectively from texts and films by Ann Petry, Toni Morrison, Lorraine Hansberry, Douglas Sirk, John Rechy, Patricia Riggen, Esmeralda Santiago, and Angie Cruz.

358

Girson, Rochelle. "Ann Petry Sets Novel in Home Town, Saybrook." *Hartford Times*, 15 August 1953 [Special Collections, Boston University].

    Reveals that *The Narrows* is set in Old Saybrook, Connecticut. Moreover, quotes Petry's responses to the critics who object to the interracial love affair between Link and Camilo and to those who call the novel propaganda. Also includes Petry's personal anecdotes on writing fiction.

359

Gittens, Seonna. "Muzzled and Mutilated: The Commodification of Black Women in Alice Walker's *In Love and Trouble* and Ann Petry's T*he Street* and Their Artful Escape from the Patriarchal System." B.A. Thesis (Senior Independent Study), The College of Wooster, 2016.

Registers as the fulfillment of an undergraduate requirement; provides examinations of Black women writers who critique the hegemony and female oppression.

360

Gloster, Hugh M. "Race and the Negro Writer." *Phylon* 11.4 (Fourth Quarter 1950): 369-373. Reprint. *Black Expressions*. Edited by Addison Gayle, Jr. New York: Weybright and Talley, 1969.

Says writers who use racial subjects have handicapped the role of "Negro" writers by lessening their "cosmic group of varied experience, philosophical perspective, literary range, [and] contributions to cultural integration." Says Petry is an exception.

361

Godfrey, Mollie Amelia. "Humankinds: Humanism and Race in American Fiction, 1903-1963." Ph.D. Diss., The University of Chicago, 2010.

Argues that the mid-twentieth-century novelists who wrote about race rejected the racial exclusions of humanism. Seeks to identify and to confirm authors who were active participants in American humanist discourse: W.E.B. DuBois, James Weldon Johnson, Nella Larsen, Claude McKay, Zora Neale Hurston, John Steinbeck, Richard Wright, Ralph Ellison, James Baldwin, and Ann Petry. Contends that these novelists believe that universalist ethics can help to bring into being a more racially inclusive and equitable society. Overall, revisits the following: underlying universalism via primitivism and cultural pluralism in the Harlem Renaissance; Marxism in the Great Depression; and sociology in the postwar period. Findings suggest the need for not only reevaluations of the utopian promise and practical limits of antiracist humanism, but also for attempts to restore African American writings to the center of American humanist discourse.

362

Goldsmith, Alfred. "Struggle for Survival." *New Masses* 59 (21 May 1946): 23-26.

Contends Petry's characters are "sketchy outlines of human beings."

363

Goodwin, Polly. "Kitten with Temper Short as His Tail." *Chicago Sunday Tribune*, Part 4, 13 November 1949, 6.

Takes title from Petry's *The Drugstore Cat*, which captures the existence of the featured cat, Buzzie. Calls book "a little gem . . . for children."

364

Grandt, Jurgen E. " 'Swing it, Sister': Jazz Time in Ann Petry's *The Street*." *Kinds of Blue: The Jazz Aesthetic in African American Narrative*. Columbus: Ohio State University Press, 2004.

Devotes a chapter to the aesthetic function of jazz in Petry's *The Street*.

365

Greco, Elaine Katherine. "Urban Freedom and Uncontained Space in American Literary Naturalism." Ph.D.

Diss., University of California, Berkeley, 2002.

Reminds readers that in American literary naturalism, urban space is generally a site of constrainment. Encourages readers to reconsider urban space as a forum for relative freedom. Argues that African American novelist Ann Petry and African Canadian novelist Austin Clarke portray acts of resistance and inequitable treatment as ways of affirming characters' rights and as ways accessing national ideals of freedom, equality, and justice in the United States and in Canada.

366
Green, Kim. "Routes of Resistance: Mobilizing Discoveries of Opportunity in Ann Petry's *The Street* and Austin Clarke's *The Meeting Point.*" *American Review of Canadian Studies*, 46.1 (March 2016): 93-106.

Demonstrates how Ann Petry in *The Street* and Austin Clarke in *The Meeting Point* provide important representations and affirmations of black people's use of movements, such as educational attainment and economic advancement, to create routes that resist inequitable treatment and that demand equal access to the benefits of belonging to the American and Canadian national communities. Illustrates how Petry's Lutie and Clarke's Bernice counter the boundaries, and their women refuse to be denied the benefits of American and Canadian discourses of opportunity.

367
_____. "To Be Black and 'At Home': Movement, Freedom, and Belonging in African American and African Canadian Literatures." Ph.D. Diss., Emory University, 2010.

Encourages comparative examinations of African American and African Canadian writers. Studies how Ann Petry's Lutie in *The Street* and Austin Clarke's Bernice in *The Meeting Point* provide nuanced representations of people who persistently encounter discrimination because they belong to marginalized racial, gender, and class groups. Shows how movements such as national and transnational migration, educational attainment, and economic advancement represent acts of resistance to inequitable treatments.

368
Green, Marjorie. "Ann Petry Planned to Write." *Opportunity: Journal of Negro Life* 24.2 (April-June 1946): 78-79.

Provides a "mini-portrait" of Petry, from high school graduation to the Houghton Mifflin Fellowship Award.

369
Greene, Lee. *Blacks in Eden: The African American Novel's First Century*. Charlottesville: University Press of Virginia, 1996.

Includes a chapter on Petry: "Configurations of Desire in *The Street.*"

370
Gregory, John. "Ann Petry Writes about a Negro Girl's Problems." *New York Sun,* 7 February 1946, 21.

Says Petry puts to "good use" her firsthand knowledge of Harlem and its problems, even the black man's inhumanity to other blacks. Applauds her natural intrusions to address the "Negro problem" and avoidance of "pseudo-literary" effects.

371

Griffin, Farah Jasmine. "Ann Petry's Harlem." In T*oward an Intellectual History of Black Women*. Edited by Mia Bay, Farah Jasmine Griffin, Martha S. Jones, and Barbara Dianne Savage. Chapel Hill, NC: The University of North Carolina Press, 2015.

Maps relationships of Ann Petry as political activist, journalist, and fiction writer in the 1940s. Calls Petry a committed progressive whose fiction explores the world of young urban black women who are invisible in better-known fictional, political, and sociological narratives on black urban life.

372

_____. *Harlem Nocturne: Women Artists & Progressive Politics During World War II*. New York: Civitas Books, 2013.

Provides a comprehensive narrative that tells of three women of color - three agents of change - who navigate within Manhattan's social, cultural, and political worlds and who explore the unique and progressive vision of New York City during and immediately following World War II; who use their creativity to promote access to the American Dream for "marginalized" and "everyday" people; and through activism who attempt to help the nation "[to] achieve" itself. The three women are choreographer and dancer, Pearl Primus; composer and pianist, Mary Lou Williams; and Ann Petry;

373

_____. "Hunting Community and Negroes in Ann Petry's *The Narrows*." In *Revising the Blueprint: Ann Petry and the Literary Left*. Edited by Alex Lubin. Jackson, MI: University Press of Mississippi, 2007.

Suggests the Cold War's anti-communism context shapes Perry's *The Narrows*.

374

_____. *'Who Set You Flowin'? The African American Migration Narrative*. New York: Oxford University Press, 1995.

Contends the experiences of slavery and emancipation are central to the works of African American artists of the nineteenth century; that the experiences of migration are central to literature, music, and visual arts by 20th Century African Americans.

375

Gross, Theodore L. "Ann Petry: The Novelist as Social Critic." In *Black Fiction: New Studies in the Afro-American Novel since 1945*. Edited by A. Robert Lee. New York: Barnes and Noble, 1980.

Quotes Petry from several of her works to support the following: Petry "has the heart of a naturalist and the head of a realist"; for Petry, the novel is "an instrument of social criticism"; and in all of Petry's short stories, the leitmotif is "racial identity."

376

Gunderson, Margaret T. "Transcending Oppression: The Blues Theme in African American Literature." M.A., Central Missouri State University, 2001.

Gives thematic readings to defend the function of the blues in African American writings.

377

Gustafson, Lucy. "Old Saybrook Author Will Speak on Witchcraft at Meeting Jan 23." *New Era*, 15 January

1970, 8.

>Announces that Petry will be guest speaker at a membership meeting of the Old Saybrook Historical Society. Offers quotes from Petry on what influenced her to write *Tituba of Salem Village*.

378

Hakutani, Yoshinobu and Robert Butler, eds. *The City in African-American Literature*. Cranbury: Associated UP, 1995.

>Seeks to move beyond the established canon of African American literature to reflect a diversity of views on the urban experience. Discusses the city in novels by major African American novelists, including Petry.

379

Hall, J.W. Review of *Ann Petry's Short Fiction: Critical Essays* by Hazel Arnett Ervin and Hilary Holladay. *Choice: Current Reviews for Academic Libraries*. 42.4 (2004): 658.

>Informs readers that the 14 essays in the collection range from reader-response to poststructuralist, offering approaches for examining gender, class, trauma, ritual, jazz/blues structures, folk traditions, and historical contexts in Petry's 13 tales found in *Miss Muriel and Other Stories*. Notes that four of the essays in the collection are reprints but ten are originals. Recommends the collection for lower-level undergraduates through faculty.

380

Hardison, Ayesha Ki'Shani. "Protesting Little Sister: Black Women's Sexual Politics, 1940-1953." Ph.D. Diss., University of Michigan, 2006.

>Calls Ann Petry, Dorothy West, Zora Neale Hurston, and Gwendolyn Brooks icons of black womanhood. Reexamines the tradition of African American protest in Petry's *The Street*; West's *The Living Is Easy*; Hurston's *Seraph of the Suwanee*; and Brooks' *Maud Martha*. Gives particular attention to how black women struggle for agency and for subjectivity to challenge the contentions of the protest novel. Also encourages critical discourse for "protesting subjectivity" in the black women writers' revisions, rejections, and negotiations of bourgeois ideals of black womanhood.

381

_____. *Writing Through Jane Crow: Race and Gender Politics in African American Literature*. Charlottesville, VA: University of Virginia Press, 2014.

>Examines African American literature and the representation of black women at the height of Jim Crow racial segregation. Shifts focus away from canonical texts by male writers which dominate the 1940s, 1950s, and 1960s and focuses on understudied works by well-known writers, such as Ann Petry, Gwendolyn Brooks, and Zora Neale Hurston; on neglected writers such as, Curtis Lucas, Pauli Murray, and Era Bell Thompson; and on memoirs, music, etiquette guides, and comics. Initiates new conversations about the efforts of "Jane Crow" writings - the interconnected racial, gender and sexual oppression that black women experience.

382

"Harlem." In *Encyclopedia of Black America*. Edited by W. Augustus Low. New York: McGraw-Hill, 1981.

>Describes Harlem in terms of its geography. Mentions Petry's *The Street* along with Claude Brown's *Manchild in the Promised Land* as novels that reveal the role Harlem streets play in the lives of its African American residents.

383

"Harlem Made Ann Petry Write Her Novel." *PM* (3 March 1946): M4.

    Shows how Petry personally observed "the kinds of violence" she writes about. For instance, as a local newspaperwoman, Petry covers a story about the owner of a delicatessen who stabs an African American youth in the back. The youth staggers out of the store and collapses on the sidewalk. This same incident appears in *The Street*.

384

Harris, Trudier. "On Southern and Northern Maids: Geography, Mammies, and Militants." In *From Mammies to Militants: Domestics in Black American Literature*. Philadelphia: Temple University Press, 1982.

    Says in *The Street,* Lutie Johnson typifies the "transitional" or "moderate" northern maid in literature. Says that like the folklore Br'er Rabbit or Staggolee, Lutie is aware of her history and culture; that she makes "no pretense about who she is or what she thinks." According to Harris, Petry insists on the recognition of Lutie's "humility." She insists that unlike the southern maid Mammy Jane in Charles Chesnutt's *Marrow of Tradition*, Lutie Johnson "sees her job as a means to an end, not as an end in itself."

385

Harris-Lopez, Trudier. "Architecture as Destiny? Women and Survival Strategies in Ann Petry's *The Street*." In *South of Tradition: Essays on African American Literature*. Athens, GA: University of Georgia Press, 2002.

    Says Min in Petry's *The Street* inspires critical considerations of how architecture influences her characterization. Contends that as a writer Petry anticipates Toni Morrison, and like Morrison Petry's use of houses and apartments play significant roles in the construction of female characters and in shaping the destinies of these characters. Says Petry's use of architecture may be more determining than Morrison's.

386

Harrison, William. Review of *The Street*. *Boston Chronicle*. 23 February 1946 [Special Collections, Boston University].

    Describes Petry as the "most profound contemporary Negro novelist specializing in sociological fiction." Calls for examining the novel's persuasive yet its imaginative argumentation. Compares the story's "action" - action that moves without deviation to its conclusion - to the action of a Greek tragedy by Sophocles or Euripides.

387

Hartley, Daniel LeClair. "Transnational Jazz and Blues: Aural Aesthetics and African Diasporic Fiction." Ph.D. Diss., University of Maryland, 2010.

    Contends that literary criticism fails to recognize jazz and blues as more than just national forms. Urges considering jazz and blues as international forms that have influenced diverse groups of novelists. Fills gaps in current scholarship by examining well-known and lesser-known novels that depict jazz and blues both within and outside of the American context. Then provides a critical framework for understanding the influences of jazz and blues in African Diasporic fiction. Includes, among others, Petry's *The Street* in the study. References the overall discussion as "aural aesthetics."

388
Hawkins, Alfonso W. "The Nurture of African American Youth in the Fiction of Ann Petry, Alice Childress and Gloria Naylor." *CLA Journal* 46.4 (2003): 457 -477.

      Asks that readers recognize and examine the countless examples in African American literature of mothers and fathers who promote the spirit of hope via sacrifices.

389
Henderson, Carol E. "Notes of a Native Daughter: The Nature of Black Womanhood in *Native Son*." In *Richard Wright's Native Son: Critical Essays*. Ed. Ana M. Fraile. Amsterdam - New York: Rodopi , 2007.

      Evaluates how Petry in *The Street* and Gwendolyn Brooks in *Maud Martha* achieve the following: 1) the revision of domestic and urban space on behalf of women in Richard Wright's *Native Son*; 2) the undermining of Wright's rendering of womanhood in *Native Son*; and 3) the establishment of "models of [female] independence, self-reliance and self-determination" as alternative sources of consciousness and personal strength for women in *The Street* and *Maud Martha*.

390
_____. "The Body of Evidence" - Reading the Scar as Text: Williams, Morrison, Baldwin, and Petry (Sherley Anne Williams, Toni Morrison, James Baldwin, and Ann Petry)." Ph.D. Diss., University of California-Riverside, 1995.

      Reveals through research how characters in literary texts speak through the use of inanimate objects (e.g., rooms, houses, tables) and through the use of masses (e.g., water, bodily fluids, the earth). Suggests looking at how scarring is also a site for producing speech. Further adds that scarring of the body as text is not only an external (physical) act of production but also an internal (psychological) act of production.

391
_____. " ' The Man Who Cried I Am': Reading Race, Class, and Gender in Ann Petry's 'The Witness.' " In *Ann Petry's Short Fiction: Critical Essays*. Edited by Hazel Arnett Ervin and Hilary Holladay. Westport, CT: Praeger, 2004.

      Reveals that Petry explores the dynamic interpersonal relationships of people around race, class, and gender, and then because of race, class and gender she uncovers the extent of "psychic wounds and scars written on the souls of black folk."

392
_____. "The 'Walking Wounded': Rethinking Black Women's Identity in Ann Petry's *The Street*." *Modern Fiction Studies* 46:4 (2000): 849-867. Reprint. In *The Critical Response to Ann Petry*. Edited by Hazel Arnett Ervin. Westport, CT: Praeger, 2005.

      Probes the social landscape of the body as text in Ann Petry's *The Street*, paying close attention to the ways in which the body - as material substance - interacts with other social structures. Explores the figurative and literal boundaries of female wounds (i.e., prejudices of race, class, gender, obscurity, and even death) and suggests alternative ways to view the subtle and not-so-subtle ways women are examined or perceived through the veil of bodily (im)perfection. Says there are two expected outcomes for the wounded female: the "discovery and the performance of identity."

393

Henderson, Frances Dianne. "(Re)claiming Self: Motive Forces Contributing to Migration in African American Literature by Women." Ph.D. Diss., Vanderbilt University, 2009.

    Moves beyond familiar migratory themes and moments, so to emphasize how migratory moments in African American literature play out in the evolution of Black womanhood - past and present. Extends critical discourse on the theme of migration and the idea of a migration spiral. Looks closely at the main characters in literature by Ann Petry, Zora Neale Hurston, Pearl Cleage, and Octavia Butler and the different motivations of their female characters when in search of a more complete - or restored - sense of wholeness. The chapter on Ann Petry reads, "Ain't No Restin' Place For a Sinner Like Me': Reading Ann Petry's *The Street* as Narrative of a Failed Migration."

394

Henderson, Mark Joseph. "Striking Back at the New Overseer: Responses to White Panopticism in the Works of Richard Wright, Ann Petry and Ralph Ellison." Ph.D. Diss., Auburn University, 2013.

    Departs from naturalism in novels by Wright, Petry, and Ellison. Instead, examines the representation of institutional surveillance of mid-twentieth-century African American urban migrants in Wright, Petry, and Ellison. Central to this examination is the image of the "new overseer," the Orwellian twentieth-century version of the pre-bellum overseer - i.e., the sophisticated and subtle strategies of "white panopticism," or the systemic surveillance of the African American urban population in order to control.

395

Hennessy, Val. Review of *The Street* by Ann Petry. *Daily Mail* (London, UK). 24 January 2020, 57.

    Introduces an international audience to Petry's first novel. Outlines the plot and concludes that the novel "spotlights" racial injustice.

396

Hernton, Calvin. "The Significance of Ann Petry." In *The Sexual Mountain and Black Women Writers, Adventures in Sex, Literature, and Real Life*. New York: Anchor/Doubleday, 1987. Reprint. 1990. Also appears in *Wild Women in the Whirlwind*. Edited by Joanne M. Braxton and Andree Nicola McLaughlin. New Brunswick, NJ: Rutgers University Press, 1990. Reprint. *The Critical Response to Ann Petry.* Edited by Hazel Arnett Ervin. Westport, CT: Praeger, 2005.

    Concludes that *The Street* "is the first work of social realism and naturalism written from an all but complex Womanist Perspective." Says "No one until Petry, male or female, had so thoroughly portrayed black women as victims of Multiple Oppression (economic, racial, and sexual), and no one had so boldly portrayed black men as the levelers of a significant measure of that oppression." Compares and contrasts the "fear" of Bigger Thomas with the "rage" of Lutie Johnson.

397

Hicks, Heather. "Rethinking Realism in Ann Petry's *The Street*." *MELUS* 27.4 (Winter 2002): 89-97.

    Initiates an examination of how realist and naturalist engage in the theoretical project of enjoining readers to a position of spectatorship - i.e., to a mode of "seeing" implicated in "surveillance and policing" or in the "power of watching." Through in-depth examinations, illustrates the practices of "surveillance and watching" as found in Henry James and then in Ann Petry. Concludes with comparative criticism of James' and of Petry's positioning of spectatorship.

398

_____. " ' This Strange Communion': Surveillance and Spectatorship in Ann Petry's *The Street*." *African American Review*. (Spring 2003): 21-38. Reprint. In *The Critical Response to Ann Petry*. Edited by Hazel Arnett Ervin. Westport, CT: Praeger, 2005.

    Directs critical attention to the metaphoric vision or the "centrality of ocular" in Petry's examinations of race relations in *The Street*. Assists in clarifying this approach by juxtaposing the following: Richard Wright's examination of race relations via his use of "blindness" in *Native Son*; Ralph Ellison's examination of race relations via his use of "invisibility" in *Invisible Man*; and Petry's examination or race relations via her use of "looking" and the "imperial gaze" in *The Street*.

399

Hicks, Scott. " 'Thank God, People Have Got to Blow Their Noses and Wipe Their Hands and Faces and Wipe Their Mouth': The Monstrosity of Paper Goods in Ann Petry's *The Street*." *Interdisciplinary Studies in Literature and Environment* 11.2 (2004): 25-41.

    Introduces an "ecocritical " approach to Petry's *The Street*. Argues that the novelist uses the image of paper to link racial, class, and gender discriminations at the devastation of the environment.

400

Higashida, Cheryl Ann. "On the Multicultural Front: Radical Writers in the United States from the Depression to the Cold War." Ph.D. Diss., Cornel University, 2003.

    Contends that gender, ethnicity, race, and region intersect with class when determining the aesthetics of social change in radical writings from the Depression to the Cold War. Says this intersectionality remains under-theorized, and that gender and race are often treated as disjunctive categories of analysis. Addresses this problem in (re)readings of works by Richard Wright, Grace Lumpkin, Ann Petry, Dorothy West, Carlos Bulosan, and Hisaye Yamamoto.

401

Hill, Herbert, ed. Introduction. *Soon One Morning: New Writings By American Negroes 1940-1962*. New York: Knopf, 1965. Reprint. 1968.

    Displays a diversity of contemporary writings by African Americans, including Petry's "Miss Muriel." Places Petry among writers who "joined the tradition of social protest" with *The Street*. Concludes that *Country Place* "foreshadows" future novels that will deal with non-black characters and issues.

402

Hill, James L. "Parallels in Black and White: The Two Worlds of Fiction of Ann Lane Petry." *Journal of Arts and Sciences* (Albany State University) 1.3 (Fall 1996): 15-26.

    Encourages comparative studies of Petry's fiction.

403

Hill, Michael. "African American Fiction After Hiroshima and Nagasake" (Chapter, 27, Volume III). In *A Companion to American Literature*. Edited by Susan Belasco, Theresa Strouth Gaul, Linck Johnson, and Michael Soto. Hoboken, NJ: John Wiley & Sons - Blackwell, 2020.

    Surveys the fiction of African American writers who emerge during the aftermath of World War II, which includes Ann Petry. While not distinguishing applications of either "aesthetics poetics" or "critical poetics" by critics of African American literature (see #70), raises questions left by Kenneth W. Warren's on the relationship between politics and aesthetics in black writing?

404
Hill, Patricia Liggin, Bernard W. Bell, Trudier Harris, R. Baxter Miller, Sondra A. O'Neale, and William J. Harris, eds. With Horace C. Porter. *Call and Response: The Riverside Anthology of the African American Literary Tradition.* Boston: Houghton Mifflin, 1998.
    Includes Petry among other Post-World War II authors.

405
Hill-Lubin, Mildred A. "African Religion: That Invisible Institution In *African and African American Literature."* In *Interdisciplinary Dimensions of African Literature.* Edited by Kofi Anyidoho, Abioseh M. Porter, Daniel Racine, and Janice Spleth. Washington, DC: Three Continents, 1985.
    Discusses ambiguities of religion and magic in the lives of Min and Jones in *The Street*

406
Hilton, Angela. "Motherhood on Trial: Black Mothers with Incarcerated Sons Negotiating the Criminal Justice System in African American Literature." Ph.D. Diss., Purdue University, 2005.
    Proposes an interdisciplinary approach to literature, sociology, and the study of challenges faced by black mothers with incarcerated sons. Provides not only an analysis of how mothers are affected by the criminal justice system - i.e., how mothers negotiate the criminal justice system on behalf of their sons, but also how African American literature contributes significantly to the emergent field of Prison Studies. Includes in this study Ann Petry, John Oliver Killens, Richard Wright, Ernest Gaines, Gloria Naylor, Terry McMillan, and Leon Dash.

407
Hinterberg, Helen J. "Helping Teens Be Literate in History." *Christian Science Monitor*, 28 March 1989, 14.
    Says Petry allows readers "to see and [to] feel the historical realities that helped to create" *Tituba of Salem Village.*

408
_____. Review of *Harriett Tubman, Conductor on the Underground Railroad. Christian Science Monitor*, 8 September 1989, 13.
    Recommends Harriet Tubman for avid young readers who want books that are "structured with episode[s]" or that tell "what really happened."

409
Hiranuma, Kimiko. "Death in the Life: Alienated Labor and Black Life in Ann Petry's 'Like a Winding Sheet.'" アメリカ文学評論 24 (2014): 12-20.
    Demonstrates a psychoanalytical reading of Petry's short fiction. Has an international audience.

410
Hobson, Laura Z. Review of *The Narrows. Saturday Review of Literature* (15 August 1953): 6
    Announces the release of *The Narrows* by Houghton Mifflin. Admits to knowing no more than

what appears on the publisher's release: "a love story" that took "five years" to write.

411
Hoffmann, Andrew. "The City as a Trap: 20th- and 21st- Century American Literature and the American Myth of Mobility." Ph.D. Diss., Marquette University, 2019.
    Says literature and film constitute important tools for exposing how capitalist ideologies generate consent for hegemonic capitalism. Seeks to understand how urban populations are interpellated by the very capitalist machinery which fixes them in space and class while simultaneously denying them the benefits of American capitalism. Says Petry's literature makes application of the ideology.

412
Holladay, Hilary. *Ann Petry*. New York: Twayne, 1996.
    Provides new ways for considering Petry's three novels and short story collection, especially regarding the importance of relationships and neighborhoods. Also encourages comparisons of modernist aesthetics in comparative readings of Petry and twentieth-century writers Virginia Woolf and William Faulkner.

413
_____. "Creative Prejudice in Ann Petry's 'Miss Muriel.' " *Studies in Short Fiction* 31.4 (Fall 1994): 667-675.
    Is fascinated with people in Petry's short fiction who are shaped by the company they keep. Says Petry's characters take up a multiplicity of perspectives, but they share a preoccupation with race, gender, and class - all of which often incite prejudices. Insists Petry writes from the position that prejudice can be creative as well as destructive for relationships - e.g., in the short story, "Miss Muriel," the very tensions that polarize the community also paradoxically keep the townspeople engaged in endless debates with each other.

414
_____. "Holding Together, Breaking Apart: Communities and Relationships in Ann Petry's Fiction." Ph.D. Diss., University of North Carolina - Chapel Hill, 1993.
    Discusses Petry's portraits of community life in her novels and short fiction. These portraits suggest that relationships emerge as the community's life-blood; that a town's identity hinges on the ideas of its individual members, especially on what the community is and what it should be.

415
_____. "Narrative Space in *Country Place*." *Xavier Review*, 1996. Reprint. In *The Critical Response to Ann Petry*. Edited by Hazel Arnett Ervin. Westport, CT: Praeger, 2005.
    Discusses how central is Petry's detailed portrait of community in her novels, including *Country Place*. Encourages comparative studies of community portraits in works by Petry, William Faulkner, Toni Morrison, Alice Walker, and Gloria Naylor.

416
Holt, Shakira C. "On Speaking Terms: Spirituality and Sensuality in the Tradition of Modern Black Female Intellectualism." Ph.D. Diss., University of Southern California - Los Angeles, 2009.
    Takes an interdisciplinary and womanist-feminist approach to the intellectual life of modern black

women. Raises specific questions for the study: Who gets to be an intellectual? Why do elite black women continue to carry the representation of black female intellectuals? What is gained when we choose to view non-elite black women as intellectuals? Next, argues that working-class black women characters from short stories by Marita Bonner and from novels by Ann Petry (*Country Place*), Zora Neale Hurston, Dorothy West, and Gwendolyn Brooks have been just as deeply intellectual as their elite counterparts and should be brought into formal studies of modern black women intellectuals.

417

Holzman, Robert. Review of *Harriet Tubman, Conductor on the Underground Railroad*. *Kirkus* 23 (1 June 1955): 366.

  Details the biography of Harriet Tubman as being "poignant and sensitive reality," especially when compared to other such attempts by other writers.

418

Home, Chelsea L. "The Street as a Distorting Lens in Ann Petry's Novel." The National Conference On Undergraduate Research (NCUR). Ithaca College, 2011.

  Student argues "the street" is seen through distorting lens, exaggerating and exacerbating black disillusionment. Says such a view warps reality by distancing images of the world around protagonist, Lutie Johnson. Says "the street" creates a hostile and volatile environment which actively entraps; it is a negative influence; and it is an ideology and not just a geographical space. NCUR is for undergraduate students.

419

Honey, Maureen. *Bitter Fruit: African American Women in World War II*. Columbia, MO: University of Missouri Press, 1999.

  Provides literature in an anthology of fiction, essay, and poetry about and by African American women as well as history of their World War II experiences. Draws from four major African American periodicals: *Opportunity*, *Negro Digest*, *Negro Story,* and *The Crisis* - all of which include early stories by Petry. Also encourages future reviews of the "autobiographical" voice in Petry.

420

hooks, bell. *Remembered Rapture: The Writer at Work*. New York: Owl Books. 1999.

  Provides essays on process and politics of writing. Includes the Chapter, "The Legacy of Ann Petry."

421

Houck, Anne Cleaver. "Plot Keyed to Social Taboo Lacks Punch." *Gazette* (Little Rock), 23 August 1953 [Special Collections, Boston University].

  Contends that while *The Narrows* reveals "errors in our civilization," its projection of an "affairs de Coeur between an educated Negro and a wanton young matron of the haut monde" lacks realism.

422

"Houghton Mifflin Awards Tenth Annual Fellowships." *Publishers' Weekly* (March 1945): 1201.

  Identifies Petry as the recipient of the tenth annual Houghton Mifflin Literary Fellowship Award in fiction; says she receives $2,400.

Secondary Works

423

Howard, Jennifer. "Paperbacks." *The Washington Post*, October 10, 1999, X10.

    Introduces writers who are in paperback and are a must read. Offers interesting comparative critiques of Petry's *The Street* and *The Narrows*.

424

Hsu, Hsuan L. "Naturalist Smellscapes and Environmental Justice." *American Literature* 88.4 (2016): 787-814.

    Focuses on writings by Frank Norris, Ann Petry, and Helena Viramontes within the context of environmental justice. Says Norris' interest in the latter draws connections between smell, health, and stratified air and allows for studies that show how these issues intersect with racially uneven geographies. Cites Petry for the latter.

425

Hughes, Carl Milton. "Common Denominator: Man." In *The Negro Novelist: 1940-1950, A Discussion of the Writings of American Negro Novelists 1941- 1950*. New York: Citadel, 1953. Reprint. 1970.

    Maintains that in *Country Place,* Petry exhibits "a high level of competence in fictional writing." Discusses influences on the novel: Sinclair Lewis's *Main Street*; Victorian standards; and Dickensian creations. Focuses on plot, characterization, and language. Criticizes shifts from narrator to characters - cites as "cumbersome."

426

_____. " Portrayals of Bitterness." In The Negro Novelist: 1940-1950, A Discussion of the Writings of American Negro Novelists 1940-1950. New York: Citadel, 1953. Reprint. 1970.

    Provides first book-length critical analysis of *The Street*. Focuses on characterization, setting, point of view, and plot. Is convinced that Petry's thesis is naturalistic but calls her techniques refreshing and advanced, especially in comparisons to contemporaries like Wright (*Native Son*) and Fannie Cook (*Mrs. Palmer's Honey*). Concludes that Lutie is a "tragic figure" in a "modern tragedy."

427

Hull, Kenneth G. "Treatment of Prejudice by Four Novels: Richard Wright, Sinclair Lewis, Lillian Smith, and Ann Petry." M.A., Fort Hays Kansas State College, 1966.

    Introduces a theme in Petry's longer fiction that later becomes a critical theme in later articles and dissertations on Petry: the prejudices of Petry's characters.

428

"Hunt Beauty for Ann Petry Film." *Pittsburgh Courier*, 15 September 1956, 44.

    Advertises a call for the " beautiful and blessed with acting ability" to consider trying out for the leading feminine role in Virgo's proposed movie production of Ann Petry's *The Street*.

429

Hyde, Yvette Rachele. "Articulating Situated Knowledge and Standpoints in our Responses to Contemporary Street Fiction: A Book Club Case Study with African American Women." Ph.D. Diss., Louisiana State University and Agricultural and Mechanical College, 2015.

    Provides significant background information on popular contemporary street fiction - e.g., urban context; experiences of oppressed groups; catalyst for articulating the concept of the mentality of a single mother; sought-after improvements in school literacy skills; and opportunities to revise concepts such as the American Dream - all to learn about social issues impacting the lives of women and children.

Reveals a strategy for realizing such a study: Collect and evaluate data through transcribing book club discussions and individual interviews. Also, draws from reader-response and feminist standpoint theories to further substantiate the research for the study.

Last, suggests introducing audiences to contemporary street fiction: "[sell it] in venues such as independent bookstores, the internet, barbershops, beauty salons, flea markets, street vendors, and churches." Suggests connecting Petry to this genre via the writer's depictions of the black mother's struggles to survive in inner-city - i.e., her depictions of tough inner-city locations and the realities of "the street" that are central to plot development; and via the writer's incorporation of language, music, fashion, and attitudes.

430

"Ill Home Life as Worse than Lynching." *Afro-American* (Baltimore), 30 March 1946 [Special Collections, Boston University].

Reiterates Petry's reasons for writing *The Street*: "to show why colored people [have] a high crime rate, a high death rate, and little or no chance of keeping [their families] intact in large Northern cities."

431

"In Memory of Ann Petry." *Congressional Record - Daily Edition*. U. S. Congress Gov: Government Document, September 5, 1997.

Memorializes the life of America's prominent Connecticut writer- citizen in the Senate and in Congress' Congressional Record as follows: "In Memory of Ann Petry"; Issue and Section: May 09, 1997; Senate (Vol 143.No 60); Page S4277 (pdf). The document begins as follows: "Mr. Dodd, ironically in the same town of Old Saybrook, CT, we have a sadder piece of news about a wonderful constituent of my state." Extensive reflections follow Petry's family, work, and life. The document ends as follows: "We express our sorrow for the loss of Ann Petry." https://www.congress.gov/crec/1997/05/09/CREC - 1997-05-09-pt1-Pg54277-2 pdf

432

Ingram, Elwanda Deloris. "Black Women: Literary Self-Portraits." Ph.D. Diss., University of Oregon, 1980.

Says that black women characters have often been portrayed as one-dimensional figures in the literature of some black male writers and some white writers - e.g., the patient, the long-suffering servant; the matriarch; the religious fanatic; and "the nigger wench." Seeks to prove that "black women writers have created black women characters who are full-dimensional and more realistically drawn than other writers have done." Says Petry's Lutie Johnson of *The Street* is one example of a more realistically drawn black, female character.

433

_____."The Suspended Black Woman in Literature." *MAWA Review* 1.1 (Spring 1982): 20-23.

Defines the suspended woman as one who is powerless and unfulfilled, leading a life of blind or numb existence. Examines four black characters as suspended women: Nanny in *Their Eyes Were Watching God*; Mariah in *This Child's Gonna Live*; Sula in *Sula*; and Lutie in *The Street*.

434

Inquiring into the Theme of Early New England Colonies: Based on Ann Petry's T*ituba of Salem Village*.

Logan, Iowa: Perfection Learning, 1994.

    Provides historical accounts of Tituba aligned with Petry's fictional portrayal .

435
Issacs, Diana Scharfeld. "Ann Petry's Life and Art: Piercing Stereotypes." Ph.D. Diss., Columbia University Teachers College, 1982.

    Provides a critical look at Petry's life and art, acknowledging her definitive contributions to African American literature and to American literature overall.

436
Isaacs, Kathleen T. Review of *Harriet Tubman: Conductor on the Underground Railroad*. *Book Links* 15.1 (2005): 40.

    Provides a review of the juvenile publication.

437
Ivana, Dragos. "Writing the City, Narrative Identity." *American, British and Canadian Studies.* 34.1 (2020): 1-7.

    Reflects on Joe Varghese Yeldho's "Sounding Harlem: Ann Petry's T*he Street* and the Experience of 'Dwelling' " and the "experiences of dwelling" in Petry's *The Street* such as noise, sound, music of "everyday life" in black communications, and on jazz as a metaphor for living anew. Applies Heidegger's theory of dwelling to suggest a complex analysis of nomadic dwelling in Harlem. (see also Yeldho in 904)

438
Ivey, James. "Ann Petry Talks about First Novel." *Crisis* 53.2 (February 1946): 48-49. Reprint. In *Sturdy Black Bridges: Visions of Black Women in Literature*. Edited by Roseann P. Bell, Bettye J. Parker, and Beverly Guy Sheftall. Garden City, NY: Anchor/Doubleday, 1979.

    Introduces Petry as a new artist in the 1940s. Quotes the writer on why she wrote *The Street*. [See full interview in this bibliography].

439
_____. "Mrs. Petry's Harlem." *Crisis* 53.5 (May 1946): 154-15.

    Renders an unfavorable review of *The Street*. Questions Petry's "portrait of Harlem" - i.e., the street and her failure to depict "normal and responsible people in the [African American] community." Attributes Lutie's failure to naivete and poor choice of male friends.

440
Izard, Anne. Review of *Tituba of Salem Village*. *Grade Teacher*, February 1965, 29.

    Calls Petry's story about a West Indian woman, who is tried as a witch in Salem, as a vivid presentation. Attributes the success of the work to Petry's "controlled style."

441
Jackson, Blyden. "A Review of J. L. Dillard's 'Black English.' " *Journal of Negro History* 58.1 (January 1973): 90-96. Reprint. *The Waiting Years.* Edited by Blyden Jackson. Baton Rouge: Louisiana State University Press, 1976. Reprint. 1977.

    Uses his own "ready references" and the "speech patterns" of ordinary black characters in fiction to rebuke aspects of Dillard's study of Pidgin English. Then, he identifies Petry as an exemplary creator of such black characters.

442
_____. "A Survey Course in Negro Literature." *College English* 35 (March 1973): 631-636. Reprint. *The Waiting Years.* Edited by Blyden Jackson. Baton Rouge: Louisiana State University Press, 1976.

Advocates a required comprehensive and general course in African American literature at the college level. Calls for the inclusion of an "Age of Wright," or a "golden age" because writers from the 1940s, like Petry, present the "[Negro], new or old, as he actually [is]."

443
_____. "An Essay in Criticism." *Phylon* 11.4 (Fourth Quarter 1950): 338-343. *The Waiting Years*. Edited by Blyden Jackson. Baton Rouge: Louisiana State University Press, 1976.

Calls for "the development of an energetic scholarly criticism" from African American critics - a criticism that will also be an "integrative factor" in America. Encourages critics to "reflect upon the life-giving quality of Ann Petry's imagination in *The Street*."

444
_____. "Of Irony in Negro Fiction: A Critical Study." Ph.D.Diss., University of Michigan, 1952.

Provides the earliest dissertation on Petry (the only available copy is located in the Petry Collection in the African American Center at Shaw University). Provides a working definition of irony, then suggests that because irony is a continuum in American society, African American artists seem to have difficulty being called satirists or ironists. Thinks, however, that Petry in *The Street* and Gardner Smith in *Last of the Conquerors* are more successful than Jessie Fauset in *Comedy, American Style* and Walter White in *The Fire in the Flint*.

445
_____. "The Ghetto of the Negro Novel: A Theme with Variations." *NCTE* (from the Discovery of English: NCTE 1971 Distinguished Lectures. Urbana, IL: National Council of Teachers English). Reprint. *The Waiting Years.* Edited by Blyden Jackson. Baton Rouge: Louisiana State University Press, 1976.

Writes that the "ghetto of the Negro novel has served the Negro novelist as an objective correlative for his [her] disdain of the pretensions of color caste." Discusses novelists' variations of the ghetto - including Petry's. Insists that "Negro" novelists have had one distinguishable "common voice" when addressing such a theme.

446
_____. "The Negro's Image of His Universe as Reflected in His Fiction." *CLA Journal* 4.1 (September 1960): 23-31. Reprint. *Images of the Negro in America*. Edited by Darwin T. Turner and Jean M. Bright. Boston: D. C. Heath, 1965. Reprint. *The Waiting Years.* Edited by Blyden Jackson. Baton Rouge: Louisiana State University Press, 1976.

Suggests there are "distinctive" characteristics in the universe of "Negro fiction": a ghetto and a non-ghetto; irony which causes pleasure and pain; and a static world. Uses Petry's *The Street* and *Country Place* to help support this thesis.

447
_____. "The Negro's Negro in Negro Literature." *Michigan Quarterly Review* 4.4 (October 1965):

290-295.

 Points to *The Street* and *The Narrows* as "changing reflection[s] of discontent." Provides a literary history of the "dominant character" in black fiction, suggesting that in *The Street,* Lutie is like her contemporaries in *Native Son, If He Hollers Let Him Go,* and *Last of the Conquerors* - that is, she is "embittered and brutalized by the experience of life forced upon [her] by America"; or, she is "full to bursting of pent-up violence and venom." Concludes that the "dominant character" in black fiction changes with the main character in *Invisible Man* and with Link Williams in *The Narrows* - i.e., each character "withdraw[s]" and "search[es] for [his] identity."

448

Jackson, Lawrence B. *The Indigent Generation: A Narrative History of African American Writers and Critics, 1931-1960*. Princeton, NJ: Princeton University Press, 2011.

 Provides a literary history of writers and critics from 1934 to 1960s, tracing artistic success and intellectual reputations. Discusses Petry in Chapter 9: "Black Futilitarianists and the Welcome Table (1945-1947)." Includes the following illustrations: photo of Petry; dust jacket of Petry's *The Street* from 1946, and cover details of *The Street* from 1946.

449

Japtok, Martin. " A Neglected Study in 'Whiteness' : Ann Petry's *Country Place.*" In *The Critical Response to Ann Petry.* Edited by Hazel Arnett Ervin. Westport: Praeger, 2005, 345-365.

 Calls for a renewed interest in Petry's *Country Place*, published in 1947, especially on Petry's contributions to today's emerging studies of "whiteness." Points to literary scholarship on "whiteness" and illustrates how conceptualizations of "whiteness" also permeate throughout Petry's 1947 narrative.

450

_____. " ' The Gospel of Whiteness': Whiteness in African American Literature." *American Studies* 49.4 (2004): 483-498.

 Provides an historical account of "whiteness" studies with significant attention given to attitudes of white audiences; to expectations of African American audiences; and to critics of the African American literary canon. Reminds readers that the implicit definition of what is African American literature has served to sideline works focusing on characters who are not African American. Calls for a reconsideration - for an inclusion - of African American works which explore whiteness in the canon of African American literature. Seeks to illustrate how in "white - life" texts by African American writers whiteness is theoretically configured as a kind of religion, or, as a worship of materialism. Argues also that some conceptualizations of whiteness are complementary to some conceptualizations of blackness in canonical African American works.

451

Jarrett, Gene Andrew. "Introduction: Not Necessarily Race Matters."*African American Literature Beyond Race: An Alternative Reader*, edited by Gene Andrew Jarrett. New York: New York University Press, 2006.

 Edits a significant volume of critical essays and excerpts that reveal there are "unknown, unavailable, infrequently-taught and under-critiqued works" by 15 major African American writers of African American literature. Petry is included. Emphasizes the diversity, multi-dimensional and postmodern possibilities of inclusive African American literature beyond race. Hazel Arnett Ervin contributes an article on Petry's *Country Place*.

452

_____. "Little Known Documents - 'Marie of the Cabin Club (1939).' " *Publication of the Modern Language Association of America (PMLA)* 121.1 (2006):245.

Centers a discussion of pseudonymity by African American writers and why they might choose to select anonymity when publishing: writers must account for the politics of race among other African American writers; they seek to produce marketable literature by overcoming disadvantageous and racial inequities in pay rates; they seek acceptance for publication; or they desire critical recognition or acclaim as well as commercial distribution. Suggests Ann Petry uses the pseudonym Arnold Petri to publish "Marie of the Cabin Club" - her first published short story - for any of the reasons above, or merely for the desire to offer literary entertainment through romance and mystery.

453

Jaskoski, Helen. "Power Unequal to Man: The Significance of Conjure in Works by Five Afro-American Authors." *Southern Folklore Quarterly* 38.2 (June 1974): 81-108.

Examines the significance of "conjure" in *The Street*. Says Petry depicts a less ambiguous practice of the root doctor - to solve the problems of minor character Min. Says Min's first attempt to take control of her own life is when she seeks the root doctor.

454

Jenkins, Candice Marie. *Private Lives, Proper Relations: Regulating Black Intimacy*. Minneapolis, MN: University of Minnesota Press, 2007.

Draws attention to dangerous domestic situations in which African Americans have become associated - e.g., "racist accusations of sexual and domestic pathology." Discusses how Petry as well as Nella Larsen, Toni Morrison, Gayl Jones, and Alice Walker bear the double social burden in their literature of uplifting the race and of claiming bourgeois subjectivity and responsibility for the black community.

455

Jenkins, Donald Ray. "Playing by the Rules and Losing: The Merit Myth in Selected African American Fiction." Ph.D. Diss., University of North Carolina at Greensboro, 2002.

Challenges the "merit myth" in the black experience via select fiction by African American writers Charles Chesnutt, Kenneth Harper, Walter White, Ralph Ellison, and Ann Petry. Illustrates how over the centuries, black persons have "played by the rules," were willing to start at the bottom, and were willing to work hard to achieve promotion and rank - only to be hampered in their quests to achieve the fruits of democracy because of skin color and social designation, and not by "merits." Demonstrates how characters learn from their experiences, and how racial characterization often nullifies the idea of individual merits.

456

Jimoh, A. Yemisi. "Ann Petry." *Literary Encyclopedia*, 25 October 2002.

Provides biographical information. Errors exists with Petry's birth year.

457

_____. *Miss Muriel and Other Stories*. The Literary Encyclopedia, 25 October 2002.

Provides great background information on Petry's short stories - e.g., concepts/ ideas for the stories; cultural influences; 'changes' in stories from first publication to the Miss Muriel collection;

canonization of the short stories by black women writers, including Petry; plot summaries, settings, points of view, and literary history. Also includes quotes by Petry on writing practices. Found here is also a great companion reader to the essays written earlier by Gladys Washington and to the collected essays on Petry's short fiction, edited by Muriel Brailey, Hazel Ervin, and Hilary Holladay (see elsewhere in this collection).

458
_____. *The Narrows*. *The Literary Encyclopedia*, 25 October 2002.

Provides historical context for the time in which the novel was written. Provides plot summary, character sketches, and themes; looks at sub-plots and motifs such as gender ambiguity, human complexity, timelessness, and varying social classes (from wealthy whites and middle-class black women to working-class blacks and whites).

459
_____. *The Street*. *The Literary Encyclopedia*, 25 October 2002.

Provides historical and biographical background information; acknowledges translations of the novel; and offers plot summary.

460
_____. *Country Place*. *The Literary Encyclopedia*, 25 October 2002.

Provides plot summary, character sketches; and quotes by Petry on concepts/ ideas for writing *Country Place*.

461
_____ and Francoise N. Hamlin. "African American Perspective on War and Citizenship from Colonial to Present Day." *These Truly are the Brave: An Anthology of African American Writings on War and Citizenship*. Gainsville, Fl: University Press of Florida, 2015.

Confirms there is a tradition of African American literature on war, liberation, and citizenship. Includes more than 80 African American writers who have focused on heroes, martyrs, patriots, and natural heroes. In the anthology, under "Part 3: The Double -V Campaign Challenges Jim Crow: World War II," includes Petry and her short story "In Darkness and Confusion."

462
Johns, Robert L. "Ann Petry." In *Notable Black American Women*. Edited by Jessie Carney Smith. Detroit: Gale Research, 1992.

Discusses thematic makeup of Petry's novels and Petry's philosophy as a writer. References Petry's criticism from 1940s to the 1980s. An incorrect year of birth is given.

463
Jones, Amy Robin. " 'There is no Place': Geographical Imagination and Revision in Novels by Ann Petry and Jo Sinclair." Ph.D. Diss., University of Colorado, 1996.

Examines the concepts of "home" and "place" in two social protest novels - Petry's *The Street* and Jo Sinclair's *The Changelings* to determine how "space" and "place" might expand understanding of racial and gendered constructions of place in geographical studies. Concluding that subversions and revisions of home and community by Petry and Sinclair are challenges to identity, position, and history.

464
Jones, Gayl. "Jazz/Blues Structure in Ann Petry's "Solo on the Drums." In *Liberating Voices: Oral Tradition in African American Literature*. Cambridge, Mass: Harvard University Press, 1991. Reprint. *Ann Petry's Short Fiction: Critical Essays*. Edited by Hazel Arnett Ervin and Hilary Holladay. Westport, CT: Praeger, 2004.

    Examines Petry's "Solo on the Drums" and her application of techniques from African American oral traditions such as jazz and blues, so to shape the structure of her story, to organize events in the story, and to present characters.

465
Jones, Loretta L. Dowdy. "Constructing the New Black Woman: Reading Gloria Naylor's Women through Ann Petry's Lutie in *The Street*." M.A., Virginia State University, 2000.

    Encourages comparative readings of Petry through the works of other African American women writers.

466
Jones, Patrina C. "Characterizing 'Minor' African American Women's Everyday Singing in African American Literature." Ph.D. Diss., Stony Brook University, 2011.

    Encourages a different approach to reading African American womanhood in African American literature - by centering daily vocal communiques by women (i.e., through singing). Turns to Ann Petry's Lutie Johnson in *The Street* who takes up singing as a justifiable means to earn a wage. Illustrates how as cultural and critical practices, singing for African American women can become non-visual subversive reality for cultural survival, for expressing facts about the respective female nature, and for communicating the concerns and conflicts which perpetuate female marginalization.

467
Jones, Tayari. "In Praise of Ann Petry." *The New York Times* (online), 10 November 2018.

    Identifies Petry's *The Street* as her favorite. Calls it "literary with an astonishing plot." Provides a plot summary. Mentions briefly Petry's third novel, *The Narrows*; her juvenile work *Tituba of Salem Village*; and her short story collection.

468
_____. "*The Street*: The 1940s African American Thriller that Became a Hugh Bestseller." *The Guardian*, 14 December 2019.

    Announces the reissuance of Petry's *The Street*. Speaks of conflicting covers of *The Street* which seem to be "crossing the line between belles-lettres and pulp."

469
Joyce, Joyce Ann. Ann Petry. *Nethula Journal* 2 (1982): 16-20.

    Contends that African American and American literary communities have failed to trust the *donnee* in Ann Petry's work, and as a result, Petry has drifted somewhat into obscurity. Offers ways critics might approach Petry's novels and still respect what and how Petry has chosen to write. Exemplifications come in lengthy comparisons of Ellison's *Invisible Man* and Petry's Link Williams from *The Narrows* - two men who struggle from early adolescence to come to terms with relationships and white society.

470

Kaiser, Ernest. "The Literature of Harlem." *Freedomways* 3.3 (Summer 1963): 276-291. Reprint. *Black Expressions*. Edited by Gayle Addison, Jr. New York: Waybright and Tally, 1969.

    Correlates sociological and literary materials that make up a chronological overview of Harlem. Mentions in the section, "Literature of the War Years," that Petry's *The Street* is "an honest attempt to sum up what the author saw and heard." In the section, "Other Writers about Harlem," discusses Petry's article "Harlem" in *Holiday*, calling the article a "kind of cooks" [sic] tour" of Harlem with some interpretations displayed with pictures - "beautiful . . . [and] in rich colors."

471

Kamarah, Sheikh Umarr. "Ann Petry and African Poetics: A Review of "Solo on the Drums." In *Ann Petry's Short Fiction: Critical Essays*. Edited by Hazel Arnett Ervin and Hilary Holladay. Westport, CT: Praeger, 2004.

    Takes the position that Petry's "Solo on the Drums" encourages a closer look at Petry's creative genius and skillful use of oral techniques "to generate rich, crisp, intimate, and dramatic prose - prose that enhances understanding of characters, specifically their hopes, difficulties, and triumphs."

472

Kamme-Erkel, Sybille. *Happily Ever-After? : Marriage and Its Rejection in Afro-American Novels*. New York: Peter Lang, 1989.

    Exploring the rejection of marriage in African American novels, primarily written by women, Kamme-Erkel looks at causes for "breakdowns." Using Petry's *The Street*, concludes that marriage breaks down "solely because of economic problems."

473

Kang, Nancy. "A Must-Read List: The Enduring Contributions of African American Women Writers." *The Canadian Press*, February 22, 2019.

    Introduces Petry's *The Street* to Canadian audiences as a social, realist novel. Introduces protagonist Lutie Johnson as "weathering sexism, racism, classism, poverty and intense personal frustration as a single mother." Says that the "brutality of the environment" gives the novel "its loaded name."

474

Karno, V.A. "Legal Topographies." Ph.D. Diss., University of Southern California, 2000.

    Charts the intersections between literary, legal, and architectural discourses in 18th-, 19th-, and 20th- Centuries, and then uncovers overlapping and recurring rhetoric of spatiality and visibility in legal opinions and in American and African American literatures. Traces literary and legal narratives to inform representation of tension between an idealized and a pragmatic American geography. Includes in the study Petry's *The Street*.

475

Karrer, Wolfgang and Barbara Puschmann-Nalenz. *The African American Short Story, 1970-1990: A Collection of Critical Essays*. Wissenschaftlicher Verlag Trier, 1993.

    Introduces the African American short story within the context of history and signifying intertextuality. Includes critiques of Petry's short story, "Mother Africa" by editor Puschmann-Nalenz.

476

Kaufmann, Peter S. "Ann Petry." *Portrait Collection.* New York: Rapid News Photo, 1945.
    Provides portrait of Petry and photographs autographing *Country Place.*

477

Kaywell, Joan F. and Kathleen Oropallo. "Young Adult Literature: Modernizing the Study of History Using Young Adult Literature." *The English Journal* 87.1 (Jan 1998): 102-107.
    Highlights Petry's *Tituba of Salem Village*. Talks historically of Petry's story about Tituba and her husband John, tracing their experiences working for the Reverend Parris in Salem Village during the witchcraft trials. Also highlights Petry's *Harriet Tubman: Conductor on the Underground Railroad*. Speaks historically of how Petry provides a moving account of the courageous woman's journey to lead hundreds of slaves to freedom.

478

Kazin, Alfred. "Brothers Crying Out for More Access to Life." *Saturday Review*, 2 October 1971, 33-35.
    Compares Petry with the young "race" writers from the 1960s, explaining how Petry's *Miss Muriel and Other Stories* collection is "different" and "slow" in "rhythm." Praises Petry's efforts, however, as a writer, particularly her artistry in "Miss Muriel."

479

Kent, George E. "Struggle for the Image: Selected Books by or about Blacks during 1971." *Phylon* 33.4 (Winter 1972): 304-311.
    Surveys books that are recovering, consolidating, or intensifying black images for greater understanding. Includes *Miss Muriel and Other Stories* collection, citing Petry as highly competent with her shorter fiction.

480

Kiken, Jonas. "Love under an Evil Star." *Post* (Denver), 13 September 1953 [Special Collections, Boston University].
    Cites Petry among a number of African American writers who once lived among the people in their novels. When reviewing *The Narrows*, calls attention to plot and characters, particularly the editor of the local newspaper, Pete Bullock, who strongly resembles Sinclair Lewis's "targets of the ulcerated strivers" and to Mamie Powther (for Petry's depiction of "the earthy side" of women).

481

Kilgallen, Cara Elana Erdheim. "The Greening of American Naturalism." Ph.D. Diss., Fordham University, 2010.
    Calls for a focus on nature as it pertains to culture in the socially activist prose of Theodore Dreiser, Jack London, Frank Norris, Ann Petry, Upton Sinclair, and Richard Wright. Argues that the politically charged and traditionally naturalistic writings of these writers cannot be understood apart from environment ethics which inform their literature. In short, encourages "ecological studies" - e.g., critical conversations about hunger and social stratifications or accesses to food, to air quality or about waste, water use, and land - all as found within the traditional naturalistic texts of Dreiser, London, Norris, Petry, Sinclair

and Wright. Incorporates terminology such as "green reading of literature" and "environmental ethics" which are informing literature.

482
Kissko, Jennifer Joyce. "The Narrative of American Poverty in the Twentieth Century: A Critique of Space in Ann Petry's *The Street*. Marilynne Robenson's *Housekeeping*, and T. Coraghessan Boyle's *The Tortilla Curtain*." M. A., Villanova University, 2002.
    Critiques poverty and space in Petry's *The Street*; Robinson's *Housekeeping*; and Boyle's *The Tortilla Curtain*.

483
Knadler, Stephen. "Exceptional Minds, Unstated Exceptions: Intellectual Disability and Post-War Racial Liberalism in African American "White Life" Novels." *Studies in American Fiction* 43.2 (2016): 231-257.
    Reveals new forms of exclusion, stigmatization, and hierarchy in white - life novels, often in ways that re-enforce class, racial, and/or gender divides of the past. Includes Petry's *Country Place* in the study.

484
Kniffel, Leonard. "New Hall of Fame Honors Writers of African Descent." *American Libraries* 30.2 (Feb 1999):52-53.
    Identifies the first 39 inductees into a new Hall of Fame for writers of African descent. Among the inclusion of well-known poets, novelists, juvenile literature writers, and essayists is Petry, the author of poems, novels, juvenile literature, and essays.

485
Koenen, Anne. "Zeitgenossische Afro-amerikanische Frauenliteratur:Selbstbild und Identitat bei Toni Morrison, Alice Walker, Toni Cade Bambara und Gayl Jones." (Campus Forschung, Band 442) Frankfurt/Main: New York: Campus, 1985.
    Requires translation. Provides introductory and historical reviews of the black women writers' literary tradition via critics and authors. Lists Petry.

486
Koster, Rick. "Groundbreaking 1946 Novel by Old Saybrook's Ann Petry back in New Edition." *The Day and TCA Regional News* [Chicago], 27 February 2020.
    Reminds readers that Petry's 1946 novel *The Street* has never been out of print. Provides an expansive historical re-introduction to Petry and the 1946 novel. Provides quotes from the editor at Houghton Mifflin Harcourt; from Petry's daughter (Elisabeth); and from the book's editor (Tayari Jones) who together are responsible for Houghton's 2020 reissuance of the novel.

487
Kothari, Reena. " The Tropes of Migration and Counter Migration: A Study of Ann Petry's "The Street," Gloria Naylor's "The Women of Brewster Place," and Toni Morrison's "Song of Solomon." Ph.D. Diss., Gujarat University, 1999.
    Encourages a chronological study of the tropes of migration and "counter-migration" in writings by Ann Petry, Gloria Naylor, and Toni Morrison.

488
Krementz, Jill. *The Writer's Desk.* New York: Random House, 1996.
    Delineates Petry's writing processes and literary practices.

489
Krstovic, Jelina. *Children's Literature Review* (2017): 123-190.
    Includes criticism of Petry's children's literature.

490
Kruckmeyer, Katherine Ann. "But Some of Us Are Classics: An Investigation of the Reception of Novels by Ann Petry and Gloria Naylor." Honor's Thesis, Brown University, 1990.
    Provides analytical research on Petry and the outcomes of her publications to meet Honor's thesis requirements at the undergraduate level.

491
Kunitz, Stanley and Vineta Colby, eds. "Ann Petry." *Twentieth Century Authors: A Bibliographical Dictionary of Modern Literature*. New York: H. W. Wilson, 1955. 776.
    Includes biographical as well as bibliographical information on Petry as novelist and writer of short stories.

492
Kushwaha, M.S. and Kamal Naseem. *Indian Doctoral Dissertations in English Studies, A Reference Guide.* Atlantic Publishers and Distributors. India: New Delhi, 2000.
    Is a bibliographical listing of doctoral dissertations in English studies (American and British) that are published at Indian universities and institutes. One focus is American literature (poetry, fiction, drama, and criticism) which lists Petry.

493
L'Engle, Madeleine. Review of *Tituba of Salem Village*. *New York Times Book Review*, Section 7, Part II, 1 November 1964, 8.
    Says Petry's work on Tituba goes beyond historical accounts and deals with universal issues like race and Christianity. Calls the book a tribute to Petry's "artistry."

494
LaForge, Jane Rosenberg. "The Civil Death of Mrs. Hedges and the Dilemma of Double Consciousness." *Western Journal of Black Studies* 32.1 (Spring 2008): 30-41.
    Investigates Mrs. Hedges in *The Street* as business savvy and a physically strong woman within the contexts of legal and metaphysical conditions (i.e., civil death), and within the DuBoisian notion of double consciousness and its effects on Mrs. Hedges' pursuit of the American dream.

495
Lancaster, Iris. M. "From Fragmentation to Wholeness: A Phenomenological and Psychological Analysis of Ann Petry's *The Street*." M.A., Texas Southern University, 2001.
    Suggests a Jungian reading of Petry's female characters who strive for individualization.

496

_____. "Unmasking the Black Female Cultural Hero: A Jungian Analysis of Min's Journey from Invisibility to Identity in Ann Petry's *The Street*." In *The Critical Response to Ann Petry*. Edited by Hazel Arnett Ervin. Westport, CT: Praeger, 2005.

Examines the themes of journey and reinvention with black female characters using Jung's "individuation process " from invisibility to identity. Demonstrates how Petry picks up on the themes of journey and reinvention with black females, such as Min, a woman who willingly commits to a heroic journey that takes her from invisibility to identity. Through Min, the black female character becomes "a person, an individual, a totally integrated personality."

497

Lapides, F. R. and D. J. Burrows, eds. *Racism: A Casebook*. New York: Crowell, 1971.

Aims to serve as a resource for creating adult learning environments. Belief is that educators can use resources that direct focus on perceptions, beliefs, attitudes and personal views of race, gender, etc., especially with white adult educators in mind. Provides 14 essays, six short stories, and comments from Petry, James Baldwin, Alex Haley, John Williams, and Malcolm X on racism, prejudices, and stereotypes.

498

Latimore, Grace Olivia. "Freedom Seeking and Self-Making in Twentieth Century Black Women's Literature." Ph.D. Diss., Georgetown University, 2018.

Discusses ways that black women have directed their efforts to make spaces, homes, and communities for and among themselves - i.e., self-determination and "self-making." Returns to women in Petry's *The Street*, Nella Larsen's *Passing*, and Toni Morrison's *Sula* for examples of "self-making." Also studies relational identities while also questioning limitations and possibilities.

499

Lattin, Vernon E. "Ann Petry and the American Dream." *Black American Literature Forum* 12.2 (Summer 1978): 69-72. Reprint. In *The Critical Response to Ann Petry*. Edited by Hazel Arnett Ervin. Westport, CT: Praeger, 2005.

Urges re-readings and re-evaluations of Petry's works. Says critics fail to see Petry as a "rebel." Forcefully contends that Petry is a "significant critic of American values" in all three of her novels.

500

Laurel, Jeanne Phoenix. "Double Veil: Cross-Racial Characterization in Six American Women's Novels, 1909-1948." Ph.D. Diss., Indiana University, 1990.

Provides close readings of American novels by African American and White American authors who portray well-developed characters of the opposite race. Includes Petry for *Country Place*. Finds common threads among these authors, such as cross-racial characterization and sophisticated attacks on racism and classism.

501

Lebow, Diane. "Selfhood in Free Fall: Novels by Black and White American Women." Ph.D. Diss., University of California, Santa Cruz, 1985.

Contends there are novels by African American women writers and novels by White American women writers that suggest a new development of the Bildungsroman tradition - i.e., female characters who have evolved with a stronger sense of self. Furthermore, this new development of the Bildungsroman is a "casting off of old traditional patterns of being a woman in order to formulate new ones," or in order to formulate a "free fall."

502
Lee, Amy. "The Narrator as Feminist Ally in Ann Petry's "The Bones of Louella Brown." In *Ann Petry's Short Fiction: Critical Essays*. Edited by Hazel Arnett Ervin and Hilary Holladay. Westport, CT: Praeger, 2004.

    Aligns Petry, Virginia Woolf, Alice Walker, and others as female critics who "see their mission as rescuing the hidden voices from a patriarchal literary history and [as] reinstating the memory of the silenced women and their stories."

503
Lee, Robert A. "Harlem On My Mind: Fictions of a Black Metropolis." *Costerus* 178 (2009): 427-455.

    Includes Petry's *The Street* as an academic inventory. Reminds readers that Petry allows Harlem to be introduced or reintroduced through the viewpoint of a woman whose observations are many - e.g., Harlem is narrowed down precisely to a street, and on "the street" is the commodifying reduction of its people and their lives; boxed-in humanity; a community both injuring and self-injuring; social realism; and echoes of urban blues.

504
Lenz, Gunter H. "Symbolic Space, Communal Rituals, and the Surreality of the Urban Ghetto: Harlem in Black Literature from the 1920s to the 1960s." *Callaloo* 2.2 (Spring 1988): 332-335.

    Discusses the "literary strategies" or "patterns" used by African American writers in their responses to the transformation of Harlem from "Negro Capital" of the 1920s to "ghetto . . . of the 1950s and 1960s." Concludes that when "dramatizing the tensions between social structure and communities in *The Street*, . . . [Petry] poses the question of whether there [is] any meaning and strength left at all in the black writers' cherished and stubborn dream of Harlem as the place and incorporation of black urban culture and community."

505
Leonard, Kandi Kay. "The American Novel after World War II: Early Postmodernism." Ph.D. Diss., University of California - Riverdale, 1993.

    Centers on thematic characteristics of postmodern American literature - e.g., unmitigated despair, experimentation, unanswered questions, alienation, radical contradictions of optimistic visions, etc. Centers discussions on women writers Ann Petry and Tillie Olsen. Submits that each writer tells the story of women struggling to survive in post-World War II America, and each describes aspects of society that radically contradict the optimistic visions created by mainstream media and marketed to public.

506
Lespinasse, Patricia G. "The Jazz Text: Wild Women, Improvisation, and Power in 20th Century Jazz Literature." Ph.D. Diss., Columbia University, 2010.

    Explores gender, improvisation, and power in African American literary narratives by Ann Petry, Toni Morrison, and Gayl Jones which might be studied as "call and response" or "revisionist narratives." Also explores ways these black female writers engage elements of music differently from their male counterparts in narrations. Encourages reading jazz literature through both feminist and transnational lens, so to understand better the significant role of jazz music in constructing a discourse of power and self-efficacy for women throughout the African Diaspora.

507

Levy, Tedd. "Ann Petry: On the Street Where She Lived." *Remarkable Women of Old Saybrook*. Charleston, SC: The History Press, 2013.

    Captures a community of women who were born or lived a formative or meaningful time in Old Saybrook, a small town on Long Island Sound in Connecticut. Listings include, among others, English colonist settlers; a founder of a woman's college; a missionary; physician; psychologist; educator; several advocates of women's rights; a universally known actress; school administrator; historian; successful businesswomen; druggists (including Petry's Aunt Anna James); and novelists (including Petry).

508

Lewis, Barbara William. "Taking the Cake: Ann Petry's "Has Anybody Seen Miss Dora Dean?" In *Ann Petry's Short Fiction: Critical Essays*. Edited by Hazel Arnett Ervin and Hilary Holladay. Westport, CT: Praeger, 2004.

    Provides historical timeline and dance techniques of the cakewalk. Includes both history and dance techniques of the cakewalk in an analysis of Petry's short story, "Has Anybody Seen Miss Dora Dean?" which captures in its title the name of the famous cakewalk dancer, Dora Dean.

509

_____. "Prodigal Daughters: Female Heroes, Fugitivity and "Wild" Women in the Works of Toni Morrison." Ph.D. Diss., University of Southern California, 1996.

    Promotes stylistic and thematic analysis of prodigal daughters in black texts by black women writers (e.g., female characters who leave home; question why they leave home, and why (and if) they return; the notion of "the divided self"; and the female voice of language). Establishes connections between fictional female heroines, actual heroines, and fugitives; then determines how writers of such daughters set out as creative artists.

510

Li, Stephanie. "Whiteness and Narrative Authority in Ann Petry's *Country Place*." *Playing in the White: Black Writers, White Subjects*. New York: Oxford University Press, 2014.

    Includes a chapter on Petry: "Whiteness and Narrative Authority in Ann Petry's *Country Place*." Explores white-life novels written by major, mid-twentieth century black writers of the 1940s and 1950s. Demonstrates how postwar black novelists are at the forefront of contributing to what is commonly understood today as Whiteness Studies.

511

Lincoln, S. Abraham. "The Theme of Oppression in Ann Petry's *The Street*." *Language in India*. 19.3 (March 2019): 4-10.

    Explores characterization in the novel, *The Street*. Also explores the following: the Harlem community and its endless suffering; objectives of feminism; and challenges faced by black women.

512

Lindfors, Bernth. "The Larson Collection at the Harry Ransom Center." *Journal of the African Literature Association* 5.1 (2010):198-203.

Cites Petry's *The Street*. Provides leads for other research on the author.

513

Literary Ladies Guide to the Writing Life. "6 Fascinating Facts About Ann Petry, Author of *The Street*," 11 October 2017 (web-based).

Provides detailed facts about Petry's life and works. Includes earlier and recent photographs of Petry and earlier and recent book covers for *The Street*, *Country Place*, and *The Narrows*.

514

Littlejohn, Amonte. *Hopeful Hostility: An Analysis of the Evolution of American Naturalism*. Cleveland, OH: Cleveland State University Press, 2011.

Traces the evolution of American Naturalism's narratological methods and expansions. Proposes moving beyond the particulars of deterministic texts. Rather, promotes intersectionality - a look at multiple components that make up American naturalism. Also looks at the individual role of the text and its relationships with other naturalistic texts. Illustrates intersectionality at work in Petry's *The Street* and in Max Brooks' World War Z.

515

Littlejohn, David. Introduction. *Black on White: A Critical Survey of Writing by American Negroes*. New York: Viking, 1966.

Makes special pleas in the introduction and in Chapter Seven for Petry to be reviewed as a "careful, wise and sympathetic" writer. Considers Petry's style to be masculine, crisp, and energetic with threads of irony, but thinks that when it comes to characters, "out of the female wisdom, [Petry] creates her characters." Says, like Victorians, Petry also creates "sordid plots." Concludes that Petry's details of Harlem are "convincingly complete," but considers *The Street* "quasi-protest literature."

516

Llorento, Manuela Matas. "The Other City: Harlem in Ann Petry's *The Street*." *Revista de Estudios Norteamericanos* 11.4 (1996):107-112.

Re-tells the plot of the narrative in *The Street* to underscore subjectively of a Harlem that is defined by difference - the symbol of material prosperity and the form of a new way of colonization. Recurring phrases include: "a city within a city" and "Harlem is nowhere and anywhere."

517

Locke, Alain. "A Critical Retrospect of the Literature of the Negro for 1947." *Phylon* 9.1 (First Quarter 1948): 7.

Looks back over literature by African American writers of 1947. Says Petry's *Country Place* "has neither the surge nor the social significance of her first novel."

518

_____. "Reason and Race: A Review of the Literature of the Negro 1946." *Phylon* 8.1 (First Quarter 1947): 17, 21.

Includes *The Street* in a review of a host of books written by African American writers in 1946.

Hails *The Street* as the "artistic success of the year." Also calls the work "quiet, courageous, unsentimental realism." Disagrees with critics who call the novel's ending defeatist. Rather, says the work is the "cleverest kind of social indictment—Zolaesque."

519

"Lost Persons in Love." *Nation* 177 (August 29. 1953): 177.

    Criticizes structure and style in *The Narrows*, citing both as too varied in a single work. Says Petry means well with a "violent and passionate" story about two lost souls.

520

Lowney, John. "Do You Sing for a Living?" Ann Petry, *The Street*, and the Gender Politics of World War II Jazz." In *Jazz Internationalism: Literary Afro-Modernism and the Cultural Politics of Black Music*. Urbana: University of Illinois Press, 2017.

    Includes a rereading of works by writers such as Ann Petry (*The Street)*, Claude McKay, and Langston Hughes, giving attention to the influences of jazz on critical social discourse and modes of artistic expressions in Afro-modernist literature. Regards *The Street* as an important jazz novel and suggests studying Petry's critical engagement with racial and gender politics through jazz in the life of main protagonist, Lutie Johnson and the lives of other women of the 1940s. Also encourages a critical study of representation in African American literature, such as Lutie's name - i.e., the musical "lute" and the monetary "loot."

521

Lubin, Alex. *Revising the Blueprint: Ann Petry and the Literary Left.* Jackson, MI: University Press of Mississippi, 2007.

    Examines Petry's relationship with left-wing political critics in years following World War II. Seven of the contributors to the collection return to Petry's *The Street, Country Place,* and *The Narrows* to address the literary left.

522

_____. *Romance and Rights: The Politics of Interracial Intimacy, 1945-1954.* Jackson, MI: University Press of Mississippi, 2005.

    Informs discussions of political intimacy - who you date and who you marry. Also challenges limitations due to the politics of interracial intimacy and the legacy of miscegenation and racial and sexual violence in America. Praises the fiction of Ann Petry, William Gardner Smith, and Chester Himes for understanding the limitations and politics of interracial intimacy and for using the issue to discuss the legacy of romance and rights.

523

Lucy, Robin Jane. "Fables of the Reconstruction: Black Women on the Domestic Front in Ann Petry's World War II Fiction." *CLA Journal* 49.1 (2005): 1-27.

    Contends that on behalf of black women of the 1940s, Petry's fiction focuses on how capitalism wages a war on black women and their children. Demonstrates how Petry attacks the capitalist system and demands the recognition of black women as catalyst for political and social changes in the United States economy - an economy that still exploits the labor of work.

524

_____. " 'Now is the Time! Here is the Place!': World War II and the Black Folk in the Writings of Ralph Ellison, Chester Himes, and Ann Petry." Ph.D. Diss., McMaster University, 1999.

Regards African American literature produced between the end of the Depression years and the end of World War II as literature of a distinct period in African American letters. Studies how writers of this period employ black folklore - i.e., a usable folk past - as a strategy for portraying and critiquing the struggles of African Americans for self-determination within the United States during this period.

525

"Lutie's Nightmare: Deconstructing the 'American Dream' in Ann Petry's *The Street*." 인문논총 59 (2008): 3-28.

Re-evaluates *The Street* in light of cultural readings. Says protagonist Lutie Johnson does not internalize the 'American Dream' and is aware of the fictionality of the discourse of the 'American Dream.' Says Lutie embodies the DuBoisian double-consciousness. Encourages reading *The Street* as a theoretical precedent to Bercovitch's theorization of the critique of the 'American Dream.' Says Petry's novel refuses to be contained but rather subverts the existing order, contending Bercovitch's argument that the narrator's challenges to the 'American Dream' are already and always contained.

526

Lyttle, Deborah Sue. "Ann Petry's *The Street*: Situating Social Protest in the Canon." M.A., University of Texas at Austin, 1988.

Promotes *The Street* as social protest and as a canonical work of literature.

527

M.C.R. "An Eloquent Statement of a Racial Problem found in Harlem's Streets." *Sunday Star* (Washington, DC), 10 February 1946, 3.

Applauds Petry for not idealizing her characters. Thinks Petry, like Shakespeare, presents characters with feelings. However, disagrees with Petry's position that Lutie's situation is limited only to young black women. Also disagrees with Petry's "too-violent climax" in the novel.

528

M.P. "Evil Results of Crowding." *Worcester Telegram*, 10 February 1946 [Special Collections, Boston University].

Insists in *The Street*, Petry is angry and that she has "an attitude of mind and with the conditions which breed immorality and crime."

529

_____. "Sordid Side of Town Life." *Worcester Sunday Telegram*, 28 September 1947 [Special Collections, Boston University].

Compares Petry's second novel, *Country Place*, with her first. Says both works "are powerfully written and [that] their characters haunt one." Concludes, however, that neither of the novels presents "a pretty picture of life." Urges Petry to write another book - "wholly from the druggist's view."

530

M.W. "The Latest Negro Novel." *Christian Science Monitor*, 8 February 1946, 14.

Calls *The Street* "ugly and revolting in the extreme." Questions why Petry as an African American woman would write such a violent treatment of Harlem life and give the impression that overall Harlem is "deplorable."

531

MacCann, Donnarae. "Black Americans." *Christian Science Monitor*, 1 May 1969, B7.

Calls Petry's *Harriet Tubman, Conductor on the Underground Railroad* and *Tituba of Salem Village* distinguished biographies that are for a change "from [the] Black American's viewpoint."

532

McBride, Kecia Driver. "Fear, Consumption and Desire: Naturalism and Ann Petry's *The Street*." *Tennessee Studies in Literature* (2003): 304-322. Reprinted. In *Twisted from the Ordinary: Essays on American Literary Naturalism*. Edited by Mary E. Parke. Knoxville: University of Tennessee Press, 2003.

Explores naturalistic techniques and themes in Petry's *The Street* within the contexts of American naturalism.

533

McCarthy, Dorsey. " ' *The Street*' Effective Weapon on Racial Bigotry." *Chicago Bee*, 17 March 1946, 16.

Thinks there is a race between Lutie and "the street" for the possession of Bub. Praises Petry for her depictions of unforgettable persons rather than types. Calls on every woman's club in America to review *The Street*.

534

McClurg, Jocelyn. "Ann Petry, Author of 'The Street,' Dies at Age 88." *Hartford Courant* (Hartford, CT), 30 April 1997, A.1.

Continues to support Connecticut's native with feature articles; this time it is to report Petry's death. Uses biographical and bibliographical information to trace Petry's life and writings from Old Saybrook, Connecticut, to Harlem, New York, and back to Old Saybrook, Connecticut. Announces that donations are to be made to the Authors League Fund, 330 W. 42nd St., New York, NY 10036.

535

McCreary, Micah L. and Richard C. Wright. "The Effects of Negative Stereotypes on African American Male and Female Relationships." *Journal of African American Male* [Special Issue/Part I: Psychological Perspectives on African American Men] 2.4 (1997): 25-46.

Centers an analysis of the "brokenness" of African American females and males in literature. Uses current research to study the intersections of racism, sexism, and economic oppression; to trace origins of the Bad Man and Bad Women stereotypes of African American relationships; and to offer recommendations for moving away from "brokenness" and toward positive nurturing relationships. Uses characters in Petry's *The Street* to exemplify a psycho-social analysis of the vulnerability and resiliency of African American women and men.

536

McDowell, Margaret B. " '*The Narrows*': A Fuller View of Ann Petry." *Black American Literature Forum* 14.4 (Winter 1980): 135-141. Reprint. *The Critical Response to Ann Petry*. Edited by Hazel Arnett Ervin.

Westport, CT: Praeger, 2005.

    Provides an extensive critical assessment of Petry's third novel within three fully developed themes: "the oppressiveness of guilt; the effects of historiography, tradition [and[time on the attitudes of contemporary people towards race; and the limited veracity of sensory apprehension." Looks specifically at techniques: flashback, symbolism, and other literary elements such as point-of-view and characterization.

537

McGuire, A. B. Review of *Harriet Tubman, Conductor on the Underground Railroad*. *New York Herald Tribune Book Review*, Section 6, Part II, 13 November 1955, 8.

    Applauds Petry's biography of Tubman. Says it is convincingly well written.

538

McInerney, Kathleen. Review of *The Narrows*. *Belles Lettres*. 4.2 (1989): n.a.

    Calls Ann Petry's *The Narrows*, a novel about the power of the story and the telling of the story as recreative acts that give substance to one's experience. Celebrates the re-publication of Petry's 1953 novel.

539

McKay, Nellie. "Ann Petry's *The Street* and *The Narrows*: A Study of the Influence of Class, Race, and Gender on Afro-American Women's Lives." In *Women and War: The Changing Status of American Women from the 1930s to the 1950s.* Edited by Maria Diedrich and Dorothea Fischer-Hornung, 1990. Reprint. In *The Critical Response to Ann Petry*. Edited by Hazel Arnett Ervin. Westport, CT: Praeger, 2005.

    Reminds readers not to take lightly the black woman as central character in *The Street* and *The Narrows* and that race, class, and gender intersect to become dominant forces in the fate of the black woman.

540

_____. Introduction. *The Narrows*. Boston: Beacon, 1988.

    Provides a lengthy critique of Petry's "creative vision" in *The Street* and *Country Place*. Calls Petry's creative vision in *The Narrows*, "sharpened," with "complex and entangled relationships - demonstrable implications for contemporary feminist criticism."

541

_____. "Reflections on Black Women Writers: Revising the Literary Canon." *The Impact of Feminist Research in the Academy*. Edited by Christie Farnham. Bloomington: Indiana University Press, 1987.

    Concludes that "what black women as writers have consistently provided . . is the rendering of the black woman's place in the world in which she lives, . . . shapes and defines ... from her own impulses and actions." Cites Petry .

542

McMahan, Elizabeth, Susan Day, and Robert Funk. *Nine Short Novels by American Women*. New York: St. Martin's Press, 1993.

    Includes Petry for her short story "Miss Muriel" for its discussions of social life.

543

McParland, Robert. "Native Sons and Daughters: Richard Wright, Chester Himes, Ann Petry, James Baldwin and Ralph Ellison." In *From Native Son to King's Men: The Literary Landscape of 1940s America*. Lanham, MD: Rowman and Littlefield, 2017.

Uses biography, social and literary criticism, and cultural history to analyze a wide range of American writers and their works, and to illustrate how the writers and their works collectively display the American dream, hopes, anxieties, and cultural imagination of the 1940s.

544

McSherry, Elizabeth. "Moses of Her People." *Hartford Courant*, 14 August 1955, 19.

Reviews *Harriet Tubman, Conductor on the Underground Railroad* at length. Provides plot summary and character sketch of Petry's portrayal of Tubman as "vital and magnetic"; predicts that students in American history will profit from Petry's biography.

545

Machlan, Elizabeth Boyle. "Diseased Properties and Broken Homes in *The Street*." In Representing Signification: Toward an Aesthetics of Living Jim Crow, and Other Forms of Racial Division. Edited by Brian Norman and Piper Kendrix Williams. Albany, NY: State University of New York Press, 2010.

Says segregation is a touchstone in African American literature and that it shapes group's identity and belonging in the United States, and that it is traceable to the slave narrative tradition in the canon. Seeks, therefore, to uncover and to identify a "segregation narrative tradition," traceable to the slave narrative tradition. Through collected essays, seeks also to promote the question of aesthetics, giving focus to literary and theoretical representations of segregation. See essay, "Diseased Properties and Broken Homes in The Street," which under Section III: Inside Jim Crow and His Doubles appears and seeks to underscore the aesthetic sensibilities of the tradition.

546

_____. "Panic Rooms: Architecture and Anxiety in New York Stories from 1900 to 9/11." Ph.D. Diss., Princeton University, 2004.

Explores the relationship between New York City's domestic architecture and its fiction, from the rise of the apartment building to the fall of the World Trade Center on September 11, 2001. Explores how twentieth-century authors and film-makers juxtaposition literary and architectural forms to explore the instability of traditional ideas of home in urban environments. Relies on images and tropes reminiscent of the Gothic genre to engage and to deconstruct New York's "actual" and social attributes both in architecture and in fiction. Petry's fiction contributes to the New York stories.

547

Madden, David. "Ann Petry: 'The Witness.'" *Studies in Black Literature* 6.3 (Fall 1975): 24-26.

Thinks Petry's short story addresses the illusions of assimilation and the prejudices that may exist among middle-class African Americans. Calls the short story social protest, but with a "balanced perspective."

548

Magill, Frank N. *Masterpieces of African American Literature.* New York: Harper Collins, 1992, 869-874.
    Focuses on Ann Petry's *The Narrows*.

549

Maja-Pearce, Adewale. "Beyond Blackness." *Times Literary Supplement* (London), 2 May 1986, 479.
    Considers Zora Neale Hurston and Ann Petry to be "significant American writers of the [twentieth] century," primarily because they are truthful to their visions and because they move beyond the rhetoric of race, respectively in *Their Eyes Were Watching God* and in *The Street*.

550

Majors, Clarence. *Calling the Wind: Twentieth Century African American Short Stories.* New York: Harper Perennial, 1993.
    Introduces Petry and her short story, "Has Anybody Seen Miss Dora Dean?"

551

Mallegg, Kristin and Thomas E. Barden. *Short Stories for Students.* Vol 44. Farmington Hills, MI: Gale/Cengage, 2016.
    Provides historical and critical overviews of short stories from all cultures and time periods. Presents contextual analysis as well as discussions of plot, characters, themes and structures in commonly studied short stories. Includes Petry.

552

Mann, L.S. "Ann Petry's Novel of Negro and White in New England Community." *Springfield Republican*, 13 September 1953, 8.
    Writes that there are "two powerful stories" in conflict in *The Narrows*: the character study of Abbie Crunch and the tragic love affair between Link Williams and Camilo Sheffield - a black man and a white woman. Finds fault with Petry's characterization of Link as a tragic figure. Says, instead, a character like Abbie "awakens this emotion."

553

Marcus, Sybil. *A World of Fiction: Twenty Timeless Short Stories*. White Plains, NY: Pearson/Longman, 2006.
    Includes Petry's "Like a Winding Sheet" as one of twenty timeless short stories.

554

Margolies, Edward. "Struggles for Space: Stephen Crane, James Baldwin, Ann Petry, Bernard Malamud." *New York and the Literary Imagination: The City in Twentieth Century Fiction and Drama*. Jefferson, NC: McFarland & Co, 2018.
    Presents a collection that focuses on the myths of New York City and its paradoxes (e.g., contradictions and ambivalences; the same and different). The collection is divided into three parts: Part One: Mythmakers examine New York from the perspectives of New York aristocracy, immigrants, and African Americans. Part Two: An American dream with variations which includes a chapter on Ann Petry. In Part Three, there is a century of theater.

555
Markau, Ulrike. *Setting, Protagonists and Relationships between Black and White in Four African American Novels: Claude McKay's Home to Harlem, Ann Petry's The Street, Ralph Ellison's Invisible Man, and Louise Meriwether's Daddy Was a Number Runner.* Freiburg Schw, 1995.

    Illustrates international interests in setting and protagonists in *The Street*.

556
Martin, Allie Beth. Review of *Tituba of Salem Village*. *Library Journal* 89 (September 15, 1964): 3498.

    Summarizes very briefly the plot. Thinks the theme will entice young people to read other works with similar themes.

557
Martinez, Brenda Giselle. "Letters to Ourselves: Literary Representations of Intersectional Resistance and Radicalizing Collective Healing." M.A., Lehigh University, 2017.

    Explores the plight of being a woman of color in America through Black feminist lens. Refers to Anne Spenser's "Letter to My Sisters" as a love letter which introduces and passes down the notion of "intersectional resistance" so to dismantle intersectional oppression. Contends that one recipient of Spenser's letter is Ann Petry in *The Street*.

558
Maund, Alfred. "The Negro Novelist and the Contemporary Scene." *Chicago Jewish Forum* 13 (Fall 1954): 28-34.

    Assesses Petry's achievements in *The Street* and in *The Narrows*. Considers *The Street* to be slightly "feminist." Thinks of Lutie as "the female counterpart" to Bigger Thomas. Likes the different ways in which Petry handles the theme of "the idle rich" in both novels.

559
May, Claudia. "Prisms and Refractions: Portrayal of Domestic Laborers in Ann Petry's *The Street* and Alice Childress's *Like One of the Family: Conversations From a Domestic Life*." *Reconstruction:Studies in Contemporary Culture* 13.2 (2013):2-2.

    Examines portrayals of female African American domestic workers in fiction and how the women confront racial, gender, and class inequities. Also critiques the conduct of those who condone the margination of African Americans.

560
_____. "Railroad Blues: Crossing the Tracks of Gender, Class, and Race Inequities in the Blues and Ann Petry's *The Street*." In *Trains, Literature and Culture: Reading/Writing the Rails*. Edited by Steven D. Spalding and Benjamin Fraser. Lanham, MD: Lexington Books, 2012.

    Traces the history, relevance, and theoretical functions of the train device as a blues metaphor in African American literature. Focuses on protagonist Lutie Johnson's commute to work by train and then interrogates the metaphor, questioning whether the train enables her to escape and to achieve financial independence, or like the infrastructure of a train system, does the train device function like a blues metaphor which foreshadows the paradox of Lutie's narrative. Hence, Lutie actually does not escape inadequate housing, bankrupt social services, or racial inequities which characterize her neighborhood.

561

Meacham, William Shands. "Race and The Novel." *The Virginia Quarterly Review* 30.1 (Winter 1954): 134-139.

    Examines analytically Petry's *The Narrows,* illustrating the results of "dark currents of racial conflicts run[ing] . . . beneath the surfaces of contemporary society."

562

Meldon, John. " '*The Street*' - A Powerful Novel of Harlem Tragedy." *Daily Worker* (New York), 20 March 1946, 11.

    Urges audiences to read *The Street* without delay. Says the novel shows white Americans how others might see them. Calls the novel a "shock treatment" for complacent white Americans. Applauds Petry for telling "the truth" - that is, for telling what is good and what is bad about her race. Dislikes, however, the novel's "too pessimistic" ending.

563

Mickenberg, Julia. "Civil Rights, History and the Left: Inventing the Juvenile Black Biography." *MELUS* 27.2 (Summer 2002): 65-93.

    Contends that children's literature between 1945 and 1965 by women authors Shirley Graham, Ann Petry, Dorothy Sterling, and Emma Gelders Sterne becomes the important vehicle for civil rights activism. Says such literature fills voids in American history which have either excluded African American history or diminished its relevance.

564

Mittlefehldt, Pamela Klass. "A Politics of Transformation: Women and Story in American Culture." Ph.D. Diss., University of Minnesota,1990.

    Examines the power of the story in women's writings between the 1930s and 1960s. Illustrates functions of storytelling in powerful ways in women's lives. Concludes that women's storytelling - oral and written - is often politically charged; is social criticism; and is transformative at individual or cultural levels. As a tool, storytelling establishes context and also provides grounding, affirmations, and community.

565

Mobley, Marilyn Sanders. "Ann Petry." *African American Writers*. Edited by Lea Baechler and A. Walton Litz. New York: Scribner's 1991, 347-59.

    Examines what is called Petry's unique "double perspective" in all three of her novels. Defines "double perspective" as Petry's way of bringing to her literary works her middle-class upbringing in a small New England town and her years of living and working in NYC among impoverished African Americans.

566

Mock-Murton, Michele. "*Country Place*." *Masterplots II: African American Literature*. Revised edition. December, 2008, 1-3.

    Provides for *Country Place t*he following: in-depth and useful plot summary; descriptive character sketches; obvious and not-so-obvious themes and meaning; critical contexts that advance analytical critiques; and an annotated bibliography.

567

Moffett, James, and Kenneth R. McElheny. *Points of View: An Anthology of Short Stories*. New York: Mentor, 1966.

    Includes Petry's "Doby's Gone."

568

Moody, J. N. "Review of *The Street*." *Commonweal*, 43 (22 February 1946): 486.

    Questions whether a white girl who is as attractive as the protagonist Lutie Johnson in *The Street* would not have encountered similar tragic circumstances? Argues against blaming Lutie's handicaps on race hatred. Applauds Petry, however, for her "sensitivity to detail" and for her ability to tell a "powerful" story.

569

Moody-Freeman, Julie E. "Review of *Ann Petry's Short Fiction: Critical Essays*," edited by Hazel Arnett Ervin and Hilary Holladay. *CLA Journal* 48.1 (2004): 103-107. Also, in *Choice Review's* (online) 42.4 (2004): 42.

    Applauds the collection, especially its introduction which contextualizes Petry's literary development as a short story writer. Calls the collection a great companion to Petry's collection *Miss Muriel and Other Stories*.

570

Moon, Bucklin. "Both Sides of the Street." *New Republic* 114 (February 1, 1946): 193-194.

    Thinks Petry's "feeling of inner warmth and understanding" makes her characters come alive. Calls her bar scenes, however, contrived. Introduces the notion that Petry could become a pulp writer.

571

Moore, Steven T. "Black Rage in African American Literature before the Civil Rights Movement: Frederick Douglass, Harriet Jacobs, Charles Chesnutt, Nella Larsen, Richard Wright and Ann Petry." Ph.D. Diss., University of Nebraska - Lincoln, 2007.

    Traces the gender differences of black rage expressed in African American literature, from Frederick Douglas to Ann Petry. Emphasizes, among others, the following themes: white silence and black rage; buried anger; physical lash-outs; biracial battles; and murderous rage.

572

Morgan, Stacy I. *Rethinking Social Realism: African American Art and Literature, 1930-1953*. Athens: University of Georgia Press, 2004.

    Examines select African American mural and graphic artists, poets, and novelists of the mid-twentieth century who emphasize the theme of social realism. Refers to the artists and writers as the generation that identifies with the poor and disenfranchised and regenerates themselves as cultural workers from the left - e.g., endorsing pro-labor progressivism; anti-capitalism; attacking corporate greed; emphasizing regionalism. Says that in the 1940s and early 1950s, novelist Ann Petry, artist John Wilson and poet Robert Hayden were among the few African American cultural workers who debut an engagement with social realism.

573

Morris, M. Aldon. Review of *Country Place*. *Boston Chronicle*, 22 May 1948 [Petry Collection, Schomburg].

    Calls the theme in *Country Place* "commonplace and the characters not too articulate." Still says Petry holds the reader's attention " down to the very last word …."

574

Morris, Wright. "The Complexity of Evil." *New York Times Book Review*, Section 7, 16 August 1953, 4.

    Calls some parts of *The Narrows* disappointing and more of a "first draft" and other parts imaginative and credible. Suggests comparing Mamie Powther and James Joyce's Molly Bloom.

575

Morrison, Allan. "Women in the Arts." *Ebony* (August 1966): 90-94.

    Includes Petry in its Who's Who of African American women in the arts.

576

Morrissette, Sandra G. " 'Have You Stolen Anything:' Images of Motherhood in the Novels of Ann Petry, Toni Morrison and Alice Walker." M.A., Roosevelt University, 2001.

    Offers images of motherhood for critical analysis by major novelists.

577

Morsberger, Robert E. "The Further Transformation of Tituba." *New England Quarterly* 48.3 (September 1974): 456-458.

    Discusses Petry as an historical revisionist. Considers Tituba in *Tituba of Salem Village* to be a "new addition to the pantheon of black heroines."

578

Mott, Shani Tahir. "Masquerade Narratives: Writing Race and Imagining Democracy in American Literature,1930 - 1955." Ph.D. Diss., University of Michigan, 2005.

    Studies African American and White American writers who create political novels with protagonists and/or central secondary characters of a different racial identity. Calls such writings "masquerade narratives." In such narratives, writers free themselves from the racial boundaries and burdens that language and national structure place on creative vision. Supplementals attempt to understand better the criticism of political writings by select writers - e.g., journals, diaries, essays, manifestos, etc. Includes Petry's *The Narrows* and her criticism of the novelist within the novel.

579

Moynihan, Sinead. "Ann Petry's Cakewalk: Domestic Workers and The New Yorker at Mid-Century." *MELUS* 44.1 (2019): 1-21.

    Promotes the "literary cakewalk" in African American narratives as a dance that offers the following for characters: psychological and cultural space; allowances for resistance; and allowances for reversal of stereotypes. Incorrectly refers to "Has Anybody Seen Miss Dora Dean? (1958) as Petry's first short story. Petry's first short story, however, is "On Saturday the Siren Sounds at Noon" (1943). Also see Arnold Petri's "Maria of the Cabin Club."

580

Mullen, Bill V. "Object Lessons, Fetishization and Class Consciousness in Ann Petry's *The Street*." In *Revising the Blueprint: Ann Petry and the Literary Left*. Edited by Alex Lubin. Jackson, MI: University Press of Mississippi, 2007.

    Discusses how Petry's novel uncovers the social relations that have historically contributed to the exploitation of laboring black female bodies.

581

_____. " 'A Revolutionary Tale': In Search of African American Women's Short Story Writing." In *American Women Short Story Writers: A Collection of Critical Essays*. Edited by Julie Brown. New York: Routledge, 1995, 191-208.

    Writes that Alice Walker's road to her "mother's garden" as well as to her crossover in commercial success is well-paved in the period between 1946 and Walker's work *In Love and Trouble,* yet so are numerous other works by black women writers. Says Petry is "foremost" among such women writers - e.g., Petry's "Like a Winding Sheet" is collected in *The Best American Short Stories of 1946,* edited by Martha Foley and in subsequent reprints. Also, it's Petry's story form which becomes black women's "quotidian concerns and inner lives" and it is her successful mainstream publication which opens up the "flood of short fiction collection[s] by black women."

582

Musser, Judith. *"Girl, Colored" and Other Stories: A Complete Short Fiction Anthology of African American Women Writers in The Crisis Magazine*. Jefferson, NC: McFarland & Company, 2011.

    Includes in the collection Petry's "Olaf and His Girlfriend."

583

_____. *"Tell It To Us Easy" and Other Stories: A Complete Short Fiction Anthology of African American Women Writers in Opportunity Magazine (1923- 1948)*. Jefferson, NC: McFarland & Co., 2018.

    Contextualizes the African American short story - historically, culturally, and theoretically published in *Opportunity Magazine*, from 1923 to 1948. Cites Petry.

584

Myles, Lynette D. "Beyond Borders: Black Women, Space, and Female Subjectivity in African American Women's Narratives of Enslavement." Ph.D. Diss., Arizona State University, 2006.

    Reviews crossroads that focus on the following: digression as resistance; space for black female subjectivity; disruptions of black female consciousness; black female support for survival; demystifying the American Dream; locating safe space for survival and renewal; and female autonomy. Literary works included in the study are Petry's *The Street* and Nella Larsen's *Quicksand*.

585

Myree-Mainor, Joy. " 'I'm Craving for That Kind of Love': Loss and Desire in Ann Petry's *The Street*." *Obsidian* 12.1 (Spring 2011): 47-59, 149.

    Encourages re-readings of *The Street* with focus on protagonist Lutie Johnson's unconscious expressions of sexual desire - e.g., her sense of morality and self-definition as an upstanding "married" black woman, and the restraints and challenges that she faces. Insists Lutie - not Min or Mamie Powther in *The Narrows* - is Petry's first sexualized protagonist. Encourages comparative examinations.

586

_____. "Re-reading the Social Protest Tradition: Progressive Race, Gender, and Class Politics in the Fiction of Ann Petry and Dorothy West." Ph.D. Diss., University of Kentucky, 2004.

Says Ann Petry and Dorothy West are central to appreciating the protest tradition in African American letters. Reviews Petry's *The Street, The Narrows* and short stories from *Miss Muriel and Other Stories* as well as West's *The Living Is Easy, The Wedding,* and short stories from *The Richer, The Poorer* to illustrate how both writers promote racial advancement - informed by aspects of Black nationalism, especially racial solidarity, self-definition, determination, and reliance on Black cultural traditions.

587

_____. " 'The Story of Race Relations': Reading Black Nationalism in Ann Petry's *The Street.*" *CLA Journal* 54.2 (December 2010): 176-197.

Says Petry's *The Street* prefigures and revises the legacy of 1960s nationalism, especially its association with sexism, heterosexism, and patriarchal and essentialist gender roles. Urges closer scrutiny of how Petry navigates "the story of race relations" in her narratives which explicitly promote social protest.

588

Nakitoshi, N. Tadashi. "Summation of the NASSS International Graduate Students Literature and Culture Workshops." *Nanzan Review of American Studies*, 30 (2008): 241-243.

Identifies student participants from Japan, United States, and Philippians in an international graduate school literary and cultural workshop. Cites Ms. Hiranuma Kimiko of Doshisha University, for focus on the community used by post-war African American women writers, especially Ann Petry. In her study "Reexamining the African American Women's Sense of Community: Ann Petry and Her Community in *The Street*," Kimiko stresses re-reading Petry's *The Street* in appropriate historical and social contexts.

589

Nance, Merle. "Four-Star Novel." *People's Voice*, 16 February 1946, S-6.

Call *The Stree*t a "novel of circumstances." Compares Petry's work with Hardy's *Return of the Native*, saying that like Egdon Heath, the street "is the acting." Believes Petry "builds her plot [and] interweaves her characters with an architectural solidity." Defends Petry against those critics who claim she is defeatist. Writes that Petry merely fails to render solutions at the end of her novel.

590

Nargis, Nargis. "Identity Politics in the Works of Afro-American Women Writers: A Study of the Selected Works of Jessie Fauset, Nella Larsen and Ann Petry." Ph.D. Diss., Panjab University, 2007.

Registers scholarly international critiques of identity and interracial politics in works by major black women writers from the Harlem Renaissance to Petry.

591

Naviaux, Julie A. "Distinctly American: Performing Humanity in African American Literature From Proto to Post New Negro Renaissance." Ph.D. Diss., University of Kentucky, 2016.

Draws on recent literary scholarship, performance studies, and early critical writings on African American art and performance from the 1910s through the 1940s to demonstrate the creative use of "art and performance," by "spectator and performer", so to 1) create space; 2) investigate social and cultural constructions; 3) critique performances of race, gender, and class; 4) critique the audiences' reactions to the artistic product against the racial identity of audiences and performers; 5) reveal the problematic nature of being both "American" and "African American"; and 6) show problems with binary racial lines and class distinctions. The early critical writings used in this study include the following: public speeches and musical displays in James Weldon Johnson's *Autobiography of an Ex-Colored Man* (1912); classical and modern dance as seen in Jessie Fauset's *There is Confusion* (1924); variety show stages in Walter White's *Flight* (1926); and vocal concerts in Ann Petry's *The Street* (1946).

592

Nedoma, Jeannette. R*ace, Racism and Violence in Ann Petry's 'The Witness': From Miss Muriel and Other Stories*. Verlag: Grin Publishing, 2009.

Traces the historical beginnings of prejudice, discrimination, violence, and struggle for African Americans in the United States of America. Reminds readers that racism should have ended with the end of the Civil War in 1865, but as suggested by Petry's main character of suburbia Connecticut in the short story, "The Witness," the long and tortuous way of life for African Americans continues.

593

Nelson, George. "Review of *Harlem Nocturne: Women Artists and Progressive Politics During World War II*" by Farah Jasmine Griffin. *International Herald Tribune* (Paris), 25 September 2013, 10.

Confirms international interests in novelist, Ann Petry; choreographer and dancer, Pearl Primus; and composer and pianist, Mary Lou Williams. Provides biographical and critical contexts for each of the female subjects. Is critical of Griffin's task in some parts of her narrative, but then calls the work "a heartfelt tribute to three remarkable artists." Ends paraphrasing Griffin and James Baldwin: These artists "were not willing to forget or wholly forgive America's historical transgressions," but were devoted "to helping this nation 'achieve' itself."

594

Nelson, Lisa K. "Racing the Rebel; Romancing Rebellion." Ph.D. Diss., Columbia University, 2005.

Uses two master narratives to promote understanding of masculine subjects in twentieth-century American literature: the Oedipus complex and the cultural fantasy of the black rapist. Examines the figures of the rebel - mythologized, racialized, sexualized, and politicized in works by Faulkner, Malamud, Bellow, Mailer, Roth, Ellison, Himes, and Petry. Also anticipates the rebel that is by the 1960s revised as motorcycle outlaw and is appropriated by subversive gay writers.

595

Newlin, Keith. *The Oxford Handbook of American Literary Naturalism*. New York: Oxford University Press, 2011.

Provides a literary history of American literary naturalism, from its beginnings in the 1890s to the present; identifies leading American naturalists; and introduces major African American naturalists (DuBois, Chesnutt, Pauline Hopkins, Wright, Petry and Baldwin). Defines their contributions (e.g., tropes of brute and spectator; horrors of mob violence; and naturalistic musical forms of the blues).

596

Nichols, Charles H. "New England Narrative." *Phylon* 14.3 (Fourth Quarter 1953): 437.

Criticizes Petry's style in *The Narrows,* calling its overall effect somewhat "disappointing," particularly with its lack of "profound emotional involvement." However, says the novel is more than about race because of its questioning of integrity and personal convictions, moral values, and materialistic standards.

597

_____."The Forties: A Decade of Growth." *Phylon* 11.4 (Fourth Quarter 1950): 377-380.

Says Petry's literary achievements as well as the literary achievements of other African American writers are attributable to "craft" and "varieties of subject matters."

598

Nielson, David Gordon. "Black Ethos: The Northern Urban Negro 1890-1930." Ph.D. Diss., State University of New York at Binghamton, 1972.

Seeks insight into the ethos of ordinary black America; describes a characteristic spirit woven into the web of northern black urban existence during 1890-1930; looks at how the existence of a black ethos has changed.

599

Noble, Jeanne. *Beautiful, Also, Are the Souls of My Black Sisters: A History of the Black Woman in America*. Englewood Cliffs, NJ: Prentice-Hall, 1978.

Traces literary development of African American women in fiction, from domestic workers to self-sustaining individuals. When discussing the African American woman as the domestic worker, Petry's character Pink from "In Darkness and Confusion" and Lutie from early portions of *The Street* are included. Noble regards *The Street* as an early work which "Speak[s] the Truth to the People" about African American women and their "struggles in the urban setting."

600

Noh, Jongjin. "Dream Deferred or Dream Defeated?: Ann Petry's *The Street*." *The New Korean Journal of English Language and Literature* 56.1 (2014): 127-147.

Confirms an international interest in the African American novelist. Provides a summation of Petry's plot and offers several character sketches from *The Street*. Theorizes about Petry's critiques of male-dominant ideology and the politics of it in the novel. Concludes by citing Petry as one black woman writer whose strong voice has helped to define the African American literary tradition.

601

Norman, Elizabeth J. *African American Connecticut Explored*. Middletown, CT: Wesleyan University Press, 2014.

Provides a collection of essays on African American Connecticut history which includes, among others, the following subjects: black governors of Connecticut; prominent black abolitionists; community responses to the Amistad trial; Civil Rights work of Jackie Robinson; and best-selling author Ann Petry for her novels with New England settings - *Country Place* and *The Narrows*.

602

Norris, Keenan. *Street Lit: Representing the Urban Landscape*. Lanham, MD: Scarecrow Press, 2014.

Provides a forward by Omar Tyree and an introduction by Keenan Norris, to chronicle a literary critique of early "street lit[erature]" and contemporary "urban street lit." Outlines lineages of the writers; the role of "street lit" writers; and its function.

603

O'Banner, Bessie Marie. "A Study of Black Heroines in Four Selected Novels (1929-1959) by Four Black American Women Novelists: Zora Neale Hurston, Nella Larsen, Paule Marshall, Ann Lane Petry." Ph.D. Diss., Southern Illinois University of Carbondale, 1981.

    Investigates the "old preoccupation of blacks trying to make it" according to white standards. Concludes that such standards found in Nella Larsen's *Passing* are replaced by concerns for "self-fulfillment," particularly among black women in Zora Neale Hurston's *Their Eyes Were Watching God*; Ann Petry's *The Street*; and Paule Marshall's *Brown Girl, Brownstones*.

604

O'Conner, Patricia T. "Review of *The Street*." *New York Times Book Review*, 5 January 1986, 26.

    Announces the reprint of *The Street*. Reiterates the novel's favorable reception in 1946 with quotes taken from numerous reviews that followed the 1946 publication. Reemphasizes Petry's use of "strong characterization."

605

O'Donnell, Heather. "Ann Petry." *Voices from the GAPS: Women Writers of Color*.
    Visit: www.voices.cla.umn.edu

606

"Obituary of Ann Petry, American Novelist Who Used Her Experiences as a Reporter to Write of Life on the Mean Streets of Harlem in the 1940s." *The Daily Telegraph* (London, UK), June 10, 1997.

    Celebrates internationally the life of Ann Petry and praises the writer for her "closely observed style" and "sharp eye for local details" in *The Street* and in *Country Place*.

607

Ochoa, Peggy Ann. "Culturing Subjectivity: Revisions of Identity in Cross-Cultural Literatures." Ph.D. Diss., University of Southern California, 1997.

    Contextualizes identity formation through the theoretical lens of Louis Althusser, Sigmund Freud, Antonio Cramsci, Gloria Anzaldua, Homi Bhabha, and Michel Pecheux. Includes W.E.B. DuBois's concept of "double consciousness" and Virginia Woolf's sense of split consciousness. Then through contextual and theoretical underpinnings, investigates texts by Petry, Morrison, Kingston, Sahgal, Suleri, and (James) Joyce, exploring how these writers delineate the processes of identity formation.

608

Olsen, Tillie. "One Out of Twelve: Writers Who Are Women in Our Century." In *Silence*. New York: Delacorte/Seymour Lawrence. 1965. Reprint. 1972. Reprint. 1978.

    Questions the domestic and literary lives of women writers of the twentieth century, and why only one out of twelve achieves critical recognition equal to that of men. Contends that many of these women are "silenced" by the "traditional silencers of humanity: class, color, gender," or by other silencers such as: "imposed guilt," or the fact that "a man can give full energy to his profession, a woman cannot." Discusses women as writers who "work on a paid job," or "who are mothers as well as writers," or whose "books of great worth suffer the death of being unknown or, at best a peculiar eclipsing." Petry is mentioned among such women.

609
"On the Author." *New York Herald Tribune Book Review.* Section 6, 16 August 1953, 2.
  Offers quotes by Petry on her experiences as a newspaper woman and as a recreation field specialist in New York; reflects on how Petry came to win a Houghton Mifflin Fellowship Award; and identifies the writers who continue to influence Petry.

610
Orr, Lisa Marie. "Re-Working Class: The Body and "Difference" in Working-Class Women's Writings." Ph.D. Diss., University of California, Los Angeles, 1997.
  Argues that class is performative and that it is always represented as deliberate political acts in working-class women's writings. Provides evidence of such a conclusion by focusing on twentieth-century American working-class women's writings which are counter-representative to arguments that gender, race, and sexuality are constructive. Examines the works of writers such as Stephen Crane, Edith Wharton, Theodore Dreiser, William Faulkner, Van Vorsts, Tillie Olsen, Sandra Cisneros, Edith Summers Kelly, Paule Marshall, Mary Doyle Curran, and Ann Petry.

611
Ottley, Roi. "Famous People." Review of *Harriet Tubman, Conductor on The Underground Railroad. Chicago Sunday Tribune*, Part 4, Section 2, 13, November 1955, 50.
  Offers quotes by Petry on why she wrote Harriet Tubman's biography. Calls the biography "superb . . . [and] starkly honest."

612
"Out of a Fog." *Newsweek* (17 August 1953): 94-95.
  Calls Petry's setting in *The Narrows* theatrical and her style "subdued lyricism." Considers Petry's subsidiary characters, with their "long memories and frozen poetry," to be the most interesting.

613
Page. Ernest R. "Black Literature and Changing Attitudes: Does It Do the Job?" *English Journal* 66.3 (March 1977): 29-33.
  Pulls from his dissertation to showcase the success of high school teachers who use African American literature as means "to change . . . negative attitudes towards blacks." Introduces "A Black Literature Package (BLP)" and includes one novel, seven short stories, eight poems, one play, and five portions of autobiographies. Petry's short story "In Darkness and Confusion" is included.

614
Page, James A. "Black Literature." *English Journal* 62.5 (May1973): 709-717.
  Writes that "[some] of the best novel-writing of the 1940s [is] done by two women." Cites Petry as one of the two for her *Country Place*.

615
_____. *Selected Black American Authors: An Illustrated Bio-Bibliography*. Boston: G. K. Hall, 1977.
  Petry is included.

616

"PBS News Hour - New York Times Book Club," Canvas, PBS News Hour Art Hub, January 1, 2020.

Announces the May 2020 pick for the PBS News Hour - New York Times Book Club, which is Petry's *The Street*. The book is chosen by Tayari Jones who has written an introduction to one of the newest re-issuances of the novel.

617

Pakditawan, Sirinya. *An Analysis of The Street by Ann Petry*. Verlag: GRIN, 2014.

Provides the contents of a Seminar Paper on Petry that is published by a German publisher. Includes analyses of the following: the novel's ending and Lutie's move to Chicago; Lutie's disillusionment in the second part of the novel; and the implications of the novel's ending.

618

Panish, Jon. *The Color of Jazz: Race and Representation in Postwar American Culture*. Jackson, MI: University Press of Mississippi, 1997.

Examines how Petry as well as Amira Baraka, Ralph Ellison, James Baldwin, John A. Williams, and Albert Murray use black expressive culture (i.e., jazz) from the community's collective and aesthetic tradition.

619

Panton, Rachel and Stephanie Y. Evans. " 'Sassin' Through Sadhana." 2.1 *Race and Yoga*, 2017.

Features personal narratives by black women who practice and/or teach yoga. Identifies almost 50 black women writers who mention yoga in their memoirs. Writer Ann Petry is included because she does yoga to recover from a back injury.

620

Pappy, Esther Walls. "Review of *Harriet Tubman, Conductor on the Underground Railroad*." *Saturday Review of Literature* (12 November 1955): 75.

Contends that the style in Harriet Tubman is "quiet and evocative." Briefly compares the work with other biographies on Tubman, calling all others "meager." Says Petry's summation of related historical events at the end of each chapter is an attractive feature.

621

Parascandola, L. J. "Review of *The Radical Fiction of Ann Petry by Keith Clark*." *Choice: Current Reviews for Academic Libraries*. 51.8 (April 2014): 1398-1399.

Praises Clark for his efforts to expand understanding and appreciation of Petry's entire oeuvre. Says most interesting is Clark's use of gothic critical theory to analyze Petry's lesser-known novel *Country Place* and several of her short stories. Recommends Clark's critical work as an invaluable study of Petry and African American literature.

622

Parham, Marisa. *Haunting and Displacement in African American Literature and Culture*. New York: Routledge, 2009.

Defines haunting as follows: a nameless anxiety that African Americans may experience; disturbing memories; and even social haunting. Suggests that African American people are often viscerally affected by the past and touched by the after-life of the past in the present. In Chapter Six, applies definitions of haunting in an analysis of nameless anxiety and disturbing memories that are experienced by male protagonists in both Richard Wright's *Native Son* and Petry's "Like a Winding Sheet."

623

Park, Stephen M. "Subjectivity in the American Protest Novel." *Modern Fiction Studies* 58.2 (Summer 2012): 403-406.

Provides a lengthy close reading of Kimberley S. Drake's *Subjectivity in the American Protest Novel* (Palgrave, 2011). Applauds Drake's success in surveying and reframing the history of the American protest novel; in presenting a new definition of protest - one that is rooted in the internal struggles of characters. Says Drake's scholarship redirects attention to the psychological landscape in protest fiction and how writers bridge public activism and individual subjecthood - i.e., to the internal struggles of characters. Gives adequate attention to Drake's examinations of protagonists in works by Richard Wright, Ann Petry, Tillie Olsen, Sarah E. Wright, and Chester Himes - protagonists who assert their subjecthood against otherwise repressive environments.

624

Park, You-me and Gayle Wald. "Native Daughters in the Promised Land: Gender, Race, and the Question of Separate Spheres." *American Literature*. 70.3 (September 1998): 607-633. Reprint. *No More Separate Spheres! A Next Wave American Studies Reader*. Edited by Cathy N. Davidson. Durham: Duke University Press, 2002.

Says minority literature represents the boundaries between public and private spheres in the United States; boundaries both reinforce and overlap class and gender.

625

Parray, Ashaq Hussain. "*The Narrows:* An Exposition of Petry's Racial Protest, Quest for Identity and Repercussions of Blind Adherence to American Dream." *Language in India*. 17.12 (2017): 61-75.

Reminds international readers that African American narratives expectantly explore the bruised consciousness of race. Says there are, however, fiction writers who are matchless in terms of their literary thrust and originality. Places Petry in this category for her novel, *The Narrows*. Reviews of the novel include: exceptional, superior, and original; a masterpiece; and an exceptionally heart rending interracial love affair of the 1950s. Also provides plot summaries and characterizations.

626

_____. "Ann Petry: A Victim of Canonical Representation." *International Journal of English and Education* 1.2 (October 2012): 249-254.

Promises to apprise readers of African American literary history and of the contributions of African American writers who delineate the impacts of racism, sexism, and classism in novels and short stories. Identifies Petry as one of the writers, but argues that Petry is a victim of canonical oversight, especially in light of writers Toni Morrison and Alice Walker.

627

Parson, Margaret. "Absorbing Story of Negro Section in N. E. Town." *Telegram*, 16 August 1953 [Special Collections, Boston University].

Reviews *The Narrows*. Finds Petry's "vivid and sensitive" portrayals of various characters more absorbing than the main plot. Along with a brief plot summary, concludes that the book is "strong in its ideas."

628

Patrick, Diane. "Black Literary Hall of Fame Founded." *Publisher's Weekly* (15 February 1999): 17.

    Announces The Literary Hall of Fame for Writers of African Descent, a national organization honoring distinguished black authors. Founded by Haki Madhubuti, numerous black publishers, and academicians at Chicago State University, the mission of the organization is to provide "black writers and their philosophies with proper acclaim." Each year two living and two deceased writers are inducted. Petry is among the first, posthumous honorees.

629

Peden, William H. "Of War and Peace and Other Matters." In *The American Short Story: Front Line in the National Defense of Literature*. Boston: Houghton Mifflin, 1964.

    Identifies Petry's "Miss Muriel" along with short stories by James Baldwin, Frank Yerby, and Paule Marshall as "really good recent stories by and about American Negroes."

630

_____."The Black Explosion." *Studies in Short Fiction* 12.3 (Summer 1975): 231-241.

    Surveys and then recommends collections of modern short stories by African American writers - from Langston Hughes to Henry Dumas. With explanations, recommends Petry's *Miss Muriel and Other Stories,* particularly "Miss Muriel," "The New Mirror," and "Mother Africa."

631

Penzler, Otto. *Black Noir: Mystery, Crime and Suspense Stories by African American Writers*. New York: Pegasus Books, 2009.

    Provides an introduction, followed by Petry's "On Saturday the Siren Sounds at Noon."

632

Perkins, Annie. "The Effects of Evil in Ann Petry's *The Street*: Invoking Biblical and Literary Traditions." In *The Critical Response to Ann Petry.* Edited by Hazel Arnett Ervin. Westport, CT: Praeger, 2005.

    Introduces less obvious themes in Petry's *The Street* which invoke biblical and literary traditions - evil with its deleterious and sinful effects on human nature, pride, lust, envy, and greed.

633

Perrin, T. " 'It Offers No Solutions': Ambivalence and Aesthetics in the Social Problems Novel." In *The Aesthetics of Middlebrow Fiction*. New York: Palgrave Macmillan, 2015.

    Argues that with the exception of Petry's *The Street,* the social problem novel has been dismissed as a middlebrow genre - a genre which insists on preaching a message, or a tone that is watered-down and ambivalent at best. Contends that the social problem novel's ambivalence is not as confusing as it is more precise. Encourages theory of social ambivalence, social powerlessness, and subversion.

634

Perry, Alison M. "Jay-Walking in the City: Violence Against Women, Urban Space, and Pedestrian Acts of Resistance." Ph.D. Diss., University of Texas at Austin, 2007.

    Concentrates on literary Harlem as a central public site; contextualizes Harlem's histories of abusive, domestic experiences, and characters/residents, especially the interventions and securities (or lack of securities) for Harlem's residents. Includes in the discussion: Ann Petry's *The Street*; Gloria Naylor's *The Women of Brewster Place*; Audre Lorde's *Zami: A New Spelling of My Name*; and Sapphire's *Push*.

635
Peterson, Rachel. "Invisible Hands at Work: Domestic Service and Meritocracy in Ann Petry's Novels." In Alex Lubin. *Revising the Blueprint: Ann Petry and the Literary Left.* Jackson, MI: University Press of Mississippi, 2007.
    Discusses how Petry uses women's labor and domestic services as ways to commit indictments of postwar racial, gender, and class politics.

636
_____. "Adapting Left Culture to the Cold War: Theodore Ward, Ann Petry and 'Correspondence.' " Ph.D. Diss., University of Michigan, 2008.
    Considers a variety of literary texts, published between 1945 and 1960, as politically left - i.e., engaging gender relations, civil rights, and the labor movements in the context of McCarthyism. Includes Petry because of her depictions of repressive injustices and marginalization of characters during the Cold War era.

637
Petry, Elisabeth. *At Home Inside: A Daughter's Tribute to Ann Petry.* Jackson, MI: University Press of Mississippi, 2008.
    Blends biography and memoir, and synthesizes Ann Petry's journals and family letters to provide a tribute to Petry's life. Also provides glimpses into Ann Petry's "complex humanity." See also *Can Anything Beat White? A Black Family's Letters*.

638
_____. *Can Anything Beat White? A Black Family's Letters.* Edited by Elizabeth Petry. Jackson: University Press of Mississippi, 2005.
    Uses over 400 family letters and other documents to portray the African American middle-class life of Ann Petry and her ancestors - starting from the 1890s.

639
_____. An Interview. "Liz Petry on Her Mother, Ann Petry: Private But Dedicated to Service - and Her Art." *Library of America Newsletter,* April 4, 2019.
    Using email, Petry's daughter answers questions about her mother's life and career.

640
_____. " 'Just Like Georgia Except for the Climate': Black Life at Mid-Century in Ann Petry's *The Narrows*." In *African American Connecticut Explored.* Edited by Elizabeth J. Norman. Middletown, CT: Wesleyan University Press, 2014.
    Explores New England settings in Ann Petry's *The Narrows* and *Country Place*.

641
Pettis, Joyce. "Reading Ann Petry's *The Narrows* into Black Literary Tradition." *Recovered Writers,*

Recovered Texts. Edited by Dolan Hubbard. Knoxville: University of Tennessee Press, 2005,100-120.

    Says Petry's *The Narrows* deserves re-evaluations within historical, cultural, and critical contexts. Discusses meticulously developed characters in the narrative.

642

Phillips, Kimberley L. "Keeping a Record of Life: Women and Art during World War II." *OAH Magazine of History* 19.2. Reprint. *Recent Directions in Gender and Women's History.* New York: Oxford University Press, March 2005, 20-24.

    Examines art forms used to challenge racial and ethnic prejudices portrayed in popular culture during the 1940s by singer, Kate Smith; writer, Ann Petry; and artist, Mime Okubo. Uses their texts 1) to expose the prejudices and barriers that minorities faced despite the wartime rhetoric about advancing democracy abroad; 2) to provide important glimpses into the inner lives of people of the 1940s who traditionally were presented through racist stereotypes; and 3) to agitate for fundamental change the status of women and minority groups as citizens. Petry's text is her short story, "In Darkness and Confusion."

643

Phillpotts-Brown, Kristina. "American Dreams/American Abjection: Systematic Oppression in F. Scott Fitzgerald, Ann Petry, and Marlon James." Senior Thesis, Princeton University, 2017.

    Cites a review of works by Fitzgerald, Petry, and Marlon James. Says a copy can be obtained as follows: http://arks.princeton.edu/ark:/88435/dsp01j6731636f

644

"Pile Them under the Tree." *Christian Century* (16 December 1970): 1516.

    Gives a one-sentence review of *Legends of the Saints*: It is "refreshing."

645

Pinconnat, Crystel. "Traduire La Puissance du Blanc. Du Gothique dans "Native Son" de Richard Wright et "The Street" d'Ann Petry." *Classiques Garner*, 2013.

    Requires translation. Includes two major protest novels by two major novelists for analysis: *Native Son* de Richard Wright and *The Street* d'Ann Petry. Illustrates continued international interest in Petry.

646

"Play Schools' Conference to Hear Ann Petry, Others." *New York Amsterdam News*, 4 April 1946, 24.

    Announces the appearance of Petry as guest speaker at the April 13, 1946 annual conference of the Play Schools Association, held at Hotel Pennsylvania. The theme for the speakers and for the discussion groups that follow is the same: "Building a World to Believe In - For All the Children All the Time."

647

Podcast (Apple): Grading the Nutmeg: The Podcast of Connecticut History. "Novelist Ann Petry and Exploring the Family Tree," 2020.

    Is Petry's daughter, Elisabeth, on the Podcast about the family's tree of four generations.

648

Poirier, Suzanne. "From Pharmacist to Novelist." In *Pharmacy in History*, 27-33. Madison, WI: American Institute of the History of Pharmacy, 1986.

    Classifies the role of the pharmacist in several of Petry's short stories and the novel, *Country Place*. Traces the development of one recurring theme that is relevant to Petry and to her characters who are pharmacists - and that is, "making distinctions between professional and private lives."

649

Pollock, Channing. "The Problem of Poverty." *Pictorial Review* (2 June 1946): 2:P.

    Cites a scene from *The Street* which Petry uses to indict society for the death of a jobless and starving black man. Cites facts and statistics to argue that poverty "is as old as civilization" and has yet to be solved using, perhaps, a redistribution of wealth.

650

Poore, Charles. "Books of the Times." *New York Times Book Review*, 7 February 1946, 21.

    Suggests that because of Petry's convincing scenes and characters, readers, regardless of race, "won't forget that Harlem street." Is convinced that because of the goodness of Lutie and Bub, their portrayals are superior to the other characters in the book.

651

Posten, Ted. "Cheers for Ann Petry - Good Job!" *New York Post,* 23 August 1953 [Petry Collection, Schomburg].

    Looks briefly at Petry's characters in *The Narrows*. Says above all, Petry's characters, who just happen to be black, have problems and concerns that are common to all people.

652

Pratt, Louis Hill. Review of *Ann Petry: A Bio-Bibliography* by Hazel Arnett Ervin. *CLA Journal* 38.2 (December 1994): 261-265.

    Concludes his review of the collection using the following quote taken from Alice Walker: "A people do not throw their geniuses away. And if they are thrown away it is our duty as artists and as witnesses for the future to collect them again for the sake of our children, and if necessary, bone by bone." Expresses contentment that Petry has now been added to the list of African American women writers "discovered" or "rediscovered" in bibliographical works.

653

Prescott, Orville. "Outstanding Novel." *Yale Review* 35 (Spring 1946):574-575.

    Says the problems experienced by African Americans "are illuminated through the characters and not the other way around" in Petry's Harlem. Calls the characters "significantly individualistic" with their own "savagely engrossing" stories. Believes Petry's success lies in part in her "brutal frankness."

654

Price, Emerson. "Tragedy in Harlem." *Cleveland Press*, 12 February 1946 [Special Collections, Boston University].

    Compares *The Street* to Richard Wright's *Native Son* and Chester Himes *If He Hollers Let Him*

Go. Says Petry's novel is "artistically superior." Also says that unlike "most women writers ... [Petry] skillfully interprets the profoundest of human emotions."

655

"Prospects: LeRoi Jones?" In *Native Sons*. Edited by Edward Margolies. Philadelphia: Lippincott, 1968.

    Mentions Petry favorably. Notes the importance of a writer such as Petry who includes in her works, "technical proficiency and a freshness of outlook."

656

Pryse, Marjorie. " 'Patterns against the Sky': Deism and Motherhood in Ann Petry's *The Street*." In *Conjuring: Black Women, Fiction, and Literary Tradition*. Edited by Marjorie Pryse and Hortense J. Spillers. Bloomington: Indiana University Press, 1985. Reprint. *The Critical Response to Ann Petry*. Edited by Hazel Arnett Ervin. Westport, CT: Praeger, 2005.

    Says Petry uses language in *The Street* that "evokes a deistic universe" where, within this universe, there are "laws" of the street, set in motion by white people. Contends, however, there are other forces which counter these laws - Lutie's Granny, Mrs. Hedges, and Prophet David. Concludes that Petry offers "its readers an alternative in the vision . . . its grandmothers, its folklore, and the survival of human feeling."

657

Purdy, Theodore M. "The Ghetto that is Harlem." *Saturday Review of Literature* (2 March 1964): 30.

    Thinks Petry "stacks the cards unfairly" against Lutie, particularly when Petry fails to show how "the street" changes and deforms the lives of the more seditious characters in the novel.

658

Puri, Usha. *Towards a New Womanhood: A Study of Black Women Writers*. Jaipur, India: Printwell, 1989.

    Includes critical interpretations of Petry's fiction that are being introduced to an international audience.

659

Raab, Angela R. "Mangled Bodies, Mangled Selves: Hurston, A. Walker, and Morrison." M. A. Thesis., Indiana University, 2008.

    Mentions Petry and her works in this study of African American women's literature, which is said to possess landscapes of women characters with broken bodies, missing limbs and teeth, paralyzed appendages, lost hair, and other deformities. Such motifs are studied simultaneously in works by Petry, Nella Larsen, Zora Neale Hurston, Dorothy West, Alice Walker, Toni Morrison, Pearl Cleage, and Octavia Butler. There are several questions that are meant to guide the study: When does the motif originate? Why does the motif persist? Does each author use the motif in the same way? What does the trail of broken bodies reveal about how African American women authors interpret the relationship between body and self?

660

Rabinowitz, Paula. "Domestic Labor: Film Noir, Proletarian Literature, and Black Women's Fiction." *Modern Fiction Studies* 47.1 (Spring 2001): 229-255.

    Adds Ann Petry and Gwendolyn Brooks to the study of "domestic labor" in film and literature. Says Petry in *The Street* and Gwendolyn Brooks in *Maud Martha* are concerned with new kinds of social relations forged during the Depression and World War II. Says each writer locates black women's labor within proletarian literary culture by linking domestic melodrama to female bildungsroman.

661
_____. "Pulping Ann Petry: The Case of *Country Place*." In *American Pulp: How Paperback Brought Modernism to Main Street*. Princeton, NJ: Princeton University Press, 2015.

Includes Petry's novel *Country Place* in the examination of the following: 1) the literary impact of pulp paperbacks between the late 1930s and early 1960s; and 2) how such writings democratized literature and ideas, spurred social mobility, and helped readers fashion new identities. Comparisons are made of the fiction that fits the latter categorizations, from James Cain to Petry, Sherwood Anderson, and Faulkner.

662
Rahming, M. B. "Phenomenology, Epistemology, Ontology, and Spirit: The Caribbean Perspective in Ann Petry's *Tituba of Salem Village*." *South Central Review* 20.2/4 (2003): 24-46.

Says Petry attempts to raise Tituba from the philosophical and cultural expendability to which her blackness and her slave status consigned her in the white, puritan community; from where blackness is associated with the devil. Applauds Petry for the "complexity" of Tituba's character - unmatched by any other Caribbean portrait of Tituba. Confirms as others: Petry's Tituba is "a more convincing and human character."

663
Ramadan, Wafa Darwish. "Ann Petry's *The Street*: A Novel of Race, Class, and Gender." M.A., Hebrew University, 1992.

Looks at the intersectionality of race, class, and gender in Petry's first novel.

664
Ramm, Hans-Christoph. "Modell fur eine literarische Amerikakunde: Zugange Zum modernen Schwarzamerikanischen Roman am Beispiel von Ann Petry's *The Street*, James Baldwin's *Go Tell It On The Mountain*, und Ralph Ellison's *Invisible Man*." Ph.D. Diss., Frankfurt (Main) University, 1988.

Confirms an international audience for major, modern authors such as Ann Petry, James Baldwin, and Ralph Ellison.

665
Randle, Kemeshia Laquita. "Revising the Concept of Black Female Sexuality in American Literature." Ph.D. Diss., The University of Alabama, 2014.

Evaluates literary and historical discourse that circumscribe black female sexuality. Says there is diminishing discussions of black female sexuality in the academy because of negative experiences of protagonists in works by major female writers within the canon. Calls for an evolution of feminism that is intergenerational and has an inter-media approach to utilizing popular fiction in the literary classroom. Suggests "Maverick feminism" as an alternative for evaluating historical and modern texts.

666
Rasberry, Gary Vaughn. "In the Twilight of Jim Crow: African American Literature, Totalitarianism, and the Cold War." Ph.D. Diss., University of Chicago, 2009.

Examines how literary productions by a variety of African American writers have collectively advanced critiques of totalitarianism and Cold War ideology through the lens of colonial and racial violence. Says such literary productions are by W. E. B. DuBois, Richard Wright, Gwendolyn Brooks, James Baldwin, and Ann Petry.

667

_____. "The 'Lost Years' or a 'Decade of Progress'?: African American Writers and the Second World War." *A Companion to the Harlem Renaissance*. New York: Wiley, 2015, 402-422.

Provides a chapter discussion of Ann Petry and her work under "Part V: Beyond Harlem: New Geographies and Lasting Influences." Clarifies the 1940s as a fertile but under-studied period.

668

Ravichandran, Sugannya, "Fiction as Negotiation Between Ideology and Literary Aesthetics: A Study of The Novels of Ann Petry." Ph.D. Diss., University of Madras, 2015.

Examines how Petry negotiates ideology and literary aesthetics in her three novels. Defines ideology and literary aesthetics, and then gives illustrations, using Petry's essay "The Novel as Social Criticism" and the positions of 'art for art's sake' by Charles Dickens, D. H. Lawrence, and Chinua Achebe. Helps to illustrate the growing international interest in Petry.

669

Raynor, Deirdre. " ' Ain't No Room for Us Anywhere': Reading Ann Petry's 'In Darkness and Confusion' as a Migration Narrative." In *Ann Petry's Short Fiction: Critical Essays*. Edited by Hazel Arnett Ervin and Hilary Holladay. Westport, CT: Praeger, 2004.

Reads "In Darkness and Confusion" as a migration narrative, citing also constructions of racial identity and the intersections of race, class, and gender.

670

_____. " Race Trumps All Other Identity Markers: Reading Ann Petry's *The Narrows* as an Anti-Lynching Text." In *The Critical Response to Ann Petry*. Edited by Hazel Arnett Ervin. Westport, CT: Praeger, 2005.

Provides an analytical frame for viewing and discussing Petry's *The Narrows* as an anti-lynching text. Referencing literary and sociological research, identifies perpetrators of lynching (e.g., white males, white females, the "big lie" myth, the media); illustrates how Petry expands on such perpetrators in her narrative.

671

Rayson, Ann. "Ann Petry." In *American Women Writers: A Critical Reference Guide from Colonial Times to the Present*. Edited by Langdon Lynne Faust. Vol 2, M to Z. New York: Frederick Ungar, 1983. First printed in 1979.

Agrees *The Street* is "gripping yet simplistic"; *Country Place* is Petry's "most successful novel"; and *The Narrows* is "simultaneously sophisticated and melodramatic." Believes, however, Petry's short stories succeed better than her novels.

672

Reckner, Judith Pendall. "The Men and Women of Two Black Novels." M.A., University of Wisconsin – Eau Claire, 1978.

Promotes an analytical focus on gender in African American fiction.

673

Redding, J. Saunders. Review of *The Narrows*. *Afro-American* (Baltimore) 12 September 1953, 2.

Compares *The Narrows* to Petry's first and second novels and concludes that the third novel shows "greater narrative skill" and "tighter, sounder thematic structure." Says all of Petry's literary works suggest that she has been working towards a "creative philosophy" and an "artistic creed" - realistic idealism - that is, she writes as if there are no fundamental differences between the races.

674

_____. "The Problem of the Negro Writer." *Massachusetts Review* (Autumn-Winter 1964): 57-70. Reprint. *Black and White in American Culture: An American Culture: An Anthology from the Massachusetts Review*. Edited by Jules Chametzky and Sidney Kaplan. Amherst: University of Massachusetts Press, 1969.

Concludes that the problem of dual commitment created by African American writers can be transcended "positively." For example, looks to Petry and Ralph Ellison "with a recognition of the fact that Negro behavior - character, sensation, thought - is dredged from the same deep mine of potentials which is the source of all human behavior."

675

Reich, Steven A. "The Great Migration and the Literary Imagination." *Journal of The Historical Society* 9.1 (2009): 87-128.

Defines historically, sociologically, artistically, environmentally and scientifically the literary imagination that supports writings of the Great Migration. Reveals that Petry and Wright pulled not only from their journalistic experiences but also from their research and investigations of The Chicago School of Sociology and their studies of environmentalists of the 1920s, 1930s, and 1940s.

676

Reid, E. Shelley. "Beyond Morrison and Walker: Looking Good and Looking Forward in Contemporary Black Women's Stories." *African American Review* 34.2 (2000): 313-328.

Surveys contributions made by women to a tradition of women's writings, beginning with Jessie Redmon Fauset, Zora Neale Hurston, Paula Marshall and Ann Petry; followed by Alice Walker and Toni Morrison; and continued by Bebe Moore Campbell, Terry McMillan, Sapphire, and A. J. Yerdella. Includes also with the latter, Susan Straight, a white, contemporary.

677

Reid, Margaret Walraven. Review of *Harriet Tubman, Conductor on the Underground Railroad*. *Library Journal* 80 (15 September 1955): 45.

Recommends, highly, this juvenile work. Calls it historical, objective, and superior, especially when compared to previous books on Harriet Tubman.

678

"Remember Salem?" *Old Saybrook Pictorial*, 28 January 1970, 30.

Repeats much about what influences Petry to write *Tituba of Salem Village*.

679

Review of *Country Place*. *New Yorker* (11 October 1947): 122.

Concludes that the novel's ending is plagued by a "couple of improbabilities." But also concludes that Petry has joined other novelists who write about the "bigotry, marital infidelity, and astounding malice" that exist in the American small town.

680

Review of *Country Place*. *Wisconsin Library Bulletin* 43 (November 1947): 154.

Provides a very brief review of *Country Place*. Offers plot summary and concludes that the novel is "completely different . . . from *The Street*."

681

Review of *Harriet Tubman, Conductor on the Underground Railroad*. *Best Sellers* 30 (1 February 1971): 482-483.

Announces under subtitle "History and Biography" that Harriet Tubman has been released in paperback. Calls the biography a "great story."

682

Review of *Harriet Tubman, Conductor on the Underground Railroad*. *Booklist* 52 (15 September 1955): 39.

Calls the biography a "lifelike and poignant portrait."

683

Review of *Harriet Tubman, Conductor on the Underground Railroad*. *Commonweal* 63 (18 November 1955): 182.

Concludes the biography has been written both "skillfully and warmingly."

684

Review of *Harriet Tubman, Conductor on the Underground Railroad*. *Grade Teacher* (September 1971): 158, 160.

Announces that the biography of Tubman is now in paperback. Calls the work "good news in Black history." Says that Petry's book is more in-depth compared to other biographies of Tubman.

685

Review of *Harriet Tubman, Conductor on the Underground Railroad*. *New Yorker* (26 November 1955): 216. [Also appears in some issues with different page number - p. 228].

Says Tubman's biographer - Ann Petry - provides an "evocative portrait."

686

Review of *Legends of the Saints*. *Horn Book Magazine* (December 1970): 611.

Criticizes Petry's writing style, calling it "flat." Is impressed, however, with the expressive illustrations and the scholarly research for *Legends of the Saints*.

687

Review of *Legends of the Saints*. *Kirkus* 38 (15 October 1970): 1137.

Says the book expresses "human integrity" and the greatness of the "traditional hero."

688

Review of *Legends of the Saints*. *Library Journal* 96 (15 January 1971): 44.

    Praises the book's form, calling it "familiar, significant, and pleasing."

689

Review of *Miss Muriel and Other Stories*. *Booklist* 68 (15 September 1971): 83.

    Finds the stories about the Layen family to be "fresh and poignant," but considers some of the other stories, especially those with ghetto settings, to be less than appealing.

690

Review of *Miss Muriel and Other Stories*. *Kirkus* 34.22 (1 June 1971): 587.

    Criticizes Petry's style in *Miss Muriel*, calling it "not quite up to rough-grained urban realities." Concludes, however, that overall the collection is "superb."

691

Review of *Miss Muriel and Other Stories*. *Library Journal* 96 (July 1971): 2348.

    Encourages librarians to display the collection. Calls it "evocative with descriptive writings."

692

Review of *Miss Muriel and Other Stories*. *Library Journal* (Special Section) 96 (November 1971): 3915.

    Emphasizes that while Petry's stories in this collection first appear in magazines from the 1940s, the stories "still have appeal for today's readers." Says Petry has a well-founded view of characters and their communities.

693

Review of *Miss Muriel and Other Stories*. *Publishers' Weekly* (July 1971): 66.

    Finds Petry's stories set in Harlem didactic, but overall "exquisitely" composed.

694

Review of *The Drugstore Cat*. *Booklist* 46 (15 November 1949): 105.

    Promises that the adventures in the book will entertain younger children.

695

Review of *The Drugstore Cat*. *New York Herald Tribune Book Review*, Section 7, November 1949, 13.

    Concludes that the book has a "fresh, sensitive and witty" style. Feels that the story about a cat that learns to "control" his temper provides a moral for its young readers.

696

Review of *The Drugstore Cat*. *Saturday Review of Literature* (12 November 1949): 32.

    Provides a brief summary of plot. Praises Petry's narrative and drawings by Susanne Suba.

697

Review of *The Narrows*. *American Literature* 60.4 (December 1988): 709.

Announces the reprint of *The Narrows.* Calls the new Introduction by Nellie McKay "convincingly appreciative" and capable of rekindling "interest" in the book.

698
Review of *The Narrows. Booklist* 50 (1 September 1953): 14.
Describes Link's murder as "shameful." Praises Petry for writing a clear story about "good, misguided, [and] genuinely vicious" characters who are without personal "condemnations."

699
Review of *The Narrows. Catholic World* 178 (December 1953):235.
Thinks the structure of *The Narrows* is "thesis-laden." Calls the climax "incredible."

700
Review of *The Narrows. New Statesman and Nation* (London), 14 August 1954 [Special Collections, Boston University].
Dislikes adamantly the use of flashback in *The Narrows.* Thinks Petry - a "first-rate story-teller" - does a disservice to herself with the flashback technique.

701
Review of *The Narrows. New Yorker* (August 29, 1953): 78.
Criticizes Petry's style and structure, particularly her many points of view; her "impossibilities" in characters; and her melodramatic ending. Concludes, however, Malcolm Powther is a "beautifully constructed character."

702
Review of *The Narrows. Star* (Washington, DC), 16 August 1953 [Special Collections, Boston University].
Calls Petry an "extremely gifted writer," who has the "eye and ear of the born novelist." Contends, however, that despite her "vibrant narrative," her "observation and humor," and her "richness of character" (e.g., Abbie Crunch, the Treadway butler, the newspaper editor, and Camilo), *The Narrows* has its shortcomings. There are interior monologues that are not in sync with the main dialogue, and there is an improbable romance that allows its lovers to cross the color line.

703
Review of *The Narrows. Wisconsin Library Bulletin* 49 (September- October 1953): 212.
Provides a brief summary of the plot.

704
Review of *The Street. Booklist* 43 (1 March 1946): 213-214.
Provides a very brief plot summary. Comments on Petry's "remarkable lack of bitterness."

705
Review of *The Street. Catholic World* 163 (May 1946): 187.
Calls *The Street* an extended short story. Predicts Petry's focus on sex and other vices will be objectionable to some African American readers.

706

Review of *The Street*. *Columbus Citizen*, 24 February 1946 [Special Collections, Boston University].

Refers to Petry as an exemplar of "Negro realists" who demands from her race "higher codes of ethics" - as one of the "first steps" towards a better life. Same review appears in *Washington Post*, February 17, 1946.

707

Review of *The Street*. *Negro Story* 2 (April-May 1946): 65.

Calls *The Street* an "unforgettable indictment of a system that creates and perpetuates ghettos for its most wretched minority group, the Negro." Concludes the novel is "a must" for those who have escaped "the street" or who are unacquainted with it. Criticizes the novel for not having at least two "decent strong characters."

708

Review of *The Street*. *New Yorker* (February 9, 1946): 98.

Declares the novel is "an oppressive but moving account" of Lutie Johnson's struggle to survive in Harlem and to retain her self-respect. Criticizes, however, Petry's "tendency to overwrite."

709

Review of *The Street*. *Washington Post*, 17 February 1946 [Special Collection, Brown University].

Refers to Petry as an exemplar of "Negro realists" who demands from the race "higher codes of ethics" - one of the "first steps" towards a better life.

710

Review of *The Street*. *Wisconsin Library Bulletin* 42 (April 1946): 60.

Provides a very brief plot summary. Calls the novel "well written . . . impressive and moving."

711

Review of *Tituba of Salem Village*. *Atlantic Monthly* (December1964): 163.

Calls Tituba "an absorbing story."

712

Review of *Tituba of Salem Village*. *Booklist* 69 (1 May 1972): 839.

Considers the work a "good historical narrative based on facts."

713

Review of *Tituba of Salem Village*. *Saturday Review of Literature* (7 November 1964): 55.

Calls the book the strongest and the best written about witchcraft for young readers. Acknowledges Petry's research for the book. Summarizes the plot.

714

Reynolds, Clarence V. "Ann Lane Petry" (A Tribute). *Black Issues Book Review* 4.4 (July/August 2002): 79-81.

Profiles Petry as author of three novels and several short stories. Says Petry's portrayals are "brave and truthful characters," confronting racism and struggling with personal failures and fears.

715
Reynolds, Guy. "Dysfunctional Realism: Ann Petry, Elizabeth Hardwick, Jean Stafford, Jane Bowles." *Twentieth-Century American Women's Fiction: A Critical Introduction*. New York: St. Martin's Press, 1999, 146-167.

    Provides history of idealization, denunciations, propaganda, political realism, and re-education surrounding traditional family and sex roles, home, and women's movement.

716
Rhone, Nedra. "Black History Month: Delve into History with a Book." *The Atlanta Journal - Constitution*, 1 February 2018, D.1.

    Announces re-issuance of Petry's award-winning biography, *Harriet Tubman: Conductor on the Underground Railroad* with updates, new foreword, and educational activities at the back of the book.

717
Rickman, Ray. "Ann Petry Revisited." *American Visions* (February 5, 1990): 56.

    Anticipates new readership for Petry's reprinted novels and short stories. Revisits Petry through her biography and select bibliography. Calls *The Street* a "forerunner" of works by Toni Morrison, Alice Walker, and Gloria Naylor.

718
Riethuis, Jochem. "Work, Race, and the Performance of Gender in Ann Petry's *The Street*." *Working Women in American Literature*. Edited by Miriam Gogal. Lanham, MD: Lexington Books, 2018.109-120.

    Focuses on how American working women have been presented, represented, misrepresented, and underrepresented in naturalistic and realists fiction. Insists that despite prejudices and stereotypes regarding working women from post-Civil War era to the first half of the twentieth century, there is much to be learned from literature with working-class women. Says Petry's *The Street* adds to the discussions.

719
Riis, Roger William. "A Story of 'Hemmed In' Lives." *Opportunity: Journal of Negro Life* 24.3 (July-September 1946): 157.

    Questions "poetic distribution . . . poetic justice" in *The Street*, particularly when one unsuspecting character commits suicide on Christmas morning and when the "half-way decent characters" end up "in jail or in flight" while wicked characters are left "flourishing."

720
Roberts, Margaret Olivia. "Writing to Liberate: Selected Black Women Novelists from 1859 to 1982." Ph.D. Diss., University of Maryland, 1987.

    Contends that "in the nearly one hundred years between Iola Leroy and *The Color Purple*, the nature and kinds of oppression are described "more graphically and the women suffer more intensely in the later works." When exploring reasons for contradictions, particularly since history proves the 1890s were more restrictive and oppressive years for black women than the present, Roberts seeks answers by examining seven African American novelists who wrote between *Iola Leroy* and *The Color Purple*. Petry's *The Street* is included.

721

Roberts, Nora Ruth. "Artistic Discourse in Three Short Stories by Ann Petry." *Women & Language* 22.1 (Spring 1999): 29-36. Reprint. *Ann Petry's Short Fiction: Critical Essays*. Edited by Hazel Arnett Ervin and Hilary Holladay. Westport, CT: Praeger, 2004.

    Predicts future readings of Petry will be in the context of a multi-cultural community. To support her position, examines the fusion of art and experience in Petry's short stories "Mother Africa," "Olaf and His Girlfriend," and "Solo on the Drums."

722

Robinson, Ted. "Reviews of the Latest Books, with Sidelights on Authors." *Cleveland Plain Dealer*, 24 February 1946, 14.

    Warns the reader that there is "no palliating beauty . . . no optimistic philosophy, no relieving humor" in *The Street*. Says there are instead conditions which "constitute national scandal."

723

Robinson, William H. *Black New England Letters: The Uses of Writings In Black New England*. Boston: Trustees of the Public Library of the City of Boston, 1977.

    Includes lectures on black New England writings. Supported by the National Endowment for the Humanities and the Boston Public Library.

724

Rogers, W. G. "Ann Petry's New Novel Disappointing." *New York Post*, 27 September 1947 [Special Collections, Boston University].

    Disapproves of "unconvincing characters" in *Country Place* and the lack of "great passion" found in *The Street*.

725

Rosado, Treza. "*The Street*: An Adaptation of the Novel by Ann Petry." Antonian Scholars Honors Program, School of Humanities, Arts and Sciences, St, Catherine University, 2011.

    Focuses on the playwright's adaptation of Petry's novel *The Street*.
https://sophia.stkate.edu/shas_honors/3

726

Rose, Mary. "Depth and Dignity, Pathos and Humor." *New York Herald Tribune Book Review*, 16 August 1953, 3.

    Summarizes the plot in *The Narrows*. Calls the work "powerfully imaginative and deeply insightful." Insists the book is neither an "apologia for the Negro nor . . . an indictment of the white race."

727

Roses, Lorraine Elena and Ruth Elizabeth Randolph, eds. "Ann Petry." *Harlem Renaissance and Beyond*. Boston: G. K. Hall, 1990, 258-264.

    Provides literary biographies for 100 women. Includes Petry.

728

Rosenblatt, Paul C. *The Impact of Racism on African American Families: Literature as Social Science*. Burlington, VT: Ashgate, 2014.

Examines in Chapter 4 of the work the various ways in which novelists Ann Petry, James Baldwin, and Toni Morrison enhance understanding of the effects of racism on African American families, and how racism has influenced relationship commitments.

729

Rosenblatt, Roger. "White Outside." In *Black Fiction*. Cambridge: Harvard University Press, 1974.

Contends that unlike most white writers, black writers have taken care "not to reduce [their] white characters to stereotypes." Rather, "there . . . emerges within black fiction a consistent picture of white America." Says Petry's characters in *Country Place* serve as examples.

730

Rottenberg, Catherine, ed. *Black Harlem and the Jewish Lower East Side: Narratives Out of Time*. Albany: State University of NewYork Press, 2013.

Provides a collection of essays that are concerned with the two famous and well-researched New York City neighborhoods. Essays in the collection are by and about African Americans and Jewish Americans. Both anchor identity formations of the two communities; identify community-informed literature; and recommend materials for broader comparative studies. Treatments of Petry's novels are included.

731

Royster, Beatrice Horn. "The Ironic Vision of Four Black Women Novelists: A Study of the Novels of Jessie Fauset, Nella Larsen, Zora Neale Hurston, and Ann Petry." Ph.D. Diss., Emory University,1975.

Says Jessie Fauset, Nella Larsen, Zora Neale Hurston, and Ann Petry write from "a black perspective, a female perspective, and a world perspective." Reacting differently to their worlds, the writers are said "to display a range of unmistakable qualities of irony."

732

Rozzelle, Sarah Cathleen. "Exploring the Connections Between Family and Work: Texts by Black Women Writers in Pre-Civil Rights America." M.A., Wichita State University, 2005.

Registers through research Petry's interest in family and work.

733

Rubin, Rachel and James Smethurst. "Ann Petry's 'New Mirror'." In *Revising the Blueprint: Ann Petry and the Literary Left*. Edited by Alex Lubin. Jackson, MI: University Press of Mississippi, 2007.

Suggests Petry's short stories should be reappraised as important bridges between the "Old Left" of the 1930s, 1940s, 1950s and the Black Arts Movement. Suggests the question of race in Petry's work is both a class question and a national question. Offers other queries of representation and self-presentation.

734

Rudisel, Christine and Robert Blaisdell. *Great Short Stories by African-American Writers*. Mineola, NY:

Dover Publication, Inc., 2015.

Offers diverse perspectives of the African American experience, using thirty (30) influential authors and their outstanding short stories.

735

Ruffin, Carolyn F. "In All Shades of Black." *Christian Science Monitor*, 19 August 1971, 10.

Praises Petry for her objectivity, diversity, and lack of didacticism in her short stories found in *Miss Muriel and Other Stories*.

736

Russell, Emily S. "Embodied Citizenship: Disability in National Imagination." Ph.D. Diss., University of California, Los Angeles, 2007.

Draws from diverse texts of American literature to explore body politic as metaphor; to demonstrate that physical difference is an enduring problem of twentieth century American culture. Includes Petry's *The Street* in the discussions.

737

Russo, Maria. "*The Street*" by Ann Petry (paperback). *New York Times Book Review*, 12 January 2020, 2.

Relies on other critics to confirm that Petry has had her hand on the pulse of the community and that her "kind of talent will always feel startling and sui generis."

738

Sacks, Sam. "Petry's Novels '*The Street*' and '*The Narrows*' are Masterpieces of Social Realism - Volatile but Exacting, Heartbreaking but Often Brutally Funny." *The Wall Street Journal* (online), 22 February 2019.

Illustrates close readings of Petry's novels, providing detailed and critical discussions of plot, characters, motifs, and themes. Theorizes about new approaches to Petry's novels.

739

Sackschewsky, Leisl, "Orientations in Time: Music and the Construction of Historical Narrative in 20th- and 21st - Century African-American Literature." Ph.D. Diss., University of Washington, 2016.

Argues that the intersections between African American literature and music have been influential in the development of hip-hop aesthetics. Explores the role of hip-hop aesthetics - e.g., to animate, write, rewrite, rupture or reclaim the past for the present; to disrupt the linear narratives of progress; or to draw the past into immediate conversations with the present. Among the present texts that are included in the study are Petry's "Solo on the Drums"; Langston Hughes' *The Weary Blues*; Richard Wright's *12 Million Black Voices*; Toni Morrison's *Jazz* ; and Colson Whitehead's *Sag Harbor*.

740

Sanders, Tammy L. "The Long Tradition: Black Women and Mothers in Public Discourses." Ph.D. Diss., University of Maryland, 2009.

Investigates the ideals of black domesticity and moral motherhood via the rhetoric of scholars; public discourse involving social sciences, films, and novels; and popular images of black mothers. Includes examinations of black domesticity and moral motherhood, based on Moynihan Report; Petry's *The Street;* and Lorraine Hansberry's *A Raisin in the Sun*.

741

Sapphire and Sharifa Rhodes-Pitts. "Thalia Book Club: *The Street* by Ann Petry." Audible Audiobook – Original Recording, July 31, 2013.

        Documents an audio reading of Petry's *The Street* by the two contemporary authors.

742

Schlichenmeyer, Terri. "Harlem Nocturne." *New Pittsburgh Courier,* October 2013, B6.

        Provides an informative and persuasive review of "Harlem Nocturne" - Farah Jasmine Griffin's narrative on three women who use their talent to change society: choreographer and dancer, Pearl Primus; novelist, Ann Petry; and composer and pianist, Mary Lou Williams. Says the objections are minor. Encouragingly says that in addition to an academic audience, the book will attract music fans, political historians, and women interested in the roots of social justice.

743

Schmidt, Tyler T. *Desegregating Desire: Race and Sexuality in Cold War American Literature.* Jackson, MI: University Press of Mississippi, 2013.

        Studies the interdependence of race and sexuality in American literature from 1945 to 1955 to understand and to articulate better desegregated places and emergent identities in America in the aftermath of World War II. Looks at strategies used by eight (8) poets and novelists who help to discuss desegregated places and emergent identities. Petry who published her novels in the 1940s and 1950s is included.

744

_____. "Dreams of an Impossible Blackness: Racialized Desire and America's Integrationist Impulse, 1945-1955." Ph.D. Diss., The City University of New York, 2008.

        Interrogates the concept of integration by exploring the subtle shifts in social understandings of race and sexuality found in poems, letters, and novels in American literature and African American literature of the late 1940s and early 1950s. The following emerge: interracial desire, queer desire, non-normative sexualities, and re-imaging identities of whiteness. Petry who published her novels in the 1940s and 1950s is included.

745

_____. "White Pervert: Tracing Integration's Queer Desires in African American Novels of the 1950s." *Women's Studies Quarterly* 35.1-2 (2007): 149-171. Reprint. *Desegregating Desire: Race and Sexuality in Cold War American Literature*. Jackson, MI: University Press of Mississippi, 2013.

        Traces African American interest in post-World War II understandings of interracial sex, gender identities, homosexuality, racial deviance, and the responses of African Americans in black press, films, journals, and literature. Petry who is a journalist with New York's *Amsterdam News* and authors *The Narrows* in the 1950s is included.

746

Schneck, Peter. "Reflection of Race and Law in African American Literature." *A.S. Journal* (51), 2008. https://www.asjournal.org/51-2008/race-and-law-in-african-american-literature.

        Offers very useful comparisons of legal perspectives of protagonists in Charles Chesnutt's "The Webs of Circumstances" and Ann Petry's "The Witness." Says the effectiveness of Chesnutt and of Petry is enhanced by their understandings of their references to the law, concepts and rituals. In sketches of

Chesnutt's and Petry's works, the famous lawyer features reflections of law and race in African American culture and literature.

747
"Schomburg Center for Research in Black Culture: Archives of Angelou, Petry, Collins, Hadley Jeannette Available for Research." *Targeted News Service* (Washington, DC), 4 February 2020.

    Announces Ann Petry archives (professional, social, and family life) to be located at the Schomburg Center for Research in Black Culture, Manuscripts, Archives and Rare Books Division within The New York Public Library: Journals and Diaries, 1920 - 2006; Correspondence, 1920 - 2006; and Manuscripts, 1939-1987 (note: unpublished manuscripts include two incomplete drafts of the short stories "Checkup" and "The Wayfarer" as well as drafts of poetry); Clippings and Printed Matter, 1922 - 2012; and Artifacts and Memorabilia, circa 1980s, 1990s.

748
Schraufnagel, Noel. "The Protest Tradition in the Forties." In *The Black American Novel*. Deland, Fl: Everett/Edwards, 1972.

    Criticizes Petry's ending in *The Street,* citing psychological nuances that would dictate an alternate ending. Calls Lutie a metaphysical rebel who is fallible, and who destroys the black matriarch myth. Compares Petry's novel with other literary works that illustrate the "effects of environment and oppression on an individual."

    Calls *Country Place* an assimilationist novel, which, like *The Street*, places its characters against the hostile environment.

    Sees *The Narrows* as a combination of Petry's first two novels - that is, she reflects the effects of racism and analyzes the human condition. Summarizes plots.

749
Scott, Traci L. "Revising Maternal Myths: Reading Mothers and Violence in Contemporary Women's Narrative." M.A., University of Vermont, 1998.

    Registers academic interest in revising maternal myths that are included in Petry's literature.

750
Scott, William. "Material Resistance and the Agency of the Body in Ann Petry's *The Street*." *American Literature* 78.1 (2006): 89-116.

    Says the failures of Petry's protagonist as a black woman who attempts to resist economic forces and social categorization can be attributed to the ultimate production of modern bio-political powers.

751
Seets, Myrtle Nance. "The Maturation of the Negro Novelist as Revealed in the Novels of Richard Wright, Ann Petry, Chester Himes, and Frank Yerby." M.A., Fisk University, 1949.

    Provides one of few early analyses and evaluations of *The Street* and *Country Place*, particularly on characters and plots.

752

Sehgal, Parul. "Two Novels by Ann Petry, a Writer Who Believed in Art That Delivers a Message." *International New York Times*, 22 April 2019.

    Announces to an international audience the reissuance of Petry's *The Street* and *The Narrows* and the inclusion of literary criticism. Offers observations of Petry as an artist: Says she is a creator of unabashed protest art which endows the fullness of each character; says she has an unerring sense of psychology, and the illumination of clarity, strength/artistry - evidenced in the music of her sentences.

753

_____. "May's Book Club Pick: Two Novels by Ann Petry, a Writer Who Believed in Art That Delivers a Message." *New York Times* (online), 16 April 2019.

    Announces the existence of an online Book Club and its pick for the reading group in May of 2019: The combined collection of Petry's novels *The Street*, *The Narrows*, and the select criticism of the writer.

754

Seidman, Barbara Kitt. *The Narrows*. *Magill's Survey of American Literature*. Revised edition. September, 2006, 1-2.

    Offers critical summations of elements of the novel, *The Narrows*.

755

Sen, Nandana. " ' The Language that Keeps Breaking in my Hands': Power and Self-Representation in Ann Petry's *The Street*." A.B. Honor's in English and American Literature and Language, Harvard University, 1991.

    Registers a critical study of Petry's *The Street*, so to fulfill requirements for the undergraduate Honor's Program.

756

Shachter, Jacqueline. "Writing Resources: Videotaped Authors Advise Student Writers." *The English Journal* 69.3 (March 1980): 85-86.

    Videotapes Petry who can be found commenting on her writing methods as follows: "Usually I begin with people, because they make the plot, and the plot should really stem from the kind of people they are. I have to know how the story is going to end before I start, because then the whole thing builds to the ending." Also, "Research carefully before writing."

757

Shea, J. Vernon. *Strange Barriers*. New York: Pyramid Books, 1961.

    Includes analysis of seventeen (17) short stories of the twentieth century. Includes Petry's "The Necessary Knocking at the Door."

758

Sherrard-Johnson, Cherene. "City Place/Country Place: Negotiating Class Geographies in Ann Petry's Writings." In *Black Harlem and the Jewish Lower East Side: Narratives Out of Time*. Edited by Catherine

Rottenberg. Albany, NY: State University of New York Press, 2013.

    Draws attention to Petry's use of representation in *The Street* and *Country Place*, particularly Petry's representations of place, race, and class. Also draws attention to Petry's intersectionality of place, race, and class in these novels. Suggests to critics a different critical approach to Petry: "placing Petry's 'black novel' in conversation with her 'white novel.' " Thinks that such an approach would "explode simplified racialized categorizations of Petry's writing."

759

Shinn, Thelma J. "Women in the Novels of Ann Petry." *Critique, Studies in Modern Fiction* 16.1 (1974): 110-120. Reprint. *The Critical Response to Ann Petry*. Edited by Hazel Arnett Ervin. Westport, CT: Praeger, 2005.

    Argues that in *The Street*, *Country Place*, and *The Narrows*, " Petry shows . . . the sordidness of reality, the inequities and false illusions of society, and the inadequacies of the possibilities for women [black and white] . . . for personal development . . . ."

760

Shockley, Ann. *Living Black American Authors: A Biographical Directory*. New York: Bowker, 1973.

    Includes Petry.

761

Shockley, Evelyn Elayne. "The Tyranny of Domesticity: Identity and the Gothic in British Victorian and Twentieth-Century African American Literature." Ph.D. Diss., Duke University, 2002.

    Promotes a comparative analysis of domesticity ideology and gothic conventions in select British Victorian and twentieth-century African American literary works. Uncovers a variety of tropes, figures, and plot devices in the select literary works, which then are used to center the study of identity (particularly race, class, gender, sexuality, and nationality) in modern society. Includes Petry.

762

Shockley, Evie. "Buried Alive: Gothic Homelessness, Black Women's Sexuality, and (Living) Death in Ann Petry's 'The Street'." *African American Review* 40.3 (Fall 2006): 439-460.

    Recognizes the centrality of Petry's engagement with gothic conventions in *The Street*, and her use of language, tropes and metaphorical figures to communicate heroine Lutie Johnson's fight to control her body and her right to sexual self-determination.

763

Showalter, Elaine. "Women and the Literary Curriculum." *College English* 32.8 (May 1971): 855-866.

    Illustrates how women in the academy are estranged from their own experiences because of male-oriented reading lists being generated in general college literature classes. Provides as an alternative a "Syllabus for English 235: The Women Writer in the 20th Century." Under black women writers, includes Petry for T*he Street.*

764

Si, Stephanie. "White and Narrative Authority in Ann Petry's *Country Place*." *Playing in the White: Black*

Writers, White Subjects. New York: Oxford University Press, 2015.

Provides an insightful and engaging introduction that promotes close readings of African American fiction about white life. Seeks to avoid the familiar "kind of excuse-making analysis" or the treatment of whiteness as a polarizing term - either "as a simplistic manifestation of evil or as a racially transcendent point of sympathy." Invokes Robert Fikes' position regarding African American writers on white life (see elsewhere in this book).

765

_____. " The Presumption of Whiteness in Ann Petry's *Country Place*." In *Narrative, Race and Ethnicity in the United States*. Edited by James J. Donohue, Jennifer Amitto, and Shaun Morgan. Columbus: The Ohio State University Press, 2007.

Includes Petry in studies of critical intersections of narrative theory and race/ethnicity theory.

766

Sibara, Jay. "Disability and Dissent in Ann Petry's *The Street*." *Literature and Medicine* 36.1 (Spring 2018): 1-26.

Illustrates in *The Street* how Petry portrays chronic illness, disfigurement and disability as embodied effects of racism, resulting from labor exploitation, crowded and unsafe housing conditions, and lack of access to nourishing foods and effective health care. Insists Petry challenges Western medical institutions, Western medicine (as practiced in the United States), medical professionals, law enforcement officials and their institutions, and others, as she calls for a recognition of the embodied effects of racism.

767

Sibara, Jennifer Claire Barager. "Imperial Injuries: Race, Disease, and Disability in North American Narratives of Resistance 1908-2006." Ph.D. Diss., University of Southern California - Los Angeles, 2013.

Seeks to chart a new direction for disability studies. Provides directions by identifying "narratives of resistance" by novelists and journalists - e.g., Sui Sin Far; Ann Petry (*The Street*); and Vicky Funaria and Sergio de la Torr (the documentary "Maquilapolis").

768

Sielke, Sabine. "Fighting 'forced relationship': Rape and Manslaughter in Ann Petry's *The Street*." In *Reading Rape: The Rhetoric of Sexual Violence in American Literature and Culture*, 1790-1990. Princeton, NJ: Princeton University Press, 2002.

Promotes comparative readings of modernist representations of rape in fiction. Allows Petry's rhetorical approach to representing rape in her fiction to be studied against the approaches taken by William Faulkner, Richard Wright, and Djuna Barnes. Suggests Petry emerges, challenging modernist critics' aesthetician of the female body.

769

Sillen, Samuel. "Ann Petry's 'Country Place' - Novel of Small-Town Life." *Daily Worker*, 8 October 1947, 11.

Focuses primarily on summary of plot, characterization, and point of view in *Country Place*, calling the former melodramatic and the latter confusing. Considers all of Petry's characters static, with the exception being Johnnie Roane.

770
Silva, Liana M. "Acts of Home-Making: Home and Urban Space in Twentieth-Century African American and Puerto Rican Cultural Productions." Ph.D. Diss., SUNY Binghamton, 2012.

    Argues that through "acts of homemaking" in cultural productions, African American and Puerto Rican artists strive to make New York City "a home space" where they can express a sense of humanity, community and citizenry. Underscores yearnings to make New York City a home - a trend that intersects the experiences of minorities in U.S. cities.

771
Silverman, Fran. "Writer Praised for Courage, Determination." *Hartford Courant*, 15 November 1992.

    Summarizes Gloria Naylor's speech at a special, daylong conference to honor Ann Petry at Trinity which is co-sponsored by Trinity and the Connecticut Humanities Council. Excerpts of Petry's work is later heard on Connecticut Public Radio during "Connecticut Voice." Naylor, who insists that "you must honor those who have gone before," lauds Petry for giving a generation of black American women an identity and black American women writers a voice. The article is filled with other accolades for Petry and *The Street*.

772
Simoneau, Elizabeth. "Subjugated Citizenship: The Politics and Psychology of Domesticity in 'The Street' by Ann Petry, 'The Dollmaker' by Harriet Arnow, and 'The Changelings' by Jo Sinclair." Ph.D. Diss., Emory University, 2011.

    Raises several questions about Ann Petry's *The Street*; Harriet Arnow's *The Dollmaker*; and Jo Sinclair's *The Changelings* - including the following: 1) Do the novels offer any insights into the politics of American citizenship? 2) Do they illuminate or challenge conventional knowledge regarding the political contexts of the 1940s and 1950s? 3) Can contemporary political analysis - particularly those concerned with autonomy, individualism, and liberalism - be useful in interpreting mid-century literary texts?

773
Sims-Wood, Janet. "African-American Women Writers: A Selected Listing of Master's Theses and Doctoral Dissertations." *Sage* 2.1 (Spring 1985): 69.

    Offers a listing of general and collected works (master's theses and doctoral dissertations) that emerge during a period in literary history when academic critics collectively and analytically define the black women writer's literary tradition. Petry is a subject in this literary tradition.

774
Skeeter, Sharyn J. "Black Women Writers: Levels of Identity." *Essence* (May 1973): 58-59, 76, 89.

    Chronicles a literary tradition and what Black women have written about themselves. Includes Petry's three novels and singles out *The Street* for its themes of marriage and motherhood; *Country Place* for its interpersonal relationships; and *The Narrows* for its ambition.

775
Smith, Alexander V. "Writing the Street: Discourses of Choice, Agency, and Mobility in Twentieth Century

Street Literature." Ph.D. Diss., University of Washington, 2019.

Rejects the general notion that "the street" in Petry's *The Street* is mere physical and material space in literature. Points to a group of diverse and multi-ethnic writers who center "the street" in their literature to challenge familiar rationalizations of physical and material spaces. When such literature is aligned, "the street" is introduced as a space that subverts, evades, and contests.

776

Smith, Barbara. "A Familiar Street." *Belles Lettres* (January/February 1987): 4

Acknowledges the reprint of *The Street* with praise, calling it a "classic if only because of its vivid descriptions, strong characterizations, and involving plot." Concludes that Petry inspires readers to question the system that hinders Lutie from succeeding. As a reviewer/reader, Smith ends with similar hope found in the novel - hope for political changes.

777

_____. "Doing Research on Black American Women." *Women Studies Newsletter* 4 (Spring 1976): 4-7.

Provides ideas for doing research on black women writers. In addition, suggests thematic approaches to reading fiction by black women writers. Includes Petry's *The Street* under the following thematic approaches: "Independent Black Women"; "Black Women and Black Men"; and "Black Women Working."

778

_____. "Toward a Black Feminist Criticism." *Conditions: Two* 1. 2 (October 1977): 25-42. Reprint. *All the Women Are White, All the Blacks Are Men, But Some of Us Are Brave*. Edited by Gloria T. Hull, Patricia Bell Scott, and Barbara Smith. New York: The Feminist Press, 1982.

Contends that there is a need for black feminist criticism. Cites examples of how male critics have misunderstood or misrepresented Petry's *The Street* due to the lack of established black feminist critical perspectives.

779

Smith, Beverly A. "Ann Petry's "In Darkness and Confusion" and the Harlem Riot of 1943: Fictional Insights into the Causes and Nature of Collective Violence." *Women and Criminal Justice* (London, UK) 12 (2001): 1-20. Reprint. *Violence & Abuse Abstracts* 8.1(2002): 3-84.

Says Petry's short story "In Darkness and Confusion" provides a fictional portrayal of the causes and the nature of the Harlem Riot of 1943. Substantiates Petry's authority on writing about the Harlem riot: Hence, she works as a journalist during World War II and captures the frustrations and grievances felt by residents toward the police, city officials, and segregated military. Compares Petry as a journalist and as a writer of fiction with those of historians and sociologists who studied both the 1943 Harlem Riot and the more deadly and destructive riots of the 1960s and beyond.

780

Smith, Bradford. "Glandular Imbalance." *Saturday Review of Literature* (18 October 1947): 17-21.

Reviews *Country Place*. Finds much fault with the novel: Says the "good" characters are "shadowy"; says the "bad" characters, beyond their lust or greed, "lack motivation or background."

Concludes that often both "good" and "bad" characters are "at the mercy of their glands" and "cannot develop or change"; thus, the characters provide no basis for sympathy or emotional engagement from the reader. Says Petry's overall design of the novel is contrived and melodramatic.

781

Smith, Eleanor Touhey. Review of *The Narrows*. *Library Journal* 78 (July 1953): 1232.

Says Petry's thesis which proclaims cultural equality cannot alone erase "race" prejudices in America. Calls her plot and characterizations "absorbing."

782

Smith, Harrison. "Writers Are Unhappy." *Saturday Review of Literature* (20 December 1946):16.

Reviews Martha Foley's *The Best American Short Stories*, and includes a brief review of Petry's "Like a Winding Sheet" - a short story that is included in Foley's collection. Calls Petry's story "most forceful and memorable" but "funereally titled."

783

Smith, John Caswell, Jr. Review of *Country Place*. *Atlantic Monthly* 180 (November 1947): 178, 182.

Gives a plot summary of the novel, emphasizing how the hurricane in the story "whip[s] up the story's "onset, climax, and departure." Contrary to most critics, thinks Johnnie is "not filled out to real-life believable proportions." In congruence with other critics, however, finds the narration by the druggist to be a distracting technique.

784

_____. Review of *The Street*. *Atlantic Monthly* 117 (April 1946): 172.

Reiterates Petry's account of the "instability of the Negro family" in the urban North in the 1940s. Says characters are only partially fictional, particularly because studies by sociologists confirm that black fathers cannot get adequate work and that black mothers, trying to keep the family intact, enter the most available work outside of the home - domestic.

785

"So, Hard Work and Virtue Guarantee Success? Dream On." *New York Times* (online), 4 April 2007.

Announces the PBS series, American Masters, which presents seven novels by writers from Theodore Dreiser and Ann Petry to Saul Bellow who expound on this title.

786

Solomon, Asale Najuma. "Dark Maternal Specters in Twentieth Century African American Literature." Ph.D. Diss., University of California-Berkeley, 2002.

Questions why the black maternal body has become the representative cause of racial misery, provoking both repulsion and longing in novels by African American writers Chester Himes, Richard Wright, Ann Petry, Gayl Jones, and Toni Morrison? Applies, among others, psychoanalysis approaches, gothic conventions, and black masculinist protest to arrive at responses.

787

Solomon, Irvin D. and Marty Ambrose. "Race and Gender Conflict in Ann Petry's *The Street*: Lessons in

Symbolic Interaction from the Middle Period of Black Literature." *McNeese Review* 37 (1999): 1-13.

Anticipates criticism and paves the way for critiques which look closely at interactions of race and gender in black female experiences in Petry's *The Street*.

788
Sorett, Josef. *Spirit in the Dark: A Religious History of Racial Aesthetics*. New York: Oxford University Press, 2016.

Gives an overview of key black writers (novelists, poets, playwrights, and preachers) from 1920s to 1960s whose conversations and interactions help to interlock histories of religion, secularism, and spirituality in the study of racial aesthetics and which help to shape decades of African American intellectual discourse. In Chapter 4: "As the Spirit Moves," cites the competing norms at play in works by major African American novelists and playwrights of 1940s and 1950s. Petry is included.

789
Sorgenti, A. "La letteratura della working-class afroamericana:paradigmi di lavoro in Chester Himes, Ann Petry, Alice Walker, and Octavia Butler." Ph.D. Diss., Universita Di Pisa, 2018.

Examines literature by Petry and others on the working-class in America. Registers continued international interest in Petry and her works.

790
Southgate, Robert I. *Black Plots and Black Characters: A Handbook for Afro-American Literature*. Syracuse, NY: Gaylord Professional Publications, 1979.

Provides a summation and analysis of the plot in *The Street*. Is also briefly bibliographical.

791
Sowinska, Suzanne. "American Women Writers and The Radical Agenda, 1925-1940." Ph.D. Diss., University of Washington, 1992.

Studies well-known and neglected writers of the 1940s as agents of the social transformation of regressive race, class, ethnic, and gender discourses operating in the 1940s. Demonstrates how debates by social realists (writers and theorists) on the "Negro Question" and the "Woman's Question" of the 1930s and 1940s create a new aesthetic sensibility. Identifies Petry as an African American woman writer who interjects "blackness," "women," and "class" into a radical discourse.

792
Sparrow, Lamont. "Displacement of Gender Identities in Alice Walker's *The Color Purple*, Ann Petry's *The Street*, and Zora Neale Hurston's *Their Eyes Were Watching God*." M.A., Fayetteville State University, 2008.

Registers interest in Petry's focus on gender identities.

793
Spencer, Nicholas. *After Utopia: The Rise of Critical Space in Twentieth-Century American Fiction*. Lincoln: University of Nebraska Press, 2006.

Is said to offer valuable insights into Ann Petry's ancestry and her important contributions to American realism.

794

Spilka, Mark. "Ann Petry's Determinist Dilemma: 'Like a Winding Sheet.'" *Eight Lessons in Love: A Domestic Violence Reader*. Columbia: University of Missouri Press, 1997.

Introduces a "domestic violence" reader which applies professional understandings of domestic violence and fictional treatments of men who are threatened or have lost commands of relationships. Literary texts examined are by Petry, James Joyce, D. H. Lawrence, T. S. Eliot, Ernest Hemingway, John Steinbeck, John Cheever, and others.

795

Springer, Gertrude. Review of *The Street*. *Survey Graphic*. 35.6 (June 1946): 230-231.

Criticizes Petry's novel for suggesting that its setting is the epitome of "all of Harlem." Says Lutie is "not very smart," primarily because she fails to turn her hatred into productive ways to use the white people and their institutions for her own purposes.

796

Standard, Dorothy. Review of *The Street*. *Punch* (London), (12 February 1986): 72.

Announces the reprint of *The Street*. Calls the novel "grim realism." Thinks the plot helps to place the work within the "Hardyesque chain of doom." Also says Lutie has the "depth and poignancy of a Tess." Introduces Petry to an international audience.

797

Starke, Catherine Juanita. *Black Portraiture in American Fiction: Stock Characters, Archetypes, and Individuals*. New York: Basic Books, 1971.

Considers Lutie to be an archetype; calls her a "sacrifi[cial] symbol or victim of cultural and environmental determinism."

798

Stepto, Robert B. "*I Thought I Knew These People: Richard Wright and the Afro-American Literary Tradition.*" In *Chant of Saints: A Gathering of Afro-American Literature, Art, and Scholarship*. Edited by Michael S. Harper and Robert B. Stepto. Chicago:University of Illinois Press, 1979.

Examines Richard Wright's place or his "lack of one" in the African American literary tradition. Points to African American women writers whose works revise the Mrs. Thomases, Bessies, and Bigger Thomases. For example, Petry is thought to have been "about the task not only of redeeming Bessie but of revising Bigger as well."

799

Stewart, Carolyn H. *The Narrows*. *Midwest Journal* 6.1 (Spring 1954): 4.5.

Takes a formalistic approach to *The Narrows*. Writes that "the form of the narrative reinforces the sense of leisurely, spontaneous development." Concludes, however, that due to structural interruptions, the love story between Link and Camilo is "deprived of emotional continuity and intensity." Nonetheless, finds Petry to be honest and fresh in her approach to inter- and intra-racial conflicts.

800

Stewart, Pearl. "A Woman's Tragedy in Harlem." *San Francisco Chronicle*, 21 February 1992.

Summarizes the plot in *The Street* as a tragedy, using operative words such as: revenge, betrayal, illegal schemes, manipulations, and villain.

801

Stoever, Jennifer Lynn. "The Contours of the Sonic Color-line: Slavery, Segregation, and the Cultural Politics of Listening." Ph.D. Diss., University of Southern California - Los Angeles, 2007.

Using theoretical analysis, close reading, and archival research to draw attention to African American writings as literary and aural. Draws attention to the "sonic color-line" in American culture, calling it an interpretive site where racial difference is produced and policed through "the ear."

802

_____. *The Sonic Color Line: Race and the Cultural Politics of Listening*. New York: New York University Press, 2016.

Promotes the notion that race and racism can be constructed from sound and maintained through the listening ear. Contends that American ideologies of white supremacy or racial politics are just as dependent on what is heard as are skin color or hair texture. For justification and application, see writings by Petry, DuBois, Douglass, Jacobs, and Chesnutt.

803

_____. "Black Radio Listeners in America's "Golden Age." *Journal of Radio & Audio Media*. 26.1 (May 2019): 119-133.

Argues that U. S. black listenership has been largely ignored in radio scholarship of the 1930s, 1940s, and 1950s. Says such scholarship provides a context for addressing racism in America. Includes Petry's fiction which suggests listening can look and sound different for black listeners.

804

Streitfeld, David. "Petry's Brew: Laughter and Fury." *Washington Post*, 25 February 1992, E 1- E 2.

Interweaves biography, bibliography, and comments by Petry and her daughter into a lengthy and intriguing introduction (or reintroduction) to the writer and her first novel, *The Street* - first published in 1946 by Houghton Mifflin and now being reissued. Two recent photographs are included.

805

_____. "Ann Petry's Storied Life." *Washington Post*, 3 May 1997.

Provides an endearing eulogy for the writer, whom he interviewed once and visited "unofficially, a few times."

806

Sullivan, J.J. "Homosexuality and Marginalization in Selected Post-World War II American Fiction." Ph.D. Diss., Columbia University, 1993.

Examines the intersections of race, class, and gender issues that contribute to the socially marginalized status of homosexuals in the twenty years following World War II. Contends that literary depictions of marginalized communities and individuals by major African American writers (male and female) ultimately marginalize homosexuals. Includes a reading of Petry's *The Narrows* to demonstrate the homosexual in particular who emerges as a literary index to social marginalization throughout the post-World War II period.

807

Sullivan, Oona. Review of *Legends of the Saints*. *New York Times Book Review*, 29 November 1970.

    With an exception to the story of Saint Christopher in the collection, calls Petry's stories about saints "a bit tall."

808

Sullivan, Richard. "Injustice, Out of Focus." *New York Times Book Review*, 28 September 1947, 12.

    Compares *Country Place* to *The Street,* calling the former "quiet . . . carefully and economically phrased." Dismisses "switched point-of-view" in *Country Place* as a weakness. Hails the novel's style as "bright and vigorous." Hails characterizations as "forceful."

809

Sumpter, Vanessa Simone. "The Woes of Working Women: Economic Subjugation in Ann Petry's *The Street*." M.A., Howard University, 1998.

    Registers Petry's concerns about the economic trials of black, working-class women.

810

Sundstrom, Kristina M. "It Wasn't Make-Believe Like the Movies": Performing the Future of African American Female Identity." Ph.D. Diss., Villanova University, 2012.

    Applies theories of gender, sexual, and racial performances to readings of Ann Petry's *The Street*, Nella Larsen's *Passing*, and Toni Morrison's *Sula*. Studies the outcomes when performances are used by the writers to recreate black female identity. Predicts the qualities of gender, sexual, and racial performances will influence future revisions of black female identity.

811

Sutherland, Amy. "When Setting is Inspiration." *Boston Globe*, 1 December 2019, N.12.

    Interviews Jeffrey Colvin following publication of his debut novel, Africaville. Colvin cites Petry among a host of major and internationally read authors for inspirational influences. Says setting in Petry's *The Street* has had a big impact on his writing.

812

Svendsen, Kester. "Another Negro Family Finding Life Too Harsh." *Daily Oklahoman*, 24 February 1946 [Special Collections, Boston University].

    Calls *The Street* not just another problem novel. Says "any honest novel about the Negro is almost inevitably a racial problem novel." Notes how Petry avoids the "stereotyped" and the "symbolic" problem novel. Emphasizes that Lutie searches for "a home and security" but fails to secure either, in part because she lives in the ghetto.

813

Sweeting-Trotter, Tarah. "Mother of Earth: Mothering Towards Reciprocity in a Patriarchal Capitalist

Framework." Ph.D. Diss., Saint Louis University, 2014.

Conducts comparative readings of matriarchal narratives by Agnes Smedley of the 1920s and writers of the twentieth century, including Ann Petry (*The Street*). Provides diverse experiences of "mothering" in a system that values material labor and production rather than human care, work, and reproductions. The critiques span across different geographical, economic, and racial conditions and also point to subversive females who emerge due to economic determinism in patriarchal environments in the narratives.

814

Tait, Althea. "Tell Them: The Premise for African American Female Children's Literature." *The Language of Diversity: Restoration Toward Peace and Unity*. Edited by Mary Alice Treat, Trevor Grizzle, and Andrew Lang. Newcastle upon Tyne: Cambridge Scholars Publishing, 2009.

Says Petry, along with other female forerunners, has preserved the future of African American children's fiction. Also provides for study and discussion the following headnotes: Petry within the context of Children's Literature; Petry and History within Children's Literature; Forms of Education; A New Day, A New Education, A New History; and The History of African American Children's Literature is steeped in the contention of truth telling.

815

Tally, Justine and Juana Herrera Cubas and Maria Cruz Exposito. "A Meeting of Minds and Cultures: Teaching Black Women's Literature in the Canary Islands." *Sage* 6.1 (Summer 1989): 63.

Addresses the revamping of graduate programs at Spanish universities in 1985. Cites the English Department at the University of La Laguna in the Canary Islands for seizing the opportunity to establish a graduate program in Anglo-American Literature, and for adding Black American women writers. Adds Ann Petry under Pre-Civil Rights and Civil Rights eras.

816

Taylor, Frances Grandy. "The Novelist and Miss James: Ann Petry Left Aunt's Store to Find Fame as Writer." *Hartford Courant*, 2 February 2001.

Announces the sale of Ann Petry's estate, which is said to offer a glimpse into Petry's life as well as offer a time capsule set by a vintage pharmacy. One finds an informative narrative about the Lane family from the arrival of Petry's father to Old Saybrook, Connecticut, to the opening of his pharmacy in the early 1900s and to Petry's death in 1997. In between, added are many historical and applaudable moments, such as the licensing of Miss Anna James as Connecticut's first black pharmacist or the historical registry of the Lane's pharmacy. While a number of items from Petry's estate are forwarded to the Schomburg Center for Research in Black Culture in New York City, the auctioneer, Peggy Maraschiello of River Wind Antiques in Deep River, Connecticut, promotes a sale of the highest interest: Petry's extensive library; china; antique carved chairs, tables, and chests; African American artifacts; and numerous items from the James Pharmacy.

817

Taylor, Ivan E. Review of *The Narrows*. *Current Literature*. 23.1 (Winter 1954): 60-61.

Discusses many critical aspects of *The Narrows*: its explosive themes; its humor; its commonplaceness yet universality; and its use of propaganda, particularly commentary on how daily newspapers manipulate news about crimes committed by African Americans.

818

Tetsuo, Yamaguchi Midori. *Feminine Fiction from Across America.* Tokyo: Bunri Company, 1978.

Includes the works of five authors as well as biographical sketches of each author. For Petry, provided is a biographical sketch and her short story, "The Migraine Worker." Further confirms Petry's international audience.

819

Tettenborn, Eva. "Traumatic Reenactment and the Impossibility of African American Testimony in Ann Petry's 'Like a Winding Sheet' and 'The Witness'." In *Ann Petry's Short Fiction: Critical Essays.* Edited by Hazel Arnett Ervin and Hilary Holladay. Westport, CT: Praeger, 2004.

Introduces "trauma theory" to contextualize the in-depth analytical readings of Petry's "Like a Winding Sheet" and "The Witness" and to illustrate how for marginalized people, trauma resides in everyday racist practices as well as in singular and horrific events and experiences.

820

_____. "Melancholia as Resistance in Contemporary African American Literature." *MELUS* 31.3 (Fall 2006): 101-121; 189-190.

Calls for further analysis of physical differences and disabilities in African American literature, especially in light of American history's traumatic impact on the African American body. Encourages the use of trauma theory to contextualize analytical readings of Petry's short stories, "Like a Winding Sheet" and "The Witness."

821

"'The Street' Still Unchanged." *Hartford Courant,* 7 March 1969, 32.

Offers quotes by Petry who concludes that after thirty years, she could write the same book about "any American ghetto." The writer reaffirms her reasons for writing *The Street.*

822

Thomas, Robert McGee. "Ann Petry, 88, First to Write a Literary Portrait of Harlem." *New York Times,* 30 April 1997, 89.

Announces the death of Petry who dies in a convalescent home near Old Saybrook, Connecticut. Reminds readers that the writer took a single street in Harlem and brought it "vividly and disturbingly to life."

823

Thomas, Toni Renee. "The Evolution of the Strong Black Woman Persona in African American Literature." M. A., Fayetteville State University, 2003.

Traces the mental, spiritual, and physical growth of black women protagonists in African American literature from 1932-1982 (from Hurston's Janie Crawford to Petry's Lutie Johnson to Walker's Celie). Also examines and showcases myths and merits of black female characters.

824

Thomson, Rosemarie Garland. "Ann Petry's Mrs. Hedges and The Evil, One-Eyed Girl: A Feminist Exploration of the Physically Disabled Female Subject." *Women's Studies* 24.6 (September 1995): 599-614.

Focuses on formal aspects of disability - its perceptions by others and reactions to those perceptions. Offers analytical characterization of Petry's Mrs. Hedges.

825

_____. "Disabled Women as Powerful Women in Petry, Morrison, and Lorde." *Extraordinary Bodies: Figuring Physical Disability in American Culture and Literature.* New York: Columbia University Press, 1997, 103-104.

   Explores representation of physical disability in nineteenth century America (e.g., Harriet Beecher Stowe, Rebecca Harding Davis, and Elizabeth Stuart Phelps) and in twentieth century America (e.g., Ann Petry, Toni Morrison, and Audre Lorde). Raises questions to scholars interested in gender, race, and problems of identity in American Culture.

826

_____. "Aberrant Bodies: Making the Corporeal Other in Nineteenth- and Twentieth-Century American Cultural Representations." Ph.D. Diss., Brandeis University, 1993.

   Interrogates ways in which "physically disabled" becomes a form of cultural otherness. Critiques the master-narrative, which sorts physical differences into antinomies of normal and abnormal. Provides a comprehensive review of literary writers and their works that intertwine as nineteenth- and twentieth-century productions of the social identity we know as "physically disabled."

827

" To the Reader in Chief ... Some of our Favorite Feminists Recommend Books for the next U.S. President's Reading List." *The Women's Review of Books* 33.2 (March/April 2016): 16-22.

   Sixteen women (Alicia Ostriker, Ana Louise Keating, Beverly Guy-Sheftall, Callie Crossley, Courtney E. Martin, Ellen Feldman, Jennifer Camper, Kate Clinton, Katie Grover, Layli Maparyan, Yi-Chun Tricia Lin, Marjorie Agosin, Martha Nichols, Moya Bailey, Robin Becker, and Rochelle Ruthchild) make recommendations to the next U. S. President regarding a reading list. One recommendation comes from Bailey to read Petry's *The Street*. Says Petry's book is a master-class, offering a real world impact of capitalism on those most marginalized in the country. Calls the narrative "deep sociological theory" disguised as a brilliant novel. Says Petry expertly renders in her tragic but beautifully told story how when you are black and poor, racism, sexism, and classism contribute to your impossibility of the American Dream. Concludes that if the president were to take the book to heart, [he or she] would surely have to transform the economy and end racism and sexism - all while creating a new plan for city living.

828

Todd, Diane M. "The American Dream in Literature: Woman and Ethnics Need Not Apply." Ph.D. Diss., Indiana University of Pennsylvania, 2000.

   Examines seventeen (17) authors of diverse ethnicity and their portrayals of the American Dream. Reveals that in Petry's *The Street* the African American woman is defeated from the very beginning of her pursuit. Shows, however, in Lorraine Hansberry and August Wilson that African Americans do achieve modest versions of the dream. Says that in the writings of Petry, Hansberry and Wilson, one common thread is that a more fulfilling version of the American Dream lies within the ethnic community.

829

Trilling, Diana. "Class and Color." *The Nation* 162 (9 March 1946): 290-291.

   Reviews Petry's *The Street* and Fannie Cook's *Mrs. Palmer's Honey*. Concludes that neither "challenges the prestige of Lillian Smith's *Strange Fruit*." Thinks, however, that *The Street* states better than Mrs. Palmer's *Honey* how "class feelings are as firmly ingrained in the colored population . . . as in the white."

830

Troupe, Quincy. "A Conversation with Terry McMillan." *Emerge* (October 1992): 51-56.

    Asks McMillan to name her literary influences: McMillan includes Petry. Says that in *The Street*, Petry teaches her to write in her own voice.

831

Turner, Darwin T. " ' The Negro Novel in America': In Rebuttal." *CLA Journal* 10.2 (December 1966): 122-124.

    Refutes a number of Robert Bone's literary conclusions, including that writers like Petry who wrote the non-Negro novel were "assimilationist[s]."

832

Turner, Washella Neurett. "Unity or Dissension?: African American Literary Perspectives on Twentieth-Century Interracial Organization and Relations." Ph.D. Diss., University of Florida, 2005.

    Contends that the psychological, after-effect of slavery on blacks and whites plays the subconscious and conscious roles of limiting group members to work together. Uses non-fiction to explore historical oppression and uses fiction to examine the dissensions of interracial, educational opportunities and other social situations. Includes in the study Petry's *The Street*.

833

Tuszynska, Agnieszka. "Strangers from Within, Strangers from Without: Negotiations and Uses of Space in African American and Immigrant Literatures and Cultures, 1900–1950s." Ph.D. Diss., University of Illinois at Urbana-Champaign, 2013.

    Explores the relationship between cultural constructions of space and literary visions of ethnicity and Americanness in fiction. Provides parallel readings of African American immigrant novels to illustrate how the disciplinary boundaries which are often drawn between African American literature and white ethnic literature can be imaginatively negotiated by examining the constructions of space and place in black and white ethnic writings. Employs geocriticism, focusing on literary spatiality as being key to cross-ethnic reputations - e.g., see Chapter III: Signifying on the Margins: Jazz Improvisation in the Marginal Spaces of Ann Petry's *The Street*, Billie Holiday's "Lady Sings the Blues," and …."

834

Unruh, Kendra. "From Kitchen Mechanics to 'Jubilant Spirits of Freedom': Black, Working-Class Women Dancing the Lindy Hop." *The Journal of Pan African Studies* (online) 4.6 (2011): 213-233.

    Examines the use of dance such as the Lindy Hop during the Swing era as a means of escape, freedom, and rebellion by Black, working-class women characters in works by writers, including Rudolph Fisher and Ann Petry.

835

―――. " 'Jubilant Spirits of Freedom': Representation of the Lindy Hop in Literature and Film From the Swing Era to the Revival." Ph.D. Diss., Purdue University, 2012.

    Draws on cultural history to study how changes in racial ownership have affected the type of liberation associated with dance such as the Lindy Hop.

836

Uzurin, Deborah L. "Representations of Hustling Women: The Figure of the Black Sex Worker in Ann Petry's

The Street and Louise Meriwether's *Daddy Was a Number Runne*r." M.A., City University of New York, 2020.

Provides close readings of Ann Petry's *The Street* and Louise Meriwether's *Daddy Was a Number Runner* and how both women write about the economic impacts of institutionalized racism, segregation, and discrimination in urban black communities - e.g., about the lack of economic opportunities in general and, more specifically, about the complicated representations of particular forms of black women's labor experiences in the 1930s and 1940s in Harlem - i.e., domestic labor and sex work.

837

V.P.H. "New England Novel Fine Despite Central Theme Flaw." *World Herald* (Omaha), 6 September 1953 [Special Collections, Boston University].

Suggests Petry entwines the past - Abbie who symbolizes "all the old-fashioned virtues" - with the present - i.e., a romance. Finds fault with "the present" in Petry's novel. Thinks that the interracial love affair between Link and Camilo is almost totally "unconvincing" because of the times. Insists *The Narrows* is not a "race novel" but a "New England novel" of spirit.

838

Van Dore, Edrie. "Yankees Bear South's Social Problem." *Hartford Times*, 15 August 1953 [Special Collections, Boston University].

Recognizes Link and Camilo in *The Narrows* for their courage, but thinks Camilo is never in love with Link. Encourages critical attention to the minor aspects of the novel, particularly the "casual romancing" of Mamie Powther and the "prim uprightness of the typical New England widow Abbie Crunch." Insists the unexpected and violent ending of the novel has a deeper meaning, particularly in terms of black-white relationships in the North.

839

Van Gelder, Lawrence. "Events." *New York Times*, 14 December 1998: E1.

Announces that the following people are all starring in Max Roach's adaptation of a tale of a jazz love triangle found in Petry's short story, "Solo on the Drums": Max Roach, the internationally known drummer, composer, musicologist, educator, and MacArthur Fellow; the So What Jazz Quintet; and actors Ruby Dee and Ossie Davis - all are participants. The event takes place at the 92 Street Y, which is also the centerpiece of Roach's series "Max Roach's America." Also announces the New York premiere, "Theater Pieces," which includes adaptation from this short fiction by Petry.

840

Varga-Coley, Barbara Jean. "The Novels of Black American Women." Ph.D. Diss., State University of New York at Stony Brook,1981.

Looks at what might be considered similar African American experiences that have been examined in novels by a host of African American women writers, including Petry.

841

Vechten, Carl Van. "A Portfolio of Photographs." In *Amistad 3*. Edited by John A. Williams and Charles F. Harris. New York: Random House, 1971.

Includes a photograph of Petry from the 1940s.

842
Vickery, John B. "American Literature: The Twentieth Century." *The Year's Work in English Studies* 61.1 (1982): 425-459.
    Focuses on dissertations, symposia, and critical books which offer "fresh and informative assessments" of Wright, Hughes, Petry, Baldwin, and Amiri Baraka.

843
Vigilleti, Elyse R. "Reading the Middle: U. S. Women Novelists and Print Culture, 1930-1960." Ph.D. Diss., University of Illinois at Urbana Champaign, 2016.
    Appeals to gender studies, digital humanities, American literature, and print culture on reading mainstream fiction of the 1930s, 1940s, and 1950s. Questions the passively productive exercises in intellectual stimulations.

844
Vilato, Claudia. "Internal Colonialism and *The Street*: The Black Power Movement through Lutie Johnson." M.A., Pennsylvania State University, 2007.
    Provides an analysis of internal colonialism and ideology, spanning from Petry's Lutie Johnson in *The Street* to the Black Power Movement.

845
"Violence against Black Women." In *All the Women Are White, All the Blacks Are Men, But Some of Us Are Brave*. Edited by Gloria T. Hull, Patricia Bell Scott, and Barbara Smith. Old Westbury, NY: The Feminist Press, 1982.
    Insists that violence is largely against the black woman because of her "position under patriarchy," and that "black men as well as white men violate and attack her." Under the subcategory "Battering," exemplifies as an example Petry's female victim from the short story, "Like a Winding Sheet."

846
Vizcaino-Aleman, Melina. "Counter-Modernity, Black Masculinity, and Female Silence in Ann Petry's Fiction." In *Revising the Blueprint: Ann Petry and the Literary Left*. Edited by Alex Lubin. Jackson, MI: University Press of Mississippi, 2007.
    Illustrates how Petry's fiction invokes the trans-Atlantic Slave Trade as a formative history of post-War II race relations. Also illustrates how Petry's fiction is an anticipation of the Black Arts Movement and its interest in anti-colonial struggles.

847
Voiles, Jane. "A Bookman's Notebook." *San Francisco Chronicle*, 19 December 1947 [Special Collections, Boston University].
    Provides a very brief review of *Country Place*. Basically, disapproves of the novel's melodrama and its lack of "stark dramatic quality."

848
_____. "A Bookman's Notebook." *San Francisco Chronicle*, 26 August 1953, 17.
    Criticizes the style of *The Narrows*, particularly its "overworked flashback soliloquies . . . and

[its] long redundant passages." Concludes, however, that Petry "knows her race, its strengths and its weaknesses."

849
Wade-Gayles, Gloria. "Going Nowhere Immediate." In *No Crystal Stair: Visions of Race and Sex in Black Women's Fiction*. New York: The Pilgrim Press, 1984.
    Focuses on black women characters in *The Street* who are "overworked in menial jobs, underpaid, humiliated, used, abused, and ignored" and then looks to Min and Mrs. Hedges as examples of such women.

850
_____."Journeying from Can't to Can and Sometimes Back to Can't." In *No Crystal Stair: Visions of Race and Sex in Black Women's Fiction*. New York: The Pilgrim Press, 1984. Reprint. In *The Critical Response to Ann Petry*. Edited by Hazel Arnett Ervin. Westport, CT: Praeger, 2005.
    Uses in-depth analysis to defend the thesis that *The Street* is not a "carbon copy" of *Native Son*. Calls Petry's novel "an explosion of the sounds of racial and sexual agony."

851
_____. "She Who Is Black and Mother: In Sociology and Fiction, 1940-1970." In *The Black Woman*. Edited by La Frances Rodgers-Rose. Beverly Hills, CA: Sage, 1980.
    Suggests correlating Petry's *The Street* with the sociological studies of sociologist E. Franklin Frazier. Says the divergent paths of the sociologist Franklin and the novelist Petry "intersect and converge" - e.g., the specifics from Frazier of "real life" do "add weight" and "enlarge the imaginative realities" of Petry's novel.

852
_____. "The Narrow Space and the Dark Enclosure: Race and Sex in the Lives of Black Women in Selected Novels Written by Black Women, 1946-1976." Ph.D. Diss., Emory University, 1981.
    Examines the African American woman protagonist within an enduring racist and capitalistic society - within a "narrow space" as mother, as woman of hopelessness, and as woman who struggles for wider options in life. Encourages readings of such a woman in the writings of Dorothy West, Sarah Wright, Gayl Jones, Toni Morrison, Alice Walker, Gwendolyn Brooks, and Ann Petry.

853
Wald, Alan M. *American Night: The Literary Left in the Era of the Cold War*. Chapel Hill: The University of North Carolina Press, 2012.
    Is the final volume of a trilogy on a multigenerational history of Communist writers. Although Petry never joined any politically Left groups, critics here contend that she has a sensitivity to left ideology in some of her 1940s literature.

854
Wall, Cheryl. *Changing Our Own Words: Essays on Criticism, Theory and Writing by Black Women*. New Brunswick, NJ: Rutgers University Press, 1989.
    Includes essays, literary criticism, and writings by Black women. Includes Petry as a female subject.

855

_____. "On Collectors and Collecting: The Joanna Banks Collection." [Repository. University of Pennsylvania, 2020].

Is focused on African American women, cookery, and children's literature. Advertises as a collection "full of possibilities" for "graduate students in search of a dissertation topic." Includes Petry's *Tituba of Salem Village* under the listing of women writers of children's literature.

856

Wang, Lili. "Critical Reception of African American Women Writers in Mainland China." *Journal of Ethnic American Literature* 9 (2019): 62-79, 121.

Introduces Petry to an international audience and focuses on her writing style.

857

Ward, Jerry W., Jr. "Everybody's Protest Novel: The Era of Richard Wright." *The Cambridge Companion to the African American Novel*. Edited by Maryemma Graham. New York: Cambridge University Press, 2004, 173-188.

Provides an extensive analysis of the elements of the protest novel from the differing perspectives of James Baldwin and Ann Petry. Says Petry "confronts what Baldwin ignored" and in *The Street* she "champion[s] *Native Son* as [a] fine example of the novel as social criticism."

858

Warfel, Harry R. " Ann Petry." In *American Novelists of Today*. New York: American Book Company, 1951.

Is biographical and bibliographical. Several dates, however, are incorrect.

859

Washington, Ada L. "A Comparative Study of Fear in Richard Wright's Bigger Thomas, Ann Petry's Mrs. Lutie Johnson, and Willard Motley's Nick Romano." M.A., Prairie View A&M College, 1953.

Looks critically at a similar theme in Wright, Petry, and Motley - "fear."

860

Washington, Gladys J. "A World Made Cunningly: A Closer Look at Ann Petry's Short Fiction." *CLA Journal* 30.1 (September 1986):14-29.

Takes a comprehensive look at style, structure, and characterization in Petry's short stories found in *Miss Muriel and Other Stories*. Concludes that the stories might be divided into two distinct groups: those that depict a "small town world with people enjoying simple pleasures" and those that depict the inner city and "all the tensions and frustrations . . . associated with the urban scene." Thinks Petry's characters reflect "a multiplicity of tendencies, attitudes, desires, and determinations." Calls Petry's world one that is crafted with the skill of artistry by a writer "keenly attuned to the nuances of [the] world about her."

861

_____. "Folk Traditions in the Short Fiction of Ann Petry." In *Ann Petry's Short Fiction: Critical Essays*. Edited by Hazel Arnett Ervin and Hilary Holladay. Westport, CT: Praeger, 2004.

Says Petry is "keenly aware of the many nuances of African American folk culture." Examines how she almost effortlessly "weaves folk traditions into the very fabric of her fiction, enriching the narratives and giving them depth and color."

862
Washington, Mary Helen. "Black Women Image Makers." *Black World* 23.10 (August 1974): 11.

Believes African American women writers are projecting "powerful" and "realistic" images that combat stereotypes of black women. Names Petry as one of those writers.

863
_____. " 'Infidelity Becomes Her': The Ambivalent Woman in The Fiction of Ann Petry." In *Invented Lives: Narratives of Black Women, 1860-1960*. Garden City, NY: Anchor/Doubleday, 1987.

Criticizes Petry's "insistence on environmental determinism as an explanation for her characters' dead-end lives." Says such an approach ignores "deeply felt realities" such as women's "relationships with their families"; women's "own suppressed creativity"; or women's "conflicts with black men and with patriarchy." Concludes that in *The Street* and "In Darkness and Confusion," Petry writes about Harlem "as an outsider," but in a story like "Miss Muriel," Petry is "the insider [with] a vantage point of power which her characters share."

864
_____. "Teaching Black-Eyed Susans: An Approach to the Study of Black Women Writers." *CLA Journal* 11.1 (Spring 1977): 23. Reprint. In *All the Women Are White, All the Blacks Are Men, But Some of Us Are Brave*. Edited by Gloria T. Hull, Patricia Bell Scott, and Barbara Smith. Old Westbury, NY: The Feminist Press, 1982.

Provides suggestions for thematic approaches to the study of literature by African American women writers. Suggests Lutie from *The Street* is to be placed under the subcategory "The Suspended Woman."

865
Washington, Zenobia. "Portraits of Four Black Women in Selected Novels by Zora Neale Hurston, Ann Petry, Gwendolyn Brooks, and Paule Marshall." M.A., Wichita State University, 1977.

Registers portraits of biography and bibliography for four, major black women writers. Petry is included.

866
Watkins, Mel. "Sexism, Racism and Black Women Writers." *New York Times Book Review*, 15 June 1986, 1, 35-37.

Argues black women writers have had much impact on American literature since the 1960s, the feminist movement, and the publication of *The Flagellants*. Suggests that despite their "ascendancy and success," black women writers have been persistent in their negative portrayals of black men. Says talented black women writers such as Ann Petry, Alice Childress, and Paule Marshall " . . . have avoided these attacks [these negative portrayals]," but, in return, " have not been as successful." See Thulani Davis in her rebuttal.

867
Watson, Carole McAlpine. *Prologue: The Novels of Black American Women, 1891 - 1965*. Westport, CT: Greenwood, 1985.

Provides analyses and annotated bibliographies for fifty-eight of the sixty-four novels written by African American women between 1891 and 1965. Includes in Chapter III, "works of universal meaning," and discussion of Petry's *The Narrows*.

868

Wattley, Ama S. " 'Beating Unavailing Palms Against the Stone': Spatiality, Sexuality, Stereotyping, and the Myth of the American Dream in Ann Petry's *The Street.*" In *The Critical Response to Ann Petry*. Edited by Hazel Arnett Ervin. Westport, CT: Praeger, 2005.

Examines how sexual stereotyping of the black woman is an issue that is addressed in Petry's *The Street*. Illustrates how Petry uses physical spaces that are narrow, small, and confining as well as harsh in social realities such as racism and sexism in order to relate the ways in which protagonist Lutie Johnson, who attempts to realize the American Dream, is trapped and constricted within her urban environment.

869

Weir, Sybil. " '*The Narrows*.': A Black New England Novel." *Studies in American Fiction* 15.1 (Spring 1987): 81-93. Reprint. In *The Critical Response to Ann Petry*. Edited by Hazel Arnett Ervin. Westport, CT: Praeger, 2005.

Claims that Petry's *The Narrows* illustrates the writer's indebtedness to Nathaniel Hawthorne and Richard Wright, to New England women writers, and to her experiences in Harlem in the 1940s. Says *The Narrows* provokes African American realities, particularly the blues tradition; double consciousness - i.e., the African American with "two souls" [one American, the other African); and the support of community.

870

Weiss, Jacqueline Shachter. *Profiles in Children's Literature: Discussions with Authors, Artists, and Editors*. Lanham, MD:Scarecrow Press, 2001.

Provides discussions with authors, artists, and editors about children's literature. Includes Petry.

871

Wesling, Meg E. " The Opacity of Everything Life: Segregation and Iconicity of Uplift in '*The Stree*t.' " *American Literature* 78.1 (March 2006): 117-140.

Goes to the final passage of Petry's *The Street* where Lutie Johnson is found on a train from Harlem to Chicago. Concludes that Lutie is defeated 1) because of challenges due to skin color, gender, and class and 2) because of Lutie's embracement of Ben Franklin's ideology for upward mobility. Says Lutie might be read as a central figure in the story of modern American life.

872

_____. "State of Culture: Pedagogy and The Making of American Citizen (Philippines, Puerto Rico, Cuba, Hawaii, United States)." Ph.D. Diss., Cornell University, 2004.

Studies the didactic discourse of citizenship in the United States in the first half of the twentieth century. Explores "state of culture" through literary works by Ann Petry, Carlos Bulosan, and Americo Parades, applying feminist literary criticism and postcolonial studies to situate the gendered and racialized formations of American citizenship within the material and discursive contexts of U.S. imperialism. Provides discussions of the following: compulsory public education; paradigm of colonial tutelage; democratizing discourse of education; forming national subjects by "subjecting" them to the state's pedagogical authority; model of citizenship submission to state pedagogy, molding subjects into citizens.

873

Wheeler, Kathleen. "High Modernism and Other Experiments and the Continuing Development of the Socio-

Moral Novel, 1918-1945." In *A Critical Guide to Twentieth-Century Women Novelists.* Malden, MA: Blackwell Publisher, 1998.

Analyzes narrative practices and stylistic devices of twentieth-century fiction. Discusses theoretical influences on the fiction, such as psychoanalysis, postwar genre, post-structuralism, post-modernism, magic realism, and feminist.

874

Whitbeck, Doris. "Women Artists at U Conn Fest." *Hartford Courant* 25 March 1979, IG, 5G.

Highlights Petry's participation as guest artist at a week-long arts festival held at the University of Connecticut. Includes vitals of Petry.

875

Whitlow, Roger. "1940-1960: Urban Realism and Beyond." In *Black American Literature: A Critical History.* Chicago: Nelson-Hall, 1973. Revised. 1976.

Is convinced that like Wright's *Native Son*, Petry's *The Street* is concerned with the "effects of environment . . . on people." Compares Lutie to Bigger Thomas. Calls Lutie "trapped" and reactionary. Places Petry in the "urban realism" movement.

876

Whitt, Margaret Earley. "At Home Inside: A Daughter's Tribute to Ann Petry by Elizabeth Petry." *Callaloo* 34.4 (Fall 2011):1104-1106; and 1118.

Underscores the presence of an informative narrative on Petry and family. Says, however, that many questions go unanswered in Liz Petry's *At Home Inside*, but applauds the daughter for using her own memories of growing up in Old Saybrook, Connecticut, and her mother's thirty-three journals to recreate "a woman larger than the literary author known most widely for her novels, short stories, children and juvenile literature."

877

Wichelms, Kathryn. "Black Realism Matters; Or, a Syllabus Is Still a Terrible Thing to Waste." *American Literary Realism* 53.2 (Winter 2021): 100-105.

Says "the national prominence of the Black Lives Matter Movement calls for self-examinations by other institutional actions." Contends that Black writers invite students [of color] to become informed participants in conversations that really include them, whether they know it or not. Cites Petry's *The Street* as one motivating illustration.

878

Wiebe, Paul. " ' Miss Muriel ' : Rewriting Innocence into Experience." In *Ann Petry's Short Fiction: Critical Essays*. Edited by Hazel Arnett Ervin and Hilary Holladay. Westport, CT: Praeger, 2004.

Relies on texts from William Blake's *Songs of Innocence* as follows:
1) to illustrate the complexity of plot which is found in the primary and counter-narratives located in Petry's "Miss Muriel"; and
2) to underscore the significance of the steps necessary for Petry's young narrator who moves in the short story from a state of innocence to a state of experience.

879
Wilhite, Keith M. "Framing Suburbia: United States Literature and the Postwar Suburban Region, 1945-2002." Ph.D. Diss., University of Iowa, 2007.

    Returns to writers of color and questions the framing of the central voice in U.S. regional and environmental writings. Critiques a recast of relationships between literary practices and the environment at the turn of the twenty-first century.

880
Wilkie, Jacqueline S. with David Faldet. "The Staying Power of a Little Known Novella: Ann Petry's 'In Darkness and Confusion.'" In *Tradition and Innovation: Select Plenary and Panel Papers from the Third Annual Conference of the Association for Core Texts and Courses*. Edited by Scott Lee and Allen Speight. Lanham, MD: University Press of America, 1999.

    Promotes Petry's novella, "In Darkness and Confusion" as an appropriate work for the common core curriculum. Shares observations that support Petry's work as a required common core text. Says the text "aesthetically engages and models deeply, moral dimensions of human experience while it [also] engages students in a deeper understanding of a clearly defined historical moment." Thinks that because of Petry's characterizations, the work allows white mainstream students to see African Americans in recognizable life experiences rather than as exotics. Further observes that the work "draws students into deeper understandings of the past and its relationship to the present." Pedagogically, promotes teaching the novella because of its amenability to teaching readings skills (skimming, posing questions, summary). Also notes that the novella offers other significant topics regarding the African American experience such as race matters and northern migration. Finally, notes that Petry's work proves to be an alternative to the familiar common core readings by Frederick Douglass and Booker T. Washington, or to the works from the Harlem Renaissance.

881
Williams, Jennifer Denise. "Black Mourning: Readings of Loss, Desire, and Racial Identification." Ph.D. Diss., University of Texas at Austin, 2006.

    Explores a diverse archive of literary and cultural African American texts, so to reveal "loss" as a condition of racial identification. Texts studied are by Jean Toomer, Ann Petry, Marlon Riggs, and Danzy Senna. Also makes application of "trauma theory." In Chapter Two, " 'Nobody Knows My Name': Ann Petry's *The Street* and Black Women's Blues Protest," the focus is on blues aesthetics, so to access hidden texts on black and female sexual trauma.

882
Williams, John A. and Charles F. Harris. *Amistad 2*. New York: Random House, 1971.

    Lends a male voice to discourse on "violence against" black women.

883
Williams, Sherley Anne. Review of *The Street*. *MS* 23 (September 1986): 23.

    Announces reprint of *The Street*. Says the "real power" of the novel lies in Petry's ability to understand the "roles that gender and sexuality play in the exploitation of black women." Claims the novel earns Petry "an abiding place among American naturalist novelists."

884
Willis, Susan. "Eruptions of Funk: Historicizing Toni Morrison." In *Black Literature and Literary Theory*. Edited

by Henry Louis Gates, Jr. New York: Methuen, 1984, 263-283.
>Makes references to Ann Petry.

885
Wilson, Mark. "A *MELUS* Interview: Ann Petry - The New England Connection." MELUS 15.2 (Summer 1988): 84.
>Discusses Petry's role as storyteller in both her short and long fiction. (See full interview in this bibliography).

886
Wilson, Sonia Alverez. "Beyond the Burdens of Exile: Exile, Immigration and Migration in U.S. Women's Writing." Ph.D. Diss., University of North Carolina at Greensboro, 2015.
>Argues for exploring representations of trauma, healing, and memory rather than ethnicity or national origins in literature of exile, so to transcend cultural borders and to deepen literary critiques of migration and immigration.

887
"Witchcraft Topic for Author's Talk." *Middletown Press*, 17 January 1970 [Special Collections, Boston University].
>Duplicates information from other articles, explaining how Petry comes to write *Tituba of Salem Village*.

888
Winter, Molly Crumpton. "The Multiethnic American Short Story." *A Companion to the American Short Story*. Edited by Alfred Bendixen and James Nagel. Malden, MA: Blackwell, 2010, 466-481.
>Captures Petry's conversations about the literary tradition of the American short story, and her focus on her short story, "Like a Winding Sheet."

889
Winters, Kari J. "Narrative Desire in Ann Petry's *The Street*." *Journal X: A Journal in Culture and Criticism* 4.2 (Spring 2000):101-112.
>Inspires a new critical approach to the familiar plot in *The Street* by applying theories of Roland Barthes. Instructs readers to contextualize narrative desire as a critical study of Petry, raising two central questions: What do characters in the novel want? What narrative desires do Petry arouse, reproduce, or frustrate for her readers? Enters structurally into discussions with some of Petry's most prominent literary critics about the readerly desires of Petry in T*he Street*. Also, enters discussions with Petry by reexamining *The Street* for structural discussions of desires (i.e., of subversive desires) and of Petry's characters in the novel. Indirectly provides readers with a glossary via definitions and illustrations of literary terms in Petry's award-winning novel: image, theme, motif, parody, metaphor, subjectivity, and magical realism.

890
Wolfe, Barbara. " ' The Narrows' Breeds Life Full of Turmoil, Confusion." *Star* (Indianapolis), 13 September 1953 [Special Collections, Boston University].
>Thinks Petry should have ended her story in *The Narrows* halfway through the novel. Says the novel

becomes anti-climactic and melodramatic. Calls Abbie and Link detailed characterizations but says Powther and his wife Mamie warrant "exclusive attention."

891
Woods, Brandon Teray. "Dangerous Accumulations: Representing Black Rage in the Protest Era of 1936-1946." Ph. D. Diss., University of Pennsylvania, 2011.

Says "black rage" is a given, especially when responding to systemic racial oppression. Prefers focusing on the "nature of rage" and the ways it has entered cultural imaginations. Using works by Arna Bontemps, Chester Himes, Richard Wright, and Ann Petry, explores and responds to the following questions: 1) Is "black rage" merely a visceral reaction or a violent lashing out against racial oppression? 2) Can "black rage" be harnessed into a legitimate form of political protest in literature?

892
Woods, Paula L. *Spooks, Spies, and Private Eyes: Black Mystery Crimes and Suspense Fiction*. New York: Doubleday, 1999.

Includes Petry in a study of African American writers of mystery and suspense fiction, namely by Chester Himes, Richard Wright, and Walter Mosley. For Petry, includes the short story, "On Saturday the Siren Sounds at Noon."

893
Woolfork, Lisa. "Trauma and Racial Difference in Twentieth-Century American Literature." Ph.D. Diss., University of Wisconsin-Madison, 2000. Reprint. *MELUS* 15.2 (1988): 71-84. Reprint. *Ann Petry's Short Fiction: Critical Essays*. Edited by Hazel Arnett Ervin and Hilary Holladay. Westport, CT: Praeger, 2004.

Calls for a psychoanalysis of Petry's characters and their African American experiences. Cites as motive for the study: psychic trauma caused by race relations.

894
Wordworks, Manitou and Laurie Dimauro. *Modern Black Writers*. Detroit: St. James Press, 2000.

Includes bibliographical texts and excerpts of criticism that collectively contextualize the critical receptions of major African American novelists, poets, and dramatists of the twentieth century. Includes novelist Petry.

895
Wormley, Margaret Just. Review of *Country Place*. *Current Literature* 17.2 (Spring 1948): 169.

Pays tribute to Petry as follows: "[I]n an age in which we aim to support the thesis of one world, it is wholesome to note that some [Negro] creative artists [e.g., Petry] are apparently concerned with art." Concludes that *Country Place*, with its "compactness of style," "increased fluidity of dialogue," and "convincing character analysis" is a "marked advance" over *The Street*.

896
Wright, Lee Alfred. "Identity, Family, and Folklore in African American Literature." Ph.D. Diss., University of Toledo, 1992.

Revisits the thematic role that African American folklore plays in defining personal, familial, and/or community identity. Includes in the study, a closer look at the break-up of the black family - from slave narratives to narratives by Petry, Alice Walker, and Toni Morrison - as well as a closer look at the use of the blues tradition which includes improvisation and recurring motifs and which enhance African American storytelling.

897

"Writer Credits Success to Customers of Father's Old Saybrook Drugstore." *Hartford Courant*, 26 September 1947, 1.

Quotes Petry to suggest that the druggist-narrator in *Country Place* is her "father made over"; that the novel's setting is "partly that of Old Saybrook"; and that the characters in the novel are much like the customers who came into her father's drugstore.

898

Wurst, Gayle. "Ben Franklin in Harlem: The Drama of Deferral in Ann Petry's *The Street*." In *Deferring a Dream: Literary Sub-Version of the American Columbiad*. Edited by Gert Buelens and Ernst Rudlin. Basil: Berkhauser, 1994.

Uses the ideological framework of the 'American Dream' to highlight contrasts between the realities of colonization and exploitation. Suggests subverting and reconstructing the 'American Dream' when contrasting Ben Franklin in Petry's Harlem.

899

Wyatt, David. "Love and Separateness: Welty, Petry, Douglas, Mary McCarthy, Friedan, Steinbeck." *Secret Histories: Reading Twentieth Century American Literature*. Baltimore, MD: Johns Hopkins University Press, 2010.

Provides a formalistic reading of twentieth century American writers, outlining the American usable past found in works of writers such as Welty, Petry, Douglas McCarthy, Friedan, and Steinbeck. Says this past becomes part of the reader-writer act of creation - an understanding among writers that fiction can do something that history sometimes refuses to do.

900

Ya Salaam Kalamu. "It Didn't Jes Grew: The Social and Aesthetic Significance of African American Music." *African American Review* 29.2 (Summer 1995): 351-375.

Fosters understanding of the aesthetic influences of African American music (blues, gospel, jazz, and hip hop) on African American writings.

901

Yarborough, Richard. "The Quest for the American Dream in Three Afro-American Novels: *If He Hollers Let Him Go*, *The Street*, and *Invisible Man*." *MELUS* 8.4 (Winter 1981): 33-59. Reprint. In *The Critical Response to Ann Petry*. Edited by Hazel Arnett Ervin. Westport, CT: Praeger, 2005.

Writes that after "four decades of innumerable promises upon which America has almost inevitably reneged, the dialectical tension in Afro-American thought between hope and despair begins to produce new synthesis: the agonizing recognition that white racism may forever keep the American Dream out of the black's grasp." To support this thesis, Yarborough points to reactions evoked by the failure of the Dream in Petry's *The Street*; Himes's *If He Hollers*; and Ellison's *Invisible Man*.

902

Yates, Elizabeth. "To Freedom by the Underground." *Christian Science Monitor,* 25 August 1955, 11.

    Provides a brief and favorable review of Petry's first edition of *Harriet Tubman, Conductor on the Underground Railroad.*

903

Yates, Sharon B. "Ann Petry: Social Critic and Literary Artist." M.A., Virginia State University, 1985.

    Registers an academic evaluation of Petry as social critic and as literary artist.

904

Yeldho, Joe Varghese. "Sounding Harlem: Ann Petry's *The Street* and the Experiences of Dwelling." *American, British, and Canadian Studies.* 34.1 (2020): 1-7.

    Encourages a shift of focus in reading Petry's *The Street* - e.g., to the practices of listening, to sound, to noise, and to music, or to other parts of a racially-informed urban dwelling. Also encourages approaching Harlem as a site of habitation rather than of occupation. (See also Dragos Ivana).

905

Yglesias, Jose. "A Classy-Type People." *New Masses,* 9 December 1947 [Special Collections, Boston University].

    Provides a lengthy critique of *Country Place*, focusing on Petry's "matter-of-fact" style and "familiar" characters. Questions whether *Country Place* is a "morality tale."

906

Young, Lisa. "Lethal Housing: Reading Restrictive Covenants and Urban Black Women's Grassroots Health Activism, 1930-1980." Ph.D. Diss., Purdue University, 2017.

    Provides an eco-literary study which includes archival data from the radical Black press, trial transcripts from restrictive covenant court cases, and decades of literature by Black women writers such as Ann Petry, Lorraine Hansberry, Gwendolyn Brooks, Gloria Naylor, Toni Cade Bambara, and Paule Marshall. Re-directs literary critics to focus on the following: health politics of Black women writers; literary historiographies that illuminate issues of race, health and gender by intertwining the national and urban worlds; bio-political violence; and sustained attention to Black health care needs from the grassroots.

907

Young, Tiffany Ann. "Rape in Contemporary American Literature: Writing Women as Rapeable." Ph.D. Diss., Florida State University, 2007.

    Says looking at the cultural representation of rape in literature helps audiences to understand the cultural fear and the fascination with rape while also soliciting respect for the victim. Includes analyses that deconstruct hegemonic discourse of rape in select novels starting in the late 1930s. Includes *The Street*.

908

Zak, Deborah Jeanne. "Redefining Female Identity in the American City: A Study of Selected Twentieth-Century American Urban Novels by Women." Ph.D. Diss., Northern Illinois University, 2002.

    Studies eighteen (18) select urban novels by twentieth-century women writers, giving specific attention to female protagonists and their relationships to urban spaces such as apartment/home; city streets; community;

and how social structures either foster or limit positive female, self-development. Includes Petry's *The Street*.

909

Zhang, Weihua. "Ann Petry." *Masterplots II: American Fiction Series*. January, 2000,1-3.
      Provides strong analytical approaches to Petry.

910

Zidan, Mahmoud Nimer. "Internal Displacement and Non-Civil Novels in African American Literature." Ph.D. Diss., State University of New York at Binghamton, 2015.
      Establishes analytical lens through which to view and to critique internal dis-placement within Black Migration or diasporic literature. Fosters studies of writers Ann Petry (*The Street*); Chester Himes (*Lonely Crusade*); Richard Wright (*The Outsider*); and Toni Morrison (*Home*). Claims that personal experiences of internal displacement and close attention to that displacement allows these writers to produce the radical novel form called "non-civil" - a form that does not conform to typical generic classifications; that does not revolve around the logic of civil-rights; and that eludes domestication for the deeply conscious of global struggles.

INTERVIEWS

Ann Petry Talks about First Novel (1946)
James W. Ivey

One day in October, 1943, I was going through a batch of manuscripts when I picked out one with the teasing title "On Saturday the Siren Sounds at Noon." It turned out upon examination to be a short story by Ann Petry. I had not known the name before, but a glance at the first paragraph told me that the woman was a writer. I went to my editor with enthusiastic praise for the story and we both agreed that it was "good stuff" and should be printed. We scheduled the story for our December, 1943 issue. This was the first published story of a young writer of remarkable talent. Further interest was aroused in the story when one of the editors of the publishing house of Houghton Mifflin asked for copies of the December issue.

This was my first introduction to the writings of Mrs. Petry. But I never met Mrs. Petry until the winter of 1946, almost three years later. In the meantime, she had submitted for publication a long-short story on the Harlem riot of August, 1943. Though a brilliant psychological analysis of the frustrations, the pent-up emotions, and the tensions which provoked the outbreak, the story was too long for *The Crisis* and we had regretfully to suggest that it be offered elsewhere. In May, 1945, however, we carried her study in affection,"Olaf and his Girl Friend." And in November we published "Like a Winding Sheet."

Mrs. Petry thus joins that company of brilliant young writers Langston Hughes, et al., who first received publication in the pages of *The Crisis*.

After one of the Mifflin editors had read "On Saturday the Siren Sounds at Noon," he asked Mrs. Petry if she were working on a novel. She was (1) and the following year she submitted the first five chapters and a complete synopsis of *The Street*. She was then awarded the $2,400 Houghton Mifflin Literary Fellowship for 1945. This enabled her to devote the next ten months to finishing the novel.

The Street was published in January and its appearance gave me an opportunity to meet Mrs. Petry. My appointment was for 11:30 A.M. in the offices of Richard Condon in East 57th Street, just off Fifth Avenue. Mrs. Petry met me cordially and was eager to record that her first published story in *The Crisis* had given her [her] reputation.

In person Mrs. Petry is of medium height, [with] pleasant manners and intercourse, and possessed of a sense of companionable good humor. She has a creamy-brown complexion; alert, smiling eyes; and a soft cultivated voice. We entered at once into the intimacy of talk and the first thing I wanted to know was how she had come to write her first published story.

"Did you have any particular message in that story? What were you trying to show?" I queried.

"Nothing in particular. I wrote it simply as a story. But it came to be written in this way. One Saturday I was standing on the 125th Street platform of the IRT subway when a siren suddenly went off. The screaming blast seemed to vibrate inside people. For the siren seemed to be just above the station. I immediately noticed the reactions of the people on the platform. They were interesting, especially the frantic knitting of a woman on a nearby bench.

"I began wondering," continued Mrs. Petry, "how this unearthly howl would affect a criminal, a man hunted by the police. That was the first incident. The second was a tragedy I covered for my paper. There was a fire in Harlem in which two children had been burnt to death. Their parents were at work and the children were alone. I imagined their reactions when they returned home that night. I knew also that many Harlem parents, like Lilly Belle in the story, often left their children home along while at work. Imaginatively combined the two incidents gave me my story."

I then asked her where she got her knowledge of the West Indian background for "Olaf and his Girl Friend." Many of her friends and acquaintances, she explained, are West Indians, and they often tell her stories about the islands and discuss West Indian customs.

"I wrote that story to show that there can be true affection among Negroes. That Negroes can love as deeply as anyone else. So many people impute to Negroes an unhampered sensuality that I felt it time to tell the truth. Now the idea of Olaf's (the chief character in the story) seeking Belle Rose through the sailor's grapevine, I got from a friend."

"What writers have influenced you?" I asked

"Really," replied Mrs. Petry, smiling. "I have read so many authors and so many books that I don't know. I have been an omnivorous reader since childhood. I was born and reared in a small town, and in a small town, you know, there is really nothing much to do except read."

I then asked her about her recently published novel, *The Street*.

"In *The Street* my aim is to show how simply and easily the environment can change the course of a person's life. For this purpose I have made Lindy [sic] Johnson an intelligent, ambitious, attractive woman with a fair degree of education. She lives in the squalor of 116th Street, but she retains her self-respect and fights to bring up her little son decently.

"I try to show why the Negro has a high crime rate, a high death rate, and little or no chance of keeping his family unit intact in large northern cities. There are no statistics in the book though they are present in the background, not as columns of figures but in terms of what life is like for people who live in over-crowded tenements.

"I tried to write a story that moves swiftly so that it would hold the attention of people who might ordinarily shy away from a so-called problem novel. And I hope that I have created characters who are real, believable, alive. For I am of the opinion that most Americans regard Negroes as types - not quite human - who fit into a special category and I wanted to show them as people with the same capacity for love and hate, for tears and laughter, and the same instincts for survival possessed by all men."

Mrs. Ann Petry was born in Old Saybrook, Connecticut, and comes from a New England family that has specialized in some branch of chemistry for three generations. Her grandfather was a chemist; her father, an aunt, and an uncle are druggists. Mrs. Petry is herself a registered pharmacist, a graduate of the college of pharmacy of the University of Connecticut. It was while working as a registered pharmacists (sic) in the drugstores owned by her family in Old Saybrook and Old Lyme that she began writing her first short stories.

If she had not married and gone to New York City to live, she would undoubtedly have continued her career as a pharmacist. Instead she sought and found jobs in New York that would give her an opportunity to write. She sold advertising space and wrote advertising copy for a Harlem weekly. She also edited the woman's page for a rival weekly, and covered general news stories.

While interviewing celebrities, covering political rallies and three-alarm fires, and reporting on murders and all other forms of sudden death, she acquired an intimate and disturbing knowledge of Harlem and its ancient evil, housing; its tragic broken families; its high death rate.

She spent nine months working on an experiment in education that was being conducted in one of the city's elementary schools and thus observed at firsthand the toll that segregated areas like Harlem exact in the twisting and warping of children's lives.

In addition to working on newspapers, she has taught salesmanship, written children's plays, acted with an amateur theatrical group. She is a former member of the now famous American Negro Theatre. She has studied painting, and plays the piano for her own amusement, claiming to be the least promising pupil of a well-known composer and pianist. At present she is executive secretary of Negro Women Incorporated, a civic-minded organization which keeps a watchful eye on local and national legislation.

Notes

1. In James Ivey's interview, we are told that Petry answered Houghton's query by saying that she was writing a novel. In the article "Street Wise," which appears in *The Hartford Courant* on November 8, 1992, Garret Condon reports that Petry responded to Houghton's query by saying she was not working on a novel but might be shortly.

The Chronology in this edition, which was edited by Ann Petry, indicates that in 1944 Houghton first asked Petry about writing a novel. At that time she replied that at the time she was not but would eventually. Petry also says that the editor who approached her was female, while Ivey writes that the editor was male. Ivey reports that *The Street* was published in January of 1946; the novel was published in February of that year.

From Interviews with Black Writers (1973)
John O'Brien

Mrs. Petry is presently working on another novel, after taking several years off to raise a family and write children's stories. We met in early November of 1971. She picked me up at the train station in Old Saybrooke [sic] and, on the way to her home, showed me the landmarks that dated back to before the Revolution. She was quick to point out disdainfully the ugly encroachments of commercialism upon her town. She lives in a house that was built in 1800 and has been preserved in its original state. Because she dislikes tape recorders, as well as interviews, she answered my questions by mail a few months after we talked in her home. Almost a year after our initial meeting, we talked briefly once more on the phone in an effort to expand on some of her earlier remarks. The brevity of her answers and her obvious hesitancy to talk about her work belie her warmth. After apologizing for what she considered to be unhelpful answers, she invited me to visit her again when I was not armed with pen and paper.

INTERVIEWER: Do you like talking about your writing?
PETRY: No. I find it painful.
INTERVIEWER: Is it just that it's unpleasant for you, or do you think a writer shouldn't discuss her own work?
PETRY: I personally don't like talking about it. My feeling is that once I've written something I don't have anything more to say about it. That's it. Talking about it isn't going to change what I did or didn't do. The classic example of the man who tried to explain his work was Shaw. Well, it seems to me that if you have to explain what you write, then you haven't done a very good job. If a critic wants to analyze it, let him. Fine. But I don't want to.
INTERVIEWER: Are you also hesitant to talk about the craft of writing?
PETRY: No. I don't mind. But I'm not an authority. I can only speak in terms of what I try to do or the problems I face.
INTERVIEWER: Do you have any particular difficulty in creating characters?
PETRY: I don't have any particular problem in creating characters. They seem to grow and develop and become alive during the process of writing. Occasionally there's something about a character I don't know. For example, I had almost finished writing *The Street* and I still did not know why Mrs. Hodges always wore a turban. One afternoon I was on the Eighth Avenue subway going to the Bronx and it suddenly came to me that Mrs. Hedges was bald. And then I worked out how she came to be bald.
INTERVIEWER: Do you have a set way in which you begin working on a character? Do you know beforehand what he or she will be doing in the story?
PETRY: There are really so many ways. I don't think that a character appears in its entirety. It's part of a process whereby you have probably surprised yourself several times by the time you have finished, because the character changes or grows or does things that you did not expect. It comes to you as you write.
INTERVIEWER: Then you never start out by thinking of a character as having to fulfill some symbolic function in the story?
PETRY: No, because I do not think of characters functioning symbolically. I hope that what starts out as a sketch will become a full-boned portrait, but that portrait is not necessarily very much related to the original sketch.

INTERVIEWER: Then the creation of a character, for you, is instinctive?
PETRY: Yes. I don't think that I can explain the origins of a character, or even why he fits the situation he's in.
INTERVIEWER: There's a complex system of imagery in your short story "In Darkness and Confusion." I wonder whether you were conscious of it as you wrote?
PETRY: I don't think I worked it in consciously. It's something that I became aware of after I finished it. That particular story almost wrote itself. I did it all at one sitting. I don't know about other people, but it seems to me that the subconscious mind is what creates such things in a story.
INTERVIEWER: Do you ever become aware that something is taking on symbolic importance while you are writing a story?
PETRY: I guess that it's always a matter of after the fact, but I always shy away from such things as symbol hunting. If they are there, they are not there because I consciously created them.
INTERVIEWER: How much do you depend upon personal experience for material in your stories? Must you experience, in some way, much of what you write about?
PETRY: I think a writer would be seriously handicapped - well, let's say limited - both as to subject-matter and the creation of characters if these were based solely on personal experience.
INTERVIEWER: I know that you worked as a reporter in Harlem for six years. Did this experience affect your writing in any way, perhaps both your style and subject matter?
PETRY: Doubtful.
INTERVIEWER: When we met at your home last November we talked about critics' frequent arbitrary grouping of black writers which is most apparent in anthologies of black literature. So often critics seem to ignore the differences between black writers in order to establish some mysterious link between them all.
PETRY: That's because we're all black. As I said, we do have a common theme. We write about relationships between whites and blacks because it's in the very air we breathe. We can't escape it. But we write about it in a thousand different ways and from a thousand different points of view.
INTERVIEWER: Does it bother you that, as John A. Williams has complained, regardless of what a black writer does in his work or what subject he may treat, he or she is always designated as "a black writer"?
PETRY: Well, it's just an indication of the fact that black people are in a minority in this country. If I lived in a country where the majority of the people were black people I would be an "author" - and the white folks would be "white authors" - if they were authors.
INTERVIEWER: I wonder whether such identification does not force a black writer always to direct himself only to black audiences? Do you find yourself writing with a particular audience in mind?
PETRY: Not at all. If I permitted myself to think in terms of the reader, I would become so inhibited I wouldn't write - at least for publication.
INTERVIEWER: In addition to the racial problems black writers face in America, they also share the problem that all American writers have - our culture does not greatly value books and reading. What do you identify with the culture you write in?
PETRY: Pro-football, beer, TV serials, and cars.
INTERVIEWER: Have you even been unable to write a story which you would have liked to write?
PETRY: I've never abandoned a story or a novel once I started working on it. I've abandoned many ideas before I ever put a pen to paper. I once planned or thought about writing a book for young people about Daniel Drayton and Edward Syres, two ships' captains imprisoned for attempting to help slaves escape from the District of Columbia on the Schooner *Pearl*. I didn't write that particular

book because I became interested in - actually fascinated by a slave, Tituba, who was one of three women charged with witchcraft at the beginning of the trials for witchcraft in Salem, Massachusetts. Another idea that I once abandoned was to write a book for young people about Jacintha de Siquiera "the celebrated African woman - founding mother of the richest of all Provinces of Brazil" [David Davidson]. I gave up this idea because of the research involved - I would have had to spend a considerable amount of time in Brazil, and I would have had to learn to speak Portuguese, or at least learn to read it. These ideas go with the territory and I hope someone else will write about these people. Feel free.

INTERVIEWER: Is there a part of a novel which is more difficult for you to write than any other?

PETRY: Sometimes. I had great difficulty writing the chapter [*The Narrows*] in which Link is murdered.

INTERVIEWER: Is there some point in the novel where you feel that you have everything in hand and the rest will fall into place?

PETRY: I never have a novel "in hand" until it is completed.

INTERVIEWER: Do you every experience any conflict between meaning and form, or between what you might like to do in a novel and what you think your reader will be able to understand? Or does the form of a novel develop on its own?

PETRY: The form finds itself.

INTERVIEWER: Do you remember how old you were when you first started to write?

PETRY: Fourteen.

INTERVIEWER: Were you anxious to show your work to people?

PETRY: I rarely ever told anyone that I was writing. And I still don't talk about what I write if I can avoid it.

INTERVIEWER: Do you think of your fiction as autobiographical?

PETRY: I could say that none of my work is autobiographical, or that all of it is - everything I write is filtered through my mind, consciously or unconsciously. The end product contains everything I know, have experienced, thought about, dreamed about, talked about, lived for. And so in that sense I am any of the characters that I create, all of them, some of them, or none of them.

INTERVIEWER: Could you say something about your writing habits? When do you work? How much revising do you do? Are you subject to moods during the time you are working on a novel?

PETRY: When I'm writing I work in the morning from 8:00 A.M. to about noon. If I'm going to do any revising I do it in the afternoon. The first draft is in longhand. The planning and the writing go hand in hand for the most part. I revise endlessly. And yet the first chapter of *The Street* was written in one sitting and that first draft was the final one - no changes. And there were no changes in a story entitled "Like a Winding Sheet" or in "Sole [sic] on the Drums." I do not work at night if I can avoid it. I am not subject to moods. I doubt if my family or anyone else can tell when I'm thinking about writing.

INTERVIEWER: One reviewer of *The Street* made a comparison between you and Theodore Dreiser. Do you see any similarity? Do you feel that you belong to a naturalistic school of writing?

PETRY: No to both questions. To be absolutely honest about it, it really doesn't interest me. I always want to do something different from what I have done before. I don't want to repeat myself. If I belong to a certain tradition, I don't want to belong, because my writing would be very boring if I always wrote in a particular style.

INTERVIEWER: Could you tell me how the conception for *The Street* came to you? After you have an idea for a novel, how do you go about starting the novel itself?

PETRY: *The Street* was built around a story in a newspaper - a small item occupying perhaps an inch of space. It concerned the superintendent of an apartment house in Harlem who taught an eight-year-old boy to steal letters from mail boxes. As far as procedure is concerned I usually make a rough outline or draft - and I break it down into chapters, and begin to write, and then revise what I've written.

INTERVIEWER: Hoyt Fuller noted in an article that a number of black writers around 1950 abandoned writing novels about blacks. He pointed to *Country Place* as an example. Why do you think this happened with so many black writers? Why did you choose different subjects and themes?

PETRY: I don't know what impelled other black writers to stop writing novels about blacks. I wrote *Country Place* because I happened to have been in a small town in Connecticut during a hurricane - I decided to write about that violent, devastating storm and its effect on the town and the people who lived there.

INTERVIEWER: A few critics have pointed out what they think are your implausible endings, especially those in *The Street* and *Country Place*. I guess what they are referring to are Lutie Johnson's act of murder and Lil's attempted murder. How do you respond to that criticism?

PETRY: I don't think there's anything "implausible" about the endings in *The Street* and *Country Place* - they're perfectly logical given the circumstances and the character of the people.

INTERVIEWER: Why did you use the druggist to narrate *Country Place* rather than having an omniscient point of view as you did in *The Street*?

PETRY: I had never used the first person, and a druggist in a small town seemed to offer great possibilities.

INTERVIEWER: One of your critics has argued that the hope of the town in *Country Place* resides in the minority figures, Neola and Portegee. One also might add the youth, Johnnie Roane. Did you intend something like this? And at the end of the novel there appears to be a restoration of moral order when several minority figures are included in the will. Were you suggesting that social and moral change must occur simultaneously?

PETRY: No to both questions. I think you're reading something into this book that simply is not there.

INTERVIEWER: What are your feelings about Weasel? His name suggests certain unlikable qualities, yet, in some crude way he brings justice to the town, even though he does not always practice it himself.

PETRY: As to the Weasel - very few people are all evil. The Weasel isn't. Mrs. Hedges isn't, nor is Powther in *The Narrows* or Bill Hod. We're all mixtures of good and evil.

INTERVIEWER: So Mrs. Hedges in *The Street* plays a kind of dual role: she rescues Lutie and Bub on two different occasions, yet she was also part of the vicious system that was entrapping them.

PETRY: Dual role? Well, perhaps. Mrs. Hedges is probably a classic example of the fact that most people are a mixture of good and evil.

INTERVIEWER: *The Narrows* seems a very different novel from the first two. Perhaps your form and content have come together perfectly in that novel. What do you think?

PETRY: I don't know.

INTERVIEWER: Is there any "correct" point of view in *The Narrows*? I think of this in relation to the themes of guilt and time. Abbie thinks that the past determines everything and that she, personally, is responsible for the evil that has occurred. Miss Doris thinks that everyone is responsible. Bill Hod and Weak Knees think of racism as being the cause of the evil. Is any one of these wholly correct?

PETRY: I suppose not, though racism comes closer to being the cause.

INTERVIEWER: Is there any implicit condemnation of Link for having undertaken the love affair with a rich white girl?

PETRY: No.

INTERVIEWER: Could you say something about the use of comedy in *The Narrows*? Some of the comic scenes seem to be steeped in "black humor."

PETRY: I have a peculiar sense of humor.

INTERVIEWER: While I was reading *The Narrows* I was struck by certain thematic similarities to Huxley and Faulkner, especially in your treatment of time. Are you conscious of any such resemblance?

PETRY: No.

INTERVIEWER: The racial conflict in *The Narrows* is minimized. Although it plays a large part in determining the outcome of the story, you seem to be treating more universal problems. Do you think that "race" is as important a theme in this novel as it was in *The Street*?

PETRY: Yes.

INTERVIEWER: Your short story "The Witness" ends with Woodruff slowing his car after he is reminded what the boys had done to him. Will he return and be a witness against them? Or is it just that he doesn't have the strength or desire to go on?

PETRY: He won't be back.

INTERVIEWER: What are your plans for writing?

PETRY: I plan to go on writing novels and short stories and one of these days I plan to write a play - or two - or three.

INTERVIEWER: Did you intend "Mother Africa" to be an allegory? For example, the protagonist is called "Man." Or is it unfair to ask you to explain your own story in this way?

PETRY: I think it is an imposition to ask me to "explain" a story or a novel.

Interviews

A Visit With Ann Petry, May 16, 1984
College of Pharmacy, University of Illinois at Chicago *

ROBERT MRTEK: Let me tell you again how grateful we are to have you here. The group that you're with now is a small class of pharmacy students, everywhere from first year students to fifth year students (fourth year professional students), and they are all taking a course called "Images of Pharmacy in the Arts." We are in the section of the course now when we are looking at writers who have either a very close association with pharmacy themselves, or who write extensively about pharmacy in their literary creations. And, we are particularly fortunate, again, to have you here because you are both a pharmacist and a very famous writer.

    As you know, I am making a tape of this and you will have the right to edit the transcript; the students have agreed that they will sign off their rights "in perpetuity" and we intend, with your permission, to deposit this in the Archival Division of the American Institute of the History of Pharmacy.

    Let me tell you that the period will be as freewheeling as you and the students are to make it. They have all read "Miss Muriel" and that chapter that we saw dramatized out of *Country Place*.

CONLIN [student]: And "The New Mirror."
MRTEK: Thank you.
PETRY: Now, if you will ask questions, I'll do my very best to answer them.
MRTEK: I think that would be fine.
PETRY: It's, I'm sure, pretty obvious that "Miss Muriel" and "The New Mirror" and another short story of mine called "Has Anybody Seen Miss Dora Dean?" are all related in one way or another to the drugstore that I talk about and write about. The question is always asked, "How much of this really happened? Did you experience this?" Well, yes, some of it did, some of it didn't. In "Miss Muriel," there was only one person who had had a real existence as far as - no, two people: one was my uncle (I think I refer to him as "Uncle Johno") and the other one is the man who arrives every summer as a guest of Uncle Johno. Now the man who arrived every summer really existed. He had been a teacher of English. He had been an actor. Usually the first thing he said to me on his arrival was, "These Yankees have destroyed your voice."
MRTEK: What did he expect?
PETRY: He said, "You're talking through your nose." But he was endlessly entertaining and really a great person to be around.

    My aunt really did exist: she was a druggist. She graduated from the Brooklyn College of Pharmacy in 1908. She was the only woman in her class. I have her diploma and that is really fascinating because every single professor that she had signed it. There are flowers depicted in the name "Brooklyn College of Pharmacy." That "B" is all decorated with flowers, and the "C's" and so on and so on. When I showed it to my daughter she said to me, with considerable puzzlement, "What have flowers got to do with pharmacy?" I said, "Well, you forget that this is a very, very old profession. It has not always been called pharmacy, but originally, almost all the things used in the treatment of illnesses came from flowers, from roots, from herbs. These days they may be made chemically, but originally came from plants - from the leaves, the seeds, etc."

As I said, my aunt really did exist. Of course, her name was not "Sophronia," but she did exist. She was very beautiful, and we did have in the town a little old man who was a shoemaker, who developed this sort of, very frightening, attachment to her. Nobody actually ran him out of town, that's all made up. He did finally marry somebody else. But before he married he came with this little bag of trinkets that had belonged to his mother. He gave these to her because he said he knew this wasn't going to work out. She was a very young woman, but then on the other hand she never did marry. And as for the piano player, he never existed but she did have a suitor that my family regarded as highly unsuitable, but that was it. Yes?

LOWRIE [student]: Were you also the only woman who graduated from your pharmacy class?

PETRY: Oh, no, there were five of us.

MRTEK: But you were the only black woman.

PETRY: Yes. My father and a friend were the first black men licensed as pharmacists in the state of Connecticut back in 1890. I still have his license. Of course, in the days when he became a pharmacist, he was apprenticed in a drugstore because there were no pharmacy schools.

MRTEK: In American pharmacy history, we find examples, particularly in the South, where pharmacy practitioners and blacks were separated by law; Negroes were not permitted to handle or manipulate any drug substances because of the racial discrimination. Now, let me ask you, in your father's time - in your own time - was that black discrimination very much there in practice? In other words, being a black pharmacist, were you set on earth to prepare pharmaceuticals for black people only?

PETRY: No.

MRTEK: That never materialized within the community?

PETRY: No, not at all. As a matter of fact as far as the community was concerned, if we had had to depend on black people for a living, we wouldn't have survived because there weren't any, except for one other family, and that was it. But, no, when my father first opened his drugstore in the town, someone who was very much like the Weasel in *Country Place* did arrive to tell him - brought him a message saying that "they" were going to run him out of town. And my father, who was a man of uncertain temper and not given to receiving such messages, promptly took him by the throat and almost choked him to death and said, "You go back and you tell them that any time they want to try, I walk on this street around nine o'clock at night. And tell them to try" - and he said - "You be sure to tell them that I come from Madagascar." And he always said that he didn't have any idea where Madagascar was or what it was. But he said he figured they'd be so frightened by the idea of confronting a man from some unknown part of the world that no one would bother him. And they didn't.

Their customers were white, all of them. If they had any feelings about us they concealed them. There was only one doctor. He served the town I lived in and five or six other towns. Quite often he was not available no matter what the emergency might be - he could be miles away. People brought anyone who had been injured to our drugstore. My father would do his best to patch them up until the doctor arrived. Oftentimes it was a mater of saving someone's life.

And when he died the whole town, well, practically the whole town, turned out, filling the church with mourners, spilling out to the sidewalks -young, old, middle-aged.

MRTEK: He was "Doc."

PETRY: Yes, Except that my father was black. "Doc" of *Country* was white.

BROSSART [student]: Was it that family influence that made you choose to go into pharmacy?

PETRY: Oh, or course, I'm sure. My family did not say, "You must study pharmacy" or anything like that when I finished high school. I was very young - only 15, and my sister who was older than I was, was already going to a fancy Ivy League college, so finally they said to me, "Why don't you try to go to pharmacy school? So I said "Sure. When?"

BROSSART: You mentioned that there was one other black family in the town that you lived in. Do you think that they might have held something against your family, that they wouldn't have anything to do with you? Do you think it might have been because of your association and professional relationship with all the white people in town?

PETRY: That hadn't developed. We had just barely moved in. We were really very [laughs] very presentable.

SUZANNE POIRIER: You mentioned - your narrator in "New Mirror" expresses some annoyance at times with being the daughter of the pharmacist, feeling "We're on display in the town, why do we have to act and behave certain ways both because we're the pharmacist's family and we're one of only two black families?" Did you yourself ever feel that your life had some inequities inasmuch as - some unfairness because - you were the pharmacist's family and your home and business were in the same building?

PETRY: Well, home and business, true, they were in the same building, but there was a very definite demarcation - my family had really literally built a wall between the society, that is the village and the people in the village, and the drugstore. The drugstore was a public thing, but our family life was not. And I would imagine that to this very day that people in that village really don't know very much about us. At all. And, as far as I was concerned, I suppose I was like any other lively youngster. I found that wall not exactly acceptable.

Let me tell you something else I still think of often. I told you that I had an aunt who was a pharmacist. And I can remember my mother saying to me and my sister and a cousin of mine that never under any circumstances in public were we ever to call her "Aunt Louise." She was always to be "Miss James," because otherwise this whole town would call her "Aunt Louise." They would prefer to call her that rather than call her "Miss James." And to this day, do you know, I refer to her as "Miss James." She lived to be ninety - ninety-four, I think.

MRTEK: When did your interest in literature and in writing first awaken and how did it - if you can remember that?

PETRY: Well, I was writing so to speak while in high school. I had an English teacher, Miss Avery. It was a small high school and the English class was up at the top of the building, which was literally like an attic. In those old buildings you can smell the oil they used to oil the floor with to keep the dust down, and it was powdery with chalk.

I used to get very bored. Miss Avery and I didn't like each other at all. Anyway, we were reading A Tale of Two Cities and because I had this terrible habit - if I really got into it I'd read the whole book. You're supposed to read a chapter every day. Then when I came to class, you see, I could spoil it for everybody.

Well, anyway, I think it was the final exam in English - we were sophomores and Miss Avery had given us what we regarded as an awful question. She did not ask us specifically about the characters, or the plot, or the author or anything that we might think she would ask. Instead she said we were to write an imaginary scene between any of the characters - it didn't make any difference which ones - and you can well imagine that any young people in any English class absolutely would have died. Well, anyway, I thought, an imaginary scene . . . . You remember Jerry Cruncher, the gravedigger? I wrote the most marvelous imaginary scene. I mean, I just sat there and enjoyed myself - making it up.

A few days later, Miss Avery arrived in class with all these papers. She looked around the room and said, "I want to read you one of these papers." She read my paper, and I thought "She's doing this because she's going to say 'This is a terrible example of what people can produce if they don't pay attention in class.' " But she didn't say that at all. She said she thought it was wonderful. And after class she gave me back my paper and she said to me, "You know," with this note of wonder in her voice, " I think if you really wanted to you could write."

I think Miss Avery had such a hard time with that English class; she later became a missionary, and she went to India.

BROSSART: Did everybody else pass?

PETRY: No, a lot of them didn't. But you asked me when I became interested in literature. I developed a love for poetry when I was in high school. We had an English teacher who, if we had a few spare moments, would read a poem to us. One day he read Robert Frost's "I, Too, Am a Swinger of Birches." Birch trees are so limber that if you would swing on them, you could swing a long distance. This is about a boy who discovers birch trees, and I was simply enchanted. I became a reader of poetry afterwards. And I was trying to think . . . .

MRTEK: Do you have a favorite poet?

PETRY: Indeed I do. But I have something I wanted to read to you.

MRTEK [to the group]: That was the journal that she keeps You see, she told us in the room downstairs to keep a journal . . . .

PETRY: Yes, but this I think is so absolutely amazing. It suggests what a long way we've come. When we finally closed that drugstore I found a great many old bottles. One of the boxes I found in the cellar contained a patent medicine. It was called "Kennedy's Medical Discovery," and it sold for a dollar and a half. Now you have to remember that in the days when they were selling patent medicines like that the average worker in a rural community earned about three hundred dollars a year, so that a dollar and a half for a bottle of medicine was a really large amount of money.

And this particular patent medicine is described as "the greatest medical discovery of the age - Kennedy's Medical Discovery. Mr. Kennedy of Roxbury, Massachusetts, discovered in one of our common pastures a weed." It's a remedy that cures "every kind of humour from the worst scrofula down to a common pimple." He had tried it in over eleven hundred cases, never failed - except in two cases - both thunder puma [?]. He has now in his possession "over two hundred certificates [sic] of its value - all within 20 miles of Boston. Manufactured by Donald Kennedy." And there's a picture of him with his mutton chop whiskers and his hair is rather long. It also says "Entered according to act of Congress in the year 1854 by Donald Kennedy in the Clerk's Office at District Court in Massachusetts." And embossed on the side, "Kennedy's Medical Discovery," and then it says also "Dr. Kennedy" embossed but it doesn't say that on the label.

This is what it says on the label: "Two bottles are warranted to cure a nursing sore mouth. One to three bottles will cure the worst kind of pimples on the face. One to three bottles will clean the system of biles. Warranted to cure the worst kind of humour in the mouth and stomach." And then he goes on to the eyes, the hair, "ulcers, corruption of the skin, ringworm, rheumatism, salt wounds, scrofula." And also, if your lungs are infected with "shooting pains" it will take care of that. It'll take care of any kind of "biliousness" and on and on and on.

MRTEK: Sounds like *Tono-bungay* --- which we have read in this class.

PETRY: But isn't that amazing, and it is a very handsome bottle, greenish in color.

MRTEK: Tell us something about the techniques of writing. How do you go about producing the works that you do? Are they all outlined first? Do you cogitate on them or do you just freewheel with the typewriter?

PETRY: Oh, no. I don't freewheel it. But in the case of *The Street,* for example, I'd written an outline - no, not an outline, a synopsis of the first five chapters. The short stories, only because I usually like to know where and how the thing's going to end. If I have an ending in view it's easier to work directly towards that. With books that I've written for children, I am usually much more careful about organizing . . . .

MRTEK: Why is that?

PETRY: Because I feel that children's books ought to have a kind of, that they should have about them something that makes you feel that they're - I guess you'd say an inevitability - that I don't think you could achieve by just shooting off. And then or course, you rewrite. And you rewrite and you rewrite.

MRTEK: We have in this class all struggled with writing this quarter and I'm glad to hear you say you rewrite, because we rewrite and throw away.

PETRY: That's right.

MRTEK: Do you throw away?

PETRY: Absolutely.

MRTEK: It doesn't come out perfect?

PETRY: It never has. In fact, I can even tell you the instances where something I wrote remained exactly the way it was when I started. The first chapter in *The Street* I wrote last. I don't think I changed anything, but that's the only thing that I can think of where that's true, because all the rest of that book I wrote and rewrote and . . . .

MRTEK: So many writers talk about writing as possessing them. Hemingway describes it that way. It couldn't be forced, or it couldn't be encouraged. It just sort of descended on the writer and then the writer had to grapple with it. Are you pretty even in your ability to write or does it . . . .

PETRY: Well, I suppose all . . . . I must say this, though: he may have said all that, about it descending on him, but I'm sure, from the way his - the things he wrote - it's perfectly obvious to me that he wrote and rewrote, because otherwise he couldn't have achieved that clean, clear kind of prose. I don't think that just comes like that.

POIRIER: Earlier, this noon, when you were talking about the characters in *Country Place,* you said that "Doc" was partly your father but your father was not as even-tempered. How can that be - the influence of the real character on created ones? Some writers talk about creating a character and then the character kind of creates him - or herself and leads the writer. Does that happen?

PETRY: Yes. or course. It does. Of course whenever that happens, I think it's wonderful because I think you get a much more believable character.

POIRIER: Do you usually start with a picture of someone or something in mind and then just kind of let it grow?

PETRY: Well, now, let me think. I - I suppose I do, I don't know. I was trying to think of the short stories that . . . . I do remember that I always intended to use that business about bats in the drugstore because that did actually happen. And I just thought it was so wonderful because all of a sudden on a hot summer's night these bats were floating around in the drugstore, creating a considerable amount of consternation. And I always thought that somehow I had to put that in a story.

LEWIS [student]: Eyes are very important in the works that I know about you, and I was wondering if somehow your characterizations some way began with the eyes. I was thinking about your minute description of bats and eyes. And then eyes - I don't remember all the eyes, but I just remember that eyes are very dominant. They almost could be a motif. You see the eyes and you know the character.

PETRY: Don't you think that's true of people?

LEWIS: Well, that's what I was wondering: if you are a very keen observer of one's eyes.

PETRY: Well, I try to be an observer of everything about people, but eyes are particularly important.

MONTELLA [student]: In "Miss Muriel" it seemed that the little girl - it just reminded me - maybe you were writing part of yourself into that character. Do you ever do that in your stories: Do you write yourself into your stories?

PETRY: Well, I think, actually, I'm in all of them. I'm even part of the Weasel. Really. I think that we all have - let's see - how am I going to say it? I think we're all sufficiently complicated as people to be able to . . . it's a matter of putting yourself in somebody's else's place. And because there is in me, or in you, well, certain qualities which may not be dominant ones or the ones that show on the surface, they are there somewhere.

CONLIN: Apart from your literary work, do you every regret leaving pharmacy and going into writing, and was there any point in your life after you have left pharmacy that you wanted to go back into that profession?

PETRY: Well, no. I never have regretted it, but the reason probably, I'm quite certain, is that I worked for my family in the afternoon when I was in high school. I worked seven days a week. The only time that drugstore was closed was on Christmas in the afternoon and Thanksgiving in the afternoon. And that's the reason - long hours and very little pay - made me pro-labor and pro-union. And once I was out of it I had no desire to return. It's true that I'm sure that if it had been a different kind of situation other than that . . .as a matter of fact, if it weren't for the experience I would probably have tried to become licensed as a pharmacist when I lived in New York City.

BROSSART: Did they pay you the going rates?

PETRY: No.

MRTEK: Oh, maybe that's the reason.

PETRY: It was that, and the hours. I mean who on earth would ever consent to working seven days a week? Good heavens, that's terrible. I'm sure you won't have to work more than thirty-five or forty hours a week. Look at all the time you have to do other things - reading, writing.

TAM. [student]: Did you enjoy it when you were in pharmacy school?

PETRY: Yes, I did

MRTEK: I want to go back to something you said about your preparation for the children's stories. You talked about the quality of inevitability. Beethoven was often described as trying to achieve that same quality of inevitability in that [sic] music. The risk of inevitability is that spontaneity goes out the window.

PETRY: Not if it's a good story. Not if it's good music.

MRTEK: How do you keep the magic and variety and yet make everything exactly "inevitable"?

PETRY: Well, I don't think that's difficult. I think if you have a kind of enthusiasm for the subject matter: for example, the more I learned about Harriet Tubman, the more I learned about *Tituba of Salem Village*, the more involved I became in the lives of these women, and the more I admired (and incidentally you know, when you talk about the healing arts, I think both those women practiced them: Tituba in Salem, which is one of the ways that she got into difficulty, and Harriet Tubman, who looked after so many people when she was on those trips North. I mean there was a nurturing quality that they had. And I think that people in what I call the healing arts, if they're really good, they have it). And if you write about people like that you don't have any problem. You get caught up in their lives, in their motivation.

The only problem that I have in writing these books is that I really and truly don't like going back in time where you have to check every single thing in terms of clothing, in terms of food, in terms of the way the houses look inside. All of that - it slows you down. But other than that . . . and you know, that's really kind of amazing, because those books, by now I don't know how many years old they are, and they still sell. They are still in print. And one of the most rewarding things about writing books for children, for young people: all year long while school is in session, all of a sudden your mail will come and there's a whole stack of letters. Yes, and it's just . . . from children who have read what you've written, and they have questions and they express their appreciation.

LOWRIE: Tell me more about the lack of distinction between pharmacy and medicine back in that era. I had a grandfather who was a small-town doctor in Graff, Ohio, and the house was attached to his office. I used to go visit him all the time. You know, I grew up in Chicago, so to me, that was the sticks. We used to go visit him, and he had this one part of his office where he would sit and make drugs.

PETRY: Sure, he was dispensing then.

LOWRIE: Yes, and then I didn't think anybody ever went to a pharmacy after seeing him, so back then there really wasn't a line of distinction at all.

PETRY: No, I'm sure there wasn't. Of course, I don't know how far back you're talking about, but originally, no.

LOWRIE: Well, the earliest I remember is late 50s, early 60s.

PETRY: Oh, there was beginning to be a distinction then because by that time there was a, I would say, gentlemen's agreement: the pharmacists did not practice medicine and doctors did not dispense.

LOWRIE: Even in small towns?

PETRY: Even in small towns. And the only reason my father was - oh, he wouldn't have said he was practicing medicine - but the only reason he was doing what he did was because there were no doctors available, so what could he do - let one bleed to death on the floor in his store? But in the early days I would say the distinction between medicine and pharmacy was nonexistent.

MRTEK: In the old days, medicine had three branches to it. One was physic, the art of diagnosis, the second one was surgery, and the third was pharmacy. They were all part of the same thing.

I wanted to ask you what your feelings are on today's attitudes toward a visual society. We have - young people claim today that they relate much more directly to an image - pictorial image - than the spoken work. And for some young people it is very difficult to even experience your art.

PETRY: I'm sure it is. But I have no - you can't do away with television; it's out of the question. The only thing that really bothers me: it would seem to me, it would be increasingly difficult, for example, to handle all the material that people have to handle in these professional schools. They have to do a tremendous amount of reading and studying and if you're not geared toward the printed word, well, I think you would have problems.

I remember one thing that bothered me and I've thought about it ever since, and that's some time ago: when Kennedy was president, he said that television is the greatest psychic destroyer in the world. And I often thought about that and what it comes down to, I guess, is that people no longer relish or welcome being alone; they no longer, if you want to use the word meditate: they don't do that. They have to have some kind of image before them, some kind of noise or sound in their ears and that is a destroyer of the self.

MRTEK: It robs us of our imagination.

BROSSART: That's why I'm having such a hard time on this paper. [laughter from class].

PETRY: Could I ask some questions? I'm very curious --- how do you feel about what I said? Is that true, do you feel that television, or that watching it, has in any way diminished your response to the printed word?

BROSSART: Well, I know from my experiences, when I read a book compared to when I see a movie, I get a lot more out of my reading because I can put my imaginary images onto people and how they're going to look and everything. After I've read a book and I go and see the movie, I feel it wasn't as deep as it was, you know; the response isn't as deep as when I was reading the book. I think you can ad lib your own feeling, your own emotions, and everything in the reading, but when you see it on the screen, it's all there and you can only accept it for what it's showing there. I think there's a big difference there, in interpretation.

PETRY: Do you write?

BROSSART: I think about it.

MRTEK: But you cannot write without thinking. How about some of the others of you? - We spent almost a full quarter agonizing over readings, plays, art work . . . .

CONLIN: I think that the visual medium takes a lot away. The movie is going to happen in an hour and a half, and if you're going to get everything out of that movie you have to get it all out of it in that span of time. Whereas, when you're reading you can stop and think about things and maybe read part of it today, and think about it, pick it back up tomorrow and continue with it and just go at your own pace, and you can get a lot more out of it than if you have to be able to get everything out of something in a set period of time. And I think that's one way that the visual medium takes it away from you.

BROSSART: Being a student, though, I think we don't really watch T.V. as much as your average . . . .

PETRY: How true!

BROSSART: It's true, when you work and you go to school and you study, you know you're lucky if you might catch the evening news. I mean, that's how it is for me and a lot of my friends.

POIRIER: You were saying in one of the conversations we had before you came that you had gone back to your writing to find references to pharmacy and things that were in there that you hadn't noticed . . . .

PETRY: Oh, I didn't find - I didn't really have the time to do that. But here and there a little - this afternoon for instance, I've mentioned *The Street* where a man had been cut and goes to the druggist, and I mentioned the fact that *Tituba of Salem Village* and *Harriet Tubman* were healers in the best sense of the word, and of course, *Country Place*. And the short stories that I have written where I used the drugstore as a background and the pharmacist appears in the pharmacy. There is also my children's book *The Drugstore Cat*. There is something though that . . . . I wrote a book for children called *Legends of the Saints*, and I looked and one segment in there has to do with St. Martin de Porres. He was a barber originally but he was also a person who dispensed medicine. He was a practitioner of the healing art. And that's - I suppose it's that really, and I guess that all came from pharmacy.

CONLIN: Have you ever written about pharmacy?

PETRY: You mean as such?

CONLIN: Yes, as a profession or a story about pharmacy?

PETRY: Well, yes, a long time ago. I wrote - there was a publication called *Drug Topics* (is it?) - Well, a good many years ago I wrote a piece I called "A Tribute to Mr. Gentry." Mr. Gentry was a purely imaginary pharmacist, and I wrote about drugstores and the way they once were and role they played in small communities and, in fact, in the large ones. Yes?

MONTELLA: What are your feelings about today's pharmacists?

PETRY: Today's pharmacists?

MONTELLA: Yes.

PETRY: Well, I mean, I don't know that I have any particular feeling. I have great respect for them professionally and I certainly think that they are far better educated and equipped to handle all the chemicals used in a very complicated world. I say complicated world as far as business is concerned.

MONTELLA: It's a lot faster-paced and productive . . . than how it was in the past?

PETRY: And, or course, I think pretty much all that life of the small-town drugstore - I think that has vanished. I think that even today, for example, you don't see the pharmacist. It would never occur to you to go in a back room and talk to him.

MRTEK: Weasel would never have had the opportunity today that he had.

PETRY: No.

MRTEK: He would have to know how to read a computer screen. What is the Ann Petry style? How do you describe yourself?

PETRY: My lifestyle?

MRTEK: No, no, not your lifestyle - unless you care to talk about it?

PETRY: Well, I live in a small town in an old, old house that was built in 1790. We shore it up here and there once in awhile. And to my daughter's disgust every time (of course, she doesn't live at home any more; she is married and lives in Philadelphia) . . . but anyway, when she was growing up if I wasn't around to answer the telephone, I'd be way off somewhere and somebody wanted me, I'd say, "Tell 'em I'm mowing the back forty." But anyway, we have gardens and grow flowers and vegetables. And I read a lot, I write a lot.

MRTEK: But in terms of literary style . . . .

PETRY: All I ever try to do is to write so that the reader will keep on reading. And I try to write so that what I've written will be remembered, whether it's a character or a situation or believable dialogue that will leave a lasting impression.

LOWRIE: Is your husband a writer also?

PETRY: Well yes, in a way. He used to write copy for an advertising agency. He is now retired. I used to tour and give lectures. I spent a year at the University of Hawaii, and naturally when you write you become an object of great curiosity. One of the first questions that people used to ask me was, "What does your husband do?" And I would look them right in the eye and say, "If I were a man, would you ask me what my wife did?" How near are we to closing because I've got something I want to read.

MRTEK: Please read.

PETRY: I'll read it right now. But first I urge you to write in a journal - almost every day, and to write short stories. Maybe write poetry. But write. You have to offset the life of chemistry and biology and all of the science that you study during these years in this school of pharmacy by developing another side of your mind and of yourselves. So I leave you with these lovely words written by Laurie Lee, a British poet: "Any bits of warm life preserved by the pen are trophies snatched from the dark, are branches of leaves fished out of the flood, are tiny arrests of mortality." You are quite young, and probably not the least bit interested in immortality, but someday you will be. Keep dreaming. Keep writing, Keep reading. Enjoy.

MRTEK: Thank you very much.

Notes

* Robert Mrtek, professor of pharmacy administration, and Suzanne Poirier, professor of pharmacy education, team-teach the course "Images of Pharmacy in the Arts" at the University of Illinois. They invited Ann Petry, a pharmacist-turned-writer, to visit and to talk about, among other things, pharmacies as settings in several of her writings.

A *MELUS* Interview: Ann Petry - The New England Connection (1988)
Mark K. Wilson

The interview took place in midsummer of 1987 in Old Saybrook, located on Long Island Sound at the mouth of the Connecticut River and aptly described by Petry as "a picture postcard of a town." We talked in the comfortable dinning room of the house where Petry and her husband, George, have lived for the past forty years, scarcely half a mile from the town green and the drugstore once owned by Petry's father when, in 1908, she was born in the second-floor family quarters. Petry speaks of her present house, built around 1790, as having "great vibes," and certainly her warm hospitality puts the visitor immediately at ease. Despite her professed discomfort with interviews in general and tape recorders in particular, she agreed to let me place a recorder on the table between us as we talked for several hours about her life and work. But no transcript can really convey the warmth of her responses, often punctuated by laughter, or the relaxed and gracious atmosphere of her home.

INTERVIEWER: Your stories are full of storytellers. There's Dottle Smith in "Miss Muriel"; in *The Narrows* there's Malcolm Powther, who, for all his primness, is a wonderful storyteller; and there's Miss Doris, who holds J. C. and the eavesdropping Abbie spellbound with the story of Mr. Orwell. You must have known storytellers as you were growing up.

PETRY: I did, yes. The first ones were right there in my own family. My father was a great storyteller, and he loved to tell stories about his family. And they were absolutely incredible stories. And sometimes I've used them in - well, in *The Narrows*, for example.

INTERVIEWER: Are they the stories of the Major's family in that novel?

PETRY: Yes, that's right. My mother's stories were not nearly as colorful or as interesting. They had to do with a household and the happenings within it. But, then, my mother had these brothers; I often make reference to them and to the stories that they used to tell. One of them had an enormous farm in Weathersfield, just outside Hartford, but the other uncles were footloose and fancy free. They never married. They had literally lived all over the world. They had been stevedores, pullman [sic] porters, barbers. And they were storytellers, and their stories were just plain wonderful. One of them, Uncle Bill, had been in the Spanish American War, and he had all kinds of stories. I grew up with these stories, and I've told them over and over again in various ways.

INTERVIEWER: You mentioned using them in *The Narrows*; are some of them also in the stories of the Layen family, the Wheeling stories?

PETRY: That's right, in those short stories. Yes definitely.

INTERVIEWER: Those stories seem to draw heavily on your own life experience as well as on the family stories you grew up with.

PETRY: They do, in many ways.

INTERVIEWER: Your maiden name was Lane, and the narrator's family name is Layen. Your father, like the narrator, was the druggist in a small New England coastal town; and both the Lanes and the Layens lived in the same building as their pharmacy, the only black families in their communities.

PETRY: Right, absolutely. Of course, I ought to tell you one of the things my mother said to me. After I started writing she said, "Please don't write about this family!" [laughs] But I did. I don't think she knew it; I don't really think she did.

INTERVIEWER: Your narrator in "Has Anybody Seen Miss Dora Dean?" remembers how as a child she created a fantasy scenario for the mysterious suicide of Mr. Forbes, and even narrated it to an imaginary audience. Did you ever do that kind of thing as a child?

PETRY: Absolutely, yes. You see, this town where I grew up was a very, very small community; and we had to entertain and amuse ourselves. Of course, naturally, we read; that was free, and available. And also here was this family of storytellers, and so it was just inevitable that as a kid I would make up stories about people.

INTERVIEWER: Do you remember particular things you read as a child?

PETRY: My mother used to read aloud to us. But I can very well remember the first book that I read all by myself, and that was *Little Women*; I think I was in the second or third grade. And all of the sudden I understood why it was people sat and read books even when it was beginning to get dark and they were still sitting there reading; that was wonderful! And then of course after that I read everything I could get my hands on.

INTERVIEWER: Do you remember what you especially liked about *Little Women*?

PETRY: Well, I do remember Jo, who was a tomboy, was a person who I could - I could understand her. For instance, there was a place in there somewhere she said that sometimes when the air was cold and the wind was blowing she could just breathe and breathe and breathe it, and it made her feel like she could run forever. I can understand that.

INTERVIEWER: And of course Jo was going to become a writer, too.

PETRY: Yes! She was, yes.

INTERVIEWER: Did you have the sense, even as a child or adolescent, that you wanted to become a writer?

PETRY: No, not really.

INTERVIEWER: Do you remember when you realized that that was what you wanted to do?

PETRY: Well, I think that it started actually when I was in high school. We read *A Tale of Two Cities,* and we had an English teacher - we weren't particularly fond of each other - and she gave us this test in which there was only one question: you were supposed to write an imaginary scene from that book. And I sat down and wrote this scene between Jerry Cruncher, who was a gravedigger, and his wife; I don't even remember what it was, but it was one of the few times that, when I was young, all of a sudden I just wrote and wrote, and it didn't make any difference whether it made sense or not - I just wrote it. And when we went back, Miss Avery, the teacher, said "Now, I've got something I want to read to you." And I sat and listened in horror, because she was reading aloud what I had written and, of course, I thought she was going to say: "This is an example of what you should never, ever do!" But instead she said that I had written it; and she said, "You know, I honestly believe that if you wanted to, you could become a writer." It never had occurred to me that I could be a writer; and even then I don't know that I ever said to myself at that particular stage that, yes, I wanted to become a writer.

INTERVIEWER: If fact, you went on to study pharmacy. Was that the result of family encouragement?

PETRY: No, there was never any pressure. I just decided that I was going to study pharmacy, and of course my family was very pleased.

INTERVIEWER: You've mentioned *Little Women* and *A Tale of Two Cities*, Alcott and Dickens. Do you remember other writers you enjoyed?

PETRY: Oh, when I was quite young, of course, I went through all the children's classics - you know, *Little Lord Fauntleroy*, *Black Beauty*, those books. And then gradually went on: I read Dickens and went on from that, particularly in fiction.

INTERVIEWER: Were there American writers in your high school courses that you remember reading?

PETRY: Yes, Poe, some of the short stories. Let's see. Oh yes, and Hawthorne. And of course poetry, a lot.

INTERVIEWER: You once mentioned Thoreau as a writer you admire, a New England writer who was important to you. Do you remember at what point you read him?

PETRY: Well, I must have been in my early twenties. I'd never felt comfortable with a lot of "things"; I don't know whether that's the right way to put it or not, but clothes and things like that just never made a very strong appeal to me. I think my mother gave me the first copy of *Walden* I ever had, and I was so impressed by it - to think that anybody would go and lead that kind of simple, uncomplicated life. And it did have a tremendous influence on me.

INTERVIEWER: Are there any black writers that you remember reading either in high school or in your own early years as a writer?

PETRY: There were two in particular: *Narrative of the Life of Frederick Douglass* and James Weldon Johnson's *Autobiography of an Ex-Colored Man.*

INTERVIEWER: Are there writers that you return to, that you go back and reread?

PETRY: Well, let's see. I read, or re-read, Faulkner. And Malamud is one of my favorite writers, especially some of his short stories, which I think are great - also a novel of his called *The Fixer*, which is very moving.

INTERVIEWER: Your third novel, *The Narrows*, is dedicated to Mabel Louise Robinson. Could you tell me who she is or was and why you dedicated the novel to her?

PETRY: Mabel Louise Robinson was a professor of English at Columbia. George was in the Army; I was working for the *People's Voice* and trying to write short stories, and I was just getting back rejection slips. I decided that there must be some better way than that, and I read a book by Arthur Train called *My Day in Court*. This was his autobiography, fascinating, and in it he said, " If I wanted to be a writer and I was young, the first thing that I would do would be to go to Columbia and see if I could enroll in Mabel Louise Robinson's workshop course in writing." And I thought, "I wonder if it still exists?" So I got hold of a catalogue, and it did, and it said to get in you had to submit a story and have an interview. So I made an appointment for an interview and took in my story in my hot little hand.

INTERVIEWER: Do you remember what the story was?

PETRY: Let me see . . . No, but in any event I had the story. I can see her now: she looked me over very carefully, and she sat and read the story in front of me, which is also embarrassing. Then she put it down and looked at me and said, "Well, that is a very good story." I thanked her, and she told me when the course met, and that was it. Well it was really and truly quite wonderful. There were only five people in that class, and they were all females; all the men had gone off to war. And so we literally did have her undivided attention. We were supposed to submit a story every three weeks. We had to read each other's stuff and talk about it. And she was really, I think, about as wonderful as it would have been possible for anybody to be. She was truly interested in us, truly committed to our becoming writers.

INTERVIEWER: Do you remember any specific things that you may have learned from her?

PETRY: Well, one of the things she used to say to us over and over again - let me see, how did she put that? "Trust is a ---truth is a millstone around the neck of a writer." People would write things and she'd say, "You can't do it this way." And they'd say, "Well, it's true." She would say, "You cannot use that exactly as it was. Sometimes maybe, but most of the time no. You have to make it dramatic."

INTERVIEWER: That makes me more curious about your own use of "truth" as she described it - actual events from your own life that may figure in your fiction. Obviously every writer does it.

PETRY: Yes, but you don't just use these things; they have to be worked into and a part of the whole. They can't just be stuck in like raisins or plums or something. They have to be mixed in.

INTERVIEWER: Can you think of specific instances, of events in your own life or outside events that you have incorporated into your fiction in this way, that you've made use of by transforming them into part of the whole?

PETRY: Well, in that story that you mentioned, "Has Anybody Seen Miss Dora Dean?," actually there was a man who did commit suicide, and my family did conjecture about it - about what happened, what caused it. So here was something that was, I hope, transformed into a believable story.

INTERVIEWER: In the stories, several times I would be reading and I would wonder -

PETRY: "Did this really happen?"

INTERVIEWER: For example, in "Doby's Gone" Sue Johnson is a first-grader and she is taunted by her white classmates and called a "nigger," and she fights back and is victorious. Did you as a child in an all - white community have a similar experience?

PETRY: Well, yes indeed. My sister and I went - you see, my sister's two years older than I am, and of course there were no kindergartens in Saybrook then. And when she was going to start first grade, I said I had to go too. And mother said, "You can't; you're too young." Because I was only four. And my father said, "Oh, let her go; they'll just send her home." But they didn't. Anyway, here we are, all decked out in our new clothes with our hair in braids and everything. And we went to school, and everything was just fine. But then when we came back home, they stoned us! Can you imagine?

INTERVIEWER: The other school children?

PETRY: Yes, they threw stones at us, and we arrived home crying, covered with bruises and cuts, and our ribbons were gone. And we said, "We don't want to go back to school!" My mother said, "Yes, you'll go back to school; it will be all right." And she took us back the next day. And when we start home and get to a certain place, all of a sudden these boys start throwing stones at us; and suddenly two of my uncles appear. And they knock the boys' heads together and threaten them with dire consequences: murder, mayhem, arson. Under no circumstances were they ever to come near those little girls again!

INTERVIEWER: And there were no repercussions?

PETRY: No.

INTERVIEWER: That sort of family solidarity is a strong element in your stories. The Layen family seems both a part of the Wheeling community and yet a separate community unto itself. Did you and your family experience that sort of double existence?

PETRY: Yes, we did. The drugstore was the public place of our lives. My parents never let it intrude on their private lives. They created a whole separate world. I always thought all families did that; I know we did. And there was always a cause for celebration: either it was somebody's birthday, or it was an anniversary, or there was *something*. There was always a great gathering. And you would not know the rest of the town existed except that we were always happy to see people and cordial and invited them to tea or something. My father sang in the church choir. He helped raise the money to build this town hall. He and three other men used to sing stuff from Gilbert and Sullivan all over the county. In other words, he was part of the community, and yet not part of it. He had a big family, warm and close-knit, and my mother did too. So we always had people from both sides of this family who were around, telling their stories and so forth. There was always this separate private world that had nothing to do with the town.

INTERVIEWER: Were there ever intruders into that world, like Mr. Bemish in "Miss Muriel"?

PETRY: Occasionally.

INTERVIEWER: Was there a real Mr. Bemish?

PETRY: Yes, there was a Mr. Bemish.

INTERVIEWER: And was he in fact run out of town?

PETRY: Well, let's say he left [laughs].

INTERVIEWER: The young Layen daughter who tells the story in "Miss Muriel" can't decide whether she objects to Mr. Bemish as a suitor for her aunt because he's white or because he's old. And then she adds something very interesting: "I do not know exactly how I've been 'trained' on the subject of race." And you put "trained" in quotation marks. Why the quotation marks?"

PETRY: Because I suppose that's not a word you would use in terms of educating a young person. I mean you don't train them in terms of race. And she did that; I mean, those are her quotes. She herself knew that this wasn't done that way. Somehow she didn't know how she had arrived at the conclusion. She didn't really know whether she objected to him because he was white or because he was old, but actually I don't think she objected to him because he was white. I think it was more because he was old.

INTERVIEWER: Getting back to Mabel Louise Robinson and her advice to transform "true" events by making them dramatic, do you recall other suggestions she made?

PETRY: Well, she told us to read plays and go to the theatre, because she said, "Here's an art, and it takes great skill to tell a story only in terms of dialogue." And she said all people who write fiction would benefit from the knowledge that they could get from reading plays and going to the theatre.

INTERVIEWER: I read somewhere that you yourself had been connected with -

PETRY: The American Negro Theatre? Yes, I was.

INTERVIEWER: And did you perform with them?

PETRY: Yes, I did, for about a year or two. It was great fun. I used to play there at the 135th Street Library. Downstairs they had the equivalent of a small theatre, and we had a play that was written by Abe Hill called *On Striver's Row*. We put it on three nights a week. And there were a lot of famous people who had their start, you know, in that theatre.

INTERVIEWER: Do you remember who some of them were?

PETRY: Oh, sure. Ruby Dee and Ossie Davis. Harry Belafonte. Let's see . . . there was Helen Martin. And Fred O'Neal, Sidney Poitier, and Hilda Sims.

INTERVIEWER: Many of your stories seem to me not only dramatic but even cinematic. The novels, particularly, seem almost made for the screen. Have you had nibbles for filming any of them?

PETRY: Oh, yes. Nibbles, and there once was an outright sale, but I guess they got terribly cold feet. I don't even remember which one of those outfits....

INTERVIEWER: What was the novel?

PETRY: *The Narrows*. And then I guess they decided that this was not something that they thought they could get away with, so to speak, because here was this love affair between this black man and a white woman. So nothing ever came of it.

INTERVIEWER: When would that have been?

PETRY: Oh, good heavens: around 1955, something like that.

INTERVIEWER: Speaking of *The Narrows*, you said to John O'Brien that you had trouble with the chapter in which Link gets killed. Do you recall why that was?

PETRY: Well, because it seemed to me that here was this man who in so many ways had to battle to survive; and he *had* survived - and had survived. I would think, fairly whole as a person. And that the end of his life should have been like that - I had trouble with that.

INTERVIEWER: It was painful to write?

PETRY: Yes, really. Because you see - as he grew up you always had this memory of this little boy who was truly abandoned by a woman who is intelligent and kindly, really, at heart; but nevertheless she doesn't even remember that he exists because she is so completely devastated by her husband's death and because she feels guilty about it. So that when it came to this young man who, I think, was great . . . . But on the other hand, the instant that he had said to these people, "We were in love," it was a death sentence; and there was no way, logically, that he would not be killed.

INTERVIEWER: You've told how you were strongly encouraged by Mabel Louise Robinson. Did you receive similar encouragement from other writers?

PETRY: I didn't know any writers, no.

INTERVIEWER: For example, Arna Bontemps reviewed both *The Street* and *The Narrows*. And you had no personal contact with him at the time?

PETRY: No, I didn't meet him until - oh, it was a long time after that. Somebody was making recordings of people who had written stuff for children, and Arna Bontemps was one of the people who were down at the place where we recorded. That was the first time I met him.

INTERVIEWER: How about Richard Wright, whose *Native Son* and *Black Boy* had gained him wide recognition by the time you published *The Street* in 1946. Did you have any contact with him?

PETRY: No, I had no contact with Richard Wright, though I read his novels and short stories as they were published. And I also read the work of Langston Hughes, James Baldwin, and Ralph Ellison - with admiration for all of them, including Wright. *Invisible Man* is a truly great novel.

INTERVIEWER: In *Country Place,* Johnny Roane feels that he has to get out of Lennox, his country place, in order to do what he wants to do. At the end of the novel he's going to New York to study painting. Did you feel that you had to get out of your "country place" in order to do what you wanted to do?

PETRY: Do you mean get out of Saybrook?

INTERVIEWER: Yes.

PETRY: No, I don't know that I did, really. The only reason I left was because I married George Petry and he lived in New York. So I went to New York to live, but I don't know that I ever thought that Saybrook was a place I had to leave.

INTERVIEWER: Do you think your writing career would have developed in the same way if you had stayed in Old Saybrook?

PETRY: I doubt it. After all, the kind of experience I had in New York in terms of work I never could have had here in Saybrook. In the first place, in New York I worked for newspapers in various capacities. And I certainly never would have been in Mabel Robinson's class; I wouldn't have been a member of the American Negro Theatre. I assume all of these things were undoubtedly helpful to me in my writing.

INTERVIEWER: What led you to come back to Old Saybrook? Was it just the end of the war?

PETRY: Well, I had suddenly become famous in a way which I think it would be very difficult to describe, and I hated it! I mean, I just didn't feel that this . . . I couldn't, I couldn't cope with it. I mean, I just didn't . . . I didn't want people asking me questions; I didn't want people interviewing me; I didn't want to have somebody always taking my picture. I decided there must be another way to live. So I left.

INTERVIEWER: And did you find what you wanted?

PETRY: Yes, I did.

INTERVIEWER: The New England town you came back to, Old Saybrook, seems very like the town of Lennox in *Country Place*, and yet it's not a very favorable picture that you paint of Lennox in that novel. Johnny Roane remembers things he disliked, in particular, "the town's smugness, its satisfaction with itself, its sly poking fun at others." I was wondering about how the novel was received in Old Saybrook in 1947. Did the townspeople recognize themselves and take offense?

PETRY: I don't think it ever occurred to them that that was Old Saybrook. I don't know.

INTERVIEWER: Have you ever had reaction from New Englanders to your portrayal of New England characters?

PETRY: No, not that I know of.

INTERVIEWER: I wanted to ask something about your relationship to New England. In his review of *The Narrows,* Arna Bontemps refers to it as "a New England novel." And Sybil Weir has recently written about that novel as a New England novel. Yet you said in a paper you read last year at the University of Massachusetts in Amherst that you do not see yourself as a New Englander. I wonder if you could comment on that.

PETRY: Well, when you consider my background, true, I guess for maybe three or four generations my family, one side or another, has lived in New England. But I think in that paper I started off by saying that if your ancestors came from England, Scotland, Wales, whatever, the chances are that when they were little somebody dandled the baby on their knees and sang "Ride a Cockhorse to Banbury Cross." But my grandfather James (that was on my mother's side) was a runaway slave from a plantation in Virginia; and so when he sang to his children, dandling them on his knee, it was: "Run little baby, run; paterollers goin' to come!" "Pateroller" was the word that slaves used for "patrols"; they never said "patrols." All right, so that's part of my background; that does not a New Englander make. In order words, this is another breed entirely. And though we take on all of the - what shall I say? - the speech patterns, we accept the kind of food, the cooking, the houses, and so forth, nevertheless truly we're not New Englanders - and never will be, as far as I can see. When you stop and think, for instance, that here we were, these little girls going to school, and were stoned! Why? Because we're the wrong color, in the wrong place, at the wrong time. And when my sister, for example, was accepted at Pembroke - you know, which is part of Brown University - and my mother took her over there to Providence with all her new clothes and things: she gets there in the registrar's office and there's great goings and comings, and rustling and whispering, and so forth. And they say she'll have to wait. And finally comes from the dean's office the dean of women and says, "Well I'm so sorry, but your daughter cannot stay in the dormitories. Black girls cannot stay in the dormitories. There's a fine nice family at such-and-such a street, and that's where those girls would have to stay." My mother of course goes and calls my father and says, "What do we do now?" "Well," he said, "you're there. Go look at the place; see what kind of family it is. If they seem to be good, decent people, she stays." So she stayed. Well, that does not a New Englander make!

INTERVIEWER: What does make a New Englander?

PETRY: You have to be, I would assume, born here for generations, and nobody ever stoned you, nobody ever told you you couldn't stay in a dormitory, nobody . . . . When my father opened his store, for example, they told him they were going to run him out of town because they did not want a black druggist in this town. That does not a New Englander make.

INTERVIEWER: Do you see a distinction between that sort of "outsiderness" and that of, say, a Hester Prynne and little Pearl, who also had stones flung at them in *The Scarlet Letter*?

PETRY: Yes, that's true.

INTERVIEWER: The racial element of course makes it different. Are you saying simply that you will never be an insider?

PETRY: No, not in my lifetime. Maybe in somebody else's lifetime.

INTERVIEWER: When you were in the Connecticut College of Pharmacy, were there any other blacks in your class?

PETRY: No, there weren't any. And when my aunt, Miss James, graduated from the Brooklyn College of Pharmacy in 1908, she was the only woman in the whole class, and the only black as well. And that was a long time ago. I often think what an extraordinary person she was. And we've all survived and flourished, but I still have this feeling that we're not really New Englanders.

INTERVIEWER: And would you like to be a New Englander?

PETRY: Well, I'm quite happy with the way I am, thank you. [laughs]

INTERVIEWER: I ask partly because it seems to me that many of the black characters in your fiction tend to fall into one of two broad and contrasting categories: the prim or the primitive. I realize I'm oversimplifying.

PETRY: Yes, I understand what you mean.

INTERVIEWER: On the other hand there are the Abbie Crunches who do seem to want to be New Englanders and, in fact, are very New England.

PETRY: Absolutely, absolutely, totally, yes.

INTERVIEWER: Malcolm Powther thinks of Abbie: "She had New England aristocrat written - "

PETRY: ". . . all over her."

INTERVIEWER: And then there's Malcolm Powther himself, and there are others in your fiction. Even Diana the kindergarten teacher in your most recent story, "The Moses Project." And Mary Lou Brown. Turner's wife in "Mother Africa."

PETRY: That's right, yes. But then there's Mamie Powther! [laughs]

INTERVIEWER: Exactly. Abbie Crunch and Mamie Powther. These two seem to epitomize the two poles I was talking about. What accounts for the difference between these two types?

PETRY: Well, you can't account for them; these are people who are the way they are. Any society has all kinds of people in it, and this one does too.

INTERVIEWER: What makes it particularly interesting is the dynamics of the interaction between these two kinds of black people - because Abbie Crunch, of course, is offended by Mamie Powther.

PETRY: Yes, her very appearance offends her [laughs]. It just happens that these people are so interesting if you take and put them together - and particularly if you take a Mrs. Crunch and put her under the same roof as Mamie Powther.

INTERVIEWER: In a way Emmanuel Turner in "Mother Africa" combines both kinds of blacks that we've been talking about: he's "Junkman, Ragman, Old Man Turner, 'Man' Turner" in his junkman phase; and then he undergoes a kind a metamorphosis -

PETRY: Right.

INTERVIEWER: - and gets his first shave in twenty-five years, or something like that.

PETRY: [laughs] And I love the fact that the barber says he knew that someday something like that would happen.

INTERVIEWER: Do you know whether Turner is going to revert to his more primitive "junkman" self?

PETRY: Oh, I think he'll revert; I think he will!

An Interview with Ann Petry (1988)
from *Artspectrum* (Windham Regional Arts Council)

Ms. Petry's work contains a remarkable range of subjects and sentiments. She writes sometimes with a sense of outrage; sometimes with exuberance. She frequently writes of white injustice toward blacks but never descends to stereotyping; she views all her characters objectively. One of her most compelling characters is Mrs. Gramby in *Country Place*, an elderly white woman. Her narrators range from an eleven-year-old black girl to a middle-aged white man. Her protagonists are young and old, white and black. Throughout her writings, Ms. Petry challenges prejudice, pettiness, and injustice at all levels of our society. She has been one of the central forces in the twentieth century demanding a reevaluation of existing stereotypes, particularly of blacks and of women, and urging the destruction of existing boundaries between individuals and between social groups. Ms. Petry s currently at work on a novel.

Following is an interview with Ann Petry.

Q. It must have been a great change moving from Old Saybrook to NewYork City after you were married.

A. Well, I had visited New York fairly often, so it wasn't a total culture shock. The part of it that was truly shocking to me was when I saw the poverty in Harlem. That was not like any poverty I had ever heard of. We lived in Harlem for quite a while. I worked for a weekly publication based in Harlem,*The Amsterdam News*. Then we moved to the Bronx. My husband was drafted and went into the army, and I lived by myself. It was at that time that I decided I would become a writer or I wouldn't. So I decided I would give myself a year in which to do it. The only kind of jobs I had were part-time jobs that didn't involve any total commitments of my time. We had a friend who was an artist in an advertising agency and was working on a catalogue for wigs. He called me and asked me if I'd do the writing, so I said, "Sure, why not?" And it brought me quite a nice sum of money. So I lived on the wig money for a long, long time. Every time I see someone wearing a wig, I feel very grateful.

Q. And this is the time you wrote *The Street*?

A. Yes.

Q. After *The Street* you wrote *Country Place*, which represents quite a change of subject matter since it describes life in a small New England town, where all but one minor character are white. What made you decide to write such a different novel?

A. I was in Old Saybrook during the hurricane of 1938. It was a frightening experience; I never forget it. I thought that I ought to use that storm in a novel, and why not place it in Old Saybrook, where I experienced it? And of course Old Saybrook is mostly white, so the novel has mostly white characters in it. Besides, I have never wanted to write the same kind of book twice.Writing such a different book was a challenge, but one that I welcomed.

Q. Then came *The Narrows*. That, too, was favorably reviewed, but I understand some readers objected to the relationship between Link and Camillo [sic].

A. If you really want to stir the flame of prejudice, then you confront someone with a black man and a white woman. The other way around nobody really gives a hoot. The book sold a lot of copies, and the critics were kind. But everyone questioned the relationship between these two people.And I don't find anything unusual about it. Men have fallen in love with pretty faces, have had passionate attachments to women who were not their Intellectual equals - there's nothing unusual about that. Personally, I think that it's a darn good story.

Q. Sometime in the late '40s, you started writing children's books. Why did you decide to do that?

A. With my parents, all my aunts and uncles, and my sister and me, we were a very old family. Then my sister, who was two years older than I, had a child. And I felt I had to do something to welcome it into this old family. So I wrote *The Drugstore Cat*. Then after that - I don't remember now exactly how or why I happened to look at some American history textbooks that were being used in the schools. I read the sections that had to do with slavery, and I was appalled. I thought, "Now, look at all these youngsters growing up in this country, whose only knowledge, really and truly, of black people is what they read in these books." The blacks were always portrayed as happy in slavery. They could all sing and dance. They were immoral, for the most part. And I thought, "Well, there has to be somewhere along the line books that portray slaves in a different way. And a good place to start is books for children." Then quite by chance, I was up in Hartford, and met a man there who asked if I had ever thought about writing a book about Harriet Tubman. I said I didn't even know who Harriet Tubman was. So I began looking up stuff about her, became fascinated, and wrote a book about her. After that I decided to write a book about the Witchcraft Trials. I did some reading on them and became very interested in Tituba, a young slave woman who was one of the women accused of and imprisoned for witchcraft, and decided to write about her. And also, incidentally and along the way, I learned more about witchcraft than people should ever know. I became fascinated, and collected all the materials I could.

Q. Most books about the Salem Witch Trials logically explain away all elements of witchcraft. But in your work, Tituba is actually depicted as having supernatural powers.

A. I did not set out to argue that witchcraft does not exist. It happens all over the world. I have had relatives with conjuring powers. The point I was making about Tituba was that she had not done anything wrong. She had not bewitched anyone; she was a good and decent person.

Q. You came from a tradition of strong and unconventional women. As you explain in your autobiographical essay, your mother and aunts were businesswomen, financially independent, who refused to be traditional housewives.

A. They were certainly not traditional women in any sense of the word. I have often marveled at how good my parents' marriage was, considering how unusual my mother was. But they loved each other very much. Perhaps my father thought all women were like that.

Q. Your novels contain many very strong women, few strong men.

A. Well, that's the way of the world.

Q. Do you consider yourself a feminist?

A. I don't like labels like that. I'm just an individual who has a special way of looking at the world. But I am an ally of feminists, there's absolutely no question about that.

Q. How has your view of the world changed over the years?

A. I don't think my views have changed much. If anything, I see the world as getting worse. As far as race relations go, worse things happen in New York now, and even right here in Connecticut. The attacks on people, that I find terrible, absolutely terrible. And I don't even remember attacks like that a few years ago. I don't know what has changed. It's frightening.

Q. So you don't think the Civil Rights Movement has changed things very much?

A. I think it did, but then I don't know what happened. On college campuses, for instance - why is there all this conflict between white students and black students? And when you read the statistics about life in Harlem - things haven't changed there.

Q. Your daughter is an attorney. You don't feel that her generation has an easier time of it than yours?

A. No, definitely not. I guess it's the same world.

Just a Few Questions More, Mrs. Petry (1989)
Hazel Arnett Ervin

In her hotel room in Philadelphia on the morning of February 4, 1989, some hours before she was to appear as the guest of honor at the Fifth Annual Black Writers' Conference, Ann Petry agreed to meet with me for an interview. Several months after our talk, she answered follow-up questions by mail. In this interview, there are no particular themes. As the title suggests, my purpose is merely to ask additional questions - questions that have arisen from previous interviews and from re-readings of her novels by other critics.

Q. In *Black Women Writers at Work*, Maya Angelou names you as a writer who has impressed her. She says she would walk fifty blocks in high heels for something you've written. And according to Ms. Angelou, for a country girl, that means a lot. How do you feel about her tribute to you?

A. Oh, what a beautiful statement! I had no idea.

Q. You are best known for *The Street*. It is your most written about work. Is there another work for which you would prefer to be remembered?

A. I'd like to be remembered for everything I've written.

Q. We have so many superb black American women writers, but are there novelists who have impressed you?

A. Women? - particularly Toni Morrison and Alice Walker.

Q. And males?

A. Ralph Ellison's *Invisible Man* is truly great. And Langston Hughes. I have enormous admiration for Langston Hughes.

Q. When did you first discover Langston Hughes?

A. I discovered Langston Hughes's poetry while I was living in Harlem — thought it was great.

Q. What about another popular person associated with Harlem - Zora Neale Hurston?

A. I read *Their Eyes Were Watching God* about five years ago.

Q. Shortly after you moved to New York City in 1938, you enrolled, first, in a writing workshop, then, in a class in which Mabel Louise Robinson was your teacher. How helpful was Robinson in shaping your writing style and technique?

A. Mabel Louise Robinson did not shape my style or technique. She did something more important than that: she taught me how to criticize my own work, and other people's work. Perhaps even more importantly, she made me believe in my own ability.

Q. So, what you're saying is that your writing career began with you learning to believe in your own ability? How, then, did you find your own voice?

A. I acquired skill in the art of writing fiction, and nonfiction, by studying, analyzing, [and] dissecting novels, short stories, plays [and] biographies created by other writers, and by rewriting my own work.

Q. Upon writing and publishing your first short story, "Marie of the Cabin Club," you used the pen name Arnold Petri. Why a pseudonym? Was it because you were then a would-be writer? Or a woman? Or…

A. Neither. I am a "private person." I did not want my friends, acquaintances, and colleagues to know that I was writing short stories.

Q. The story has one of the most favorable portrayals of a black man: Georgie Barr is a gentleman, well-traveled, successful, articulate, handsome, heroic, and something of a 007-adventurous type. There isn't a blemish. I realize I have made a comment here, but will you comment?

A. No comment is necessary.

Q. Well, is there a conscious effort after this story to portray a less romantic and a more representational black male?

A. No.

Q. Yet you never again duplicate or romanticize about the black male.

A. That's because I have no interest in writing a series of novels and/or short stories involving characters I've [already] created.

Q. But how do you develop characters and plot? Where are the influences?

A. I develop the characters in my books to the point where I could probably give a lengthy report on their likes and dislikes - including what they ate for breakfast on any given morning - their hopes and their fears, their peculiarities, what they do for a living, etc.

Q. And your plots?

A. ... from items in newspapers, from the weather, from conversations, from gossip, etc. For example, in recent years, I've been intrigued by newspaper stories about "house arrest." So, I finally wrote a short story about a man who was placed under house arrest: "The Moses Project." From the weather . . . I survived a hurricane in Connecticut. It became the source of a novel: *Country Place*.

Q. May one conclude that you maintain a rapport with your characters?

A. Yes.

Q. Do Lutie and Min from *The Street* and Abbie Crunch and Frances Jackson from *The Narrows* try to set examples for black women who might rely on fictitious black women characters for lessons about life?

A. Their commonality is gender.

Q. In *The Narrows*, Mamie Powther is like a blues lady. Then, there are jazz scenes in *The Street* and jazz scenes in the short stories "Marie of the Cabin Club" and "Solo on the Drums." How were you introduced to jazz?

A. I've been a jazz buff, or a fan, ever since I was a teenager - many a long year ago.

Q. When discussing *The Street*, many critics do not move beyond the question of form. For them, the question remains whether the work is naturalistic and protest or a tragic narrative. What form did you have in mind when you planned and wrote the novel?

A. I did not have a specific form in mind.

Q. Richard Wright mentions in "How Bigger Was Born" that he experienced "mental censorship" when writing *Native Son*, that he worried about what blacks and whites would say about Bigger and whether Bigger would perpetuate stereotypes. How much mental censorship did you experience when you were writing *The Street*?

A. None.

Q. Were there ever concerns on your part or on the part of your editor about *The Street* being overshadowed by or having to measure up to *Native Son*?

A. No.

Q. When *The Narrows* was published, many critics thought the love affair between Link and Camila was unrealistic. You, however, do not see their love affair as unrealistic?

A. Most people refuse to accept the idea that a black man and a white woman can be in love. "Miscegenation" is a buzzword - causes people to react violently.

Q. In your interview with John O'Brien, you state that you had great difficulty writing the chapter in *The Narrows* in which Link is murdered. I immediately thought of Charles Dickens, who cried as he wrote the chapter in *Oliver Twist* in which Nancy is murdered. What made it difficult for you to write about Link's murder?

A. It was like being a witness to the murder of a much loved, much admired friend.

Q. Is the ancestral link to black culture, so often found in characters in African American literature, to be found in Weak Knees and Bill Hod in *The Narrows*?

A. Well, maybe. Weak Knees and Bill Hod are trying to give Link a sense of pride in order to survive. What they are using is a survival tactic.
Q. You produced your first three novels during the literary Chicago Renaissance. Was there for you ever a sense of belonging to this movement?
A. No.
Q. Why?
A. I have no idea.
Q. Have you read any of the Chicago Renaissance writers?
A. I 've read all of them.
Q. With all that you have accomplished in your career - work in every genre - I wonder how successful you have been in securing your "own room."
A. Solitude and privacy are essential for a writer. The greatest challenge that remains [for me] is acquiring uninterrupted time in which to write.
Q. What about your actual work habits? I read once that you write from nine to noon, have lunch, and then return and write from one to two-thirty or three in the afternoon; that you write in longhand, type, and then conclude with a final draft. Have such work habits remained consistent throughout your career?
A. Yes.

Index

Note: Numbers below refer to annotations, beginning with Primary Works

A

Abston, Carmen Patrice, 66

Achebe, Chinua, 668

Adams, George, 67

Adams, William, 68

Ader, Melissa Susan, 69

African American Literary Tradition, 334

Afro-American (Baltimore), 108

Ajimuda, O.S., 70

Alcott, Louisa May, 335

Alexander, Sandra Carlton, 71

Allison, Dorothy, 225

Alvarez-Wilson, Sonia, 72

Alvarez, John, 225

Ambrose, Marty, 787

American Masters, 73, 306, 785

Aminu, O., 70

Amitto, Jennifer, 765

An, Jee Hyun, 75

Anderson, Sherwood, 661

Andrew, Joseph Hines, 76

Andrews, Larry R., 77, 78

Angelou, Maya, 80

Annas, Pamela, 109

Anonymous, 110

Arnow, Harriet, 772

"Art for art's sake," 70, 668

Artspectrum, 74

Asher, Jacqueline Colleen, 111

Asian American, 278

Attaway, William, 125

Augustan Age, 101

Authors League Fund, 102

Autry, Thea, 112

B

Babb, Sanora, 125

Babb, Valeria, 113

Babenko, Olga Alexandrovna, 114

Baechler, Léa, 565

Baker, Henry, 115

Baker, Houston, Jr., 116

Balasco, Susan, 403

Baldwin, James, 111, 112, 185, 348, 361, 390, 497, 554, 593, 629, 664, 666, 728, 857

Balliett, Whitney, 117

Balsham, Maria, 118

Bambara, Toni Cade, 208, 906

Bandi, Usha, 119

Baraka, Amira, 66, 298, 618

Barden, Thomas E., 551

Barnes, Djuna, 768

Barrett, Lindon, Intro., 120, 121, 122

Barry, Michael, 123

Bartter, George C., 124

Battat, Erin Royston, 125

Beach, Terry, 126

Belilgne, Maleda, 127

Bell, Bernard W., Intro., 128, 129

Bell, Roseann P., 438

Bellow, Saul, 594, 785

Bendixer, Alfred, 888

Benoit, Larry, 130

Benton, Loron Melinda, 131

Bercovitch, 525

Bergman, Jill, 132, 133

Bernard, Emily, 134

Bigsby, C.W.E., 339

Binggeli, Elizabeth Cara, 136, 137

Bixler, Paul, 138, 139

Black Arts Movement, 204, 733

Black, Leslie, 140

Black Lives Matter Movement, 877

Black Power Movement, 844

Blaisdell, Robert, 734

Bloom, Harold, 96

Bloomquist, Katherine Mary, 142

Bold, Christine, 143

Bonadies, Genevieve Terese, 144

Bond, E.G., 145

Bond, Gregory, 146

Bond, Gwenda, 147

Bond-Hutto, Patricia Claudette, 148

Bone, Robert, 149, 150, 219

Bonner, Emily Anne, 151

Bonner, Marita, 75, 213, 416

Bontemps, Arna, 152, 153, 154, 155

Book Clubs, 429, 533, 616, 741, 753

Bourgeois, Ashley, 156

Bowles, Jane, 715

Boyd, Herb, 157, 158

Boyle, Kay, 225, 267

Boyle, T. Coraghessan, 199, 482

Boynton, Anthony, 159

Brailey, Muriel W., Intro., 160, 161

Bramwell, Jacqueline Patricia, 162

Brauer, Bessie, 145

Brock, Sabine, 164

Brodber, Ema, 162

Brooks, Cleaneth, 76

Brooks, Gwendolyn, 75, 127, 167, 213, 380, 381, 389, 416, 660, 666, 852, 865,

Brooks, Michael W., 165

Brown, Carolina, 166

Brown, Jacqueline Elaine, 167

Brown, Julie, 581

Brown, Lloyd W., 168

Brown, Stephanie Lynne, 169

Brown, Sterling A, Intro, 170

Brown, Thomasine Corbett, 171

Brown, Tia La Shauna, 172

Bryant, Jacqueline K., 173, 174, 175

Bryfonski, Dedria, 87

Buchanan, Jemima D., 176

Buelews, Gert, 898

Buell, Ellen Lewis, 177, 178

Buelens, Carlos, 400, 872

Buncombe, Marie H., 179

Burgess, Francoise, 180

Burns, Ben, 181

Burns, Mary Patricia, 182

Burrows, D. J., 497

Bus, Heiner, 183

Busby, Margaret, 184

Butcher, Margaret Just, 185, 186

Butcher, Philip, 187

Butkovic, Matea, 188

Butler, Octavia, 151, 393, 659, 789

Butler, Robert, 378

Butterfield, Alfred, 189

Butts, Jonathan J., 190

Byrd, Rudolph P., 191

C

Cahill, Susan, 192

Cain, James, 661

Cakirtas, Onder, 193

Caldwell, Katrina Myers, 194

Callahan, Cynthia, 195

Campbell, Bebe Moore, 676

Campbell, Donna, 196, 197

Carby, Hazel, 198

Carden, Mary Paniccia, 199, 200

Carey, Alice, 201

Carter, Michael, 202

Carter-Sanborn, Kristin, 203

Cataliotti, Robert H., 204, 205

Cather, Willa, 142, 199, 335

Catlett, Elizabeth, 125

Cenage Learning/Gale, 64

Chambers, Bradford, 206

Chambers, Veronica, 207

Champbell, Bebe Moore, 676

Chametzky, Jules, 674

Chandler, Zola, 208

Charles, John C., Intro., 209, 210, 211

Chaucerian narrator, 63

Cheever, John, 794

Chenier, Felicia Antionette, 212

Cherry, Gwendolyn, 94

Chestnut, Charles, 384, 455, 571, 746, 802

Chicana, 357

Childress, Alice, 866

Childress, Paulette, 213

Choi, Yoon Young, 214

Chopin, Kate, 173

Christian, Barbara, T., 215, 216, 217, 218

Cisneros, Sandra, 269, 610

Civil Rights Movement, 74

Clark, Austin, 365, 366, 367

Clark, Graham, 219

Clark, Keith, Intro, 220, 221, 222, 223, 224, 228, 232, 317, 621

Clarke, Deborah, 225

Clarkson, Patricia, 306

Cleage, Pearl, 393, 659

Cleaver, Ethridge, 298

Cloutier, Jean-Christople, 226

Coffey, Michael, 227

Colby, Vineta, 491

Coleman, James W., 228

Collins, Patricia Hill, 229

Colson, Don, 232

Congressional Record, 431

Conn, Peter, 68

Conner, J.D., 234

Conrad, Earl, 235

Constantakis, Sara, 236

Cook, Fannie, 829

Cook, William W., 238

Cooke, Michael, 239

Corbett, Jane, 240

Cosgrove, Mary Silva, 241

Crafty, Bryant J., 242

Crane, Mary Ellen, 243

Crane, Stephen, 196, 277, 341, 554

Crescenzo, Michele, 244, 245

Crowell, Thomas Y., 95

Crucible, The, 168

Cruz, Angie, 357

Crystal, Pinconnat, 246

Cubas, Juana Herrera, 815

Cullen, Countee, 133

Curran, Mary Doyle, 610

Currier, Isabel, 247

Curry, Stephanie Juanita, 248

D

Daltry, Patience M., 249

Dandridge, Rita B., Intro, 250, 251, 252, 253

Daniel, Thomas H., 254

Dash, Leon, 406

Dante, 331

Dauterich, Edward, IV, 255

Davidson, Adenike Maria, 256

Davidson, Cathy N., 624

Davis, Amanda J., 257

Davis, Arthur P., 258, 259, 260, 261, 262

Davis, Carole Boyer, 263

Davis, Marianna W., 237

Davis, Ozzie, 839

Davis, Thulani, 264, 265,

Day, Susan, 540, 542

Debo, Annette, 266

Delano, Page Dougherty, 267, 268

Delcoco-Fridley, Lea Johanna, 269

Delph, Kyndall, 159

Demarest, David P., 270

Demmier, Monika, 271

Dempsey, David, 272

Dente, Shahara Tova V., 273

Devers, Rebecca Allison, 274

Devlin, Paul, 275

Dhillon, Nargis, 276

Dickens, Charles, 254, 668

Didon, Joan, 225

Diedrich, Maria, 539

Dimauro, Laurie, 894

Dingledine, Dan, 277

Donahue, James J., 278, 765

Dorris, Michael, 279

Douglass, Frederick, 133, 571, 802

Dow, W.T., 280, 281

Downing, Francis, 282

Doyle, Sister Mary Ellen, 283

Drake, Kimberly, Intro, 284, 285

Drake, Kimberly Sue, 286

Dreiser, Theodore, 139, 196, 277, 307, 351, 481, 610, 785

Duane, Anna May, 288

Dubey, Madhu, 289

Dubuk, Laura, 290, 291

DuCille, Ann, 292

Dudley, John, 293

Dumas, Henry, 630

Dunbar, Paul Laurence, 196

Duneer, Anita, 294

Dunne, Susan, 295

DuBois, W.E.B., 361, 666, 802

Dye, Peggy, 296

E

Eby, Claree Virginia, 297

Edgar, Anne E., 298

Egan Jennifer, 299

Eisenger, Chester E., 300

Eliot, T. S., 794

Ellison, Ralph, 75, 183, 185, 255, 275, 361, 394, 447, 455, 469, 524, 543, 555, 594, 618, 664, 674, 901

Emanuel, James, 301, 302, 303

Engel, Paul, 305

Epstein, Michael, 306

Equiano, Olaudah, 133

Erdheim, Elana, 307, 481

Erdrich, Louise, 225

Ervin, Hazel Arnett, 252, 308, 309, 310, 311, 312, 313, 314, 315, 316, 317, 318, 319, 320, 321, 326, 331, 346, 379, 392, 396, 398, 471, 496, 499, 502, 508, 536, 569, 632, 652, 656, 669, 670, 721, 759, 819, 850, 861, 868, 869, 893, 901

Euripides, 386

Evans, Stephanie Y., 619

Ewig, Elizabeth J., 322

Exposito, Maria Cruz, 815

F

Faldet, David, 880

Far, Sui Sin, 767

Farquharson, Katherine, 323

Farrell, James, 139, 351

Faulkner, William, 112, 199, 415, 594, 610, 661, 768

Fauset, Jessie, 75, 148, 173, 225, 265, 444, 590, 591, 731

Fein, Esther B., 324

Feinberg, Leslie, 225

Feld, Rose, 325

Fendt, Gene, 326

Fikes, Robert Jr., 327, 764

Fischer-Homung, Dorothea, 539

Fisher, Dexter, 329

Fisher, Rudolph, 834

Fishken, Shelley Fisher, 330

Fitzgerald, F. Scott, 643

Fitzimmons, Lorna, 331

Flagellants, The, 866

Foley, Martha, 581

Ford, Nick Aaron, 332

Foster, Frances Smith, 334

Fraizer, Franklin, 851

Franklin, Aretha, 131

Franklin, Benjamin, 111, 244,

Franklin, Marie C., 335
Fuller, Edmund, 338
Fuller, Hoyt W., 339
Fuller, James E., 340
Funaria, Vicky, 767
Funk, Robert, 542

G

Gaines, Ernest, 314, 406
Gale, Erin Nicholson, 341
Gallagher, Maria, 342
Garrett, Emma Isadore, 344
Garrett, Lula, 345
Garvey, Johanna X., 346
Gates, Henry Louis, 347, 884
Gaul, Theresa Strouth, 403
Gayle, Addison, 332, 348, 470
Gebhard, Ann O., 350
Gelder, Emma, 563
Gelfant, Blanche Housman, 351
Gerzing, Gretchen Holbrooks, 168
Gholston, Tracey Marcel, 353
Giddings, Paula, 180, 354, 355
Gilbert, Sandra M., 356
Giles, Sally Marie, 357
Girson, Rochelle, 358
Gittens, Seonna, 359
Glasgow, Ellen, 136
Gloster, Hugh M., 360
Godfrey, Mollie Amelia, 361
Goldsmith, Alfred, 362
Gogal, Miriam, 718
Goodwin, Polly, 363
Graham, Shirley, 563
Grandt, Jurgen E., 364
Greco, Elaine Katherine, 365
Green, Kim, 366, 367
Green, Marjorie, 368
Greene, Lee, 369
Gregory, John, 370
Griffin, Farah Jasmine, 63, 371, 372, 373, 374, 593, 742
Grizzzle, Trevor, 814
Groden, Suzy, 109
Gross, Theodore L., 303, 375
Gubar, Susan, 356
Gunderson, Margaret T., 376
Gunton, Sharon R., 88
Gustafson, Lucy, 377
Guy, Rosa, 350
Guy Sheftall, Beverly, 438
Guzman, Jessie Parkhurst, 260

H

Hakutani, Yoshinobu, 79, 378

Haley, Alex, 497

Hall, J.W., 379

Hamlin, Francoise N., 461

Hampton University, 101

Hansberry, Lorraine, 75, 357, 740, 828, 906

Hardison, Ayesha Ki'Shani, 380, 381

Hardwick, Elizabeth, 715

Hardy, Thomas, 323, 589, 796

Harper, Frances, 173, 720

Harper, Kenneth, 455

Harper, Michael S., 798

Harris, Charles F., 882

Harris, Trudier, 384, 385

Harrison, William, 386

Harte, Barbara, 84

Hartford Courant, 102, 104

Hartley, Daniel Le Clair, 387

Hawkins, Alfonso W., 388

Hawthorne, Nathaniel, 303, 869

Haydon, Robert, 572

Helbig, Aletha K., 90

Hemenway Ernest, 794

Henderson, Carol E., Intro., 389, 390, 391, 392

Henderson, Frances Diane, 393

Henderson, Mark Joseph, 394

Hennessy, Val, 395

Henta, Carolyn, 173

Henry, John, 314

Hernton, Calvin, 396

Hicks, Heather, Intro., 397, 398

Hicks, Scott, 399

Higgshida, Cheryl Ann, 400

Hill, Herbert, 401

Hill, James, 402

Hill, Michael, 403

Hill, Patricia Liggins, 83, 404

Hill-Lubin, Mildred A., 405

Hilton, Angela, 406

Himes, Chester, 75, 91, 112, 127, 140, 188, 219, 267, 447, 522, 524, 543, 594, 623, 654, 751, 789, 891, 892, 901, 910

Hinterberg, Helen J., 407, 408

Hiranuma, Kimiko, 409

Ho, Jennifer Ann, 278

Hoagland, Edward, 201

Hobson, Laura Z, 410

Hoffmann, Andrew, 411

Holiday, Billie, 833

Holladay, Hilary, Intro.,110, 379, 412, 413, 414, 415, 471, 502, 508, 569, 669, 721, 819, 861, 893

Holt, Skakira C., 416

Holzman, Robert, 417

Home, Chelsea L., 418

Honey, Maureen, 419

Hooks, Bell, 420

Hopkins, Pauline, 133,173

Houck, Anne Cleaver, 421

Howard, Jennifer, 423

Hsu, Hsuan L, 424

Hughes, Carl Milton, 425, 426

Hughes, Langston, 76, 520, 630, 739

Hull, Gloria T., 352, 778, 845, 864

Hull, Kenneth G., 427

Hunter, Kristin, 167

Hurston, Zora Neale, 136, 140, 164, 167,173,180, 225, 240, 255, 265, 289, 353, 361, 380, 381, 393, 416, 433, 549, 603, 659, 731, 792, 823, 865

Hyde, Yvette Alex, 429

I

Inferno, 331

Ingram, Edward Deloris, 432

Issacs, Diana Scharfeld, 435

Issacs, Kathleen T., 436

Ivana, Dragos, 437

Ivey, James, 438, 439

Izard, Anne, 440

J

Jacob, Harriet, 173, 212, 571

Jackson, Blyden, 441, 442, 443, 444, 445, 446, 447

Jackson, Lawrence B., 448

Jackson, Shirley, 145

James, Anne Louise, 130, 146

James, Henry, 111, 397

James, Marlon, 643

Japtok, Martin, Intro., 449, 450

Jarrett, Gene Andrew, Intro., 451, 452

Jaskoski, Helen, 453

Jenkins, Candice Marie, 454

Jenkins, Donald Ray, 455

Jet, 100

Jewett, Sarah Orne, 142

Jewish American, 190, 730, 758

Jimoh, A. Yemisi, 456, 457, 458, 459, 460, 461

Johns, Robert L., 462

Johnson, James Weldon, 361, 591

Johnson, Linck, 403

Jones, Amy Robin, 463

Jones, Gayl, 454, 464, 506,

852

Jones, LeRoi, 655 (see also Amira Baraka)

Jones, Loretta L. Dowdy, 465

Jones, Patrina C., 466

Jones, Tayari, 147, 467, 468, 616

Joyce, James, 574, 607, 794

Joyce, Joyce Ann, Intro., 262, 469

Jung, Carl, 248

K

Kafka, Franz, 323

Kaiser, Ernest, 470

Kamarah, Sheikh Umarr, 471

Kamme - Erkel, Sybile, 472

Kang, Nancy, 473

Kaplan, Sidney, 674

Karno, V. A., 474

Karrer, Wolfgang, 475

Kaufman, Peter S., 476

Kaywell, Joan F., 477

Kazin, Alfred, 478

Kelly, Edith Summers, 610

Kent, George E., 479

Kiken, Jonas, 480

Kilgallen, Cara, 481

Killens, John O., 406

King, Coretta Scott, 201

Kingston, Maxine Hong, 269, 607

Kirkpatrick, D. L., 301

Kissko, Jennifer Joyce, 482

Knadler, Stephen, 483

Kniffel, Leonard, 484

Koenen, Anne, 485

Koster, Rick, 486

Kothari, Reena, 487

Krementz, Jill, 488

Krstovic, Jelina, 489

Kruckmeyer, Katherine Ann, 490

Kunitz, Stanley J., 98, 491

Kushwaha, M. S., 492

L

L'Engle, Madeleine, 493

La Forge, Jane Rosenberg, 494

Lacan, 69

Lamdin, Lois S., 270

Lancaster, Iris M., 495, 496

Lang, Andrew, 814

Lange, Dorothea, 125

Lapides, F. R., 497

Larsen, Nella, 75, 133, 148, 203, 212, 265, 341, 361, 590, 603, 659, 731, 810

Latimore, Grace Olivia, 498

Lattin, Vernon E., 499

Laurel, Jeanne Phoenix, 500

Lawrence, D. H., 668, 794

Lebow, Diane, 501

Lee, Amy, 502

Lee, Robert A., 503

Lee, Scott, 880

Lemieux, Jamilah, 21

Lenz, Gunter H., 504

Leonard, Kandi Kay, 505

Lespinasse, Patricia G., 506

Levy, Tedd, 507

Lewis, Barbara William, 508, 509

Lewis, Sinclair, 425, 427, 480

Li, Stephanie, 510

Lincoln, S. Abraham, 511

Lindfors, Bernth, 512

Literary Ladies Guide to the Writing Life, 513

Littlejohn, Amonte, 514

Littlejohn, David, 515

Liz, Walton, 565

Llorento, Manuela Matas, 516

Locke, Alan, 517, 518

London, Jack, 196, 307, 481

Lorde, Audre, 634, 825

Love, Theresa R., 352

Lowney, John, 520

Lubin, Alex, 521, 522

Lucas, Curtis, 381

Lucy, Robin Jane, 523, 524

Lumpkin, Grace, 400

Lyttle, Deborah Sue, 526

M

M.C.R., 527

M.P., 528, 529

M. W., 530

MacCann, Donnarae, 531

McBride, Kecia Driver, 532

McCarthy, Dorsey, 533

McClurg, Jocelyn, 534

McComb, Morgan L., 159

McCreary, Micah L., 535

McDowell, Margaret, 536

McElhenry, Kenneth, R., 567

McGuire, A.B., 537

McInerney, Kathleen, 538

McKay, Claude, 361

McKay, Nellie, 97, 539, 540, 541

McMahan, Elizabeth, 542

McMillen, Terry, 406, 830

McParland, Robert, 543

McPherson, James Alan, 314

McSherry, Elizabeth, 544

Machlan, Elizabeth, 545, 546

Madden, David, 547

Madhubuti, Haki, 628

Maechem, William Shands, 561

Magill, Frank N., 548

Mailer, Nornan, 594

Maja-Pearce, Adele, 549

Majors, Clarence, 550

Malamud, Bernard, 554, 594

Mallegg, Kristin, 551

Mann, L. S., 552

Maquire, Roberta S., 281

Marcus, Sybil, 553

Margolies, Edward, 554, 655

Markau, Ulrike, 555

Marshall, Paule, 75, 148, 164, 179, 194, 603, 610, 629, 865, 866, 906

Martin, Allie Beth, 556

Martinez, Brenda Giselle, 557

Maund, Alfred, 558

May, Claudia, 559

Meldon, John, 562

Melville, Herman, 111

Mendelson, Phyllis Carmel, 87

Mickenberg, Julie, 563

Miller, Arthur, 168

Mittlefehldt, Pamela Kiss, 564

Mobley, Marilyn Sanders, 565

Mock-Murton, Michele, 566

Moffet, James, 567

Moody, J.N., 568

Moody-Freeman, Julie E., 569

Moon, Bucklin, 570

Moon. Rebecca, 206

Moore, Steven T., 571

Morgan, Shaun, 765

Morgan, Stacy I., 572

Morris, M. Aldon, 573

Morris, Wright, 574

Morrison, Alan, 575

Morrison, Toni, 91, 162, 180, 203, 225, 269, 273, 289, 290, 357, 385, 390, 415, 433, 454, 487, 498, 506, 576, 607, 626, 659, 676, 717, 728, 739, 825, 852, 896, 910

Morrissette, Robert E., 576

Morsberger, Robert E., 577

Mosley, Walter, 892

Mott, Shani, Tahir, 578

Motley, Willard, 859

Moynihan, Sinead, 579

Mullen, Bill, V., 581

Murray, Albert, 618

Musser, Judith, 582, 583

Myers, Walter Dean, 350

Myles, Lynette D., 584

Myree-Mainer, Joy, Intro., 585, 586, 587

N

Nagel, James, 888

Nakitoshi, N Tadashi, 588

Nance, Merle, 589

Nargis, Nargis, 590

Naseem, Kamal, 492

National Conference on Undergraduate Research, the (NCUR), 418

Native American, 278

Naviaux, Julie A., 591

Naylor, Gloria, 91, 201, 266, 388, 406, 415, 465, 487, 634, 717, 771, 906

Nedoma, Jeannette, 592

Nelson, George, 593

Nelson, Lisa K., 594

New Korean Journal of English Language & Literature, 287

Newlin, Keith, 595

Newman, Frances, 245

Nichols, Charles H., 596, 597

Nielson, David Gordon, 598

Noble, Jeanne, 599

Noh, Jonglin, 600

Norman, Elizabeth J., 601

Norris, Frank, 196, 197, 277, 307, 424, 481

Norris, Keenan, 602

Now Read This - Book Club, 107

NPR, 106

Nugent, Richard Bruce, 111

O

O'Banner, Bessie Marie, 603

O'Brien, John, 93

O'Conner, Flannery, 225

O'Conner, Patricia T., 604

O'Donnell, Heather, 605

Oates, Joyce Carol, 225

Ochoa, Peggy Ann, 607

Okubo, Mime, 642

Olsen, Tillie, 505, 608, 610

Orr, Lisa Marie, 610

Oropallo, Kathleen, 477

Ortiz, Judith, 72

Ottley, Roi, 611

P

Page, Ernest R., 613

Page, James A., 614

PBS, 73, 306, 785, 616

Pakditawan, Sirinya, 617

Panish, Jon, 618

Panton, Rachel, 619

Pappy, Esther Walls, 620

Parades, Americo, 872

Parascandola, L. J., 621

Parham, Marisa, 622

Park, Stephen M., 623

Park, You-me, 624

Parke, Mary E., 532

Parker, Bettye J., 438

Parray, Ashag Hussain, 625, 626

Parson, Margaret, 627

Patrick, Diane, 628

Passos, John Dos, 279, 341, 351

Pedan, William H., 629, 630

Penzler, Otto, 631

Perkins, Agnes Regan, 90

Perkins, Annie, 632

Perrin, T., 633

Perry, Alison M., 634

Peterson, Rachel, 635, 636

Petry, Ann
as Arnold Petri: Intro., 452
as forerunner: 91,173, 175,194, 581, 614, 717, 814
as Hall of Fame Honoree: 484, 628
as Harlem's "adopted daughter": 308, 340, 509
as journalist: 157, 158, 371, 383, 609, 767, 779
as naturalist: 79, 138, 139, 171, 197, 228, 266, 277, 293, 294, 347, 365, 397
as pharmacist: Chronology,130, 337, 507, 648, 816
as realist: 166, 247, 279, 294, 347, 375, 397
as recreation specialist: 103, 609
as screenwriter for Hollywood: 136,137, 345
as storyteller: 223, 564, 885, 896
as surname: 89, 98
in audio & video: 335, 741, 756
in autobiography: 85, 419
in biography & bibliography: 84, 89, 92, 95, 98, 141, 209, 295, 308, 309,328, 333, 337, 340, 342, 431, 435, 456, 488, 507, 513, 534, 543, 605, 606, 609, 615, 619, 637, 638, 639, 640, 646, 647, 648, 717, 727, 747, 760, 804, 805, 816, 818, 822, 858, 865, 874, 885, 894, 897,
in interviews: 65, 74, 93, 202, 207, 296, 299, 313, 336, 342, 438, 639,
in international appeals: 8, 12, 22, 114, 143, 164, 180, 184,188, 193, 246, 263, 276, 366, 367, 395, 409, 473, 485, 492, 516, 525, 549, 555, 588, 590, 592, 593, 600, 606, 617, 625, 626, 645, 658, 664, 668, 700, 752, 770, 789, 796, 815, 818, 839, 856, 872, 910
in photographs: 81, 85, 89, 99,191, 227, 237, 279, 295, 324, 328, 448, 476, 513, 804, 841
in translations: 164, 188, 193, 246, 409, 645, 664, 789, 856
in U.S. Congressional Record: 431
on writing: 70, 93, 207, 313 314, 438, 488, 668, 856, 885

Academic theses:
Ph.D.: 66, 72, 75, 76, 111, 112,122, 127, 131, 136, 142, 145, 148, 169, 173, 176, 182, 188, 190, 194, 199, 203, 205, 211, 212, 213, 234, 245, 248, 255, 267, 269, 271, 273, 274, 286, 291, 298, 307, 320, 322, 323, 341, 344, 353, 357, 361, 365, 367, 380, 387, 390, 393, 394, 400, 406, 411, 414, 416, 429, 432, 435, 444, 455, 463, 466, 474, 481, 487, 498, 500, 501, 505, 506, 509, 524, 546, 564, 571, 578, 584, 586, 590, 591, 594, 598, 603, 607, 610, 634, 636, 665, 666, 668, 720, 731, 736, 739, 740, 744, 761, 767, 770, 772, 775, 786, 789, 791, 801, 810, 813, 826, 828, 832, 833, 835, 840, 843, 852, 879, 881, 886, 891, 896, 906, 907, 908, 910
M.A.: 151, 162, 163, 167,171,172, 256, 376, 427,465, 482, 495, 526, 557, 576, 659, 663, 672, 732, 749, 751, 792, 809, 823, 836, 844, 859, 865, 903
M.S.: 140
A.B. Honors: 69, 144, 359, 490,

643, 755

Comparative Studies: 63, 66, 76, 94, 111, 112, 125,127, 133, 136, 137, 138, 140, 142, 145, 148, 151, 162, 164, 167, 173, 175, 178, 179, 180, 181, 183, 187, 188, 194, 196, 199, 201, 203, 209, 212, 213, 216, 225, 229, 230, 234, 240, 241, 245, 251, 255, 257, 266, 267, 269, 273, 275, 277, 278, 279, 281, 286, 289, 291,293, 298, 307, 314, 323, 324, 331, 335, 337, 339, 341, 344, 348, 350, 351, 353, 357, 361, 365, 366, 367, 372, 380, 381, 385, 386, 388, 389, 390, 393, 394, 396, 397, 398, 400, 401, 406, 412, 415,416, 423, 424, 425, 426, 427, 433, 444, 447, 453, 454, 463, 465, 469, 478, 479, 480, 481,482, 487, 490, 494, 497, 498, 500, 501, 502, 505, 506, 507, 508, 514, 515, 520, 522, 524, 525, 527, 529, 543, 549, 554, 555, 557, 558, 559, 563, 564, 571, 572, 574, 576, 578, 584, 585, 586, 588 589, 590, 591, 594, 595, 603, 607, 609, 610, 622, 623, 626, 634, 636, 642,643, 645, 654,656, 659, 660, 661, 662, 664, 666, 668, 673, 674, 675, 676, 677, 684, 715, 718, 720, 721, 728, 730, 731, 739, 740, 742, 743, 746, 747, 748, 751, 758, 759, 761, 767, 768, 770, 772, 775, 779, 785, 786, 788, 789, 791, 792, 794, 796, 798, 802, 808, 810, 813, 823, 825, 826, 828, 829, 830, 833, 834, 836, 839, 840, 842, 843, 844, 850, 851, 852, 854, 857, 859, 860, 865, 866, 869, 872, 875, 876, 880, 881, 884, 891,892, 894, 898, 899, 901, 906, 908, 909, 910
Supplementals:
adaptations: Chronology, 725
anthologies: 5, 6, 14, 17, 18, 20, 72, 83, 96, 184, 206, 309, 312, 330, 347, 385, 403, 404, 461, 567, 581, 582,
book clubs: 429, 533, 616, 741,753
braille: 22, 24
case studies: 429, 497, 617, 661,

668, 676
dictionaries: 71, 90, 491, 760
digital humanities: 843
encyclopedias: 95, 456, 457, 458, 459, 460, 754, 909
handbooks: 294, 310, 314, 315, 316, 595, 652, 797
public radio & television transcripts: 73,107, 306, 616, 771, 785
study guides: 64, 126, 236, 335, 350, 352, 434, 442, 462, 497, 551, 566, 613, 630, 671, 716, 738, 756, 763, 777, 842, 864, 873, 877, 880
textbooks: 6, 8, 9, 11, 16, 81, 113, 116

Criticism (Primary)
Country Place: 86, 88, 94, 135,150 186, 187, 209, 211, 290, 291, 301, 302, 303, 318, 320, 325, 327, 332, 401, 412, 414, 415, 416, 425, 446, 449, 451, 460, 483, 500, 510, 517, 521, 529, 540, 565, 566, 573, 601, 614, 621, 640, 648, 661, 679, 680, 724, 729, 748, 751, 758, 759, 764, 765, 769, 774,780, 847, 895, 897, 905
Characterizations: 325, 412, 414, 425, 500, 529, 566, 573, 640, 648, 680, 714, 729, 751, 758, 769, 780, 783, 808, 885, 895, 905, 909
Structure: 236, 303, 325, 412, 414, 425, 446, 460, 540, 565, 566, 573, 671, 751,758, 769, 780, 885,
Unfavorable reviews: 286, 847
Drugstore Cat, The: 177, 363, 489, 563, 567, 694, 695, 696, 814, 870
Harriet Tubman: 90, 105, 178,408, 417, 436, 477, 531, 611, 620, 677, 681, 682, 683, 684, 685, 716, 814, 902
Legends of the Saints: 644, 686, 687, 688, 807
Miss Muriel: 21, 67, 83, 87, 88, 114, 116, 117, 149, 160, 161, 165, 176, 205, 209, 228, 233, 248, 259, 262, 268, 271, 275, 317, 326, 329, 335, 352, 379, 401, 409, 412, 413, 414, 452, 457, 464, 467, 471, 475, 478,

479, 502, 508, 542, 547, 550, 551, 553, 569, 579, 581, 582, 586, 592, 599, 613, 622, 629, 630, 631, 642, 669, 671, 689, 690, 691, 692, 693, 721, 733, 734, 735, 739,746, 757, 779, 782, 794, 818, 819, 820, 839, 845, 860, 861, 863, 878, 880, 888, 892

Narrows, The: 88, 123, 134, 154, 166, 180, 195, 214, 230, 231, 284, 285, 298, 301, 303, 313, 317, 318, 322, 338, 358, 373, 410, 412, 414, 421, 423, 447, 458, 462, 467, 469, 519, 521, 522, 538, 638, 539, 548, 552, 558, 561, 565, 578, 586, 601, 612, 625, 627,639, 640, 641, 651, 668, 670, 673, 697, 698, 699, 700, 702, 703, 743, 748, 752, 753, 754, 759, 774, 781, 799, 806, 817, 837, 838, 848, 869, 890

Characterizations: 236, 315, 346, 358, 412, 414, 447, 469, 480, 536, 539, 552, 612, 625, 627, 641, 651, 698, 700, 701, 702, 714, 738, 759, 781, 837, 838, 885, 890, 909

Structure: 230, 236, 303, 346, 358, 412, 414, 458, 480, 519, 536, 538, 552, 561, 565, 612, 625, 627, 640, 671, 673, 699, 700, 701, 702, 703, 728, 749, 752, 754, 781, 799, 817, 837, 838, 848, 867, 869, 885, 890, 909

Unfavorable reviews: 338, 576, 848

Street, The: 64, 66, 69, 72, 73, 75, 81, 91, 94, 104, 108, 112, 119, 120, 121, 122, 124, 126, 127, 132, 133, 134, 138, 147, 148, 155, 156, 157, 158, 162, 164, 165, 167, 171, 172, 173, 174, 175, 179, 181, 182, 183, 185, 186, 188, 198, 202, 203, 205, 212, 213, 215, 217, 218, 235, 243, 245, 247, 253, 254, 257, 258, 259, 260, 266, 267, 270, 272, 276, 277, 279, 284, 287, 295, 297, 300, 301, 302, 303, 304, 306, 308, 317, 318, 319, 320, 323, 324, 330, 331, 332, 333, 336, 341, 348, 353, 354, 355, 359, 364, 366, 370, 380, 381, 384, 385, 386, 387, 389, 392, 395, 397, 398, 399, 401, 412, 414, 418, 426, 427, 428, 430, 433, 437, 438, 439, 442, 443, 444, 446, 447, 448, 453, 454, 459, 462, 463, 465, 466, 467, 468, 472, 473, 482, 486, 487, 498, 501, 503, 511, 512, 515, 516, 518, 520, 521, 525, 526, 527, 528, 529, 530, 534, 539, 540, 549, 555, 558, 559, 560, 562, 565, 568, 570, 571, 580, 585, 586, 589, 597, 599, 603, 604, 608, 616, 617, 632, 633, 639, 645, 649, 656, 657, 658, 660, 664, 668, 671, 704, 705, 706, 707, 708, 709, 710, 717, 718, 719,722, 725, 728, 730, 736, 737, 740, 741, 742, 743, 748, 750, 751, 752, 753, 755, 758, 759, 763, 766, 768, 771, 772, 774, 776, 777, 778, 784, 787, 795, 796, 800, 811, 821, 824, 828, 829, 830, 831, 832, 833, 836, 849, 850, 851, 852, 863, 868, 871, 875, 877, 881, 882, 883, 889, 904, 907

Characterizations: 75, 134, 171, 181, 243, 247, 248, 255, 256, 279, 284, 306, 308, 336, 346, 349, 353, 362, 385, 405, 412, 414, 426, 432, 433, 441, 442, 453, 473, 494, 496, 515, 527,533, 535, 539, 558, 570, 589, 600, 604, 617, 650, 653, 654, 656, 674, 707, 714, 719, 720, 738, 751, 758, 776, 784, 797, 798, 824, 849, 863, 871, 909

Structure: 236, 251, 254, 279, 300, 301, 302, 303, 306, 331, 332, 339, 343, 349, 354, 364, 383, 387, 392, 395, 412, 414, 418, 426, 443, 446, 459, 467, 515, 520, 532, 540, 565, 568, 588, 589, 606, 617, 632, 655, 657, 704, 710, 730, 751, 776, 790, 796, 800, 850, 909

Unfavorable reviews: 439, 795

Tituba of Salem Village: 90, 115, 168, 241, 249, 288, 321, 377, 407, 434, 440, 467, 477, 490, 493, 531, 556, 563, 577, 662, 678, 711, 712, 713, 814, 855, 887

Criticism (Secondary)
Stylistics: African poetics: 471; blues: 123, 166, 204, 205, 239,

250, 271, 284, 311, 346, 376, 379, 381, 387, 429, 464, 471, 503, 524, 595, 861, 881, 896, 900; cakewalk: 508, 579; call and response: 506; conjure: 405, 453; film: 166, 182, 197, 247, 274, 357, 411, 428, 546, 660, 740, 745, 835; gospel: 900; hip hop: 271, 273, 739, 900; improvisation: 506, 591, 833, 896; jazz: 117, 174, 204, 205, 223, 271, 275, 289, 311, 346, 364, 379, 387, 429, 437, 464, 471, 506, 520, 524, 618, 833, 839, 861, 896, 900; lindy hop: 834, 835; music: 205, 437, 904; performance: 341, 392, 591, 610, 718, 810; singing as communique: 466, 591; theatre: 554, 612, 725, 839

Themes: American Dream: 182, 221, 306, 372, 429, 494, 499, 504, 525, 543, 554, 584, 625, 643, 827, 828, 868, 898,901; anti-lynching literature, 670; 'apartheid': 326; archival research: 226, 747, 906; assimilationist novelist: 150, 831; automobile culture: 225; Black Arts Movement: 204, 587, 733, 846; black intimacy: 239, 454, 522; black heroine: 148, 217, 287, 305, 396, 432, 496, 509, 577, 603, 616, 762, 823; black intellectualism: 76, 416, 448, 788; Black Lives Matter: 877; Black Power Movement: 844, 846; black womanhood: 216, 336, 380, 381, 389, 393, 416, 433, 466, 720, 750, 759, 791, 823, 827, 840, 845, 849, 852, 862, 866, 868; capitalism: 411, 523, 572, 813, 852; Chicago Renaissance: 310, 590; citizenship: 736, 772, 872; city: 79, 148, 202, 351, 378, 411, 437, 516, 546, 554, 634, 779, 827, 860, 908; civil rights: 563, 571, 601, 636, 815, 910; community: 373, 413, 414, 415, 454, 463, 498, 503, 504, 507, 511, 564, 588, 601, 618, 656, 676, 692, 721, 730, 737,770, 828, 860, 869, 896, 908; criminal justice in literature: 406; 'cult of true womanhood: 285; digital humanities: 843; domesticity: 285, 389, 559, 599, 660, 740, 761, 772, 784; family: 715, 728, 732, 784, 812, 863, 896; 'forsaken race': 331; 'free will': 243, 501; geography: 382, 418, 463, 758, 813; ghetto: 445, 446, 504, 657, 689, 707, 812, 821; grassroots: 906; Harlem Renaissance: 91, 260, 361, 590; haunting: 622; health activism: 906; health and gender: 906; health politics: 906; identities: 66, 188, 193, 199, 200, 212, 229, 234, 267, 350, 375, 392, 414, 437, 447, 463, 496, 498, 545, 590, 591, 607, 625, 661, 669, 670, 730, 743, 744, 745, 761, 771, 774, 792, 810, 825, 881, 896, 908; immigration: 72, 110, 393, 554, 833, 886; incarcerated sons: 406; intimacy: 239, 454, 522; irony: 444, 445, 446, 515, 731; 'journalism as art form': 281, 767, 779; journey: 496; 'kept boy':111; labor 69, 409, 523, 559, 572, 580, 635, 660, 732, 766, 813, 836; law and literature: 298, 341, 474, 494, 746, 906; liberation and limitation: 245; literature and medicine: 766, 767; literature of exile: 72; local color: 142, 326; loneliness in cities: 243; mangled bodies: 659; marginalization: 367, 372, 466, 559, 636, 806, 819, 827; masculinity: 111,176, 199, 222, 228, 232, 786, 846; migration: 8, 72, 110, 289, 310, 346, 367, 374, 393, 394, 487, 669, 675, 886, 910; miscegenation: 214, 522; 'mother as teacher': 167; 'mothers of incarcerated sons': 406; motherhood: 69,144,181,218, 229, 269, 336, 388, 406, 473, 576, 656, 740, 784, 813, 851, 852; 'motherless': 133; mystery and suspense: 892; 'native daughters': 624; naturalism: 196,197, 228, 261, 266, 277, 293, 294, 307, 347, 365, 394, 396, 397, 399, 426, 481, 514,

532, 718, 883; neighborhood novelist: 154, 412; oppression: 79, 206, 215, 216, 222, 276, 359, 381, 396, 429, 511, 535, 536, 557, 643, 720, 748, 832, 891; 'personal epic': 189; poetic justice: 719; post war lit: 188, 194, 209, 211, 234, 274, 361, 400, 403, 404, 419, 470, 505, 510, 588, 636, 718, 806, 846, 873; print culture: 843; prison studies: 406; prodigal daughter: 509; progressive: 371, 372, 424, 572, 586, 593; protest novel, 286, 310, 315, 380, 401, 515 586, 623, 625, 645, 660, 752, 748, 786, 812, 857, 881, 891; pulp: 468, 570, 661; race and law: 474, 746; race and sexuality: 743, 744, 762; 'raceless':135, 187, 327, 451, 831; rage: 571, 891; rape: 594, 768, 907; realism: 247, 294, 347, 375, 396, 397, 421, 473, 518, 673, 706, 709, 715, 718, 793, 796, 875; regionalism: 142, 185, 572; relationships: 223, 243, 255, 371, 391, 412, 413, 414, 535, 540, 546, 555, 659, 728, 774, 794, 832, 833, 838, 863, 879, 880, 908; religion: 405, 432, 450; 'respect': 256; segregation: 341, 381, 545, 779, 836, 871; 'self-making': 286, 389, 496, 498, 501, 506, 524, 585, 586, 599, 603, 877; seven deadly sins: 632; sex work: 836; sexuality and citizenship, 268, 284, 292, 344 743, 745, 761, 762, 806, 868, 883; slavery: 832, 846; smellscapes: 424; 'social haunting': 622; social justice: 109, 190, 365, 395, 742; social protest: 286, 315, 463, 526, 547, 586, 587, 623, 625, 633, 838; social realism: 166, 396, 397, 473, 503, 572, 738, 791, 793, 796; social work and literature: 242, 270; solitude: 239; sound: 437, 850, 904; state of innocence: 878; state of experience: 878; stereotypes: 173, 175, 214, 217, 272, 384, 435, 497, 535, 579, 642, 718, 729, 812, 862, 868; subjecthood: 623; survival: 160, 165, 193, 212, 229, 231, 362, 384, 385, 466, 505, 584, 656, 708; suspense and mystery: 892; totalitarianism literature: 666; tragedy: 426, 800; uplift: 454, 871; 'unblushing realist': 155, 247, 279; urban ghetto: 206; urban realism: 378, 599, 715, 718, 791, 796, 875; urban studies in Chicano poetry: 183, 357; values: 120, 122; violence: 119, 159, 203, 215, 255, 257, 344, 383, 447, 519, 522, 527, 530, 592, 595, 634, 666, 749, 768, 779, 794, 838, 845, 882, 906; war and citizenship: 461; women war literature: 145; working women: 179, 218, 357, 559, 579, 599, 610 718, 789, 791, 809, 834, 849; youth: 388

Theoretical Approaches: African poetics 471; ambiguity, 405, 863; anxieties: 220 546, 622; archetypes: 67, 353, 797; architectural theory: 183, 286, 323, 385, 390, 474, 546, 589; art of subversion, 166, 221, 319; aural aesthetics: 387, 801, 802, 803, 850, 904; authenticity:169, 170; authority: 244, 356, 510, 764, 779, 872; Barthes: 889; binary oppositions: 120, 209, 323, 591; bio-political: 750, 906; black futilitarianist: 448; body as text, 390 392, 610, 659, 736, 743, 750, 762, 766, 767, 768, 786, 820, 825; book club's case study: 429; desires: 298, 369, 452, 532, 585, 743, 744, 861, 881, 889; dialogic: 183; difference: 172, 610; discourse on rape: 768, 907; displacement: 622, 910; dwelling, theory of: 437, 904; eco-criticism: 276, 307, 399, 906; ecology: 76, 307, 351, 481, 906; erotic: 131,170; fantasy: 127, 151, 214, 341, 594; gaze, the: 112, 398; geo-criticism: 463, 833; geography: 418,463; Gothicism: 228, 232, 248, 546, 621, 761, 762, 786; green reading: 307, 481; healing: 557, 886; Hegelian reading: 255; Heidegger: 437; humanism: 361; humanitarian narrative: 297, 591, 608; interracial desire: 298, 358, 744; intersectionality theory: 112, 120, 125, 215, 355, 356, 359, 372, 391, 400, 474, 514, 539, 557, 559, 586, 594, 624, 626, 663, 669, 739, 743, 758, 765, 787, 788, 806, 827, 850, 851, 852; intertexuality of class, race, and gender: 475, 718, 743, 744, 758, 765, 791; Jungian: 248, 495, 496; Lacanian: 69; language: 234; legal and metaphysical: 494; liberal humanism: 361; listening: 335, 801, 802, 803, 904; literacy: 244, 245, 335, 390, 407, 497; magical realism: 405 889; Marxism: 78, 125, 232, 304, 521, 580, 635, 636, 846, 853; masquerade narrative: 578; matriarchal narrative: 432, 748, 813; maverick feminism, 665; modernity: 166, 186, 219, 310, 384, 412, 416, 426, 520, 661, 664, 665, 750, 768, 846, 871, 873; narratology: 278, 514; objective correlatives: 445; pedagogical authority: 126, 872. 880; phenomenological: 495, 662; politics of listening: 801, 802, 803; postmodernist: 316, 318, 319, 505, 873; poststructuralism: 79, 319, 320, 873; psychological: 81,172, 181,193, 225, 248, 250, 390, 391, 409, 495, 535, 622, 623, 748, 752, 772, 786, 832, 873, 893; queer desires: 278, 344, 744, 745, 806; reader response: 271, 379, 429; representation: 66, 75, 111, 112, 204, 205, 212, 213, 214, 275, 277, 278, 316, 344, 356, 357, 366, 367, 381, 394, 416, 474, 520, 545, 557, 610, 618, 624, 626, 718, 733, 755, 758, 768, 786, 825, 826, 835, 836, 886, 891, 907; revisionist: 389, 506, 577; scar as text: 390, 392; signification: 66, 239, 475, 545; silence: 608, 846; sound: 802, 850, 904; spatiality: 156, 199, 474; spectatorship: 397, 398, 591; speculative: 151;

speech patterns: 441; subjectivity: 222, 285, 298, 380, 454, 584, 607, 623, 624, 808, 889; subversion: 151,166, 221,234, 290, 319, 320, 463, 466, 525, 554, 584, 594, 633, 813, 898, 889; surveillance: 394, 397, 398; teller and the telling: 223, 317,469; Todorovian 127; trauma theory: 72, 110, 379, 819, 820, 893; 'trust the donnee': 316, 469; urban aesthetics: 118, 908; usable past: 524, 739, 899; value as process: 120, 122; voice: 238, 419, 445, 464, 502, 509, 591, 600, 771, 879, 882 ; whiteness: 135, 220, 290, 291, 449, 450, 483, 510, 744, 764, 765; white panopticism: 394; womanist: 198, 213, 389, 396, 396, 416

Tropes: "Age of Wright": 442; 'bad man':535; 'bad woman': 535; bildungsroman: 501, 660; black ethos: 598; black mourning: 881; city: 79, 148, 202, 351, 378, 411, 437, 516, 546, 554; cold war literature: 274, 373, 400, 419, 666; community: 149, 190,193, 588, 770, 836; disability & lit: 659, 766, 767, 820, 824, 825, 826; domesticity: 357, 389, 599, 761, 772; double consciousness: 285, 494, 525, 565, 607, 625, 869; environmental ethics: 150, 294, 307, 399, 418, 424, 481, 546, 623, 748, 797, 836, 863, 875, 879; the forties: 318, 597, 642, 667, 748, 791, 869; 'free fall': 243, 501; 'gaze. the': 112, 166, 398; Harlem: 370, 382, 383, 437, 439, 470, 503, 504, 511, 515, 516, 527, 530, 562, 593, 606, 634, 650, 653, 693, 730, 742, 758, 770, 779, 795, 822, 863, 869, 871, 898, 904; home: 75, 257, 286, 344, 367, 463, 715, 770; identity: 66, 112, 193,199, 200, 212, 229, 234, 267, 350, 375, 392, 414, 437, 447, 463, 496, 498, 545, 590, 591, 607, 625, 661, 669, 670, 730, 743, 744, 745, 761, 774, 792, 810, 825, 896, 908; internal displacement: 910; Jane Crow writing: 381; jazz literature: 364;

kinship: 239; marriage and domesticity: 285, 292, 472,774; maternal myth: 554, 749, 786; matriarchal myth: 270, 748; memory: 72, 502, 622, 886; merit myth: 128, 455, 554, 823; migration: 8, 72, 110, 289, 310, 346, 374, 393, 487, 669, 675, 886, 910; 'mock-heroic epic': 349; morality tale: 905; mourning: 881; 'other, the': 142; performance: 341, 392, 591; place: 132, 463, 541, 743, 758, 833; poverty and space: 254, 482, 649; prejudice: 392, 413, 427, 497, 547, 592, 642,781; railroad blues: 560; rebel: 594, 748; 'returning soldier': 325; riot as ritual: 67, 110, 379, 504, 779; scars: 390, 391; space: 199, 215, 274, 284, 341, 365, 389, 411, 415, 418, 463, 482, 498, 504, 579, 584, 591, 624, 770, 775, 783, 833, 852, 868, 908; spectatorship: 397, 398, 591, 595; state of innocence: 878; 'street, the': 181, 201, 202 , 243, 273, 324, 330, 418, 503, 533, 589, 602, 606, 650, 656, 657, 707, 775, 833, 871; street literature: 429, 602; studio era narrative: 136; 'subways': 118, 165; tragic love: 338; tragic mulatto: 214, 217, 426; trains literature,560; urban spaces: 112, 365, 389, 424, 599, 634, 770, 836, 860, 875, 904, 906. 908; urban street literature: 183,190, 429, 602, 908; Victorian: 425, 515, 761; voice: 600, 605; 'woman's place': 235, 319, 539, 791; womanist: 213, 416, 389

Petry, Elizabeth (Liz), 77, 486, 637, 638, 639, 640, 647, 876

Pettis, Joyce, 641

Phelps, Elizabeth Stuart, 825

Phillips, Kimberley L., 642

Phillpotts-Brown, Kristina, 643

Pinconnat, Crystal, 645

Play Schools Conference, 646

Podcasts, 647

Poe, Edgar Allen, 181

Poirier, Suzanne, 648

Pollack, Channing, 649

Poore, Charles, 650

Porter, Dorothy, 145

Porter, Katherine Ann, 145

Posten, Ted, 651

Pratt, Louis Hill, 652

Prescott, Orville, 653

President's Reading List, 827

Price, Emerson, 654

Primus, Pearl, 593, 742

Pryse, Marjorie, 128, 656

Purdy, Theodore M., 657

Puri, Usha, 658

Puschman-Nalenz, Barbara, 475

R

Raab, Angela R., 659

Rabinowitz, Paula., 660, 661

Rahming, M. B., 662

Ramadan, Wafa Darwish, 663

Ramm, Hans-Christoph, 664

Rand, Aya, 323

Randle, Kemeshia Laquita, 665

Randolph, Ruth Elizabeth, 727

Ransom, John Crowe, 76

Rasberry, Gary Vaugh, 666, 667

Ravichandran, Sugannya, 668

Rawlings, Marjorie Kennan, 136

Raynor, Deidre, 669, 670

Rayson, Ann, 671

Rechy, John, 357

Reckner, Judith Pendall, 672

Redding. J. Saunders, 261, 262, 673, 674

Reich, Steven, A., 675

Reid, E. Shelley, 676

Reid, Margaret Walraven, 677

Reynolds, Clarence V., 714

Reynolds, Guy, 715

Rhodes-Pitt, Sharifa, 741

Rhone, Nedra, 716

Rickman, Ray, 717

Riethuis, Jochem, 718

Riggen, Patricia, 357

Riggs, Marlon, 881

Riis, Roger William, 719

Riley, Carolyn, 86

Roach, Max, 839

Robenson, Marilynne, 482

Roberts, Margaret Olivia, 720

Roberts, Nora Ruth, 721

Robinson, Ted, 722

Robinson, William H., 723

Rogers. W. G., 724

Rosado, Treza, 725

Rose, Mary, 726

Rosenblatt, Paul C., 728

Rosenblatt, Roger, 729

Roses, Lorraine Elena, 91, 727

Roth, Philip, 201, 594

Rottenburg, Catherine, 730

Royster, Beatrice Horn, 731

Rozzelle, Sarah Cathleen, 732

Rubin, Rachel, 733

Rudisel, Christine, 734

Rudlin, Ernst, 898

Ruff, Roslyn, Intro. (see also Sapphire)

Ruffin, Carolyn F., 735

Russell, Emily S., 736

Russo, Marie, 737

S

Sacks, Sam, 738

Sackschemsky, Leisl, 739

Salem Witch Trials, 241

Sanchez, Sonia, 208

Sanders, Tammy L., 740

Santiago, Esmeralda, 357

Sapphire, 273, 676, 741

Shachter, Jacqueline, 756

Schlichenmeyer, Terri, 742

Schmidt, Tyler, 743, 744, 745

Schneck, Peter, 746

Schomburg Center, The, 747

Schraufnagel, Noel, 748

Scott, Patricia Bell, 778, 845, 864
Scott, Traci L., 749
Scott, William, 750
Seets, Myrtle Nance, 751
Sehgal, Paul, 752, 753
Seidman, Barbara Kitt, 754
Sen, Nandana, 755
Senna, Danzy, 225, 881
Shachter, Jacqueline, 756
Shakespeare, William, 527
Shaw University, Chron., 444
Shea J. Vernon, 757
Sherrard-Johnson, Cherene, 758
Shinn, Thelma J., 759
Shockley, Ann, 760
Shockley, Evelyn Elayne, 761
Shockley, Evie, 762
Showalter, Elaine, 763
Si, Stephanie, 764, 765
Sibara, Jay, 766
Sibara, Jennifer Claire Barager, 767
Siegel, Robert, 106 (see also NPR)
Sielke, Sabine, 768
Sillen, Samuel, 769
Silko, Leslie Marmon, 225
Silva, Liana, 770
Silverman, Fran, 771
Simoneau, Elizabeth, 772

SIms-Wood, Janet, 773
Sinclair, Jo, 463, 481, 772
Sinclair, Upton, 279, 307, 481
Sirk, Douglas, 357
Sister Souljah, 273, 353
Skeeter, Sharyn J., 774
Small, Shayna, Intro.
Smiley, Jane, 199, 225
Smith, Alexander V., 775
Smith, Barbara, 352, 776, 777, 778, 845, 864
Smith, Beverly A., 779
Smith, Bradford, 780
Smith, Eleanor Touhey, 781
Smith, Gardner, 444, 447,
Smith, Harrison, 782
Smith, Jessie Carney, 462
Smith, John Caswell, 783, 784
Smith, Kate, 642
Smith, Lillian, 427
Smith, Venture, 314
Smith, William G., 267
Solomon, Asale Najuma, 786
Solomon, Irvin D., 787
Sophocles, 386
Sorett, Josef, 788
Sorgenti, A., 789
Soto, Michael, 403
Souljah, 273, 353

Southgate, Robert I., 790

Sowinska, Suzanne, 791

Sparrow, Lamont, 792

Speight, Allen, 880

Spencer, Nicholas, 793

Spenser, Anne, 557

Spilka, Mark, 794

Spillers, Hortense J., 128, 656

Springer, Gertrude, 795

Stannard, Dorothy, 796

Starke, Catherine Juanita, 797

Stein, Gertrude, 225, 267

Steinback, John, 125, 279, 361, 794, 899

Stephian, Barry, 68

Stepto, Robert B., 798

Sterling, Dorothy, 563

Stewart, Carolyn H., 799

Stewart, Pearl, 800

Stoever, Jennifer Lynn, 801, 802, 803

Stowe, Harriet Beecher, 173, 286, 825

Straight, Susan, 676

Streitfeld, David, 804, 805

Sullivan, J.J., 806

Sullivan, Oona, 807

Sullivan, Richard, 808

Sumpter, Vanessa Simone, 809

Sundstrom. Kristina M., 810

Sutherland, Amy, 811

Suzan-Lori, Parks, 159

Svendsen, Kester, 812

Sweeting-Trotter, Tarah, 813

T

Tait, Althea, 814

Tally, Justine, 815

Tate, Allen, 76

Taylor, Frances Grandy, 816

Taylor, Ivan E., 817

Tetsuo, Yameguchi Midori, 818

Tettenborn, Eva, 819, 820

Thomas, Ruby, 94

Thomas, Robert McGee, 822

Thomas, Toni Renee, 823

Thompson, Era Bell, 381

Thomson, Rose Marie Garland, 824, 825, 826

Todd, Diane M., 828

Tolson, Melvin, 76, 314

Toomer, Jean, 881

Torr, Sergio de la, 767

Treat, Mary Alice, 814

Trilling, Diana, 829

Troupe, Quincy, 830

Turner, Darwin T., 831

Turner, Washella Neurett, 842

Tuszynska, Agnieszka, 833

Tyler, Parker, 76

Tyree, Omar, 602

U

Unruh, Kendra, 834, 835

Uzurin, Deborah, L., 836

V

V.P.H., 837

Van Dore, Edrie, 838

Van Gelder, Lawrence, 839

Varga-Coley, Barbara Jean, 840

Vechten, Carl Van, 841

Vickery, John B., 842

Vigilleti, Elyse R., 843

Vilato, Claudia, 844

Vizcaíno-Aleman, Melina, 846

Voiles, Jane, 847, 848

Vinson, James, 302

Viramontes, Helena, 225, 424

Vorsts, Van, 610

W

Wade-Gayles. Gloria, 849, 850, 851, 852

Wald, Alan M., 853

Wald, Gayle, 624

Walker, Alice, 133, 269, 289, 359, 415, 454, 502, 576, 626, 676, 717, 720, 789, 792, 823, 852

Walker, Margaret, 314

Wall, Cheryl, 854, 855,

Wang, Lili, 856

Ward, Jerry W., Jr., 857

Ward, Theodore, 636

Warfel, Harry R., 858

Warren, Kenneth W., 403

Warren, Robert Penn, 76, 201

Washington, Ada L., 859

Washington, Gladys, 457, 860, 861

Washington, Mary Helen, 180, 862, 863, 864

Washington, Zenobia, 865

Watkins, Mel, 866

Watson, Carole McAlpine, 867

Wattley, Ama S., 868

Weir, Sybil, 869

Weiss, Jacqueline Shachter, 870

Welty, Eudora, 899

Wesling, Meg E., 871

West, Dorothy, 140, 148, 194, 213, 380, 400, 416, 586, 659, 852

Wharton, Edith, 225, 323

Wheeler, Kathleen, 873,

Whitbeck, Doris, 874

White, Walter, 444, 455, 591

Whitehead, Colson, 739

Whitlow, Roger, 875

Whitt, Margaret Earley, 876

Wichelms, Kathryn, 877

Wideman, John Edgar, 199

Wiebe, Paul, 878

Wilhite, Keith M., 879

Wilkie, Jacqueline S., 880

Williams, Jennifer Denise, 881

Williams, John, 497

Williams, John A., 882

Williams, Mary Lou, 63, 742

Williams, Sherley Anne, 390, 883

Willis, Pauline, 94

Willis, Susan, 884

Wilson, August, 828

Wilson, John, 572

Wilson, Mark, 885

Wilson, Sonia Alverez, 886

Winter, Molly Crumpton, 888

Winters, Kari J., 889

Wisconsin School of Pharmacy, 65

Wolfe, Barbara, 890

Womanist, 213, 396

Woods, Brandon Teray, 891

Woods, Paula L., 892

Woolf, Virginia, 323, 502

Woolfork, Lisa, 893

Wordworks, Manitou, 894

Wormley, Margaret Just, 895

Wright, Lee Alfred, 896

Wright, Richard, 66, 75, 91, 121, 136, 137, 138, 181, 183, 185, 188, 219, 307, 339, 361, 389, 394, 396, 398, 400, 406, 426, 447, 481, 571, 622, 623, 645, 654, 666, 739, 751, 798, 850, 857, 859, 869, 875, 891, 892, 910

Wright, Richard C., 535

Wright, Sarah E., 131, 167, 433, 623, 852

Wurst, Gayle, 898

Wyatt, David, 89

Y

Ya Salaam, Kalamu, 900

Yamamoto, Hisaye, 400

Yarborough, Richard, 901

Yates, Elizabeth, 902

Yates, Sharon B., 903

Yeldho, Joe Varghese, 904

Yerby, Frank, 140, 629, 751

Yerdella, A. J., 676

Yglesias, Jose, 905

Young, Lisa, 906

Young, Tiffany Ann, 907

Z

Zak, Deborah Jeannie, 908

Zhang, Welhua, 909

Zidan, Mahmoud Nimer, 910

Zola, 138, 139, 518

About the Editor

Hazel Arnett Ervin received her first book contract while she was a doctoral student in the College of Arts and Sciences at Howard University. Deciding early in her career to fill voids in the annals of arts and letters, so to inform writers, audiences, and literary art forms, Ervin's repertoire of publications include the following: *Ann Petry: A Bio-Bibliography* (1993); *African American Literary Criticism, 1773 to 2000* (1999); *The Handbook of African American Literature* (2004); *Ann Petry's Short Fiction: Critical Essays* (with Hilary Holladay in 2004); *The Critical Response to Ann Petry* (2005); *A Community of Voices on Education and the African American Experience – A Record of Triumphs and Struggles* (2015); *What The Scriptures, Proverbs, Maxims, Aphorisms, Wise Sayings, and Memorable Quotations Teach Us Still About Character* (2021); and *The 25th Anniversary Edition, Ann Petry: A Bio-Bibliography* (2021). In addition to her publications, the academician, senior administrator, and consultant in higher education is also Fulbright Scholar; (Aspen) Wye Fellow; UNCF/Mellon Fellow; and NEH Fellow. She is cited in *The World Who's Who of Women* (Cambridge, England) and *Who's Who in Black Atlanta*.

www.ingramcontent.com/pod-product-compliance
Lightning Source LLC
Chambersburg PA
CBHW080634230426
43663CB00016B/2868